ORGANISATIONAL INTELLIGENCE

ORGANISATIONAL INTELLIGENCE

Including upcoming

(Fourth Wave Social Change)

Dr. R.H. Tupkary
Former Prof. & Head,
Metallurgical Engineering,
VRCE, Nagpur.

Himalaya Publishing House

MUMBAI • NEW DELHI • NAGPUR • BENGALURU • HYDERABAD • CHENNAI • PUNE • LUCKNOW • AHMEDABAD • ERNAKULAM • BHUBANESWAR • INDORE • KOLKATA • GUWAHATI

First Edition : 2012

Published by	:	Mrs. Meena Pandey for **Himalaya Publishing House Pvt. Ltd.,** "Ramdoot", Dr. Bhalerao Marg, Girgaon, **Mumbai - 400 004.** Phone: 022-23860170/23863863, Fax: 022-23877178 **E-mail: himpub@vsnl.com; Website: www.himpub.com**
Branch Offices	:	
New Delhi	:	"Pooja Apartments", 4-B, Murari Lal Street, Ansari Road, Darya Ganj, New Delhi - 110 002. Phone: 011-23270392, 23278631; Fax: 011-23256286
Nagpur	:	Kundanlal Chandak Industrial Estate, Ghat Road, Nagpur - 440 018. Phone: 0712-2738731, 3296733; Telefax: 0712-2721215
Bengaluru	:	No. 16/1 (Old 12/1), 1st Floor, Next to Hotel Highlands, Madhava Nagar, Race Course Road, Bengaluru - 560 001. Phone: 080-32919385; Telefax: 080-22286611
Hyderabad	:	No. 3-4-184, Lingampally, Besides Raghavendra Swamy Matham, Kachiguda, Hyderabad - 500 027. Phone: 040-27560041, 27550139; Mobile: 09848130433
Chennai	:	No. 8/2, Modley 2nd Street, Ground Floor, T. Nagar, Chennai - 600 017. Phone: 044-28144004/28144005.
Pune	:	First Floor, "Laksha" Apartment, No. 527, Mehunpura, Shaniwarpeth (Near Prabhat Theatre), Pune - 411 030. Phone: 020-24496323/24496333
Lucknow	:	Jai Baba Bhavan, Church Road, Near Manas Complex and Dr. Awasthi Clinic, Aliganj, Lucknow - 226 024. Phone: 0522-2339329, 4068914; Mobile: 09305302158, 09415349385, 09389593752
Ahmedabad	:	114, "SHAIL", 1st Floor, Opp. Madhu Sudan House, C.G. Road, Navrang Pura, Ahmedabad - 380 009. Phone: 079-26560126; Mobile: 09327324149, 09377088847
Ernakulam	:	39/104 A, Lakshmi Apartment, Karikkamuri Cross Rd., Ernakulam, Cochin - 622011, Kerala. Phone: 0484-2378012, 2378016; Mobile: 09344199799
Bhubaneswar	:	5 Station Square, Bhubaneswar - 751 001 (Odisha). Phone: 0674-2532129, Mobile: 09861046007
Indore	:	Kesardeep Avenue Extension, 73, Narayan Bagh, Flat No. 302, IIIrd Floor, Near Humpty Dumpty School, Indore - 452 007 (M.P.). Mobile: 09301386468
Kolkata	:	108/4, Beliaghata Main Road, Near ID Hospital, Opp. SBI Bank, Kolkata - 700 010, Phone: 033-32449649, Mobile: 09910440956
Guwahati	:	House No. 15, Behind Pragjyotish College, Near Sharma Printing Press, P.O. Bharalumukh, Guwahati - 781009, (Assam). Mobile: 09883055590, 09883055536
DTP by	:	HPH, Editorial Office, Bhandup (Sunanda)
Printed at	:	M/s. Aditya Offset Process India Pvt. Ltd., On behalf on HPH.

Dedication

To all those,
who sacrificed their lives in the past,
for improving the organisationality
and
to all those,
who are presently striving hard
to organise and consolidate
the society
in tune with time
into a
mighty Indian nation

Acclaims

In the complex web of organised social world one can avoid reading this comprehensive text on organisation at one's own peril.

Dr. S.M.deshpande, Former Professor,
Electrical Engineering, Indian Institute of Science, Banglore

It is a comprehensive treatise on organisation dealing with it as a noun, an adjective in grammatical terms and as verb in the form of the very process of organisation.

Prof. Shrikant G. Kulkarni,
Amrita college of Marketing, Coimbtore

Three waves of social revolutions, as revealed by Alvin Toffler are universally accepted. But the upcoming Fourth Wave of change as decoded by the author is worth understanding to improve organisational efficiency.

P.G.Borawar, Former Prof and Head, Sociology Department,
Dharampeth Arts and Commerce College, Nagpur

The unique concept of 'organisationality' as developed by the author is worth understanding fully to appreciate the science of organisation.

Dr. I.K.Chopde, Professor, Mechanical Engineering,
Visvesvaraya National Institute of Technology, Nagpur

This is a unique account for intelligent appreciation of an organisation as a fundamental science and management in its applied form.

Dr. P.L.Joshi, Former Prof and Head,
Department of Politcal science and Public Administration,
Nagpur University, Nagpur

It explains lucidly why social life is collapsing in independent India in spite of almost copying the successful British model of organisation.

Dr. R.W.Khare, Free Lance Engineering Consultant,
Banglore.

A very fine contribution in the field of organisational science.

Dr. Sanjiv Kelkar, Master of Medicine,
Internationally Acclaimed Trainer in Debates, Nagpur

Modern society is a society of organisations. It is a complex social web at the local, regional, national and international level to meet varied human needs. Now nobody can live happily without getting involved in this web. No nation can progress without efficient organisational web. What is therefore primarily required is to acquire sufficient . . . .

Preface

The earlier title that was visualised for the present book was 'Rise and Fall of Organisations' broadly with reference to organisations and institutions like commercial, social, charity, political, research and the like. It would have been quite in tune with standard format of management science, based essentially on the five fundamental principles such as planning, organising, staffing, leading and controlling. This is how the management science is dealt with and is taught at the universities and is practiced in actual management of organisations.

Management science deals with organisations as such and does not bother much about whether any society wherein organisations are formed is organised or not. In fact it is presumed that the society is reasonably organised. The relationship of organised society and the organisations formed therein does not practically interest them from the point of view of management. But this is of great fundamental importance in consolidating organisations and thereby the nations. The present book therefore opens up with a question as to why Indians are so disorganised even after adoptng the same organisational model as has been successfully developed and adopted by the westerners, not only in developing their own nation-states but thereby ruling many other less organised societies, including India, all over the world for nearly a couple of centuries.

I therefore thought of organisation as a subject beyond the limited meaning usually presumed in the management science. I sincerely felt that organisational science is a science by itself, like any other and, management of organisations is at best its applied form like any other pair of pure and applied sciences. Organisational science therefore need not be confined to merely in terms of referring an organisation as a **'noun'** in grammatical sense. In fact it should also include organisation as an **'adjective'**, in the sense of quality of an organised state and as **'verb'** in the form of the very process of organising a group of people in the form of an organisation, society, nation or on international and humanitarian level.

With this in mind I contacted few professors of management and of sociology at the university level and explained to them what I had in mind to write about organisation. The management experts emphasised their standard approach as just described above. While the sociology experts pleaded their inability to suggest me anything worth reading except citing a small and old book entitled **'Modern Organisations'** by **Amitai Etzioni**, published in 1965 AD, which has been duly referred and quoted in the text.

I have personally and actively worked for almost 40-50 years in a number of organisations which included academic, social, charitable, national and even political ones. With such first-hand experience and the discussions I had with the above mentioned learned experts in management and sociology I wrote a Marathi book entitled ***'Sanghathana and Sanghatitata'***. It was published in 2008 AD. I was still not entirely happy about the design, contents and the lay-out of that Marathi book on the subject matter that I had in mind. I was still trying to evolve a new pattern in the understanding of organisations and organised groups. Therefore I decided to rewrite it in English in an improvised design and lay-out with additional inputs after further study and interactions with many others to put forward a new pattern of outlook on 'organisation' as such. The result is before the readers in the form of the present book.

It takes some bit of intelligence to appreciate and deal with the modern-day organised world. Earlier there were some organisations, of their own types, in various societies all over the world. But according to Amitai Etzioni, modern day societies are societies of organisations. These have now expanded from local to regional, social, national and even at the international and humanitarian level. In fact it is a complex web of organisations that form the present-day societies and the international community. Nobody can now live happily without getting involved directly or indirectly in this web of organisations. It requires intelligence to get involved appropriately in the organised world to get ones own desires and ambitions fulfilled, to the extent possible, for leading a happy, meaningful and contented life.

This perception of organisation led me to write the present book to help those interested in appreciating the organised world more intelligently, participate in it to the extent required and thereby make themselves more happy and contented. In this sense this book is not only relevant to those interested in management and sociology but is of interest to each and every individual as a *knowledge-key* for contented life-styles. This is also the basic reason why the title **'Organisational Intelligence'** has been coined for the present book. This is also the reason why I felt that I am less a author but more a developer of the pattern presented in this book, by using varieties of inputs from the existing available knowledge.

This is not a text book for any present-day university course since such a course on basic organisational science is not perhaps taught at any of the universities in the world. What is taught and what is very popular is management science which is nothing but, in my opinion, applied organisational science. The pattern developed in the present book is supposed to differentiate organisational science from management science. It would thereby be beneficial for its introduction as a course at the university level in its own right. Pending that it would certainly help to study and understand the standard courses in present-day management science. It can therefore be treated as a semi-text-book for management and sociology students and practicing managers. Equally it would be of interest to those interested in sociology because presently this subject does not find its due importance in sociology as is taught at the universities.

The present book therefore deals with why organisations are required, their origin, how these are formed, their relevance to society, what makes them grow and causes their decay and such relevant topics. It also deals with the effectiveness and efficiency of an organised effort and ways and means of improving the same. It also deals with idealised outlook towards organisation.

The present book has coined a new term as **'organisationality'** to depict the mental state of the group being organised. It is a quality of larger group like society, nation or international community or humanity as such. Unless the organisationality is adequately developed no effort in formation and management of organisations in that organisationality bears right fruits. Similarly it also emphasises that there is no alternative to adoption of Indian philosophical *advaiti* outlook to achieve effective and efficient organisations and thereby better social progress. This revolution in the perception of organisations is slowly taking place all over the world. I call it as the upcoming **'Fourth Wave of Social Change'**. It is still in its infancy and yet can be felt by those who are interested and are prepared to see it..

Several new perceptions have been developed in the present book. One such is how the religious organisations get developed and how they affect the societies and the human race as a whole. It also deals with religion-like other neo-religious or social organisations. The other unique perception developed here is the **'disciple syndrome'**, the conditions for its development and its effects on an organised effort. It is all to develop the knowledge-body or science of organisation, in all its encompassing form. All these perceptions fit in the present title of the book well. Hence the choice. It is hoped that the reader would be able to readily develop the required intelligence after going through the book.

I wanted these new perceptions pertaining to organisational science to be critically evaluated by some management and sociology experts of all-India repute. Some of their candid comments have been included in the **'acclaims'** to help throw light on the contents of the present book. I hope to get more such critical comments after the book is published and also hope to include them in the next edition.

A lot of ideas from the existing literature have been useful in developing the total text of the present book. All these have been duely acknowledged in the text alongwith the names of their authors and sources.

One may find some comments made more than once at different places. *Firstly* it is more fundamental and needs to be appreciated better to follow the entire text properly. *Secondly* what is read earlier is generally not remembered by average readers while reading the later parts, during the first reading of the book. One has to scrape through again to remember it when needed. *Thirdly* it is therefore deliberately repeated to make the subject explicit at every point rather than relying on memory or undertaking the trouble of referring back the earlier information to appreciate the new point.

Some section titles are repeated but to explain the same but from the point of view of understanding the new topic.

As usual the subject index is provided at the end of the book. But in addition, a few more unique things have also been provided at the end. The text includes references to a large number of eminent persons in terms of their contributions to social organisations, but without any specific quotable reference. Person-index has therefore been provided at the end to indicate their individual reference in the text. Similarly some Sanskrit sayings *(subhshitas)* and Sanskrit (including Marathi) terms are used in the text to illustrate the view-point. In the text these are written in Roman script. The pronunciations of these differ in India from region to region. There is therefore a possibility of confusion when written in Roman script. To avoid this confusion, glossary of these are given in the end in Devnagri script with page numbers wherever these occur in the text and thereby minimise possible confusion in understanding them.

When I approached Himalaya Publishing House, and told them that it was a semi-text-book, not only for students of management and sociology, but of interest to one and all, they readily agreed to publish the same. I am most thankful to them. I am equally thankful to their team for correcting the script with diligence. I must also thank the artists of their group who have designed the cover very elegantly.

I am associated with a group of retired faculty members from varied university colleges. We do have regular discussions on number of topics. We also organise weekly public meetings, in the form of study-circles, to discuss varied topics. I am thankful to many of my friends in this group for varied discussions on several topics that helped me to better develop the text of the present book.

I sincerely wish that the purpose of writing this book shall be best served if additional books are written to increase awareness of average people for acquiring better organisational intelligence.

Dr. R.H. Tupkary
(rhtupkary@gmail.com)

Nagpur
Dated : September 2011

Contents

Detailed Contents

CHAPTER 1

INTRODUCTION

CHAPTER STRUCTURE

- Britishers and Indians
- In Retrospect
- Exceptions
- Industrial Revolution
- Apparent Contradictions
- Feudalism
- Management Science
- Extents of Organisation
- Scope
- Design
- Organisational Web
- TNA Factor
- Dead End
- Institutions and Organisations

As one scans the history of nearly sixty years of post independent India one can not fail to notice that almost the entire social life in India has in general decayed and fairbit disintegrated beyond imagination. Many in fact believe that it has disintegrated to such an extent that it is now beyond repair. It is also interesting to note that on the one hand India is progressing on the material-wealth front whereas, on the other hand, it is socially disintegrating. Modern socio-systems are politico-centric in nature. The disintegration in politico-systems, as is evident in India, is often considered as the main reason for such social disintegration. Is it the only reason? Quite often post-independence social life is compared with the social life of pre-independence period and concluded that the pre-independence period was much better-off as compared to the post-independence Indian social life. Comparatively, some feel and perhaps quite erroneously, that the social life under British rule was better than that under our own democratically elected representatives. Why do they feel so? Why are they so much disillusioned about independent India? There is growing organisational vacuum in every sphere of Indian life and that in reality is causing the social disintegration.

It is interesting to note what has been achieved on the whole by Rashtriya Swayamsewak Sangha (RSS for short), which has been claimed, as per their written constitution, to have started for developing corporate social life in national society. What is the outcome after their eight decades of existence till now? It did somewhat succeed in the pre-independence period. But since independence the national society seems to have been more disintegrated in spite of their inputs, hard work and sacrifice. Why did it happen?

The same is the story of Marxists. In spite of their nearly a hundred year's of hard work and in spite of their uninterrupted governance in some states for nearly three decades they have not been able to reduce disparities in the society anywhere; in fact these have increased. Their organised efforts did not bear the expected results. Why?

A line of thinking seeks to find the explanation in the structural deficiencies in these institutions. Others find it as the consequences of distinctly different leadership practices and policies concerning goals in pre and post-independence India.

The reasons for such disillusionment stem basically from the utter lack of disciplined civic life, corrupt governance at all levels, criminalisation of polity as a whole, outdated academic institutions, nepotism in every walk of life, utter disregard to caliber and competency, over delayed and more often manipulated justice, confusion without any certainty, hopelessness in every sphere to the extent imaginable, busy police doing everything except maintaining the law and order or policing rightly the society as expected of them and the list can go on without any end. Everybody is thus affected by the total incompetence of the social, socio-political and socio-economic systems at large. The decay in religious systems is no less noticeable.

Whenever there is discussion even amongst the so-called educated ones, all that comes out is the description of the state of affairs and how it is going from bad to worse. But hardly anywhere the root cause is analysed and put before the public for consideration and for inspiring action in accordance with it. The only advice that is given even by the print media is that individuals must stand and do well, in whatever way they individually can, to reverse this trend. But they also do not guide as to how to motivate an individual. It appears as if the society after independence has lost the direction and will to develop national life in tune with time and in competition with other nations. Every society in the world is now organised as a nation with national government. Varieties of indices have been developed to assess the well being of a society. In the community of nations, the place of India in such ratings is simply pathetical. Why are even the democratically and periodically elected leaders unable to cope up with these problems and give decent, disciplined, peaceful and happy individual and social life to almost all their citizens? Why is the organised social life in India so much decayed and disintegrated?

Britishers and Indians

The present day social life in India, to a large extent, has evolved, by copying the British pattern of organisations and institutions. Perhaps it all started with the adoption of Society's Act in 1860 and setting up of Indian National Congress for fighting against the British rule for gaining independence. Various social and political organisations like Hindu Mahasabha and even Muslim League formed a part of this broad movement, at least in the beginning. This was followed by the Company Law of 1892 for the formation of essentially the commercial and finance related organisations, in tune with the requirements of changeover from agricultural order to growing industrialisation. In due course a number of social organisations and institutions came into existence. The most notable being the Gandhian and Ambedkarian organisations at the social level. Several organisations were also started for social upliftment particularly in Maharashtra and Bengal.

In spite of the backdrop of such lofty organisations and institutions of pre-independent India, the history of organisations and institutions, on the whole, in post-independent India, covering almost every aspect of national and social life is one of decay and death. In the last one thousand years history of India, **Shivaji** and **Ramdas Swami** were exceptions to possess exceptional organisational intelligence. They used it fully to establish **Hindavi Swarajya** and eliminated the Mughal Empire, once and for all. But this science was perhaps forgotten thereafter until the War of Independence of India in 1857, fought under the inspiring leadership of **Tatya Tope**, against the British Rule. Unfortunately the same spirit did not continue after its failure.

The same organisational intelligence was later best exhibited by **Mahatma Gandhi** in leading the independence movement. Recently world management-gurus have certified that Maharma Gandhi possessed exceptionally high organisational intelligence and he applied it in managing the crusade for freedom very well. They know Gandhi well because he is known as a great hero of India's Independence Movement and a ***Mahatma*** in correct sense of the term. But these management-gurus perhaps do not know as to what has happened to all those Gandhian Institutions after his demise. In spite of all Governmental financial help, all these institutions are now either defunct or dead. They practically exist only on paper. They inspire practically nobody except giving lip service to their originator. How come institutions established by management-guru like Gandhi came to such a sad-end, soon after his demise? The third RSS chief **Balasaheb Deoras** [1] used to say,"

Hindus do not have institutional minds and rather than building institutions they revel in destroying them". There may be some exceptions but that only proves this rule.

The Britishers did not build just their own nation but built their empire all over the world through their overall organised efforts in the form of their organisations and institutions. By adopting the same organisational setup, rather copying them, to the extent possible, the Indians could not build their nation, as desired by most citizens, in the last sixty years of post-independent India. Organisations are supposed to consolidate society but the post independent Indian society is more fractured than before, in spite of many such legally formed organisations. There is a general downfall in all socio-economic, socio-political, socio-charitable, socio-co-operative, socio-psychological and almost in every aspect of social reconstruction in post-independent India. Does it not pinch the intellectuals, academicians or the leadership and in the phraseology of **Arnold Toynbee** [2], the *creative minority*, in the Indian society? Is it not worth probing it further deeply, so that ways and means could be found out to overcome the obstacles in the way of making the Indian society well-organised for its material and social progress?

After all why we failed on this front even after adopting the model, which proved so successful elsewhere? What are the fundamental differences between the British and the Indian societies that make the model work well in one while making it inoperable in the other? Where did the Indians lack as compared to the Britishers in adopting the organisational and institutional set-up for effective social progress?

In Retrospect

What made, particularly the North-West-European nations so well organised? What factors helped them establish their empire world over? How could those who held individual freedom as almost non-negotiable, built such varied and innumerable organisations and institutions, even by forgoing some bit of their individual freedom, for organising their social life?

Why the Indians, who made progress in science and technology far ahead of any other social group in the world and, achieved once almost 33% of world trade [3], in manufactured goods in metallurgy, ceramics, textiles, etc., could not bring about energy-revolution like the Europeans did, that finally led to industrial revolution in the 18th century? Similarly after achieving the status of world ***spiritual-guru*** long before anyone could even think of it, how did it end up in slavery for almost twelve hundred years?

Exceptions

Is it not strange that when all such once lofty organisations and institutions were decaying in post-independent India, the RSS, which was just a tiny organisation in pre-independent India flourished into mighty ***Sangha Pariwar*** to occupy the centre stage in almost all walks of life and one of its members, during the period 1998-2004, even became the Prime Minister of India? Did it happen just by fluke or there is something the thinkers must ponder over? Leaving apart whether one agrees with views of the RSS or has prejudices of some or the other sort about it, is it not worth studying to understand what factors make organisations grow or decay?

Those interested in such subjects attribute the decay to the societal shortcomings like selfish character of the people. But it should be remembered that only on the basis of selfish interests that the Britishers organised themselves, to the extent that they ruled all over the world. Why can't then the Indians be organised on the basis of the same selfish character? Selfishness is a natural human trait and is universal in nature and, if it results in something somewhere, it must have broadly the same effect elsewhere. Hence the decay of organisations and organised social life, in India, can not be attributed to selfish interests alone. Many blame that all evils in the Indian society owe their origin to the obnoxious caste system, prevailing mainly amongst the Hindu society. They are not prepared to probe this further in depth and analyse the problem further, to go to its root causes.

A country with not less than almost nine to ten thousand years of uninterrupted agrarian social order, peaceful progress without much upheaval, at least not recorded in history, equally long and strong tradition of producing quality goods in textiles, metallurgy, ceramics, etc., possessing key to long and healthy individual and thereby the social life using Ayurvedic medicines, treatments and ***yoga***, earning tremendous wealth through almost one-third international trade, upholding human and social values through liberal and tolerant ethos and all such lofty ideals, to the extent that this land was once known as the only ***Golden and Spiritual Land*** of the then known world. Why such an extra-ordinary society possessing all the required scientific and technological base of those days, did not transform itself into something like the modern and prosperous industrial society, through industrial revolution and its inalienable multifarious organisations and institutions, as did the British society without possessing any such prior social, scientific and technological base as India had? The efforts to eliminate the caste structure, in the last sixty years, have in fact consolidated them more and deteriorated the social organisational order. Why is it so?

Religious havoc

Similarly in spite of growing consumerism, as a result of industrialisation, with globalisation, openness and liberalization, the proportion of time, energy and money being spent by individuals and groups for religion related matters is also increasing. These activities are not distinctly individualistic attempts, as it ought to be, to realise the supreme. On the contrary these religious activities are getting more and more organised and thereby more and more intolerant and belligerent, posing increased threat to social peace, almost all over the world. It is true with all religions, without exception. It has therefore become imperative to understand these paradoxes as well and develop the science of religious organisations, as a specialised area of knowledge.

Industrial Revolution

Although organisations did exist before industrial revolution, it is a fact that these formed more rapidly, in numerous varieties and numbers, after industrial revolution, to cater to the enormous demands created by the industrial revolution. In India, besides the governmental administrative and defense organisations, there hardly existed any other form of organisation prior to the coming of Britishers. Therefore, in order essentially to understand the formation of organisations and institutions it is necessary to understand why did industrial revolution at all occur? What factors led it to occur? [4] Why and how it transformed the agrarian society into a modern society? Why did it occur mainly in North-Western Europe or Britain, in particular? Why did it occur in eighteenth century, neither earlier nor later? Should not the Indian sociologists probe this in all its possible depths, with reference to Indian context to understand the science of social-progress in general and that in India, in particular?

India adopted to transform itself into a modern industrial society soon after getting independence, by adopting, in fact copying, the organisational and institutional set-up of Britain, on a massive scale, through required legislations and other supports. In spite of this, at the end of sixty years of post-independent efforts, India has failed to transform itself into a modern industrial society, with democratic governance, all pleasing polity, all pleasing civic discipline, orderly social development, decreased disparity, upholder of human dignity, regaining the old drive and motivation for progress and so on. These are all the attributes of modern western societies arising out of industrial revolution. Why did we fail on this front?

Apparent Contradictions

In the present day Indian scenario, organisations are formed in various segments of society for varied purposes, more on parochial basis. It is not generally seen that organisations are formed wherein the Hindus and Muslims participate together. Similar is the story of different language people, people belonging to the so called high and low castes and so on for common purposes. Such groups come together generally in the form of organisations only under legal compulsions and not on their own sweet will. Why such a state of affairs exists when all are citizens of the same common nation? What basically is the hurdle that prevents them from forming organisations together? This is particularly intriguing when the same people are happy to be associated with anybody in organisations on international, humanitarian and human rights level. Why does their humanitarian outlook disappear and take the very sectarian perception in the Indian context? Has it got anything to do with the general impression that such international organisations are presumed to be run by the white superior people and hence worth joining? Many Indians are very enthusiastic and proud for being associated with such international organisations, particularly when such people are not seen active in any local organisations. Why does this happen? What is this mental make-up like?

Feudalism

Traditionally the Indian society had been feudal as all agrarian societies all over the world had been. This was enforced deep in to the psyche of Indians perhaps more due to its subjugation for over the last twelve hundred years, first under the Muslims and then under the British rule. The age-old social structure, based on four ***Vernas*** wherein the ruling and governance was left specifically for the ***Kshatriya Verna*** also helped consolidate this feudal psyche through ages [5]. The concept of elders, being more experienced, are always right, was cultivated in the Indian society for too long. The teaching that king is God's incarnation ***(Avatar)*** might also have helped in cultivating the feudal psyche still deeper.

Similar feudal psyche prevailed in no less a degree all over Europe. But organisations were formed and they functioned well even under the feudal set-up there; the typical examples being the organised efforts to discover the world, East India Companies of various nations to trade with the east, Banks, Stock Exchanges and so on, much before the advent of industrial revolution. Why should feudal psyche then prove to be an obstacle in India? **King Rajendra Chol** from southern India did organise expeditions into the south-east Asia but these were exceptional attempts and did not continue any longer. Why did we fail on that front? Organisational intelligence is required to provide adequate answer to this dilemma. India was subjugated for over twelve hundred years before getting again complete independence. Does it suffer from something that came in the way of developing excellent organisations in the past and which continues even in the post independent India?

Is there anything missing in the Indian society that prevents it from getting properly organised? This does worry some of the thinkers. But average man is least concerned about it, why? A true corporate social and professional world seems to be a mirage to an average Indian. Even in modern times the average Indian is quite comfortable in his feudal unorganised world, why so?

Social system is a sort of mosaic group in constant dynamic interaction with each other. Was it responsible for development of organised society in Europe? This dynamism was certainly missing in Indian society because of the long, stable, peaceful and contented agrarian social order.

Management Science

Management science was developed in the western world based on their historical progress of social development in general and for developing better defense organisations, for ensuring safety, at least initially, in particular. It later on developed more against the backdrop of industrial revolution and its requirements [6]. There was no reason to develop such a science in India because there was no professional organisational order ever present in India, except perhaps somewhat in the administration of kingdoms and therefore in defense. In India, all social, charitable and commercial activities, involving production and marketing, though well developed, were almost entirely family centric activities, as far as organisational set-up is concerned. The family unit proved to satisfy the required needs then. The political set-up was essentially feudal, even with ***Ramrajya*** as their ideal of governance, with super and sub-ordinates. Wisdom of a king in the form of a single individual can never be equated with wisdom of a corporate group, in modern sense and yet it is cited even now by many as an ideal mode of governance with Ramarajya as its ideal. This was so until getting independence from the Britishers. During the freedom movement Mahatma Gandhi had put it in no uncertain terms that he was all for bringing back Ramrajya and for which he was spearheading the independence movement. Contrary to his expectations the first Prime Minister of India, **Jawaharlal Nehru** however decided to develop India along the lines of industrial revolution that had earlier taken place in the west. Hence for industrialisation the same western approach was adopted, to generate human resources, through teaching and training, in western style management subjects at the university level. There was not much of an alternative left.

The basic difference in historical processes of development of social structures in India and in the west was not taken into account while training Indians in management to cater to the requirements of local industrialisation. Like many other things this was also copied from the west considering it to be of superior variety and of universal applicability, anytime, anywhere and everywhere.

In the western world, it is generally observed that whenever any one becomes a part of any organisational set-up, he/she at least broadly identifies himself/herself with the aim of that organisation. Normally he/she may not join any organisation if he/she does not have, at least such broad identification. The situation in India is almost the opposite. Here generally a very strange phenomenon is observed. Here the participants in an organisation, in general, do not identify themselves with the aims of that organisation. They most often have their own agenda to follow within the organisation they join. For example, a teacher in most of the academic institutions in India feels that he has nothing to do with the running of that academic organisation, which may be a school or a college or a university. In his opinion running of such an academic institution is a job solely of its Chairman, Director, Manager, Vice Chancellor, etc. as the case may be, and it has nothing to do with him. Here a Government employee does not identify himself with the mission of running that sector of Government, where he is employed. Here a member of a co-operative society does not identify himself in the running of that organisation for the benefit of all. Here members of a democratic political party willingly accept that it is a personal property of some individual or his family, who is considered to be responsible for its management and progress. He in fact behaves that he is a bonded labour in all such organisations. The participation is entirely looked upon as a means of personal sustenance and nothing else.

Here we have to manage an organisation wherein the participants or constituents have almost nothing to do with the aim of that organisation. In other words it means that it is to be formed and run with participants, who are not associates but practically slaves, may be part time, working just for their sustenance in return. Does not the contrast in western and Indian socio-historical processes worth probing further to evaluate better management strategies, particularly under Indian context? Can both be managed and administered by the same management techniques? Will the western style human resource development be able to cope up with the problems of managing organisations in the Indian context? Is it not necessary to go to the very roots of such problems? No wonder British style organisations have failed and consequently it has deccelerated much of the expected social progress in post independent India.

Extents of Organisation

The word organisation is a noun in grammatical terms and is used likewise to describe the ordered structure of a group of people. It is also used in material world to describe likewise the ordered material structures. It has generally been used as a pronoun in the present text. It is also used as a verb to describe the process that creates organised formats of people. At times it is used as an adjective, as distinctly different from its connotation as noun to describe the quality of order. In material world this order is described in terms of long and short-range orders, meaning thereby that the atoms, molecules or other phases are ordered over a short or long distance of the material entity. In this sense organisation is also used to denote the quality of ordered state of various groups of people, extending over small or widely spread human population. It is not merely structurally mechanical in nature. It is related to mental cohesion of the participants. To illustrate this point, family is a short range order and society or humanity is a long range order of human population. Unfortunately there is no separate term to describe this quality of order by a specific term in English literature. A new term has therefore been coined in the present book to differentiate it from noun and to specifically describe the quality of organised state of the group. This has been termed as ***organisationality*** of any group. It describes the mental state of being organised. This will come up in greater details later. On the whole organisation is dealt with here in its broadest possible extents.

Scope

Attempts have been made in the present book to resolve the above inconsistencies, self contradictions and paradoxes by developing the fundamentals of science of organisation, and in its applied form as the management science. Organised forms of people are tangible manifestations, which can almost be felt physically, as groups of people working together. There is something more than mere physical existence of human beings. They also have mental existence. **How do we recognise when people are mentally together? What kind of an organised form does it take?** The present day organisational knowledge does not take note of this abstract notion. There may be some exceptions. It is discussed in the present book, at length, as the most fundamental aspect for understanding the science of organisations. It is supposed to throw light on the very process of organisation itself. This is where the organisational intelligence comes in to appreciate the organisational web.

Presently everything related to organisations is treated as management science in general and business management in particular. The present book does not discuss only the underlying principles of organisations like the companies, academic institutions, the charitable organisations, political and social organisations and the like but also those underlying the ordered forms of groups of people of all kinds. In this respect it is wider in its approach than the present day management science that is generally taught at the university level. Management in general and business management in particular, as is taught formally at the university level, is more about running, growth and development of organisations that are already established. The present book is not restricted to this aspect alone. It attempts to cover all possible human group-forms with respect to their formation, growth, decay, alterations, transformations and so on.

This is because there are several other human groups, besides the standard organisations, which need better understanding from the fundamental standpoint. In general, **human beings in natural course have and always will, get together to give life some meaning and purpose by forming varied types of organic relationships.** They believe that their efforts in forming such relationships have a purpose and that these do make a difference to all those so connected and perhaps to all those not directly so connected. The present book includes in its purview all these organic relationships.

The present book also attempts to analyse all the above with reference to organising the Indian society through organisations and institutions, and explain why, in spite of adopting the British pattern of organising the society, it could not achieve even the semblance of success. Further it envisages explaining, what needs to be done to achieve success in India in this respect.

Some theory has also been developed to explain not only these phenomena but to put forward the very fundamentals of science of organisation, to explain the requirements for the formation and growth of organisations and the organised state of the society, in view of the future needs. It also discusses how and what factors cause decay in any organisation, to finally end up in their closure, merger or disbanding. In short it is basic theory to explain the rise and fall of organised state of the society and organisations in any society. It is this basic organisational intelligence that everybody needs to acquire. Whole of the discussion, in the present book, veers round all important aspects of organisations and organised state, taking examples mostly from Indian context. It also takes into account the historical developments in the formation of organisations in basically the western and the Indian societies and also on national and international levels.

Design

The present book is designed in a particular way. Human beings basically have the herd instinct. But, being more intelligent and innovative, human beings give some meaning for their coming together. Formation of organisations or the ordered format has some meaning and it is the very *reason d'etre'* for individuals to opt for organised form of living. Broadly it fulfils human needs. What are all different needs of human beings? The answer is hidden in the biological and sociological evolution which will have to be understood to appreciate human needs in its full perspective and it is only there-from that the organisations can be understood properly.

Are these needs as visualised in different societies different? The answer to this question, at least to some extent, is affirmative. The organisational forms therefore may differ as per the individual societies. Is it normal for human beings to get readily fitted into an organised form? How does it finally translate in actual practice in forming and management of organisations? The present book attempts to explain this.

Biological evolution is fairly well agreed universally. However no such agreement exists with respect to social evolution. **Alvin Toffler** [7] has put the social evolution, as it occurred in the west with respect to production, distribution and marketing of goods and services or basically in terms of material well being or economics. It is primarily meant to satisfy the bodily or biological needs of human beings. No doubt this is bound to be a dominant basis for forming organisations. But evolution has not been limited to this aspect alone. There has been mental and psychological evolution of human beings as well. Formation of organisations has to take these into account, with their due appreciation. Similarly there has been intellectual evolution as well. Do organisations consider it as their underlying driving force?

To a vast majority spirituality is an inalienable part of their existence. Though it is individual connection between human being and the supreme power or as God in some form, most need some form of organised help in this regard. Organisations have therefore been formed to cater to these needs as well. The religious organisations, besides contributing to help individuals in this direction, have also caused fair bit of havoc in the past [8]. Should we not study them from the point of view of its underlying science? Attempt has also been made in this direction.

Organised efforts have to deal with individuals, societies, nations, international communities, nature and perhaps the whole universe. The science of organisation has to explain the interconnectivity, if any, between these entities and therefore will have to draw not only from all social sciences like anthropology, history, politics, economics, psychology and so on but also from general natural sciences and technology as well to form its main body of knowledge. It therefore starts with appreciation of evolution with reference to organisation.

Organisational Web

Practically all human needs are now met through organised efforts and not by discreet individual efforts. Individuals, whatever they can, contribute it mainly through organised efforts. Human requirements have become so varied and for which so much of complex processing of tangible goods and equally complex intangible and varied services are required such that all these efforts form a very complex web of organised efforts at the local, regional, national or international level. Every one is entangled in this web even without asking, under compulsion of living a happy life. Now social life means living in this web. Living in such a web will be easier and fruitful if everyone understands this web at least to some extent. One can miss it only at his own peril. The present book is intended to help everyone understand intelligently this web and also to recognise ones own path in this complex web for progress and thereby happy and contented living.

TNA Factor

The industrialisation in its original form and that aided by the information technology in its present form, has definitely improved the life styles of even the common man, by reducing many of his day-to-day hardships, by providing increasingly improved quality of goods and services at ever decreasing costs and by improving its economics of production. But it has in general, certainly increased the human greed as well, as an inevitable and inalienable side effect, beyond imagination. Overall human life has become too wealth-centric to the extent of even dehumanizing human beings to a large extent. The natural sympathy and empathy amongst human beings have been very adversely affected. It has also destroyed the family structure which tends to support an individual or a group in times of need. This has led to increased tensions in individual and social lives. The worst part is that these two come as a package deal and material pleasures alone, as it appears, can not be achieved in isolation. The traditional humanistic life-style has been its first victim. The situation acquires alarming proportion since it is being felt on organised level. The situation is almost heading to a state with not much of any alternative in sight [9]. Progress made so far has been due to organised efforts on ever increasing scale, on the one hand, but in achieving this progress, it has given rise to unnecessary tensions, in ones own lives, on the other. In order to appreciate all this and to find the way out to enjoy the fruits of industrialisation, without tensions, it is imperative to understand the science of organisation fairly thoroughly and act accordingly.

Dead End

Industrialisation and development of organisations went hand-in-hand. The early organisations were more pyramidal in structure and bureaucratic in their style of management. It worked well so long as the industrialised European nations had their niche market and captive sources of raw materials in the form of their colonies all over the world. But the situation suddenly changed after the Second World War when they had to liberate their colonies. Now many of the same former colonies are challenging and competing with them in production of goods and services. The effectiveness and efficiency of organisation has therefore come to the centre stage for their progress, more so even for their survival. This has led them to understand the organisational science for evolving more effective organisational structures and better management practices, through appropriate changes. The organisation is thus undergoing a paradigm change. In spite of sincere efforts it has not been possible to evolve any standard format of organisational structures and management styles, which can guarantee expected results, any where in the world. It has been and is still a trial and error experiment, in every individual case, which costs a lot when failures occur. In a way it is always a shot in the dark. When someone achieves success it is trumpeted as *eureka* but soon it appears that it was more of a chance, that too highly subjective, rather than any creative scientific breakthrough. Often it is seen that what style works at one place does not succeed elsewhere. There seems to be a dead-end and everybody is only trying and correcting himself every time. Even those who prove to be very successful managers at one place often fail elsewhere. In spite of our right endeavours and putting in the best possible brains, for more than one hundred years, no standard management practice has yet been evolved that can guarantee success. Is it due to our overall failure in understanding the organisational science itself? Once organisational science is known, right applied technology in the form of management could possibly be worked out.

Institutions and Organisations

In English vocabulary two different words are used to describe the deliberately organised entities, namely organisations and institutions. Quite often these are used quite synonymously without understanding the fine nuances that distinguish them. There are some fine distinctions between them. Generally an ***institution*** (referred to as ***sanstha, sankaya*** in Indian parlance) means an organisation that has been formed for some overall lofty social or national or even international cause and that the objective is fairly well defined in a focussed form. It also implies that there is no personal or selfish motive in any form in forming an institution. When the motive is more selfish in terms of some people, it is commonly referred to as an ***organisation*** (***sanghatana*** in Indian parlance). When the body is supposed to form many sub-organisations under its umbrella then it may be called as an *organisation* like United Nations Organisation or any government organisation. In this book the term organisation is used to denote all such organised forms without differentiating them in any way as organisations or institutions.

References

1. Deoras, M.D. alias Balasaheb, Third Chief of RSS, *From his discourses.*
2. Toynbee, Arnold, *A Study of History*, Abridged Edition, Oxford (1972).
3. India Watch Foundation, *Bulletin,* (www.india.watch.com)
4. Grey, David, *Farewell to Alms,*
5. Sharma, R.S. from net.
6. Taylor, Frederick, W., *Principles of Scientific Management,* Harper (1947).
7. Toffler, Alvin, *Third Wave,* Bantam (1085).
8. Cogley, John, *Preface by Arnold Toynbee on Religion,* Encyclopaedia Britanica, page 441.
9. Kendurkar, M.P. *A Letter* Written to Alvin Toffler, 23rd Octo, 1998.

General References

1. Tupkary, R.H., Marathi book on organisation *(Sanghatana ani Sanghatitata),* Mangesh Prakashan, Nagpur (2008)
2. Koontz,H. and Weihrich,H., *Essentials of Managements*, McGraw-Hill, N.Delhi, (2007)
3. Toffler, Alvin, All Books
4. Capra, Fritjof, *The Web of Life,* Flamingo, London, (1997).
5. Weihrich, Heinz and Koontz, Harold, *Management – A Global Perspective,* Tenth Edition, McGraw-Hill, Singapore (1993)

CHAPTER 2

EVOLUTION

CHAPTER STRUCTURE

It is necessary to understand intelligently the already described paradoxes and problems, typified by the Indian example, in organising any society, primarily in terms of evolution of human beings to the present day civilizational level. This would indicate how the individual and the group characteristics have been evolved during the social evolution, in every society. It would easily pave the way to intelligently understand the total body of knowledge pertaining to organisations or the science of organisation in its proper evolutionary perspective. Biological evolution means development of life forms essentially in the direction of better appreciation of the world around, better sustenance and living, through the development of the brain. Similarly social evolution means understanding relationships between technologies (or economics), social structure and values in a society and how and why they change with time.

Biological Evolution

In the long process of evolution innumerable different life-forms were evolved ending ultimately in the human specie. The striking characteristics of the biological evolution are the evolution of the brain coupled with evolution of sense and motor organs. There seems to be three major stages of brain development in the entire evolution process. The first major life-form with characteristic brain to appear were reptiles and these had only the brain-stem which was responsible for respiration, food digestion, procreation and such other life sustaining functions. When they fought amongst themselves it was more often fight to finish. They did not possess the emotional aspects. This is the reason why the female reptile may eat her own progeny after their birth. The young ones are left to themselves immediately after their birth to sustain on their own. The differences in early and later reptiles are ignored here for the sake of simplicity.

Broadly the second stage of development was the mammals that were provided with brain consisting of reptile's brain-stem and above it additionally the limbic system. This is typified by the cheetah brain in brain biology [1]. In the limbic system the brain's were hard wired to spot and recoil immediately from objects hurtling towards oneself., threatening facial expressions, snarling animals and the like dangers in the near surroundings. It helped to survive the life forms possessing this till the present. It excels at handling threats in a moment. This is besides the reptilinean functions as provided by the brain-stem. That is why they would either fight or flight depending upon the adversary and the situation. They nurse their young ones at least for some time after their birth, before they can be left, to sustain themselves, on their own. Here again this is a highly generalised description. But it serves the present purpose.

The third and the most important stage of brain development was the development of cortex above the limbic system. This is the characteristic of hominids and in its fully developed form this is the human brain. It consists of all these three parts, viz the brain stem, the limbic system and the cortex. The cortex is capable of learning, logic, language, abstract thinking, innovation, creation and many such functions [2]. Along with the brain evolution, the life-forms were provided with various sense and motor organs to judge the world around and to act accordingly, ensuing essentially ones own sustenance and safety. Human being has been provided with the maximum of these senses that is, five sense organs and five motor organs, to sense and act accordingly.

Human being has also been provided with the sixth organ called mind and the sixth sense or intuition to judge things independently of any logic. Man has been provided with brain weighing nearly 1300-1400 gms and has the highest brain to body weight ratio. The evolution of brain and its functions are shown in Fig. 2.1 [3].

It is believed by anthropologists that anatomically similar to the present day humans, was evolved some 40-50,000 years ago itself. It was preceded by evolution of few million years, starting perhaps from gorilla or chimpanzees, passing through Australopithecus, Homo-erectus, Homo-habilis, Homo-sapien and Homo-sapien-sapien (perhaps through Neanderthal in some cases) to finally evolve into modern human being [4]. Has the biological evolution stopped since then, that is since last 40-50,000 years? The answer is emphatically no. The evolution then on, that has taken place, is in the form of social evolution or evolution of mind.

Social Evolution

During the evolution from chimpanzee to man, human being transformed himself, from walking on four legs into a bi-pedal animal, transforming the front two legs into two hands and along with the evolution of characteristic thumb, which made him capable of doing many different activities, not endowed with any other animal. During this evolution itself the hominids perhaps discovered fire and the art of cooking as well. Unlike animals, human babies had to be nourished, for sufficiently long, perhaps 10-12 years, to make them fit to live in this world. It required a long period during which the female was not available for any other work except nourishing the young ones. Since there was no birth control as is possible today, neither other relevant facilities, almost entire active life of female was confined to house hold duties only looking after many children. Man therefore had to take on himself the entire job of food collection through hunting and gathering [5]. The early dimorphic human had almost per force to become mono-morphic and attached to his female and the progeny during this evolution. The limbic system, the emotional seat in the brain must have helped in this evolution, to a large extent. All this culminated into formation of some kind of loose family life styles. Along with all this, human beings also had to live in the form of tribes, for effective hunting and food gathering, as it was not readily possible on individual basis, like many other animals.

But even after full anatomical evolution, the human being still was closer in life styles to animals only. This lasted for nearly the first 30-40,000 years of human existence. This period is now referred to as stone-age wherein man did evolve more and more to live in families and groups as nomads. Man was then essentially a food gatherer through hunting and through foraging. Inventions in the form of stone-tools, some form of hut construction, etc. did occur in this period [4].

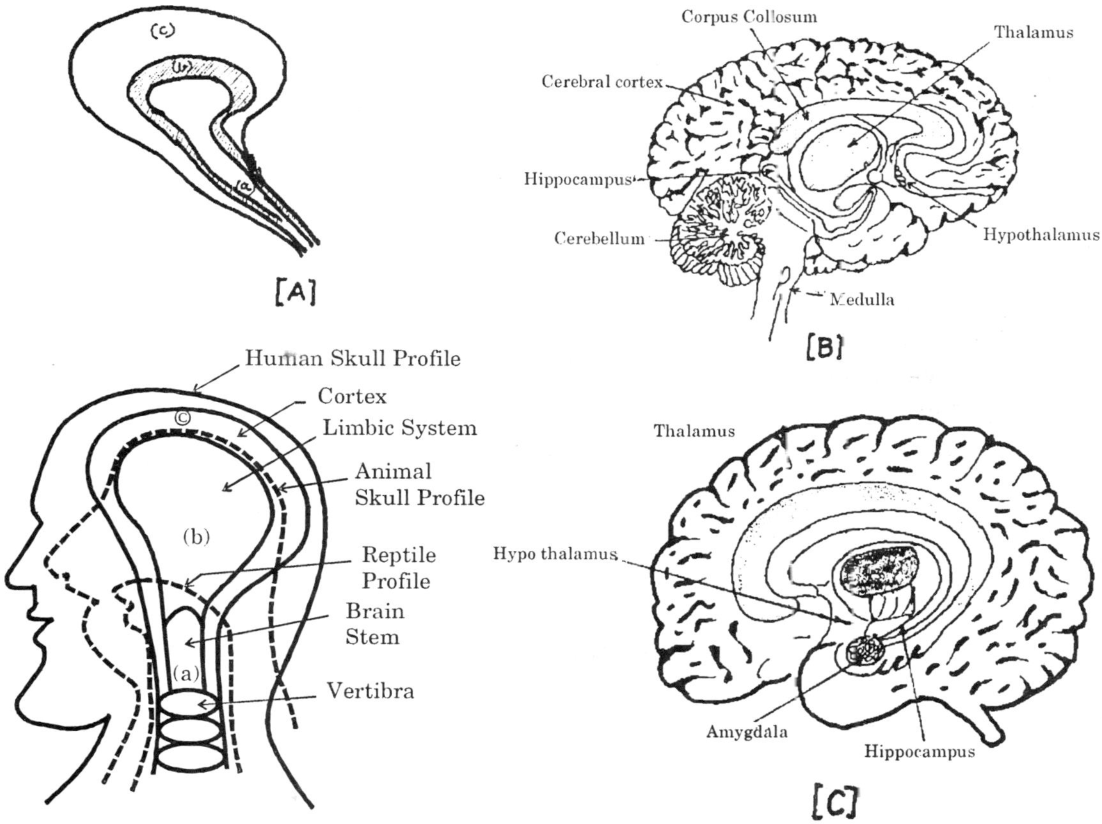

Fig. 2.1 : (A) Depicts the evolution of brain broadly in three stages. (a) shows the reptilian brain stem, (b) shows the limbic system and (c) shows the human cortex, as growing one over the other with evolution from reptile to animal to human. The [B] and [C] show the details of major parts of human brain

Agricultural Revolution or First Wave of Change

Until the advent of human being with cortex brain and the characteristic thumb, all the species that lived on this globe, including the now present animals, sustained themselves using whatever was available in nature in its natural form. They had no capability to alter the natural forms to make them more suitable, for their sustenance and happy life. Human form is the first animal form that does not entirely sustain itself using only the naturally occurring things, but processes natural things, alters them suitably, so that these can be better used for their sustenance and security and thereby make life happier. It requires energy in some form to bring about such alterations in materials occurring in nature. The story of social evolution is in a way the story of how humans harnessed energy to suit their ever increasing requirements. Even the very first somewhat human specie did process stones, using mainly own energy in the form of hands and perhaps legs, and converted them into better tools, for hunting and so on [4].

Then perhaps accidentally, man must have understood the methodology of agriculture by planting seed and cultivation of the crop. This marked the beginning of agricultural revolution. It was indeed revolution because it changed the life styles completely. The nomad had to give up his roaming and wandering life-style and, settle around some cultivable piece of land. This obviously made him settle near the rivers. This life style was not taken by all the tribals instantly and simultaneously. The agricultural men, being intelligent enough, somehow got attached to their cultivable piece of land. Whereas the nomads still wanted to freely roam around for hunting, without any hindrance. This obviously must have resulted in clashes and perhaps wars between those who settled and those who continued roaming. The instinct of fight to finish, unlike the animals, might have evolved at that stage itself out of the instinct of ownership of cultivable land. These wars must have taken a very long time until a vast majority left the nomadic style and became agriculturists.

The description of wars between the ***Aryas*** and the ***Dasyus***, as described in ***Vedas*** in India are nothing but the wars between the nomads and those who took up settled life style for cultivation. The cultivation is represented by the symbol ***ar*** meaning plow in Sanskrit language and hence plowers became synonymous with ***Aryans,*** the holder of ***ar***. This has nothing to do with the name of the tribe having migrated into India from somewhere outside. It is not war between the *Dravidians* and the migrated lot of *Aryans* as is made out by the colonial powers. The current archeological thinking has already ruled out the theory of *Aryans* migrating into India from somewhere, after particularly the excavations at Manikgarh in Balochistan [6].

The agricultural revolution stabilised the family structure some-what like an organisation and led to the development of self contained villages, wherein several families lived together. This was the first glimpse of proper social life seen by human beings.

Agricultural revolution occurred, quite independently at, maybe a dozen different areas, around the globe, at some or the other stage of evolution, in the range from 10,000 years BC till 3000 years BC. This paradigm change in life style due to the advent of agriculture is referred to by **Alvin Toffler** [7] as the ***First Wave*** of change in social evolution and the agricultural society as its product as the ***First Wave Society***. The first wave society still exists in most parts of the world even today. There are societies like the north-western European nations where the agricultural revolution did not change the life style completely as elsewhere. It remained as semi-stone-age, semi-agricultural format till the next social revolution.

The first wave society for the first time became, instead of just a food gatherer, a net food producer, via agriculture. Human beings have not looked back since then in terms of production activities. The sole source of energy available to them, for doing any such job, was human muscle strength, perhaps aided by animals.

Industrial Revolution or Second Wave of Change

By the term western it is generally meant as Anglo-Saxon race. But in due course, amalgamating with others in the north-western Europe, it has now evolved into many of the original north-western European societies that are now represented by France, Germany, Spain, etc of the main land Europe, Britain and Scandinavian countries, their settlements like USA, Canada, Australia, new-Zealand and so on. These societies did develop through the first agricultural revolution in Greece, around fifth century BC. It has also been influenced by the Roman Empire, in the first few centuries of AD, evolving typically in the form of present day Greece, Italy, etc. When this revolution occurred and flourished the north-western Europe was still in semi-stone age. It continued almost until the end of first millennium of AD. Thereafter it transformed into some kind of semi agricultural societies. Agriculture was difficult in north-western Europe and hence their societies continued to be more as food gatherers than food producers, as in stone-age, until the advent of industrial era.

Out of the compulsions of sustenance in north-western Europe, a different revolution occurred in the 17-18th century and which is now called the industrial revolution. There were many more reasons for such a revolution to occur in north-western Europe, in 18th century (for further details see Appendix A). It was primarily based on harnessing of energy, through inter-conversion of various energy forms, for changing the forms of naturally occurring materials into useful forms. This could not be achieved by individuals or even by families alone on a very large scale in the agricultural era.

It had to be carried out on a large scale, which required many different people to perform well defined activities at a pre-fixed place, with mutual co-operation and co-ordination. It required many things to happen as a priori, like fixing a place for people to come together to work. Such centers came to be called as manufacturing centers or factories. People had to leave their villages, their families, to move to their work place, follow working hours and work as per requirements and so on. For the first time the manufacturing activity, being carried out on a large scale, required its proper management. Until then management was restricted to trade, carried out on large scale or for defense purposes only. All this was a paradigm shift in life styles of the society, even on a much larger scale than the agricultural revolution had brought in. **Alvin Toffler** calls this change as ***Industrial Revolution*** or the ***Second Wave*** of social change in life styles and the society evolving there-from, as the ***Second Wave Society*** [7].

This completely swept the so-called western societies with a paradigm change in its entirety. It is now sweeping the whole human race everywhere because it brought in a lot of relief in human hardships, in day-to-day life, and made life much happier than before, more predominantly since the nineteenth century.

The industrial revolution resulted in the necessity of developing innumerable different organisations to cater to the needs arising out of this change. It therefore resulted in developing the science of management of all such organisations as well. In fact it led to acquire and organise knowledge in the form of various disciplines of science and therefrom the various disciplines of technology that now pervade all the societies in the world. The development of varieties of social sciences is the net outcome of this revolution.

Information Technological Revolution or Third Wave of Change

In the mid-nineteen-fifties yet another revolution started particularly in the USA. In 1955 for the first time the population of white collared workers surpassed that of the blue-collared workers. This marks the beginning of another revolutionary social change. The then designed computer became its symbol, since it is its primary tool. It could process huge amount of data, by synthesis and analysis, to evolve some new insights or knowledge, which could be used to make the production and distribution of goods manufactured by industrialisation still more effectively and efficiently. It soon swept the entire globe and affected almost all the societies in the world, including even the first wave societies. Now no nation is free from this revolution. This is often called the ***Information Technology Revolution*** (IT for short), and ***Third Wave*** of social change and the social styles developing out of its use is now called by Toffler as the ***Third Wave Society*** [7]. It further changed the whole style of creating organisations and their management, in quite different ways from those developed out of earlier capital oriented industrial revolution.

In order to appreciate basically the modern organisational science and its applied part in the form of management of organisations, the social evolution has to be appreciated in all its encompassing implications. **The process of social evolution as it occurred in the western countries has been scientifically revealed for the first time by Alvin Toffler.** He has also shown all its attendant fall-outs, such as power shift [8], revolutionary wealth patterns [9], psychological changes and political upheavals [10], religious and spiritual considerations and the like, all of which had tremendous influence on organisational patterns. The environmental worries, as a net fall-out of industrialisation, have been brought out very clearly by **Friedman** [11]. It has no doubt swept the social lives of all societies on the globe, without exception, via almost total reorganisation of their traditional social life styles. It therefore hardly needs extra emphasis to suggest that it is imperative to understand the social evolution as depicted by Alvin Toffler to appreciate the science of organisation.

Is it the only mode of social evolution that has evolved the societies across the globe uniformly as per the above model? The answer is emphatically in the negative. The social evolution broadly occurred from stone-age to agricultural, but it has not been uniformly the same all-over. The social evolution in the oldest of living civilization, that is the Indian, has been quite different, in many ways. Let us see what it is like.

Indian Social Evolution

The model of social evolution as it occurred in the west has been depicted by Toffler and is given above. The social evolution in older societies like the Indian or the Chinese, who had a well developed society, culture and civilization in the past, in the agricultural era itself, were developed on somewhat different lines. This was well before the west was civilized.

Agricultural revolution first occurred in the world in India, some ten to eleven thousand years ago. The credit goes to **King Prithu Vainya** who understood agriculture for the first time [12]. **King Prajapati** appreciated the yearly periodic Monsoon that was necessary for crop cultivation in India in those days. The challenges of sustenance were thus solved for the first time to a great extent, through agricultural production. The agricultural era continues even till to-date in most parts of India, in spite of the fact that industrialisation of India, in the real sense, has also started after getting independence from British Raj, from the middle of twentieth century.

The social evolution after the advent of agricultural revolution took an altogether different path in India. The overall environment in India was more conducive to relaxed social life even in those olden days. The weather was neither too cold nor too hot throughout the year, unlike north-western Europe, where industrial revolution first occurred. It was mostly temperate. The alluvial soil flowing with water and getting deposited afresh every year along the banks of major rivers like Sindhu, Saraswati, Ganga and all their tributaries, provided very fertile land for cultivation at no extra labour and special inputs like fertilizers and so on. This proved very effective in getting good crop even in those days when the science of cultivation was still in its infancy. The agricultural out-put was reasonably high for those days of relatively lesser population.

The challenges for survival were therefore practically non-existent. As a result the then agricultural society in India was self contented at much less labour input and hard work. Comparatively the challenges in Europe were far too great because of the snow-fall and resulting cold, during major part of the year, which made their agriculture rather difficult. Hence in spite of agricultural revolution everywhere, north-western Europe could not experience the same for quite some time. Their life style was still exhibiting the late stone-age characteristics, as late as until the 13-14th century AD. The challenges for survival were too great. But the exception was at the shores of the Mediteranean Sea, where the weather was just like in India, readily amenable to agriculture. This is the reason why agricultural society in the form of Greeks and later Romans developed there, but not in north-western Europe.

In such self contented and relaxed mood, as it prevailed in India for a very prolonged duration, it was a ripe environment for cortex brain to show its full potential in creative and innovative understanding of the world around. This must be the origin of more abstract thinking in Indian society, far ahead of any other society in the world. Everything was favourable for curiosity to rise to its peak, go crazy and perhaps berserk to seek answers thereat.

Curiosity of Nature

In the beginning of the agricultural civilization itself several questions must have haunted the Indian thinkers out of the curiosity of the very pleasant nature around. How does the sun rise and set everyday and that too in a particular direction? How does the moon get larger/or smaller everyday? How are human beings and for that matter all live forms born? Why do they die after some time? There must have been an endless series of such questions which finally led perhaps to ask the following very basic philosophical questions:

1. **Who am I as an individual human being, quite different from animals? Where have I come from at birth and where am I heading to, after death?**
2. **What is this world around? Where did it come from? Where is it heading and what for?**
3. **What have I to do with this world? What is my relationship with this world? Is it an accident that we two exist together or there is something else?**
4. **In this constantly changing world, is there anything that is eternal, non-changing and if so what is it?**
5. **As an individual sometimes I feel happy and some other times unhappy. What is this all? What is meant by happiness? Can it last for ever and if so how?**

Brahma Concept

A prolonged meditation by many along with extensive discussions amongst themselves, over a very long time span, those such questions finally led to the development of understanding of true nature of human being and the world around. The basic gist of that Indian thinking is somewhat as follows:

1. Behind the constantly changing apparent world around, there is one eternal element that pervades the entire universe. They called it as ***Brahma*** which neither can be created nor can be destroyed. It is manifested in the form of ***Maya*** that we see around in the form of only transient existence that is created and it gets destroyed in due course of time. In short what gets born gets decimated. Brahma remains outside the cycle of birth and death. It is a self evolving cause of this universe.
2. As a result there is no conflict anywhere in this whole world. There is everywhere only co-operation, mutual help and understanding.

3. Since the whole universe being only the manifestation of Brahma, there is only pleasure and bliss everywhere. Hence human being is essentially nothing but only pleasure and happiness. One will not however be happy unless everybody and everything around is equally conducive, helpful, caring and happy. Disregarding this, if anyone tries to enjoy alone then he is bound to end up in misery. Hence collective enjoyment along with nature is the only right culture

4. Since the whole world is Brahma, that is non-dual, it is not correct to think in terms of conquering nature for becoming happy. Nature must remain the same for enjoyment for all, including the future generations.

5. Nobody has any special rights or powers over others. Everybody is like a part of a human body in the body-society. There is therefore no place for anybody's ego, selfishness, lust, jealousy, etc. Everybody can have happy and pleasant life as a collective entity alone.

6. Though it is not readily seen outwardly, the realisation of Brahma is the only and ultimate goal of human existence.

Upanishadic Idealism

All these ideas were developed long back in the Upanishdic period itself, when the rest of the world was still groping in the dark and struggling to evolve from the stone-age The Indian thinkers in that great Upanishdic period itself had realised the true nature of human beings. That understanding shall remain as long as such humans exist on this earth. They realised that human beings need to be made happy at four different levels of their existence. In fact these were four different types of human needs or desires. The ***first and foremost desire*** is his hunger and then safety, followed by the biological needs for the adults. These were termed as bodily needs, without which human beings ordinarily would not be able to live and think of anything else. The ***second*** level is his ***mental and psychological happiness***. This is related to his expectation of being liked and taken care by others. Similarly others listen to him and give their ears for what he says and so on. The ***third*** desire is his ***intellectual hunger*** arising out of his curiosity of the world around, to reveal the unknown or create something new. Finally the ***fourth desire*** is his ***spiritual hunger*** to satisfy the desire to know the inaccessible world by human senses. These therefore constitute the four levels of human existence in this world, assuming that soul exists or when one cares for the well being of the world around. If one does not believe in the existence of soul then first three are the basic requirements of ones physical existence. All these in different proportions are to be met to make any human being happy.

The proportion of the desires that one longs for varies depending upon one's own genetic programming at birth, and his social upbringing, on individual basis. Since the genetic programming is distinctly individualistic in character, these requirements are also unique in every individual It is not necessary that these are met in any particular order like first body pleasures, then mental happiness and then intellectual followed by the spiritual happiness. These are in fact integral in character and are experienced in an integral manner, though apparently the body pleasures are felt as the most primary in nature.

Out of the four, the ***body, mind and intellect*** related pleasures are related to this world and are therefore referred to as ***physical pleasures***, in spite of the fact that, to some extent the mind and to a large extent the intellectual pleasures are more abstract or intangible in nature. The spiritual pleasure is related to the other world, beyond our common senses and, hence is referred to as meta-physical pleasures.

The interesting phenomenon about the physical pleasures is that they are felt only against the backdrop of miseries and sorrow. Conversely miseries are felt against the backdrop of pleasures alone. This is because these are not eternal pleasures, but are relative ones. They are fundamentally ephemeral in nature. The spiritual pleasure is not only intangible but has a lasting character. The Indian ***seers*** saw it as ultimate pleasure of human beings and that the attainment of such a pleasure is the ultimate aim of human beings.

All human efforts have to be directed in meeting the above mentioned four needs so as to make them happy. The Indians designed, with due care, the required social structure so that everybody would be able to get the above pleasures as per ones own individuality without casting all in a rigid social die. This social evolution is unique in the world and it therefore resulted in unique social structure in India amongst the Hindus. This will be seen in greater detail later.

Chinese Philosophy

In the Chinese philosophy the reality consists of two opposites, like the day and night, light and darkness, cold and hot, male and female, north and south poles and so on like the integral two sides of the same coin. These are known in Chinese as ***yin*** and ***yang;*** the *yin* as feminine and *yang* as masculine in nature. None of these in the individual pair has independent existence. **Fritjof Capra** [13] explains it as:

"The yang having reached its climax retreats in favour of yin; the yin having reached its climax retreats in favour of yang".

The physical pleasures are similar in character. According to **Swami Vivekananda,**

"Vedanta only explains this reality of the world,"

There is no specific social model prescribed by the Chinese thinkers to inculcate the above philosophy.

References

1. Howard, P.J., *The Owners, Manual for the Brain*, Bard Marietta, (2001).
2. Ciccarelli, S.K. and Meyer, G.E., *Psychology*, Pearson, (2006).
3. From internet.
4. Ember, C.R., Ember, Melvin and Peregrine, P.N. *Anthropology*, Pearson, (2002).
5. Pease, Allan and Barbara, *Why men Don't Listen and Women Can't Read Maps,* Manjul, Bhopal, India, (2001).
6. Rajagopalan, R. *The Secrets of Ancient Indus Valley*, CBT, N.Delhi, (1995) Possehl, G.L., *Harrappan Civilization*, Oxford, IBH, (1993).
7. Toffler Alvin, , *Third Wave*, Bantom, (1985).
8. Tofler Alvin, *Power Shift,* Bantom, (1990).
9. Toffler Alvin, *Revolutionary Wealth*, Borzoi, (2006).
10. Toffler Alvin and Heidi, *War and Antiwar*, Warner, (1993).
11. Friedman, Thomas, L., *Hot, Flat and Crowded*, Penguin, London (2008).
12. Deodhar Dilip, *Search of King Prithuvainya*, (Hindi Bulletin), Vikram Sathe, Nagpur (2000).
13. Capra Fritjof, *The Turning Point,* Flamingo, London (1982).

CHAPTER 3

ORGANISATIONALITY

CHAPTER STRUCTURE

- Social Groups
- Evolving Social Structures
- Organisationality or Chiti
- Birth of a Nation
- International Organisationality
- Birth of Organisations
- Infra-structural Form
- Indian Historical Perspective
- European Organisationality
- Administrative Control
- Social Progress
- Us and They Syndrome
- Emergent Structures
- Organisational Soul and Structure
- Limitations of Organisationality

All life forms are hard-wired in their tiny brains such that they have natural tendencies to live in groups. It is seen in very tiny life forms such as ants, insects and birds or even in animals and, is far more so with humans. According to **Yogi Arbindo** [1] there is some abstract power of attraction between human beings that brings them together. Since it is seen in other living worlds as well, it must be natural to all living forms. That is the reason why a human being is often referred to as a social animal. It is true that many therefore call humans as the only animals who wear clothes. Since human evolution, they lived in groups to make their timely needs met, as far as was possible

Presently people in groups are often seen in market place, in bazaar, while traveling, at picnic spots, pilgrimage centers and so on. These are essentially only motley crowds. In all these forms they only appear apparently together as groups. The fact however is that there is no group-existence in such forms because they do not have any relationship with each other in that form. They have practically nothing to do with each other in such crowd-forms. That apparent group form does not evolve any mutual concern amongst them either. They are definitely not mentally connected with each other in these forms in any way. Such groups are not the subject matter of the present book. The subject-matter of the present book is those groups wherein those involved live together or work together or are interconnected or may be mentally homogeneous with respect to some subject of common interest and so on.

Social Groups

We see various types of groups of people around us. Some are small while others are large in terms of the number of participants. The typical examples of relatively small groups are the traditional, practically stone-age level tribes, families, self-sufficient remote villages, castes and sub-castes in the Indian context and the like. Large groups are the society itself or the nation-state or nations. Still larger is international community or mankind as a whole. Human rights organisations may also be included in it. All such group-forms seem to form one category of social groups of people, because of some of their common characteristics. The other very common category of groups of people, that are seen everywhere, is in the form, popularly known as organisations and institutions. Both of these categories of groups of people have a pattern of people comprising these groups or a structure wherein the individual constituents are expected to remain active in their own groups. What is the basic difference between these two categories?

The first group, consisting of family, tribe, village, nation or international community, etc., is not man-made by any stretch of imagination. These groups are not pre-designed in any form either. They do not consist of, even broadly, a fixed number of participants. The strength of any one of these groups in this category varies as per natural influences. These have evolved themselves slowly in due course of time along with social evolution stretching over perhaps millennia. In fact the various groups in this category are products of social evolution and not developments brought about consciously in a pre-conceived manner. All these groups are definitely active for the well being of those forming the group, or even for larger good, but there is no clear-cut, specific, time-bound and well defined aim set forth for any one of them for being active. Any group in this category does not show any rigid pattern of order or format or arrangement. It is neither a motley crowd like those mentioned above. Those involved in any one of the groups are quite strongly interrelated and mentally connected with each other. But it appears to be a loose structural arrangement of all those involved in any individual group.

On the contrary, the category commonly referred today as organisations and institutions is positively a man-made, pre-designed orderly arrangement of, broadly certain fixed number of people, formed with a specific aim(s) to be achieved. In fact to achieve the well set-out aim, as far as is possible, right people in right number are chosen to form the group and is known as an ***organisation*** or an ***institution***. Their activities are co-ordinated and controlled to achieve mainly the aim. Hence it is man-made and pre-designed. Those involved in such groups form a fairly rigid pattern or structural arrangement.

"Designed structures are always man-made and they are created for some specific purpose and hence they embody some meaning", says Fritjof Capra. These are therefore created intelligently. The more they are created and managed intelligently the better they are bound to serve.

Similarly **Vimla Thakar,** great disciple of philosopher **J. Krishnamurthy,** also emphasises, "**structures are always human creations, since there is no structure in nature**".

Being naturally evolved, there is no specific structure, in evolved groups. However, being deliberately formed, there are specific structures in organisations and institutions.

In both of these categories there are rules and regulations that normally control the behaviour and actions of an individual as well as the group as a whole. But such rules and regulations are not very well defined or of some specific rigid pattern in the naturally evolved groups. On the contrary the rules and regulations, to the extent possible, are fairly rigid in organisational set-ups. There is a well defined controller, leader or manager, responsible for running and managing the affairs of an organisation. But the same is not very obvious in naturally evolved group-forms.

Amongst the sociologists, the functionalists do emphasise that both of these groups positively contribute towards the maintenance, integration and adaptation of the society itself at large. Therein lies the origin of organised forms. Some social scientists do refer the family or tribe also as an organisation. However when these groupings are scientifically defined the differences become very obvious and then the family, tribe, remote self-contained village, castes and sub-castes, etc. can not be classified as organisations in modern sense of the term.

Both groups have certain things in common as well. The participants in any one of them take pride in being associated with the group. This feeling of participation and pride is more dominant in the naturally evolved forms as compared to the man-made organisations. One may or may not join an organisation. It depends on his sweet will or may even by some compulsions, if any. But everybody has to be a member of one or more of socially evolved groups, almost by birth, like being a member of a family, tribe or society or nation. People can become members of any number of organisations, but at their will.

It is seen that good organisations are formed in any evolved groups, more so in larger groups like society or nation or at an international level. In the smaller evolved groups like family, tribe and self-sufficient village, organisations are formed but these are formed more often temporarily and informally, on the basis of division of work, only to execute certain emergent tasks. But in larger evolved groups like society and national and international communities, organisations are no doubt formed informally and temporarily, as and when needed but, these are more often formed, more formally, within legal framework, for executing specific jobs, on a larger scale, either on short or long-term basis of division of work, ultimately to meet larger social/human interests.

Evolving Social Structures

Animals and birds normally live and forage in groups. In the process of biological evolution, the brains of all life forms have been hard-wired to stay in flocks for ones own safety and security. This is a natural instinct. Living in groups perhaps ensures safety and makes it easier to procure food. While hominids were evolving from the animals, the group instinct seems to have remained intact and hence the stone-age humans, who were partly human and partly animal-like in their instincts and behaviour, therefore also lived in groups. This eventually led to the development of tribes as the first social group of human beings and the trait of living in group continued, since then unabated. This is the basis to consider man as a social animal. In fact something like families also developed in this period as described before. After agricultural revolution, tribes along with loose family structures settled around farm land on a more permanent basis. Here-from the families crystallized into clear-cut groups with the transformation of general and instinctive male-female relationship into more sacred husband-wife relationship. Slowly the families became more evident and the tribal form disappeared and social life evolved in the form of a self contained village, around cultivable land. With the passage of time and with increased communications, several villages came in contact with each other and such a large group acquired the status of a small society. The entire population however did not change this way. Majority did change and some small minority still continued to live as per the old style, in forests

At the tribal level itself somebody with superior muscular strength and better organising ability, in natural course, led the tribe in matters of sustenance and security. This is the origin of kingdom and the king running the affairs of groups as a tribe, which can essentially be classified as his governance. When village-form stabilised somebody with leadership qualities must have ruled in some way to lead their affairs, at least in the early age. As several villages together acquired the status of a society, the shape of kingdom and the king must have crystallized and stabilised, in due course of time.

It is natural instinct for humans to develop affinity towards increasingly larger groups of humans [1]. While living together in such associated forms, it slowly led to develop increasing affinity amongst the members. In due course, it transformed into emotional attachment and mutual inter-dependence amongst its members. So in stone-age itself the formation of tribes and families led to the development of mutual co-operation, collective group-wise working for foraging and safety and, all this evolved into abstract feeling of oneness in the group. This is the reason why, first the tribe then the families followed by self-contained villages came to be identified as homogeneous human groups with their own identity. These groups were not pre-designed in any way. They evolved out of natural evolutionary requirements. According to **Amitai Etzioni,**

"Unless sufficient integrative mechanism gets developed society does not evolve and that it is not dependent on external processes"

After the agricultural revolution such groups settled around the cultivable pieces of land and crystallized themselves more as small societies. As communication and transport system improved the size of such human groups continuously increased to finally evolve into proper society at large. Slowly the affinity that got developed in the tribe evolved into common points of faith, rules and regulations of behaviour maintaining the social life in the form of law and order in the society, collective confidence amongst the members and such things, which finally led to evolution of a common value system of the society, to which everyone agreed willingly or per force. This led to the evolution of culture and civilization on a larger scale of the society. It is the inalienable part of social evolutionary development which essentially depends on the **'collective social awareness'** or development of **'collective cohesiveness'** or evolution of **'integrated social mind'**. This can also be referred to as **'social solidarity'** of the group. This is a kind of identification of the social group and an individual in that society becomes known by that identity. The common value system did develop in some crude form in the tribe itself, more so in the form of families and self-contained villages. However it acquired its own stable form in the form of society when evolved on a larger scale.

Organisationality or Chiti

In this way every society, out of their integrative mechanism, acquires some kind of collective aim for its own existence. The realisation of such aim in the society is known as development of **'chiti'** in the traditional Indian literature [2]. It gives innermost support in the form of their collective aim for the existence of the society as a whole. This is the organised format of the society. It is not an organisation or institution in the modern sense of the term. On the whole, it is a common abstract psychological state, of all individuals in the society and, it indicates the **ordered** or the **organised- state** of the society.

There is no equivalent term in English language to describe the same. An organisation is readily understood because of its tangible existence. But there is no way to describe the mental state of the group being organised, because of its intangible existence. The word chiti describes the unified mental state of the organised social group. A new term has therefore been coined here to describe it in English. It is ***organisationality*** and that is nothing but the mental state of being organised. It indicates the orderly state of the group. In grammatical terms it is an adjective and not a noun or pronoun and that it describes the mental state of the group.

Birth of a Nation

If the organisationality or chiti continues for sufficiently long duration then in this historically long and continuous association of the social group, it broadly leads to evolution of the group as an entity rather than as just mechanical group of individuals. It also establishes mental communication amongst its members, in jointly resisting external aggression to ensure one's own safety, sacrificing for the good of the society at large, if and when so required, developing common friends and foes without discrimination, feeling the same joy or sorrow about any event, developing innate common culture, influencing the emotional behaviour of every individual and all such things finally leading to preserve and protect their own identity as a group, as distinct from the others. It finally culminates in the formation of their nation which is nothing but only a peculiar emotional state of the collective mind of the social group. It is only an emotion of oneness which makes them behave in a unified, uni-purposeful and uni-directional manner. It resembles the individual parts of the human body behaving in a similar way in protecting the body health. There is a peculiar selfish interest of the group as a whole behind this national feeling. The intense feeling of being a group as a unit against the rest slowly develops in the group and which is chiefly responsible for the evolution of first society and then nation as distinct from the others.

The identity as ***'us'*** and the rest as ***'they'*** leads to evolution of some syndrome on the basis of, some form of, differentiating characteristics or more a superiority complex of a group *vis-à-vis* the others. The more intense is this superiority complex, the easier and earlier the group may evolve into a society, may enlarge itself by assimilating other adjoining groups if possible to evolve into a nation, as distinct from the others. The evolution may also be aided by historical events related to survival and safety of the group. Historical processes can help the evolution, provided they act and react unitedly and uni-directionally in all spheres of life.

International Organisationality

Formation of nation is the first broad organised form of human society. The language, geography, culture and such things help form national organised form. When it is realised, it is quite natural to evolve still higher level of organisationality at the international level or at the level of humanity as a whole.

After the Second World War, perhaps because of the miseries and holocaust of the war, many felt the innermost and innate unity of human beings, transcendenting their national boundaries. The earlier atmosphere of some nations subjugating the others, trying to rule others, no longer could be justified. International community thus mentally came closer together. It thus paved the way for closer co-operation and mutual support for solving common problems facing the human race as a whole. The organisationality on the international level was thus evolved and as a result, organisations and institutions flourished rapidly on international level. Further extension of the same spirit and mental cohesiveness led to form human rights organisations transcendenting the national boundaries. Now human-rights have acquired organisationality of its own type at international level.

The Indians, right in the Upanishadic period itself, had realised the spirit of oneness of human beings on universal level in the form of one family or ***vasudhaiva kutmbakam,*** neigh the oneness of the entire existence. **Yogi Arbindo** only emphasized the same [1].

Birth of Organisations

Humans being more intelligent, a much smaller group from amongst these cohesive groups can be easily and deliberately formed to carry out any specific task, as and when required, to achieve desired and specific aim, normally for the welfare of the cohesive group as a whole or to meet out some of their own selfish interests. The formation of such groups, whether on permanent, quasi-permanent or ad-hoc basis, is now known as organisations and institutions.

Such organisations were in fact formed in the nomadic stone-age itself. They were more on ad-hoc and day-to-day basis. In the tribal form, the physically fit young ones would set-out, almost everyday, for hunting, for the sustenance of the whole tribe. This was in fact an ad-hoc organisation formed for a specific purpose of foraging for food by picking up specific persons as conceived to be the best, amongst the group, for the job. This precisely fits into the definition of the present day organisation. This is therefore the origin or the *Gangotri* of organisations. This continued at the family level even in the agricultural era when similar groups would go in the field for cultivation or at a later stage for carrying out any family level production activities.

If the initial cohesive group is of small size, such as tribe or family then organised groups can be formed as and when required on a mere temporary or ad-hoc basis. But when the group attains a large size like society, nation or international community, the organised groups are required more on a permanent or semi-permanent basis to perform the required functions on a regular or semi-regular basis, because the division of work has to be made on long-term basis. These smaller groups, with specific aim and preferred recruitment, and working with extended co-operation for achieving the common aim, are now known as *organisations* or *institutions.* Hereafter it is referred to as an organisation alone.

Infrastructural Form

The cohesive larger whole, in the form of evolved social structures, as society, nation or international community, from where the organisations are carved out, acts like the foundation-state of the organisation. The chiti or the cohesive-state or the organisationality as described above acts as the infra-structure for building organisations. The basic organisationality helps in the formation of good, united and cohesive organisations within themselves. As any building stands on an invisible foundation, so also organisations are created only on the invisible foundation of organisationality of the society at national or international levels. Organisations are never created in vacuum. **They are always created in a society, more truly and technically in an existing organisationality alone.** The more stronger is the organisationality the more easier it will be to form organisations for any purpose and the more there will be a chance for them to progress by being more cohesive and united for achieving the aim of the organisation.

In the absence of such infra-structure the formation of organisations and institutions will not be difficult at all, because they can still be created in the form of their own structure as per the legal provisions of the society at large. But in that case the lack of cohesiveness shall persist in the organisation, and as a result, their collective activities shall be doubtful. Formation of organisations and their growth depends on the strength and effectiveness of the organisationality of their society. The awakening of the chiti of a society is thus a precondition for its construction and reconstruction through organisations and institutions as was understood by the Indians long ago. After the Second War the chiti of the international community as a whole developed well, again out of, and as a reaction of, the historical processes of the previous two centuries. It then became readily possible to form organisations on international level. This is also the reason why international organisations could not be built before the Second World War to any discernible extent.

The international organisationality as evolved on the basis of religions is dealt with separately later.

Basically sound organisationality helps in the formation of good, united, motivated and cohesive organisations within the society. The stronger the organisationality, the more easily it will lead to the formation of organisations for any purpose and the more there will be a chance for them to progress by being more efficient and vice-a-versa. The organisationality of the British society was basically developed out of the challenges of their very existence in their history. They could therefore develop much of the required organisations and institutions, even to cater to the needs arising out of industrial revolution, to develop their society into a mighty force, which eventually not only built their own nation but once ruled over much of the globe.

This is the reason why their War-time Prime Minister **Sir Winston Churchill** once said,

"We first create our institutions and then they create us".

It requires intelligence of high order to appreciate this conviction. Nobody else in India appreciated this fact with reference to India more than the founder of RSS, **Dr. K.B. Hedgewar**. This is the reason why he started RSS to first organise the national society as a whole, to suit the times. Though he did not use any such term, he meant to first improve the organisationality of the national society, so that national reconstruction could be possible through required organisations readily. It is also the reason why he confined the RSS work, and it still confines itself, to consolidate and further develop the traditional feeble but original, cultural and civilizational organisationality as Indians, by its efforts. It is also the reason why it encompasses itself to the whole of the nation and not to any section thereof. On the contrary no such serious thought was given by any one while organising the independence movement. It was presumed that as nation-states stabilized in Europe on the basis of their constitution, so India will also stabilise as a nation on the basis of its constitution after getting independence from the Britishers, perhaps without any specific efforts.

Indian Historical Perspective

Before the arrival of Islamic invaders in India, the then Hindu society was living in a typical agrarian era in the form of small self-contained villages or small kingdoms. These villages were quite similar in their social values and culture, throughout the length and breadth of India. The *rishis, sadhus and sanyasis* who roamed throughout India, preached the same values and that is the reason why, in spite of lack of communication and transport, social life was similar all over India. The *sadhus, sanyasis* and *rishis* evolved their unanimity and updated their social understanding, by staying together and discussing threadbare, all issues of social interests, every year in the rainy season for four months*(chartur- mas),* when their movements as was possible in those days, on foot or at best on horses or bullock-carts, were even otherwise restricted. They would then roam over the entire land for the next eight months and thereafter to repeat it again year on year. This went on for hundreds and thousands of years in India which evolved the Indian civilization and culture to near human perfection, as was possible in those days.

Yet there was no system-integration of all such similar villages into an integrated society on the basis of India as a whole. At best it was a loosely integrated society. These villages or small cluster of villages were ruled by a king and such kingdoms were spread all over India. Barring some exceptions there was no integrated administrative governance in India, as a whole. This also acted as a big hurdle in developing one organisationality on the basis of India as a whole. This is a very peculiar example wherein, in spite of being socially similar, organisationality did not develop on the basis of India as a whole. The bigness of India did prove as a major hurdle, but not the sole hurdle. There are other reasons, and perhaps more dominant, which prevented the evolution of one organisationality of India as a whole. This will be discussed later when the ***us vs. they*** model is discussed.

It is often said that there existed common culture and civilization in entire India and that is the reason why it has been a nation on the basis of this culture and civilization [3,4]. This is true only up to its own limitations. There were and still are sacred places spread all over India to indicate its unity. Indians have been undertaking pilgrimage trips to places all over India to substantiate its oneness. A very small number took such pilgrimages. However this bond of integration was not strong enough to evolve pan-Indian entity in the form of ***us and they*** to evolve its own nationality vis-à-vis the invaders. When the Britishers established common administrative control all over India this cultural and civilizational commonness came in handy to evolve modern nation-state out of it. This is the reason why in pre-independence era India evolved as a modern nation, to a great extent, to fight for its freedom against the Britishers. The organisationality developed in pre-independence period was therefore essentially the extension of earlier weak organisationality based on the same culture and civilization of the past. Those who have pride in this continue to call it by the same name and hence they are opposed by those who do not believe in it

European Organisationality

In Europe the kingdoms were small like in India and spread all over Europe. The challenges of survival were so great that these kingdoms developed their own organisationality, just for survival. This consolidated further when trade assumed a significant activity. The rulers of such kingdoms in general, took special interests in protecting their own economy against the others by levying differential taxes. Later as international trade developed, these different organisationalities consolidated further, to protect their own interests as against the others. It led to improve communication and transportation within the kingdoms and without. Wars after wars were fought, amongst these small kingdoms of Europe just to maintain their own identity. All these factors improved and easily crystallized these small kingdoms, on the basis of *us vs. they* identity, into nations or nation-states in just few hundred years mainly due to single administrative control under the king. There was never any organisationality, ever established, on the basis of Europe as a whole, even on the basis of common religion like Christianity, under the undisputed leadership of Pope, over more than a millennium. That is the reason why these nations fought each other for nearly 4-5 centuries, just to prevent any one from dominating the others. It took them to two World Wars to finally realise the futility of such wars, when the international feeling of oneness was even otherwise on the rise. Now therefore it has finally culminated into the European organisationality in the form of European Community (EC for short) only after the Second War, when internationality became the order of the day, all over the world.

Administrative Control

The similarity of cultural values, and the evolution of civilization there-from, has its own impact on the formation of a nation. But it proved to be too feeble, and very specifically, in the Indian context. The organisationality of Indian society did not flourish as required with time until the advent of Britishers and understanding and appreciation of their organised social life. This is the reason why many **Macaulay-System** educated people think that there was no unified society and as a result no nation as India ever existed before the arrival of Britishers and establishment of their unified administrative control over India as a whole.

In the times of **Chandra Gupta**, the First Maurya king, some 2500 years ago, India is historically considered to have been brought under one king-rule. But in those days the establishment of empire did not mean establishment of unified administrative control over the entire population and kingdoms under the empire. It only meant that small kingdoms, with their own administrative control over their own kingdoms, accepted the status of autonomous subjugate kingdoms *(Mandlik)* of the emperor. Therefore even in Chandra Gupta's times, India was not under one administrative control. That is the reason why India, as a whole, had not experienced one organisationality until the advent of British rule. The arguments of Macaulay educated intellectuals may be disputed by others but fact remains that this lack of organisationality did not allow any other activity, more so the production and distribution activities that are so vital for social survival, to flourish much beyond the level of families. It is in a way responsible to scuttle the formation of organisations and institutions in India. On the contrary it flourished in European nations even before the advent of industrial revolution.

Single administrative control definitely improves the organisationality of any society. There should be no doubt about this. This is the reason why many colonies of Europeans, in particular of Britain's, in Africa and America, which did not have even the internal cultural similarities, like in India, spread over the entire area, developed their own organisationality during only the British rule. But mere administrative control is also not enough to develop organisationality either. Other historical processes as mentioned above must have occurred earlier for its proper development.

This is the reason why after the Britishers left these colonies, many of them suffered internal wars between various tribes, which had some independent organisationality of their own. India was no exception to this rule. The Hindus and the Muslims, the main two communities, also fought like-wise, nearly a war, finally resulting in partition of India itself and formation of two different nations on the basis of their altogether different organisationalities. This difference in organisationality was basically the culture-centric, originated from the differential religious, in fact cultural, background of Muslims and the **Dharma** concept, in cultural form, of Hindus. Many attribute it entirely to their different religions out of ignorance.

Under the British rule, because of the earlier similarity of social and cultural values, Hindus mainly developed their own organisationality quickly, strictly speaking on the basis of their traditional culture only, and fought for freedom. They wanted the Muslims also to join this organisationality and stay in united India on the basis that they had only changed their religion and not the culture. The religional differences were never any basis of cultural differences under the broader Indian context. Some exceptional Muslims did accept the argument and joined the struggle for independence unitedly under the Congress banner. But the Muslims as a society however rejected this, considering their religious (in fact religious-cum-civilizational) organisationality as overriding the territorial and cultural organisationality, devoid of religion. Finally they preferred to separate out as another nation. But even the common religious background did not prove as the sound basis for long to sustain their nation. Bangla Desh later separated from them purely on the basis of only its culture and civilization. Hence the culture and civilization plays a dominant role in evolving the organisationality. It however needs unified administrative control to evolve in its proper form, commensurate with the prevalent times. All such things together finally evolve the organisationality of any society.

The example of earlier coagulation and later disintegration of USSR can also be seen in the same perspective. The moment the central governmental iron hand of administration vanished, those who were brought under one governmental umbrella *per-force*, fled away from each other, on the basis of their original differential identity, which was nothing but different organisationalities based on their different cultures. Common administrative control of few decades did not prove to be adequate for developing their collective organisationality. Perhaps the unified USSR administration did not seriously attempt to develop it either. Whatever the earlier organisationality, that proved relatively stronger. The attempts of consolidation of Hindus and Muslims, and perhaps even of Christians, in post-independent India have not borne expected fruits because of the same reasons.

Social Progress

Organisationality by itself is of no use. It is not apparent either. It is felt only through manifestation in the form of organisations, even at times on ad-hoc basis. Organisationality is thus the soul (hence called chiti in India) of any society and as a result, organisations are formed in that social group. The description of soul or spirit or *Ishwara* as given in Shrimad Bhagwad Gita by **Lord Krishna** is,

"He is in every creation and every creation is in Him and yet He is aloof from everything in this world".

The soul of an organisation is something like this [4]. It is behind every collective effort. All collective efforts are possible only because of organisationality and yet it is neither felt nor seen readily.

If the organisationality is not adequate or sufficiently strong then the organisations formed for the development of that society shall be correspondingly weak. This is the precise reason why good organisations have been formed in the north-western-European countries on the basis of their strong organisationalities. On the contrary because of this being very weak in India, good organisations could not be formed and even if formed they did not grow and last long and strengthen the society at large, as is obvious from the post-independence scenario.

This point can be substantiated further by some more examples. Prior to World War II there were just few, perhaps only as exceptions, international organisations. These were formed more on the basis of internationally spread religions like mainly Christianity, which had its own characteristic organisationality, on international level, and because of which only such international organisations could be formed. In other social spheres, international organisations could not then be formed. That period was marked by subjugation of the world by few European nations. There was therefore no international organisationality in existence. Those were the days of rulers and the ruled on international level. Under such conditions formation of international organisationality and therefore organisations was just not possible.

The situation suddenly seems to have changed after the Second World War, more under pressure from freedom-loving USA. Humanitarian outlook developed fairly dominantly because of the holocaust of First and particularly the Second World War. Even those who had earlier subjugated other countries changed themselves, at least outwardly or apparently. Many problems were seen as problems of entire humanity, transgressing the limited national societies. People from different nationalities developed feeling of oneness, cohesiveness and a large number, at least mentally, identified themselves as one single human community. As a result organisationality on the international level was thus established to a fair extent. To develop organisationality it is not necessary for people to physically come together. The pre-condition is only that they must mentally feel their common identity and that too with pride as compared to smaller identities. At this stage, the large international community became ***us*** vis-à-vis the rest as ***they*** in the ***us and they*** syndrome. Let us first understand this syndrome as it is far more important in understanding the organisationality.

Us and They Syndrome

In spite of being nationals of the same nation there exists no organisationality in the so-called Indian society even after sixty years of independence. Mentally the Indian society is fairly well divided into linguistic, religious, Aryan-Dravidian, north-south, castes and sub-castes and such other considerations. The mental division is so sharp that they do not have generally a common social/national visions or interests. Most times these parochial tendencies dominate over national interests. This reality is always concealed under one or the other rhetoric of one nationality. It only means that organisationality at the national level is practically absent in the vast majority of Indian population. They were never exposed to it in their history either. In the absence of such organisationality how can organisations be formed out of such mentally and psychologically diverse people. In times of natural disaster or calamity or external aggression there is, more or less, a facade of national unity or organisationality wherein the original weak organisationality in the form of cultural similarity overrides all other considerations.

Now because of being independent and governed by a common democratic constitution the earlier weak organisationality has definitely improved amongst a small section of the population and which overridingly dominates at emergencies, at least. But it has always been very temporary and those opposed to such national interests prefer to keep quiet, remain obscured and mark time rather than get beating as anti-constitutional and therefore as an anti-national. Whenever the time is ripe again, all these differences come out in open without fear and consequences, often under one or the other garb of regional interests. With all this, the rhetoric is always of national unity, for essentially safeguarding against being branded as anti-national. The actions however are always fairly contradictory.

In India the 'us and they' syndrome could never be developed, in spite of having perhaps the longest history, to help crystallize the Indian society as a national entity, in modern sense. The traditional Hindu-ness or cultural similarities was not strong enough a mental force to have defined them as us and the rest as they. Indians always thought that the whole mankind is one entity in the form a family (*vasudhaiva kutumbakam*) and in fact always worked for the welfare of mankind as a whole. Their entire perception and behaviour was always underlined by this spirit of universal oneness, not just of human race but of the entire animate and inanimate existence, in the form of *permeshti.*

How can national identity arise from this mental-psychological state? In fact the need to evolve oganisationality at the national level never seems to have occurred to them, perhaps because of their understanding of the universe being one whole. The dominance of family-centric social life and self-contained village life, for several millennia, did not allow the evolution of any higher-level-evolved social structures, even to facilitate trade and manufacture, in spite of it being carried out on international level. The challenges of sustenance, being too feeble, unlike those of the Europeans, did not lead the Indians further in terms of organised efforts. The lack of means of transport and communications did not allow development of organisationality on a wider scale as required with changing times to stand against highly organised invaders. In reality the Indians did not understand the implications of invasions by barbarians because of their psychology of universal brotherhood. There were wars amongst the kingdoms in India, the great one is depicted as Mahabharata, but these were considered as *dharma yuddhas* (wars to establish just society) and therefore had nothing to do with the populations at large on either side. The great freedom fighter, thinker, philosopher and revolutionary *Swatantryavir* **V.D.Sawarkar** call this as perversion of good qualities ***(sadguna vikriti)*** in its extreme [5].

The spiritual dominance, in the form of achieving *Moksha* (discussed in detail later), made people think more in terms of individual liberation than for social identity. All these contributed in deccelerating the progress of Indian society in the direction of increasing organisationality. The present day competitiveness in declaring that the Indian society is no different or superior to any other nation in the world defeats the very spirit of us and they. The general political psyche in India of not dominating the world, unlike the Chinese, also defeats the purpose. All these in fact act as hindrances in developing organisationality at the national level, in present times. Many advanced nations are well aware of their nationality but never get tired from shouting in terms of international organisationality. However when it comes to national interests they are more pragmatic and look for national interests first to safeguard them against any international organisationality. Internally they always talk of distinct roles of their own nations in the community of nations. This is the practical world and the Indians need to understand this well.

Unfortunately the Indian leaders even like **Gandhi, Nehru, Vinoba Bhave**, and the like being encultured in the traditional ethos, lived in fool's paradise, to a large extent, as all their predecessors. They talked of great ***Panchsheel Ideals*** (ideals for world to live as one family), emphasising the humanitarian concept, when China was busy consolidating her own national boundaries, with a very long-term world view, by grabbing Tibet and part of Indian territory. Vinoba Bhave had pleaded to disband Indian army after independence, as it was not considered necessary, in a modern day world. What happened in 1962 in war against the Chinese is before us. How the Chinese are posing threats now, along the Himalayan borders, by particularly staking claim on some area of Arunachal

Pradesh is very apparent and, every right thinking Indian is worried about it. These are in fact Sawarkar's ***sadguna vikrities*** and nothing else in the real world. Societies can not be organised on such utopian ideas in the real world. They have to live with only us and they mode in action. Gullible Hindus still live in the old mental world and forget that superior culture is no guarantee of safety in this world. They have yet to learn intelligently the lesson of lack of organisational intelligence from their own history.

Emergent Structures

The Indian society is today mainly organised by copying the British or the western model of organising the society by making legal provisions under the prevailing national constitution. Therefore organisations are created as per law in the form of their formal legal structures, taking diverse elements as participants, without having any solid organisationality of their own. Such organisations remain merely as legal entities in the form of their structures. Organisations do not function properly on the basis of merely the outer legal structure. Organisations do need a mental cohesiveness of participants to function effectively, in attaining its set-out aim. **Fritjof Capra** [6] calls this inner cohesiveness as the ***emergent-structure*** of an organisation. This is because an organisation is something more than the assemblage of men, money and materials. The whole is something more than this sum. To understand any organisation is to understand this additional ingredient, what Capra calls as emergent structures. Those who join an organisation, even after admitting that they shall work for achieving the organisational objective, have to mutually help each other and work in co-operation and co-ordination as a group for achieving the objective. The inter-relationships of all required in an organisation is therefore more important. This is nothing but the same as organisationality discussed above so far. Without emergent structures only legally structured organisations do not progress well. Sometimes they soon get disintegrated, become defunct or die out easily in due course of time. The fate of Ghandian institutions after his demise is typically due to lack of emergent structures.

Prior to independence the organisationality of Indian society as a whole was slowly getting built, by using the British example as a model. It also emphasised the us and they syndrome in the form of British-rulers as ***they*** and the Indians being subjugated as ***us*** and which helped, to the extent possible, to consolidate organisationality.in the pre-independence days. That is why people feel that India was better organised prior to independence. The underlying traditional organisationality, of the vast masses, in the form of Hindu or Indian culture and civilization, though very weak, their love for their only land in this world, came in handy at that time for building the organisationality to a large extent. Let it be admitted that it was mostly the Hindu organisationality, with only token representation of those who later worked for the partition of the country, and nothing else. It however could not be nourished further on the same lines after independence because of political expediency and compulsions. Some did realise this and strove hard for achieving it. They could not succeed to the extent required and desired by them. The ***us*** and ***they*** syndrome could not be sharpened further in terms of India and the rest on the international level. Many so-called Indians then had, and even now have, a soft corner for Pakistan, on the basis of common religion. Some others (communist for instance) had a soft corner for other dominant international powers for one or the other reason. There was no common spirit of ***us vs. they*** seen all through the Indian citizens. On the other side the outwardly differences and parochial tendencies were used for political expediency to finally blur the national organisationality in post independent India, to an appreciable extent.

This is manifested in a very peculiar fashion in present-day India. When Indians were driven out of Uganda, being Gujratis, were termed as ousting of Gujratis and not of Indians. When there were problems faced by the Tamils in Shrilanka, Tamilians in India had a soft corner for them but the rest of Indians did not feel any such emotional bond. When the Bangla Deshis were driven out of Mumbai the West Bengalis did not treat them as aliens but identified with them as brothers. When the Hindus were driven out of Kashmir valley it was the Kashmiri Pandits, not Hindus that were driven out. When Pakistan team wins against the Indian team a large section of Muslims feel victorious. This is the level of Indian organisationality and yet we claim to be one nation merely on the basis of our constitution. **Legal oneness is quite different from national feeling of oneness**. After all it is necessary to understand that **nationality is quite different from citizenship**.

The result proved to be disastrous. Government organisations suffered the most from the lack of organisationality. In a socialistic pattern of social development the overall failure was alarming. However there are exceptional organisations and institutions even in public sector where the spirit of cohesiveness in the participants was consciously developed by the specific leadership. The chief example is that of the defense forces. Being intellectuals and having been exposed to the organisations in the western world and having zeal to develop the Indian nation on the world map, in modern sense, some isolated individuals were successful to some extent in this respect in their own narrow spheres. Such organisations flourished well and contributed their might in national reconstruction. But these were exceptions rather than a rule.

In the commercial world the lack of organisationality has always been a serious tumbling block in achieving the expected efficiency of work in India Monetary allurement has often been used as a substitute for lack of organisationality. Alternatively more emphasis is being laid on training or in emphasising the inherent requirement of organisationality in Indian society.

Lately attempts are underway to develop one's own organisational culture as its substitute through training and modifications in organisational structures. Notwithstanding all this, in general, organisations in India often complain about lack of organisationality. It is also true that organisationality can not be developed so readily in any such organisations in the absence of unified social-base values. It is a historical process and sufficient time is required to develop the social value system and thereby the organisationality. It can not be developed within a short time by monetary allurement or such ad-hoc attempts alone.

Organisational Soul and Structure

It is therefore imperative to understand that organisations do not mean only the formal organisational structures, whereby the power distribution, via various posts and levels, is indicated and in turn, ways and means of managing the organisation becomes obvious. An organisation means a system with definite objective to be achieved based on some philosophy. Organisation therefore also means basic integration of body, mind and intellect of all individuals, in the organisation, in carrying out, as best as is possible, the organisational tasks allotted to every individual participant. It also means identifying oneness with the organisation as a whole, or the group behaving as an integral organisational body. Just by forming the organisation as per the legal norms does not automatically lead to evolution of the emergent structures as suggested by **Fritjof Capra**. These are either there in the form of evolved structures in which the organisations are formed or are deliberately cultivated.

The management of any organisation, in the modern sense, in a way, aims to develop the emergent structures required for their organisation. This is precisely the soul of any organisation and it is nothing but the *chiti* as discussed above. If the body, mind and intellect of an individual participant in any organisation are evolved in the form of an integral individual, he/she is useful to the organisation to maximum possible extent. If this is not so, then the organisation will have to develop it so that the individual participant becomes ideally useful to the organisation. This has to be viewed against the general experience of the day. It is seen that participants often complain of not being paid adequately or not provided with adequate facilities for work and so on and hence they do not remain active as they could. This is the case of the participants being physically present, but not mentally, in the organisation. Intellectual presence may be still far off. This is how individuals will have to be first integrated with respect to their individual body, mind and soul while working in an organisation. Then only the group integration shall be possible.

Utmost efforts are expected from all participants to achieve the aim of the organisation. It will be possible only if all the participants, though individually quite different, like various organs of a human body, feel integrated as a one single entity like the human body. Attempts are made in modern times to achieve this by suitable training. It is therefore absolutely necessary to understand that the apparent form of an organisation is quite different from the underlying organisationality or the emergent structure. Though there appears to be a duality in this, it is in fact non-dual in its essential form because these two can not be separated from each other. They are inalienably and inseparably interlinked as the two sides of the same coin.

Limitations of Organisationality

We have seen the role of organisationality in the form of infra-structure for the development of organisations in any society. However it is no sure guarantee that if proper organisationality exists good organisations shall automatically be formed. There are many more requirements for the formation of good, effective and efficient organisations. Unless these are also available mere good organisationality shall not be able to develop good organisations. But it is equally true that even if other things are available and good organisationality is missing then the possibility of forming good organisations is remote. The importance of the role of organisationality in developing good organisations must be clear now.

References

1. Yogi Arabindo, *The Ideal of Human Unity*.
2. Tuldharia, Badri Prasad, *Daishik Shashtra* (Hindi), Bal Gangadhar Tilak-Smarak. Publication.
3. Upaddhyaya, Deen Dayal, *Integral Humanism,* Bharatiya Vichar sadhana, Pune.
4. Golwalkar, M.S. alias Guruji, *Bunch of Thoughts*, Jagran, Banglore, (1966).
5. Sawarkar, V.D., *Six Golden Pages in History* (Indian), (Marathi).
6. Capra Fritjof, *Hidden Connections*, Flamingo, (2003).

CHAPTER 4

VARIETIES

CHAPTER STRUCTURE

- Permanent, Semi-permanent and Ad-hoc
- Project Organisation
- Profit and Non-profit Making
- Area of Operation
- Perpetual
- Extrovert and Introvert
- Federation
- Professional
- Virtual Organisation
- International
  - Economical
  - Political
  - Humanitarian
  - Sports and Games
  - Study and Research
- Social
- Religious
- Organisationality-cum-organisation

When the society expands substantially into a large size owing to increase in the means of communication and transportation, the goods produced at one place could be sold at some other places. This resulted in increased demand for different goods which then had to be produced on an increasingly larger scale. This was met by division of work. In the agricultural era goods could be produced at family level. But later it was realised that these had to be produced by groups of people working in organised fashion. This was the beginning of meeting the social material requirements through organised efforts.

Modern organisations are deliberately formed for some specific aim to be achieved, usually in the larger interests of the society or humanity as a whole. There were not many organisations in the agricultural era, except the governmental organisations of administration, of law and order maintenance and especially of defense against the invaders. In north-western Europe organisations did flourish before the advent of industrial era. In fact north-western Europe never had a clear-cut agricultural era evolved out of their stone-age, as the southern Europe or other societies elsewhere in the world had. It was more or less stone-age-cum agricultural era. In Europe small scale agricultural societies existed along with more or less semi-stone-age societies for quite some time.

The challenges of sustenance and livelihood could not be met successfully on individual basis even in the stone-age. Organised efforts on ever increasing scale were necessary for hunting, fishing and so on to earn livelihood. The challenges of sustenance and of security were so overriding that the Europeans had to respond to them by searching around the world. This led them to explore the world across the seas and thereby to increase the international trade, even before the onset of industrial revolution.

In India the entire population did not evolve into agricultural society. Some always continued in their traditional nomadic stone-age style, which can be seen even today. But those who transformed themselves into an agriculture era, continued, flourished and remained largely unaffected by the stone-age groups. In this sense, India had a prolonged and stable agricultural era. There was no other organisation, since the economic activities and the related lifestyle of the majority, in particular, was almost entirely family-centric, including the production and trade of goods.

After industrial revolution, and as a result, innumerable organisations came up to deal with mainly the economic activities like the raw material procurement, processing, production, marketing and sales of products across the whole globe, along with all the attendant service-based organisations. These changes did result in changing entirely the social structure and thereby the means of entertainment, sports, arts and almost everything. Organised efforts were required in ever increasing fashion to meet this end. These economic activities are made more and more efficient and effective through the adaptation of the information technology tool that is currently being innovated under that revolution. Knowledge is increasingly shaping the organisations and the organised format of the present day world.

It is impossible to sustain any modern day society without organisations of various types, sizes and in innumerable numbers. In fact it is no exaggeration to say that the human being is born in some organised system, he lives in some such systems, he dies in some organised system and finally is cremated in some organised system only. In the modern day world, societies being very large in size can exist only in such organised format and in no other shape. In other words society means organisations and nothing else. It is in this sense that organisations alone sustain any society in the modern day world. This was understood by the British earlier than others and hence Sir Winston Churchill said what has already been stated earlier. Overall governance of the society ensures their proper mutual interactions for peaceful social progress.

These innumerable organisations can not be studied individually to work out the underlying principles to evolve their basic body-knowledge. As is the scientific practice, and for the sake of their study, in general, it is easy to sub-divide them into groups, to reveal their group-wise characteristics, so that the body of organised knowledge about them can be put forth in the form of their science. It is thus necessary to sub-divide them into groups to bring out basically the organisational principles underlying them.

Organisations are generally formed very formally with well defined structures. Alternatively they may even be formed quite informally without much of a distinctive structure, like the one that comes into effect at times of accident or natural calamity.

There are organisations which operate as a part of governmental structure and at the same time as a private enterprise. Such organisations are often called as hybrid organisations.

The organisations can be sub-divided into groups on the basis of different criteria. It can be duration of existence, size, type of activities, field of operation, whether meant to make profit or are charity oriented, religion-based, and so on.

Organisations cannot be classified strictly according to some basis. Many organisations may fall in different categories at the same time. Yet attempt has been made to classify them, as far as is possible, to bring out their main group characteristics.

Many professional organisations have come into existence to promote arts, culture and music and so on. Similarly organisations of professionals to promote and to safeguard their own interests in their own sphere of operations have also come up lately.

Permanent, Semi-permanent and Ad-hoc

As discussed earlier and with the organisationality developed on social, national and international level, vast number of organisations are generally formed on a permanent or semi-permanent or ad-hoc basis. Examples of permanent organisations are banks, financial organisations, commercial companies, charitable organisations, academic institutions, research organisations and so on. Political parties and their various wings, trade-unions, housing co-operative societies and so on are typical examples of semi-permanent organisations. However there is always a need for some ad-hoc organisations with a specific short-term objective. These are formed for very emergent issues like celebration of somebody's birthday or anniversary or periodic events like *Ganeshotsava* celebrations or Social Gathering or Annual Sports Events and a variety of such needs. Ad-hoc organisations are at times formed within a permanent or semi-permanent organisation for a specific task to be achieved within a specific time limit. Many organisations are supposed to be perpetually, in operation like the university, the government, commercial companies, sports organisations and so on, wherein the participants go on changing regularly with time.

Those who take the initiative to form ad-hoc organisations, take most of the members of that organisationality into confidence in forming such ad-hoc organisations. Ad-hoc organisations usually get dissolved automatically or even formally closed later after their purpose is over. The entire social group is *de-facto* considered to be the participants in such organisations, many times without even their formal approval.

But when organisations are to be formed more formally for some long-term objective the prospective participants, their number, their category, etc. needs to be decided in advance. It all depends on the nature, size and type of organisations.

Project Organisations

Some organisations are created for a very specific purpose like for the completion of certain time-bound projects, within the larger area of its operations. Such organisations are called *project organisations* and are generally created within an established organisation. They get dissolved once that project is completed. Modern companies form *strategic business groups* (SBOs) which are more or less organisations formed within the main organisations for a specific purpose with focused interest, as distinct from the general organisational activities.

Project organisations need not be very formal. In times of natural calamity, disaster or accident people get organised instantly without any prior notice and start work in an organised manner. The humanitarian considerations are overriding and that drives the organised effort for help in all possible ways. Whoever dominates the operation, because of his leadership qualities, becomes the leader and guides the required operations and the others generally obey his commands. There may be instances of quarrel as well if more than one try to dominate the operation and have different perceptions of help or rescue.

Profit and Non-profit Making

Especially the Americans, divide organisations in terms of whether they are meant to make profit or not. Hence those commercial organisations that are out to make mainly profit, albeit along with some social responsibility along with their activities, are known as profit-making organisations and the rest are termed as non-profit organisations or NPOs. Companies, of all types, in general, typically form the profit making organisations in the present day world. Government, charitable, political, educational, professional, literary and those related to fine arts and such other organisations are termed as NPOs since they in some or the other form are meant to render some service to the participants or to the society without specifically bringing any monetary benefit to individual members. That is the reason why these are often called institutions, which are invariably only NPOs. In any society there would be as many profit making organisations as there would be NPOs. This reflects that the selfish nature of human being is associated equally with selfless behaviour as well.

No organisation can be NPO and profit making at the same time. However a part of either of them may be specifically designed for the other purpose like social service or profit-making business depending upon its original nature.

Area of Operation

Every organisation determines its area of operation in terms of geographical extents, units or products or some aspect of social life. Even the Government as an organisation has its own area of operation. It can be varied within certain limits, if and as and when required. It also limits its own size by way of the number of participants it would take, to achieve the well set-out aim. In the commercial world, in the last couple of hundred years, by amalgamating some others or by increasing their own area of operations, many organisations have grown into *multi-national companies* (MNCs) or more popularly now known as *trans-national companies* (TNCs) like Tata Steel, Arcelor-Mittal, Sony, Samsung, Phillips, IBM, Dell, Intel, Toyota, Honda and so on.

Perpetual

There are organisations designed to continue to operate perpetually like the Government and its various wings, universities, governmental but autonomous commercial units like Electricity Boards, Atomic Energy Commission, ISRO, Insurance Companies, Railways and Communication Organisations and so on. People may join and may leave but these will operate as perpetual units almost for ever, with due changes as per the time requirements and as the majority public desires. These are *perpetual organisations*. University of Cambridge or Oxford have been there for the last several hundred years, because of their ability and capacity to modify themselves in tune with time. The multi or trans-national companies can also be categorized under this category.

Extrovert and Introvert

Organisations can be extrovert or introvert depending upon whether they are meant to serve the interest of their members alone or of public at large. Trade unions, professional's organisations or unions, academic institutions, co-operative societies and the like are meant to look after the interests of their own members alone and that they are not supposed to bother much about the interests of public at large. These are called *introvert organisations*. Whereas companies and all such commercial organisations which serve some interests of public at large are known as *extrovert organisations*. Governmental organisations, autonomous bodies, etc. are chiefly meant to serve the society in one way or the other and hence these are extrovert organisations, by nature. NPOs in general may be extrovert in nature. Similarly all public sector organisations are extrovert in nature. Social service organisations are invariably extrovert in nature. Professional organisations like Institution of Engineers, of Architects, of Medical doctors, of Artists, of Literatures and the like are by their very nature introvert in character

Organisations are also formed even if the participants are directly competitors of one another, to serve some common interests of their individual existence or selfish interests. The typical examples are organisations of traders, manufacturers, etc. They can get their common problems solved through such organisations like reduction in government tariffs, taxes and so on. These are only introvert in character.

Federation

Altogether new types of organisations have been developed in the modern world which are called federations and confederations wherein organisations are members rather than individuals. This may also be called as umbrella organisation. The examples are CII, FICCI, ASSOCHEM, Railway-men's Federation, Federation of Government Employee's Unions, Apex Bank of Co-operative Banks, Federation of University Staff Associations and so on. In this case the member organisations operate at local level and the federation as a whole is supposed to operate, more often, on national level.

Professional

The industrial era has promoted professionals to form their own organisations to promote and safeguard their own interests, like the Institution of Engineers, of Architects and even narrower groups like those of electrical or mechanical or metallurgical engineers. Similarly organisations of Allopathic or Ayurvedic or Homeopathic doctors have also been formed on national or regional levels. There are organisations of teachers or professors. Even organisations of the academic supporting officers and workers have also been formed to look after their own interests and to see that no injustice is done to them by the government or the public at large.

Governments, both central and provincial as well as regional, and also on private level have promoted formation of organisations to deal with the problems in the field of education, sports, arts, music and so on.

Virtual Organisation

Many jobs are carried out with some pivotal person acting as the manager and taking help from various people as and when and to whatever extent required, without forming a formal organisation. The job is sub-divided by the co-ordinator into various parts to be carried out by different people as per requirements. The cost is thereby minimised since payment is made for just the contribution made by specific individuals. The job is not carried out by any individual alone, but by several others in unison, without all of them together appearing as a formal organisation. They however work in an organised manner. These are virtual organisations and shall be described in detail while describing the future organisations.

International

The end of Second World War itself resulted in the formation of United Nations Organisations, UNO for short, to solve the problems facing various nations, to the extent possible, without resorting to conflict or war. The area of its operation has been continuously expanding to cater to the emerging needs of under-developed nations and also to cater to human welfare as a whole like better health and livelihood, security, peaceful progress of all, wider education, child welfare, female empowerment and so on.

Eonomical

Economics is the crux of international relations and every nation is selfish to preserve its own interests. But a win-win situation is beneficial to all as is understood in the modern-day world.

International finance and monetary organisations like World Bank, International Monetary Fund and so on have been formed to help under-developed nations for their economic progress. Similarly World Trade Organisation, WTO for short, has been formed to evolve ways and means for effective and efficient production and marketing across the whole world. This is to ensure that each nation concentrates on making what it can make economically the best and buys the rest from wherever it is available with better quality and at a cheap rate. The basis is in the form of uniform tariffs and duties on good's movements. This is also to open up the service sector likewise to eventually make one world community. World Wide Web has reduced the world to almost a single village. The aim is to finally evolve a single world government and a single human society as its end product.

On the same lines some small group of nations have also formed their own associations to mutually help each other in general but particularly in the areas of economics. The European Community is perhaps the first one to form such an organisation. The others are FTA, ASEAN, SAARC and so on. They are slowly evolving into a still wider area of co-operation beyond just economics.

Political

The Second World War changed the political alignments on international levels and inter-governmental organisations like the NATO, CENTO, SEATO or non-aligned nations block and so on were formed to serve some or the other purpose of national security and political influence. Those who did not want to join any specific group formed the *non-aligned movement* in the form of an organisation. Here the members are the Governments to be represented by appropriate dignitaries. Similarly to look after the common interests of some nations, organisations are formed by interested Governments for some specific purposes. The examples are organisations as Nuclear Non-Proliferation Group, or of Nuclear Fuels Club and so on to prevent the destructive nuclear energy getting into the hands of backward societies.

Humanitarian

Even before UNO was born there have been some individuals who were moved by the human misery and therefore they started some humanitarian organisations disregarding their national boundaries. The Red-Cross is a typical example to illustrate them. Christianity was in the vanguard in this respect and must be given its due credit. In its original form it was meant to serve humanity only. Earlier the Red Cross was meant to nurse the wounded in wars on either side, purely on humanitarian considerations, but now it has expanded its area of operation to humanitarian work at large. Similarly there are many organisations to look after specific humanitarian aspects like human rights, women empowerment, child care, food for hungry and so on. Amnesty International is one such. But often they do not appear all that neutral and dedicated to the proclaimed cause alone. If they do they have to take into account the local social factors and not weigh or assess anything and everything only on the scale of western social perceptions, it might prove better.

Sports and Games

International Olympic Organisation is another of its types to look after and establish excellence in games and sports, and sportsmanship in particular, on international level, irrespective of any other considerations. It has been there in existence for more than a century now and has been doing excellent work. Similarly there is an organisation to look after sports interests of Commonwealth Nations as well. Cricket, Football and such individual games, are looked after by international organisations or federations of organisations for that particular game, transcending the national boundaries. All are very active and almost universally liked by the sports-lovers.

Study and Research

There are organisations formed purely for study and research in fields of interests to the entire international community as a whole or for a group of some nations for their mutual benefits. Such organised activities typically refer purely to the development of science, technology, strategic studies, environmental protection, historical and archeological monument protection, defense related matters and so on. They in a way generally help avoid wars and help maintain peace, help develop science and maintain heritage and culture around the globe.

Social

Numerous organisations have been formed by governments and on individual initiatives to cater to the requirements of education, sports, arts, charity, economics, construction, transport, entertainment and so on to cover almost the entire range of social activities including politics.

Religious

There is no need to have religious organisations in the true sense of the term since religion is related purely to one's connection or union with the supreme-power that is beyond human senses, commonly referred by the common term as God. But the Semitic religions have been formed on exclusiveness principle. It means those who belong to their religion are considered in someway superior and the rest as inferior and that they would like to convert the entire human race to their own order. This required organised efforts for the propagation of exclusively their own religions. These religions therefore were formed in a much organised way, right from their beginning. Christianity organised it through Church and the hierarchies of Pastors and, Islam organised it, on local levels, through Majsid and Mullah-Moulavis supported by the social laws. This character still continues. These are no longer that homogeneous and monistic in character as the original ones, since several different denominations have cropped up in both of these religions. Yet they have their own organisationality on the international level, transgressing the national boundaries. This organisationality exhibits itself at times as an organisation in various forms. In fact their religious interests, at times rein supreme to the extent that they do not have regard for national or regional interests in relation to their religious interests.

The religious organisations flourish by using the weak psychology of an individual and his earnest desire to know what is the world like beyond the human senses. They also flourish because they claim to propound even the social and economical order, suited for this overall purpose, for their followers, along with.

They would like to cast the human race into a huge monolithic, which is quite non-synergic with nature. Nature abhors symmetry but enjoys diversity in every aspect of human existence and in that sense their efforts to cast humanity in mono-cast is fundamentally anti-nature, for certain. These religions do form organisations within the national boundaries, under one or the other pretext to help propagate, in reality, their religions alone by increasing their number by conversion of the locals. They are at times happy in merely increasing their number mechanically in the form of some organisationality.

It must be appreciated that some 1500 years ago Christianity helped to develop some kind of organisationality based on religion in Europe and which lasted for at least a millennia before it was replaced by other forms of organisationalities. The acceptance of Christianity as their state religion by the Romans must have helped to evolve the Christianity based organisationality in Europe.

Similarly Islam also proved to be a good tool in establishing organisationality, in the area where it flourished, because their social law in the form of *shariya* was enforced everywhere through the state power only.

The religious organisations within Hindu fold are quite different from the religious organisations of Christians and the Muslims. These are well focused for attaining salvation, by some devotional path, with specific attendant rituals, prescribed by some enlightened soul. There have been many such religions, more commonly known as *sampradayas* in the Indian parlance. Some of them were decimated and new ones were born, within overall fold of Hindu cultural ethos. There are also some exceptions like Lord Buddha and Mahavir Jain who deviated fair bit from the traditional perceptions but still remained within the overall Indian cultural and civilizational fold because they propagated their teachings, on the whole, within the same social value system. Moreover they do not have their separate social code, other than that of traditional Hindus.

Organisationality-cum-organisation

It has already been shown that the formation of organisations is essentially based on the duality of organisation and the society. This distinction is usually very apparent in most organisations. But what happens when this distinction is blurred? Typical examples of when it is blurred or is not very clear are the processions, *morchas, dindi* (religious procession in Marathi) or public demonstration of anger against somebody or the government on a specific issue. In such cases scientific scrutiny fails to identify them clearly as either organisationality or as an organisation. These apparently happen to have some loose structure and objective alright, but the number of participants is anything but fixed. Many times they may not have a controller, leader or a manager; the group acts on its own. Such discrepancies do exist and hence the confusion remains whether to call them specifically as ad-hoc organisations formed within the existing organisationality.

The *Indian National Congress,* formed for liberating India from the British Rule was one such organisation. It was more a movement rather than an organisation. It considered itself as equivalent to the nation as a whole, since it always spoke on behalf of people of India as a whole. There was no rigid and specific structure, encompassing every one right down to the lower most level, to make it look like an organisation. There was a small group claiming to be their guide and philosopher. It included one and all without much insistence on any rigid discipline. The *Acharya Kul* started by **Vinoba Bhave** was another one like this, but it did not flourish much to come into the notice of all.

The best example of this category is that of RSS. It considers itself as co-extensive with the nation since it has been formed to develop basically the organisationality of the Indian society and not to develop as an organisation of some people from amongst the society, to serve the nation in some or the other aspect of national interest. It is claimed by their adherents that the interests of RSS are nothing less than only and only national interests. There is no parochial interest of any kind, except that of nation; howsoever one may disagree with their perception of nation. Hence it is not interested in any group or individuals at all. Outwardly it appears to be an organisation working for this aim but the aim itself states that it shall wither away when the national society's interests, by and large, match with that of the RSS or *vice versa.* This is an exceptional, apparently looking like an organisation, but meant to create basically the required organisationality of the

Indian national society. Organisationality is missing from the Indian society even after attaining independence as has already been highlighted earlier. This is their attempt, at least claimed by them, to increase the organisationality alone. There is no parallel example of the same elsewhere in the world. It is unique in this respect and hence deserves attention to understand basically the organisational science.

The founder of RSS, **Dr. K.B. Hedgewar** had exceptional insight into organisational science. He believed that organised state or organisationality is the natural state of any society and such a society has all the necessary strength to overcome any and every challenge that comes in the way and make further progress at any time.

"There is no alternative to the development of organisationality", emphasised Dr. Hedgewar [1,2]. He firmly believed, emphasised and acted accordingly in sacrificing his entire life for that cause in the form of RSS. The RSS, started in 1925, is his brain-child and aimed at achieving the necessary organisationality that is missing, in the Indian society. Even after his demise in 1940 the RSS continued to grow and has since then grown into a mighty ***Sangha Pariwar*** now. This is a unique organisation of its own type in the entire spectrum of organisations and hence deserves attention to understand fundamentally the science of organisation.

Karl Marx also visualised that through the state a society shall emerge wherein **'from each according to his capacity to each according to his needs'** shall take place, giving rise to a society free from high and low, superior and inferior and any such distinctions, what he referred to as the classless society. His ideas are now codified and known as Marxism. In fact it is an organisation-free society, as was imagined by him and which does not seem to be scientifically possible, in the present day world.

It however does resemble the ideal society that is believed by Indians to have existed in India in the *sat-yug* (era of truth alone) long ago, and has been described as below:

na rajyam na cha rajasit
na dando na cha dandikah /
dharmenaiva prajah sarvah
rakshanti sma parasparam //

Meaning thereby that once upon a time, in the ***sat-yug,*** ideal society did exist, wherein there was no criminal, no king to punish, everybody lived according to their duties such that they protected themselves. One can aim at such an ideal organisationality wherein ideal organisations will only be built.

References

1. Palkar, N.H., *Dr. Hedgewar,* (Biography in Marathi), Datey, Dr. Hedgewar Memorial Soc., Pune, (1960)
2. Sinha, Rakesh, *Dr. Keshav Baliram Hedgewar,* (Biography in Hindi), Publications Division, Govt of India, New Delhi (2003)

CHAPTER 5

ORIGIN

CHAPTER STRUCTURE

Selfishness and Cohesiveness

Every life form must sustain itself through some form of food intake. It provides the required energy to sustain life directly. This is a natural instinct. Food must be available at their own site for those life forms that do not possess locomotion, like plants, trees, bushes, shrubs, etc. Those life-forms who have own locomotion can move around, at least to some extent, search for food and take it, if possible. It is in the selfish interest of one's own life to keep alive. The alternative is death, which is not chosen so readily. Besides there is often worry about safety and security of one's own life. This is also a natural instinct inbuilt in every life-form. In fact there are **four distinct natural instincts** which every life form possesses as their pure and simple nature or instinctual self. These are *firstly* the food intake, *secondly* fear and security needs, *thirdly* sleep and *fourthly* sex for procreation. Out of these sleep is naturally available and almost no effort is required to get it. Similarly sex is commonly available at some age readily because of the natural attraction between the male and the female. However it can be a cause of conflict and therefore some commonly agreeable arrangement has to be made for its equitable distribution, through marriages in human beings.

But every life form has to strive, and strive regularly, to get the remaining two, that is food and security. These are not naturally available. It requires some efforts to get it. These two instincts motivate the living beings to get together in their own groups, flocks, etc. since it instinctively ensures better safety and better chance of getting food. This is seen in insects, organisms, animals, birds including human beings alike. This is instinctively the origin of cohesiveness or organisationality, as seen in all the living forms with locomotion.

Man has been evolved out of the animal world in some way and hence possesses the same flocking or group instinct for its own survival. Hence even in the stoneage humans lived in groups in the form of tribes, the glimpse of which can still be obtained today, in its remnant form, in some isolated parts of the world like Central Australia, Andaman-Nicobar islands of India, some parts of Africa and so on. Human being is the most intelligent of all living beings because nature has provided human beings with the characteristic cortex-brain. Hence man got evolved, in natural course itself, in the form of organisationality of tribe, family, self-sufficient village, society and nation and on international and human rights levels. **"But with social evolution and being very intelligent, human being, by the very nature, consciously form other required groups to achieve the desired objectives,"** according to **Aristotle**.

In Hindu ethos human beings are differentiated from the rest of the living world very articulately as below:

The similarities between human beings and animals are shown as:

Aahaar nidra bhaya maithunan cha

Saamanyametat pashubhirnaranam - *Mahabharata ShantiParva* (294.29)

which means *aahaar* (food to keep oneself alive), *nidra* (sleep), *bhaya* (fear) and *maithun* (sex for procreation) are common to human beings and animals.

But there is one difference and by stating that difference this quartet is completed as:

dharmo hi teshamaadhiko vishesho

dharmenahinaah pashubhi samaanaah -

It is the Dharma defined in Indian context (as not religion, but more as one's duties for sustaining the society in the early days and later the entire universe) which is an attribute of human beings because of their cortex brain, as different from animals. It is this additional intelligence that has endowed the human beings with the capacity to evolve organisationalities in various forms as mentioned above and also, after adequate social evolution, to evolve consciously and deliberately the varieties of required organisations.

It only means that in the absence of culture and civilization the animals and humans were more or less, on the same plane. The various attributes of human cortex makes humans capable of mutual love, dependence, sharing, co-operation, tangible and intangible relations and so on amongst themselves and which are responsible for consciously developing organised and integrated social life for the benefit of all.

Hence in its ultimate analysis purely selfish interests and needs drive humans to form organisations required for their happy, joyful and finally satisfactory living on earth.

Pleasure/Happiness Rationale

Next logical question arises as to what constitutes human happiness? This is the big question that needs to be understood properly in its all-encompassing significance, so that his needs can be assessed more rationally. All individuals are individually unique in themselves. Because of their characteristic individual genetic origin and upbringing in different surroundings and forms, they develop in themselves their own characteristic value system, which decides what is more important and dominantly to be achieved in one's own life any time. They have therefore different needs, ambitions, attitudes, desires, responsibilities, levels of knowledge, skills, potentials and above all a way of behaviour. This is a scientific fact and is unlike the politico-social rhetoric in the form of absolute equality of human beings. Yet all these needs can be broadly categorised in some common groups for considerations. Psychologist **Abraham Maslow** [1] has enumerated these needs in the form of hierarchy of their importance. These are also shown in **Fig. 5.1**. These are:

1. Physical or bodily needs in the form of food for sustenance
2. Security needs out of natural instinctual fear
3. Biological needs (sex) to satisfy urge for procreation
4. Psychological needs of love, caring, belonging, etc.
5. Affiliation and acceptance needs as being liked and loved by others
6. Esteem needs in the form of appreciation by others.
7. Self-actualization needs to ultimately satisfy one's overall ego.

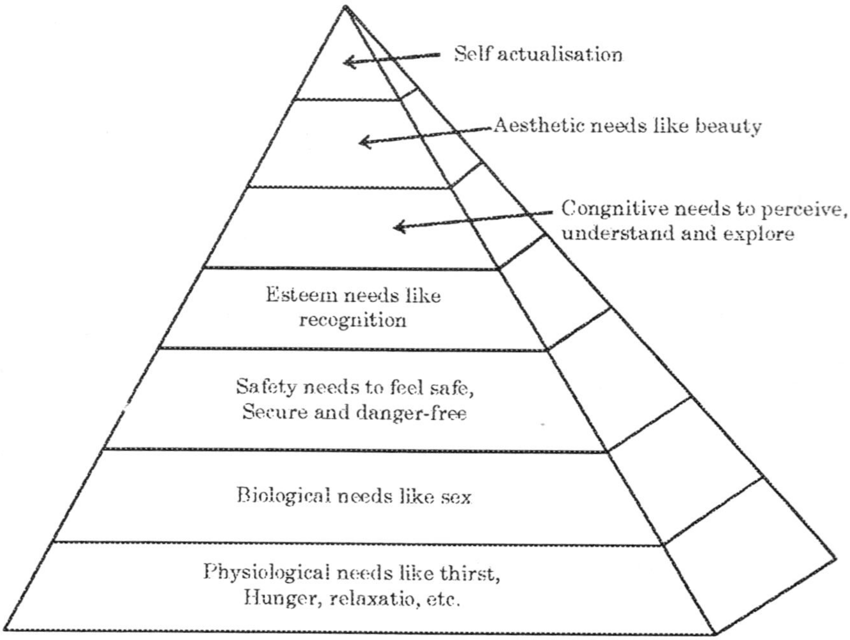

Fig. 5.1 : Hierarchy of human needs according to Abraham Maslow [1]

These needs may differ from person to person to a significant extent. Howsoever one may disagree with their hierarchical arrangement, because humans can not be fitted in such straight jackets but needs as enumerated, in general, do exist. It is true that satisfying these needs make one satisfied and happy. It is most obvious that satisfying hunger (with thirst as well) is the most primary of all needs of human beings, neigh of every living being. A hungry human being feels happy when he is fed, that's for certain. We are not certain whether the rest of the living beings feel happy this way. Perhaps they also must be feeling the same way, but they have no means to express.

However is it the only way for human beings to feel happy? The answer is emphatically no. When stomach is full human beings would later on like better quality and tasty food to fill their stomachs or that too in good surrounding, perhaps in a five star hotel with candle lights and so on. These now make him happier. But it is also equally true that even with empty stomach he would rather feed his parents or children or even at times a more hungry person and feel happy in doing so. What type of happiness does he experience this way? Even while being hungry a person would not eat, if food is thrown at him with abuse. Food remains food whether served with love or abuse. Does he not get happiness by eating such thrown and abused food? Where does the difference lie? It only means that there is something of higher level that is hurt in this process. He would forego food rather than getting his hungry stomach filled in this way. Sometimes somebody is engrossed in some work of unfolding the true nature in some respect and gets so engrossed in it, that he does not feel hungry or thirsty at all. He almost forgets it. What kind of happiness does he feel in this endeavour?

This is in fact the same story about everything that human being is capable of enjoying through all his five senses. The same thing happens with music or scenic beauty or pleasant smell. While enjoying good music in a pleasant surrounding, if suddenly a message comes that some one dear to him has suddenly expired, will he continue to enjoy the same as before? No, now he is in no mood to enjoy the same, what he was enjoying a moment ago. He is suddenly very unhappy. Where has his happiness gone? Why does it so happen? Because he is no more in a mental state to enjoy it as before. He is full of sorrow. In other words there is mental level where he needs to feel happy as well.

One more observation deepens this thought further. While enjoying these worldly pleasures one gets slowly bored by even the same enjoyment. It is referred to as the **Law of Diminishing Returns** with respect to food intake in economics. This is only partial statement of the truth. The fact of diminishing returns is that the enjoyment obtainable, through any of the five senses, decreases as one goes on enjoying the same, but at the same time the desire to enjoy it, goes on getting more and more intense. In the extreme, it is possible that the value of enjoyment becomes zero but the innate desire to enjoy the same is infinite. Where does the happiness lie then?

It only means that getting fed or getting enjoyment, through any one or all the five senses, definitely makes one happy but it is not the end of happiness. They have their own limitations to make humans happy. It holds true within those limitations alone. There are other levels as well where human being can and does become happy. In other words he needs those requirements also to be met to make him happy. Where is the end of all this?

Although it has already been explained earlier in Chapter 2 (page 23) in Section on Upanishadic Idealism, it is being elaborated here to describe human needs against the backdrop of modern perceptions in human psychology. The basic needs as explained by Maslow in the form of physiological and biological needs and the bodily desires in the form of hunger, thirst, etc. and biological needs like sex, as explained in the Upanishadic wisdom are just the same. It also includes rest, sleep, medication, etc that relieves the body from fatigue, any discomfort and pain. It is agreed by both that these are the most basic or primary needs and have to be met on priority before anything else can be considered. If stomach is empty nothing else can be thought of by ordinary human beings. It is said in Hindi that when stomach is empty one can not worship even God *(khali pet na bhaajan howe gopala)*. Maslow also talks of happiness resulting from objects of the world through senses. Esteem needs like recognition, love, etc. by others or safety and security needs or assertion and expression and, on the whole danger-free living satisfies the mental needs as explained in the Upanishadic wisdom.

The aesthetic and cognitive needs of Maslow may be close to the intellectual needs as visualized by the Upanishadic thinkers. The intellect as imagined by the Upanishadic thinkers is however somewhat different. It is the power that decides which one amongst all that is desired is worth striving for. It is more a rational and overriding force that decides as to what should be finally adopted amongst the available choices. The specific spiritual needs as explained by the Upanishadic thinkers are just not acceptable to western mind and Maslow is obviously no exception to it. But Maslow's self actualisation is definitely something higher than just the physical needs and therefore it is somewhat meta-physical in nature.

All these requirements in different proportions are to be met to make human beings happy. The proportion varies depending upon his genetic programming, at birth, and his social upbringing, on individual or social basis. Since the genetic programming is distinctly individualistic in character, these requirements are also unique in every individual It is not necessary that these are met in any particular order like first body pleasures, then mental happiness and then intellectual followed by the spiritual happiness. These are in fact **integral in character** and are enjoyed in integral manner, though apparently the body pleasures are felt as most primary in nature.

It is true that Maslow's analysis covers human needs and desires in greater details than that explained by the Upanishadic thinkers. The Upanishadic thinkers bundled up most of them as bodily needs. They concentrated more on the mental needs and probed them in depth since they felt that the mental needs are the main obstacle on the path towards salvation. That is why the most important difference between the two perceptions is in the understanding of the worldly physical pleasures. Maslow however does not see the most fundamental part and that is the relativism in experiencing the physical pleasures or its converse as sorrow or pain. Physical happiness is felt only against the backdrop of sorrow or pain and vice-a-versa as was emphatically propounded by the Upanidshadic thinkers. The spiritual pleasure is absolute and that is the reason why the Indian seers saw and felt it as ultimate pleasure that human beings can experience and must strive for and hence they called it as bliss.

This difference in fundamental perception led the westerners to focus their attention more on achieving the physical pleasures whereas the Indians focused their attention on spiritual attainment. It is worth understanding how these two fundamentally different perceptions led to the development of these two societies and their organisations.

The origin of organisational life of humans goes back to this basic human character. The bird and the animal worlds are characterised by their ***flight or fight*** syndrome. Their flocking tendency originates from this syndrome since security dominates their group character more than their food procurement. Food requirements have to be obtained by them purely individually and hence do not need group existence, in general, for that. In modern times human needs can not all be met by individual endeavours. Organised efforts are a must, to that end.

Through formation of society or nation, humans have in a way, ensured their security. Hence the body, mind and intellectual desires are to be met through organised efforts, particularly when the requirements have been increasing with increasing socialisation to almost unlimited extent.

Real Happiness

Where does the real happiness lie? As is understood by the Indian seers it is not in physical pleasures. Is it in spiritual endeavours? The answer is complex. According to

Swami Vivekanand and as propounded by his best disciple Late Shri **M.S.** alias **Guruji-Golwalkar** [2], the second RSS-Chief, the answer is as follows:

"The real happiness in reality exists in every human being himself. It does not reside in anything outside. In fact he is the embodiment of absolute happiness or bliss. Happiness is not without but within him alone. The outside physical world, with all its attractive things, is only apparent *(nimitta)* reason to feel the inner happiness. At the time of enjoying the worldly things, the existence of that very worldly thing is lost from the mind at that very moment of realisation of happiness. What is being experienced is nothing but the real pleasure residing inside oneself. Hence the desire to be happy is basically quite natural to human beings. Human being is nothing but happiness alone."

Once this happiness is realised then nothing else is left to be achieved in this world. The Indian seers realised all this, long ago and felt that it pervades the entire animate and inanimate existence. They called it Brahma which is all pervading, omniscient and omnipresent. It cannot be described by any worldly language, similes or metaphors. The Indian seers had therefore the courage to describe it as ***'neti-neti'*** (it is not this, not that, neither that). The rest of the physical world is ***'Maya'*** which has, even otherwise, a transient existence. Therefore Brahma is the only and absolute truth and is worth realising. Brahma is obscured by Maya and hence unless this veil of Maya is removed Brahma can not be realized say the knowledgeable. The realisation of Brahma was also referred to as realisation of ***Moksha***. The sole aim of human being is nothing but to realise Moksha. The same was somewhat described by some others as ***Nirvana, Arihant*** and so on. This was also referred to as elevation of man to ***Narayana*** (God). According to the Indian traditional view even if man is born as a man, he should end up as Narayana as far as is possible, in his own life and if it is not possible in this life then through the required number of rebirths thereafter. It makes no difference even if one does not believe in rebirth theory.

This is the ultimate objective of every human being as propounded by the Indian philosophy. Since the evolution of human being in the present form, what human being is longing for is this happiness or bliss as obtainable on union with Brahma, notwithstanding his inability to express it in words. This does not mean that he has to forego the happiness of earlier three, body, mental and intellectual pleasures, to obtain this ultimate and eternal happiness. In fact he has to strive to achieve happiness on account of all these fours. That is why it has been described as attainment of Moksha, through all possible worldly pleasures, the limit of which is dictated by Dharma, the rules and regulations for sustaining the universe in proper shape for the good of all. The formula is known as the four ***purusharthas*, viz *dharma, artha, kama* and *moksha,*** what are the only things worth attaining in life. The concept of Dharma here is nothing but the best organised society in tune with nature and time and affable to all without complaints. Knowingly or unknowingly all human endeavours are directly aimed at this ultimate objective. But on the way of realising Brahma, unknowingly or knowingly one gets confined to the charming worldly pleasures and all his endeavours get directed at achieving these, forgetting his ultimate destined aim. Occasionally sometimes one does get the glimpse of the ultimate happiness, but it is ignored, out of ignorance, and one gets entangled in the worldly transient pleasures. For example at the time of some accident, natural calamity, etc., one goes, at times all out, to help the victims automatically, many times even without conscious thought. This is nothing but experiencing the universal spirit that is residing in him and the victims alike, may be momentarily.

Western Psyche

The westerners so far have not reached this far, in any form. According to The Bible the world is meant for pleasure of human beings and this has influenced them in all walks of life, all through the ages. The challenges of survival before them were such that they could meet them only by organising themselves. It made them organise better for foraging in the early days itself. They therefore organised to roam around the world for earning their living and for which various organisations had to be developed and participants taught to work unitedly, with mutual help, co-operation and in co-ordinated manner towards the common goal, perhaps disregarding one's own self.

The fascist behaviour of the Church, over a long period of about a thousand years, during the period 5-16th century AD, at times contradicting even the observed scientific facts, generated in them a kind of revolt not just against the church but against the very concept of God itself. The net result was in developing scientific understanding of the world around and there-from the scientific temper in them. All this led them to believe only in the physical world knowable through senses only. They even disregarded mind as an independent entity in the beginning. Human being was considered to be merely a bundle of desires. It was their basic belief that human being could be made happy, by maximum exploitation of nature. Efforts were therefore directed predominantly in the direction of capturing nature by understanding it. It also helped them develop their own regional organisationality, as described earlier and, organisations to meet the human physical desires, collectively or individually, which was merely enumerated by **Abraham Maslow** [1], more succinctly. This outlook of life really is the origin of their organisationality and organisations in the western society.

Beginning

Hence the origin of organisationality and organisations goes to the very nature of human beings, in the form of mere physical desires as in the west or in the very clear form of body, mind, intellect and spiritual needs of human beings as realised in India and, in some or the other form of vague combination of these elsewhere in the world. This was in essence responsible right in the stone-age itself, for the formation of tribes almost all over the world. It continued after agricultural revolution, in the formation of families and eventually self-contained villagés. As transport and communication improved it further led to the formation of society and nation thereafter. It had to wait until the end of Second World War, to develop it at the international level. Whether one admits it or not the development of organisationality as described above has at its base the appreciation of oneness of all human souls and nothing else, to the extent possible to feel, as propounded by the Indians in the form of universal Brahma.

The basic fear instinct, and perhaps the intense desire to know the inaccessible and unknown, in effect resulted in the evolution of religions in some form and, organisations were formed therefor in the agricultural era itself. The credit for formation of organisations on religious basis goes to the Semitic religions alone because it is inherently their nature in the form of propagation of their religion to the exclusion of others. The adoption of Christianity by Roman kings might have had the influence of organising their religion on stronger footing. The propagation of Islam was made possible only through the use of state power and that is why their organised structure is stronger even today. The Hindus do not believe in increasing their number mechanically. On the contrary they emphasise that human beings must be upgraded spiritually on individual basis to realise the all pervading power of Brahma which does not need any organised effort for its realisation. Hence Hindus did not form spiritual organisations, at least consciously and deliberately. The Buddhist's organisation of their monks is in some way the exception. But herein also it is for training the religious teachers and not for organising the followers of Buddhism. The Ramakrishna Mission as an organisation was formed by **Swami Vivekananda** essentially to propagate the **Vedanta Philisophy** for nourishing universal brotherhood rather than to propagate any religion. This is perhaps the first of its type of organisation consciously formed in India to propagate religion-cum-philosophy. This is definitely the influence of western organised society on Vivekananda. There is however a very fundamental difference in forming such an organisation in Hindu society. Hindus considered the entire humanity as one family and hence did not bother to develop religious organisations, like those developed by Semitic religions for conversion of the rest into their own fold mechanically.

Selfishness

From the above it can be inferred that organisations may be formed to meet the bodily, mental, intellectual and spiritual needs of human beings since these are his selfish and perhaps instinctual interests. Is it limited so narrowly like this?

In the stone-age when the existence of human being was more or less at the animal level, human needs were confined more to the instinctual bodily needs alone. The other higher level needs, like mental and intellectual, were yet to be realised appropriately. It means that his selfish interests were limited to his own bodily self alone, to become happy. Soon some tribal-cum-family format evolved and from thereon the human individual-self enlarged to encompass the self of his family or tribe, as his own self. Then he would be happy if the selfish interests of members of his tribe or family are met and even at times disregarding his own personal happiness. This was the first step of enlargement of his selfish interests beyond his bodily self to become happy.

In the agriculture era the family unit developed into a strong cohesive unit and, as the variety of requirements increased and consequentially as division of labour became essential, self-contained village life also evolved around it. Now the self of an individual, enlarged decisively to include his family and, then the society in the form of his village, as well. The happiness then rested on making the whole family and the village or the society happy, alongwith.

As society developed on a larger scale, the human self enlarged to still higher level to include the well being of the society around. That is the reason why in times of need the wider social or kingdom's interests predominated over own or family's selfish interests. His happiness got somewhat equated with the happiness of the society around, at least on some accounts.

It was soon realised in India that human being can not be happy unless the flora and fauna around him are also happily sustained in its natural form, since man continuously interacts with them. His happiness therefore became synonymous with the happiness of the flora and fauna, that is the nature or the world around. Finally it was realised in India that the entire universe is pervaded by one and only one being, which they called Brahma and it is the ultimate aim of human being to realise this oneness in the entire universe. This is the ultimate desire of all human beings, whether one agrees with it or not.

This process of enlargement of one's own happiness was described in India in the form of continuously enlarging realisation from individual self pleasures, through society and then on to nature to Brahma. Since everyone first realises the reality of his existence in terms of own individual body, that bodily level was called as ***vyashti*** (individual). In the next stage, human being realises the social level of his existence and is called as ***samashti*** (to include family and society at large). Then the vision enlarges to ***srishti*** (the entire nature around) and finally ending up in realisation of ***permeshti*** (the entire animate and inanimate creation). This methodology of enlarging ones own vision and realisation through four stages as ***vyashti, samashti, srushti* and *permeshti*** is essential for the maintenance of harmony and peace in not only the human race, as a whole, but in this entire universe, for total peaceful evolution and sustenance, of the entire human race, in tune with nature. The Indians always thought of integrating not only the human race but the entire universe, animate and inanimate existence put together, in this way, to avoid individual or collective ego leading to conflict or clash of interests amongst individuals and amongst groups, capable of destroying one and all pleasures otherwise attained.

The Indians did not consider human beings as anything special and destined for superior pleasures as compared to other living beings. It considered humans as a part of total existence. That is the reason why they always thought of overall existence. Hence wherever the Indians went they taught this message of their seers and helped the society there to elevate itself in this way. There was no domination or subjugation of any society, leave apart their exploitation, anywhere in the world, wherever the Indians went. That is why ***Buddhism*** spread from India to many countries and is seen there even today, but without any Indian domination. It is therefore amazing to see that the biggest temple and that is of God Vishnu, is not in India but in Cambodia.

This is the utmost level of organisationality, in the form of oneness with the entire universe, beyond which nothing exists, and hence worth achieving. It has not been even thought of elsewhere in the world to this extent. The question of bringing it in reality, in the form of human behaviour, therefore did not arise elsewhere.

The westerners considered human being as a superior creation when compared to the rest of live-world and that the world was created for his pleasures. It naturally led to their belief in their right of exploitation of nature for human pleasure. That is the reason why, to satisfy the physical needs, the westerners formed required organisations and on the basis of their superior organised strength they exploited the societies wherever they went to the extent that some of those societies were completely exterminated from this world once and for all. As illustrations, the examples of America, Australia, New Zealand, etc can be readily cited. Where are the original human tribes that once lived there?

It is true that the urge to provide bodily pleasures alone restricted them to think essentially about individual selves. Organisations were formed to meet this individual selfish interests and in turn of their own societies. Through organised endeavours they attempted to satisfy the needs of individuals in their societies. They proved that organised efforts were best suited to meet these individual needs. That is the reason why not only organisationality flourished in their societies but varieties of orgaisations were formed readily.

The on-set of industrial revolution aggravated this desire of worldly pleasures beyond imagination. It essentially aimed at processing the naturally occurring materials into products for decreasing the hardships and increasing the physical happiness of human beings in their day-to-day lives. It however created unending human material greed. In fact the intense desire to meet bodily pleasures led to industrial revolution in their societies. It resulted in formation of still numerous and in a larger number, a variety of organisations to meet the need arising out of industrial revolution. The fall-out of industrial revolution has been the development of strong social ego to make one's own small society materially rich, as compared to the others. It led to the formation of strong kingdoms and from where the modern nation-states were born in the western world. These then dominated practically the whole world and exploited slave-societies fully for their own interests, without any human considerations.

Since the end of 19th and beginning of 20th century the western societies did realise the existence of mind as an independent entity and also realised that intellect is quite different from mere physical existence. But still they have not yet accepted the existence of soul in the body and hence spirituality is not acceptable to them as is acceptable to most Indians. Whatever world is known through human senses is all that they are prepared to accept to exist. The existence of inaccessible part of the universe is not yet acceptable to them. This extension of reality from body to mind and then to intellect have led them to think of their happiness in terms of physical, mental and intellectual pleasures. Hence organisations have slowly been formed to cater to all these three types of needs. However the dominance still remains with respect to bodily needs alone, as majority would be content with bodily pleasures and not much beyond.

The development of science and scientific temper, particularly in the last three centuries, resulted in the west, in confining the religion to a very narrow sphere of life by most. But in spite of the emphasis on the materialistic development, humanitarian interests did develop, in the west in recent past. Amassing of plenty of wealth, by exploiting industrialisation for personal gains, did not in reality lead to peace of mind. The state of affairs around did move such individuals to think in terms of miseries of the have-nots. It also resulted in feeling of compassion for the society or even for the entire human race since it is the inherent nature of human beings and in that lies the real peace of mind as discovered by the Indians. That is the reason why number of charitable organisations, with social perspective and free from religious considerations, has been developed in the west since the nineteenth century. The examples are of **Nobel, Rockefeller, von Humboldt, Bill Gate Foundation** and such trusts, at the international level, that are doing good humanitarian work. Some Indian trusts like those of **N.R. Narayan Murthy, Azij Premji, Tatas** and the like are doing similar humanitarian work in India. Now charitable trusts have been formed in millions all over the world, in every country, for one or the other purpose, for helping the have-nots and serving the society at large.

It may appear strange that there were no charitable trusts in India before the advent of British Rule in the middle of nineteenth century. These were formed only thereafter. This is because every home in India was charitable enough as per its perception of the universe as one integral whole. In ancient times the self contained village-life was so well organised that it provided living and sustenance for all residing there and also to those who occasionally visited the village for one or the other purpose.

Therefore, except the government in the form of administrative and defense organisations, practically no organisations ever existed in India even to cater to the physical needs of individuals. The effective unit in India for sustaining the society was family alone. Even the technological production, distribution and even international trade were all family-centric in structure. The families in those days were large and joint families, unlike the present-day small families. They were capable of providing the required man-power for productive purposes, like the agriculture or the manufacture and sale of goods. The activities were kept within limits as manageable by the families. Modern organisations were developed in India only after the British Rule was established. The British rulers, having no idea about the well developed civilized social life prevalent in India from times immemorial, thought India was as backward enough because of lack of organisations akin to them. Hence when they got into the command, they introduced legislations to facilitate formation of organisations in India in every sphere of life.

Environmental Compulsions

Organisations can get formed, at times, out of compulsions in the social environment. Similarly in spite of everything in order, organisations do not get formed simply because of hostile social environment. Hence the origin of organisations does lie in the nature of social environment as well. Some times the challenges posed are such that organisations get formed readily, for example at times of external aggression or natural calamity or accident, etc. Some times different people unknowingly long for some common things or their selfish interests coincide and when such people come to know of each other's such common needs, organisation is readily formed amongst them.

Organisations cannot be formed just because participants are available. They need to agree on leadership so that the necessary hierarchical structure can be formed for creating an organisation. Usually some kind of promoter fulfills this need. It is also observed that leaders, out of their charming and capable personality, somehow collect people to form organisations, though it takes little time to form such organisations. Typical examples of such organisations are those created by **Dr. Ambedkar** or **Mahatma Gandhi**. The best example is of **Dr. Hedgewar** who created the mighty organisation as RSS, starting from himself alone and that too against all possible odds.

Panthic, denominational or *sampradaya* organisations (religious) are formed, knowingly or unknowingly, by the seer who has realised the ultimate reality. Even if he does not want to form an organisation, at times, people on their own collect around him and many times that takes eventually the shape of an organisation. The best examples of these are the local or regional saints and their followers forming different organisations.

It is now common practice to form organisations facilitated by required legislation by governments. In this respect the democratic governments are always keen to organise society through such private and autonomous organisations. This is the dominant form of organising any society since the present size and the complexity of social life cannot be administered through direct governmental management of all affairs alone. The communist experiment in this direction miserably failed. A local initiative in forming fairly autonomous organisations, aided by suitable legislation, is now order of the day. The final control required to be used in emergency however, rests with the government.

References

1. Maslow, A.H., A *Theory of Human Motivation*, Psychological Review, (1943).
2. Golwalkar, M.S. alias Guruji, *Guruji Samagra,* (Hindi, Compiled Collection of His Thoughts), vol 1-12, (2006).

CHAPTER 6

CHARACTERISTICS

CHAPTER STRUCTURE

- Strength
- Equilibrium
- Individual Freedom
- Newton-Cartesian World View
- Early Modern Organisations
- Modern Organisations

Industrial revolution and its tremendous impact on overall production of goods, their distribution, marketing and sales, along with other related activities left no alternative but to carry out almost all activities in an organised fashion. The things left for individuals to do on their own went on decreasing continuously with social evolution. The organisational modern life became more and more complex with time. Individuals found it increasingly difficult to earn livelihood and ensure one's own security on an individual basis. Therefore now almost everyone spends his almost entire life in organised systems alone, earning living and ensuring own safety. Finally almost all die in an equally organised system like a hospital which tries to keep him alive till it becomes impossible to do so. There is no escape from this. The only escape is to retire from the civil society and move to the jungle for residence, if one feels happy in natural surroundings alone.

Up to the time when agricultural era was dominant and was the sole means of sustenance, one could live in somewhat isolation without any help from others. Those were the days when those who produced goods and services that were required and, were also consumers of the same. It extended at best up to family level groups only. But as requirements increased in volume and variety, division of labour became imperative and sustenance of everyone depended on others. This went on increasing with time and with increasing social cohesiveness. Some organised forms had to be evolved to cater to such needs.

"Earlier society therefore did have some ad-hoc and some regular organisations but modern society is a society of organisations alone", according to great social scientist **Amitai Etzioni** [1].

Strength

It is often seen that what can not be accomplished, on an individual basis is often readily accomplished by working in groups in an organised way. According to the well known columnist of New Yorker, **James Suroviki**,

"Larger groups of people are smarter than an elite few, no matter how brilliant, better at solving problems, fostering innovation and coming to wise decisions, when working together".

Management guru **George R. Terry** says:

"Within any group, co-ordination makes possible a total accomplishment in excess of the sum of the individual parts making up that total. The total accomplishment of a department of ten employees whose efforts are closely co-ordinated (organised) is far greater than that of the same ten employees working as individuals".

One of the great thinkers of the RSS-Pariwar, **D.B. Thengri** [2], used to describe the same concept quite humourously giving an example from algebra. He would say,

"Let us assume that the strength of A is obtained by A-square and that of B is obtained by B-square. Then the strength of A and B working together in an organised effort shall be equal to the square of A plus B together. As per well known algebra it comes out to be A-square plus B-square plus 2AB. Where from the additional strength 2AB has come when A and B work together? It is the additional strength that is obtained when A and B work in co-ordinated manner".

There is always something more than mere addition when people work together as a group. This is illustrated in Fig. 6.1.

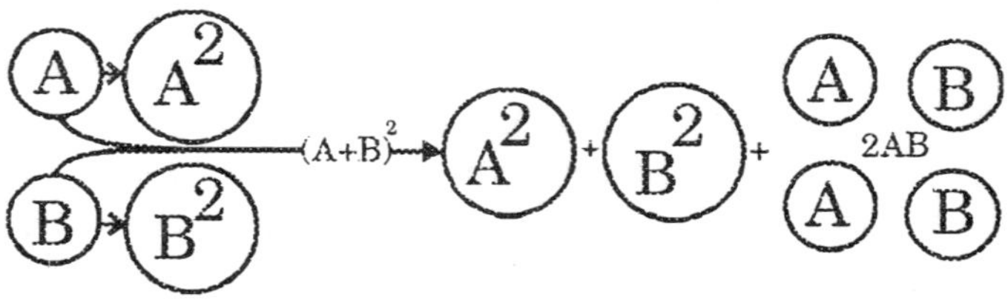

Fig. 6.1 : Schematic representation of how organisational strength improves beyond mere addition.

It happens because men consciously connect, co-ordinate and supplement each other in their actions while working in an organised manner. This brings in additional energy and strength for an individual to act. That is the reason why it is often observed that small and less smart men, working in an organised manner accomplish far greater tasks readily than what they themselves individually would have ever achieved.

Organised efforts have therefore always been thought of against the backdrop of individuals to establish its superiority. An organisation is the confluence of not just the outwardly discernible individuals in mere physical forms but of mental, intellectual and creative energies of all those participants working with co-operation in a co-ordinated fashion, for common organisational goals. Therefore the more the participants contribute their energies the more shall be the organisational strength of the same group.

Equilibrium

In a broader sense almost every organisation directly or indirectly is meant to cater to some need of the society. As a first and foremost step somebody, usually with some deeper insight, identifies such social needs. He visualises the organised effort required to meet this need and accordingly tries to set up an organisation for the proposed purpose. Formation of any organisation must therefore take into account the external social environment before deciding to form an organisation at any point of time. The planning of the organisation takes into account these external conditions, with respect to the requirements of the society at large and the type of human resource available, with whom the organised effort could be made eventually.

The organising and staffing has necessarily to be carried out from amongst the members available in the society at large. In a way this exercise aims at creating psychologically, the equilibrium conditions between the external social environments, in which the organisation is to function and the collective will of those participating in the organisation, *vis-à-vis* the organisational objective. Without this synchronisation organisations cannot even start to function properly. It also means that by and large those participating in the organisation, at least mentally or perhaps even outwardly, are committed to the objective of the organisation, at least to start with. In commercial organisations of any type the external conditions means the market, the rivals, other social and governmental restrictions and so on. The human resource means the qualities of people available at affordable payment for manning the proposed organisation. In the case of NPOs the external environment means the societal environment at large and the human resource means the psychological state and aspirations of those joining the organisation.

On forming an organisation, with proper planning, organising and staffing, some kind of psychological synergy or equilibrium is established, at least to start with, between the social environment and the human resource within an organisation. If this is lacking then the organisation may not get even going. With the progress of time, organisations lose, and definitely lose, this equilibrium because the external environment does get altered due to the external pace of change in the society and the organisational pace of change often lags behind. It may also get altered due to the changes in the psychological state of those who joined the organisation in the beginning. In social and charitable organisations the initial zeal of social service or selflessness may not last long and may even be replaced by some selfish interests, quite different from the organisational objective. This happens often because of their altered needs in the changed social environment. It is not certain that those who join the NPOs for some selfless contribution, in the beginning, shall remain so over a long period of time. They do undergo psychological changes with time and that affects the equilibrium adversely. In spite of any due precaution in the beginning, it is impossible to avoid this imbalance in any organisation in due course of time. In commercial and profit making organisations this happens rather easily.

If this was not the case there would not have been several depressions as has been seen periodically in the economic situations in any country or now even all over the world. Most get stuck in the mud and start loving the status-quo. This is precisely the reason why once lofty organisations such as Gandhian institutions in India simply fossilised after independence. Those manning these became prisoners of precedents and got locked in the custodian's conventions. The same is the story of Christian churches in European countries after the onset of scientific temper and onset of industrialisation.

The same is the sorry state of many commercial organisations over time. They also loose this equilibrium for a variety of reasons and their competitors offer better quality and cheaper products and services. They have a chance to improve or an option to get merged in some better ones, if they can not be run any more. Some however do get decimated in this process of imbalance.

Individual Freedom

It is true that individual freedom does get constrained to some extent in an organisation, since, without it, organisation can not function. The extent of this constriction of freedom depends upon the type of organisation and the style of its functioning. For example, at one extreme end like the **McDonald** type organisations or in the army, the individual freedom is practically absent. There the motto is to obey the superior's orders or quit. In the army it is not to question the superior's command, but to do or die. The individuality is totally surrendered to the organisational cause, in such cases. In the parlance of management it is often referred to as bureaucracy, meaning following orders top down unquestioningly. At the other end of this spectrum are the organised processions, demonstrations, *morcha* or *dindi* and such organised events. This organised format is so loose that individual freedom is mostly in tact. It also depends on the style of management.

Those organisations where decisions are to be taken at every stage more innovatively rather than as per orders from above, individual freedom, to the extent possible, is kept in-tact to work effectively and efficiently. This is generally referred to as flattening of organisation [3]. But in organisations like McDonalds, where there is not much of necessity for innovative actions, but to strictly follow the well thought out and laid down discipline instead, then the individual freedom is curtailed to a fair extent. The situation shall be unique for every organisation depending upon its character and the goal to be achieved and wherein the right mix of individual freedom and bureaucracy is established through the organisational structure and its management. Those who fail to choose the right mix often lead to serious organisational problems.

Newton-Cartesian World View

The renaissance in Europe in the 15-16th century initiated actions, perhaps with vengeance, against the autocracy of the church. By 17th century the scientific study of nature could explain the nature of the world in the language of science. This era is marked by unprecedented contribution in the field of science in general, and in the field of mechanics and physics in particular, by **Isaac Newton**. Similarly this period was also influenced fundamentally, in the field of philosophy, by **Rene Descartes**, the French philosopher. On the social front the ideas of evolution developed by **Darwin** and the ideas about human psychology developed by **Sigmund Freud** contributed immensely. The 17-19th century period was also marked by the onset of industrial revolution, which changed the social face of the world beyond imagination. On the whole the credit of explaining the observed facts in nature and developing there-from the unified world-model for the first time goes to Newton and Descartes.

The sociological world-model was constructed predominantly by Freud and Darwin, based on theirs and some other's observations. They had also to use some ideas of Newton and Descartes even while developing the sociological world view. However those ideas no longer explain the world as is understood in the twentieth century fully, in the light of discoveries of many in general but those of **Albert Einstein** in particular in the twentieth century. The modern world view is known as Einsteinian or more appropriately systemic world view. But the then world view, as dominant in 17-19th century, is often referred to as the **Newton-Cartesian world view,** in honour of those two great scientist/natural-philosophers, because of the dominance of natural sciences. It is therefore necessary to understand the then world view and its effects on the then society. What was this world-view or world-model like?

The Newton-Cartesian model considered the world as one giant machine in which the constituent parts were considered to be discreet, as parts are in any machine. The state of affairs is explained by **Immanuel Kant** as the parts existing for each other, in the sense of supporting each other within a functional whole. Machine can be understood by understanding the parts. It can be reduced to its fundamental parts by reductionist approach and then reconstructed again by reassembling them to understand it fully. Even biology was understood to be explicable by the laws of physics and chemistry, in the form of physico-chemical explanation of life. That was therefore the era of trying to understand the world by understanding smaller and smaller parts thereof and by reducing them to the smallest pieces. It was essentially a science of pieces.

On the whole that situation has aptly been described by **Fritjof Capra** [4] as, **"The universe is a mechanical system composed of elementary building blocks, the view of the human body as a machine, the view of life in society as a competitive struggle for existence, the belief in unlimited material progress to be achieved through economic and technological growth, and – last, not least – the belief that a society in which female is everywhere subsumed under the male is one that follows a basic law of nature".**

There was the confidence to understand the world by reducing it down to its smallest parts. This mechanical world view shaped most of the activities in the society like scientific and technological developments, management of organisations and thereby organising the society at large. Hence attempts were made to understand organisations, in terms of their parts, like human resource, finance, engineering, production, marketing and so on separately or discreetly. This view lasted almost until the end of Second World War.

Early Modern Organisations

Although organisations did exist in western societies even before the advent of industrial revolution, these flourished on an unprecedented scale only after industrial revolution, to cater to the emergent needs of industrialisation.The early organisations in the 18th and 19th century, formed to cater the early industrialisation, were therefore managed under the educational and therefore the psycho-social influence of Newton-Cartesian world view, including the then prevalent sociological ideas of Freud and Darwin.

Human beings were considered as merely bundles of desires and hence physical pleasures were considered as the final need of human beings. Hence profit in every human activity and therefore money acquired a pivotal role in every social and individual activity. Organised efforts were considered necessary to produce the required human needs. It resulted in most grasping, commercialised and calculating civilization in the history of humanity. Everything was reduced down to **contractual transactions**, including the human relations like even the marriages. It may not be any exaggeration to say that the breeding of organisations, on such a varied and wider scale, in contractual formats, is the outcome of industrial revolution only. The formation of such organisations had to be based on the prevalent overall social perceptions.

As a result organisations were **pyramidal in structures** and highly bureaucratic in style of their management. This was made possible by keeping most of the power and therefore authority at the top managerial level. Structurally the organisations had to be highly hierarchical in nature and value-free. All this **originated basically from racist, capitalists, imperialistic, anti-ecological and patriarchic mind-set** evolved out of their historical processes. It was presumed that the orders from top would convey what was expected at the top and, monetary gains of lower strata would make them work as per these orders. In short organisations were fairly rigid structures with all power concentrated at the top. Management styles that developed in those days conformed to this perception. It worked, more or less well, because the western nations had their own market niches in the form of their slave colonies spread all over the world, where their word reigned supreme and that power was fully exploited for commercial advantages. There was therefore not much of a competition in their manufacture and trade in their own colonies. It was impossible for any agricultural society to compete with industrialised society in terms of economics of manufacture and trade.

Modern Organisations

Twentieth century was marked by a paradigm shift in perception of the world, particularly in view of the scientific ideas of Einstein. The world came to be understood, not as a machine but, a holistic organic whole with parts intimately interconnected with each other in the form of a network. It has now been further extended and viewed as a deeply ecological system. According to **Fritjof Capra** [4] **"shallow ecological view is at best anthropo-centric or human-centric, which views humans as above or outside nature and ascribes only use-value to nature".**

Human is just only one of the living being and is viewed in that sense in deep ecology with spirituality at the centre. Self assertion and integration in the form of individuality and in the organised form are both essential for all living beings, more so for the rational humans. A dynamic balance between them is necessary. Power in the sense of domination over others is excessive self assertion. It can be avoided by having network style of functioning. This systemic view implies systems thinking. This has had profound impact on everything including the organisations in every field of activity. In its early format it was known as **Einstenian World-View** and now as post-Einstenian or **Deep Ecological World View** [4].

This coincidentally occurred along with the after-effects of the Second World War in the form of colonies being liberated and the western societies consequently had to compete amongst themselves and with the emerging nations as well. The efficiency of their organisations then came in question, for the first time. From this time onwards, the management styles started orienting themselves in terms of efficiency alone. The earlier pyramidal structure and bureaucratic management style had to be dispensed with more and more flat structures and less and less bureaucratic management [5,6]. Since then the whole structure and style of management has been continuously undergoing tremendous changes for improving their efficiency. Innovation has now become the focal point of all organised efforts with respect to anything and everything. It then became imperative that organisations provide maximum freedom to individuals while working in a group, to help develop organisation innovatively and continuously.

It should be noted that those who valued individual freedom the most developed the best of organisations as per the requirements, wherein there was distinct curtailment of some individual freedom, for certain. Those were the days of ***'might is right'***. But now they have realised this mistake and therefore see that maximum freedom is allowed in an organisation for better individual performance even in groups.

Having realised that the larger the organisation and consequently higher is the bureaucratic management, lower is the efficiency. Therefore now smaller organisations are being preferred in terms of efficiency. Is it not paradoxical to see that even under such perception, present day organisations have been growing into multinational or trans-national companies? On the one hand they are growing into such mega-organisations but on the other they are also decentralizing themselves. The problem is being solved by many innovative management techniques, like creating small working groups with fair autonomy or creating autonomous units on regional or product-wise basis or autonomy of working or outsourcing or developing effective vendor system and so on. Some of these are called as ***atomised organizations*** [7] and which have proved very effective. On the whole the organisational structure is being made more and more flat as the world is getting more flat [3]. It is also seen that individuality is kept in tact, to the extent possible, even while working in an organisation.

References

1. Etzioni, Amitai, *Modern Organisations,* Prentice Hall of India, N.Delhi, (1965).
2. Thengri, D.B, *From his public speeches.*
3. Friedman, Thomas, L., *The world is Flat,* Penguin, London, (2005).
4. Tom Peters and Robert H. Waterman Jr, *In search of Excellence*, Profile, (2003).
5. Tom Peters and Nancy Austin, *A Passion for Excellence,* Profile, (2003).
6. Capra, Fritjof, *Web of Life*, Flamingo, (1997).
7. Deal, T., Kennedy, E and Allan, A., *Corporate Cultures(The Rites and Rituals of Corporate Life)*, Perseus, Cambridge, Mass, (1982).

CHAPTER 7

REQUIREMENTS

CHAPTER STRUCTURE

- Fundamentals
- Definitions
- Ideal Organisation
- Organisational Structures
- Hierarchical Power Structure
- Ideal View
- Countervailing Power

Fundamentals

There are three fundamental requirements which must be met before any organisation can be formed. These are

1. **Common acceptable aim, object or task for the organisation as a whole that needs to be achieved.**
2. **Participants or members who feel that their own selfish interests, in overall sense, could be met by working in and for such an organisation.**
3. **Co-operative and integrated endeavours of the participants to achieve the common or set-out aim that is, it has some philosophical base for working together.**

It presumes that organisations shall be created for the welfare of the society at large. Therein also lies the well-being of individuals. No organisation can be created if this condition is not met even indirectly. That is the reason why organisations of burglars, dacoits or even terrorists do not meet the wider social objective and therefore can not be allowed to be formed in a society. In some religious or social societies, organisations of terrorists are considered to be legitimately in social interests and hence are promoted consciously. But this is an exception and hence besides the point. If any of these three basic requirements is missing organisation cannot be created.

There are some auxiliary requirements which should also be met for effective functioning of any organisation. These however are not essential requirements for forming an organisation. These are:

1. **Rules and regulations as to how the group shall work as an organised body for achieving the common objective. This is nothing but organising the group suitably, or setting it in order. It is essentially the organisational structure.**
2. **Controller, leader, manager and the like to chalk out the working of an organisation, in the form of planning, organising, staffing, leading and controlling functions in an integrated fashion**
3. **Financial resources for managing the organisation.**
4. **Psychological or mental energy in the form of motivation of participants or in the form of appropriate work-culture.**

Finally, it has now become necessary that organisations are legal entities and for that they have to be created under one or the other laws of the land. This is an optional requirement because organisations can be created without such legal frame work. The best examples of organisations formed without legal framework are the religious organisations, formed merely under fundamental rights of association. Similarly some project organisations are formed under the same provisions without any other specific legal sanction. In fact the constitutional provision itself is the legal provision. Burglars cannot claim the same freedom for the formation of their organisations.

In a way, society contributes, directly or indirectly, in terms of time, energy, intellect and money, for the formation and running of any legitimate organisation. It is in the interest of society; on the whole, to run such organisations to meet its larger needs, which otherwise cannot be met now on the basis of the society as a whole. The formation of small organised groups is rather easier, effective and an efficient way of carrying out various functions of the society to meet the individual and collective needs, essentially based on the principle of division of work. It helps to organise the society at large and provide means so that the individual's needs are met peacefully and effectively. This is the reason why formation of organisations is promoted through appropriate legislations by the government.

Organisation is a group activity and *ipso facto* it is an interest activity for those participating in it. Otherwise there is no reason why people should join to form organisations. Organisation is therefore an organised aggregate of people and an interest group like this thus becomes an ***interest aggregate***.

"But if these organisations are not functioning in the broad sense of social development then it is equally in the interest of society to either close them down or to exert upon them to improve as per the legal design", emphasises **John Argenti** [1].

The intelligent appreciation of organisations is perhaps the first step in this direction. This is the reason why these must be formed under the legal framework provided therefor. If this framework is not sufficiently strong then it is imperative and the duty of the legitimate government to strengthen this legal framework under which organisations may be formed.

Religious organisations are not generally formed under any legal provision because they have been there traditionally since the advent of agricultural era in perpetuation. However several laws have been introduced in almost all countries even to regulate some or the other parts of religious activities. Whenever the religious organisations get involved in financial or wealth matters or have to deal with outsiders, then these transactions are definitely regulated by enforcing them to form organisations under the existing legal framework. Time has now come to regulate them more to better suit the democratic societal formats that are evolving almost everywhere, where everything is being controlled under the constitutional provisions, except individual's worship to get connected with the Supreme Power.

Whether religious organisations are legally formed or not, does not alter their basic aim of uniting an individual with the transcendental Supreme Power. This aim has, in fact, nothing to do with any body else whatsoever except the person concerned. This rests entirely on an individual and his mental connection with the Supreme. But since it has somehow evolved in the form of an organised activity, which is capable of helping or even damaging the society at large, it becomes imperative to get them also registered and thereby regulated. This is more important, particularly when the society is illiterate and poor and needs to be protected against the exploiters, in the name of religion. In an ideal situation religion should not be used for their exploitation in any way. The government has no alternative but to intervene in such organised exploitative activities that are going on in the name of religion.

In order to illustrate an organisation a diagram, in the form of three similar but entangled circles is used all over the world. Who first drew this figure and where and when it was drawn is not known. But it is universally accepted and used to depict an organisation, as per **John Adair** [2]. There are three circles, one each depicting one of the three basic requirements. These three circles entangle in each other to indicate that these basic requirements are inalienably interlinked. They are not only interrelated but they affect each other substantially and effectively. This figure has been modified to explain more of the related things and is shown in **Fig. 7.1** to include organisational relationship with the society to indicate their inescapable connection with and as an inalienable part of the society. The prime position of the leader, as an overriding one, is also indicated therein. The three circles in this figure are shown to be of the same size and they cut each other symmetrically. This is to depict that all, *inter se*, ought to be balanced for any organisation to function.

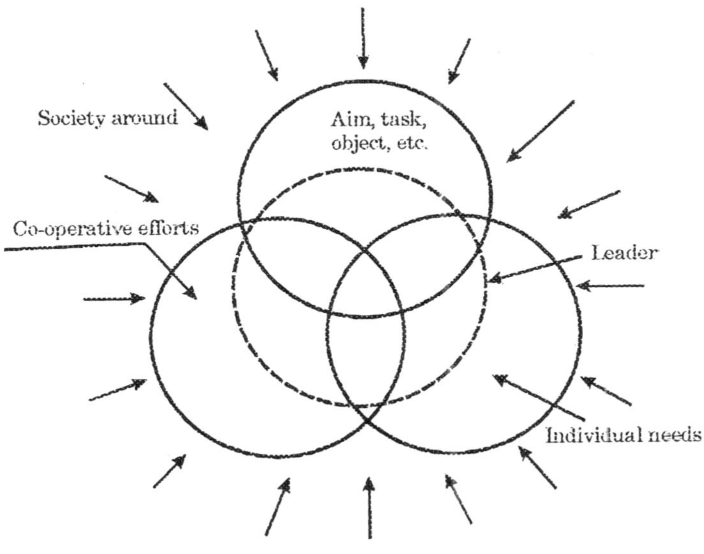

Fig. 7.1 : Schematic of an organisation along with the position of leader and the society at large.

Organisation is formed out of a larger social group by selecting some of them for a specific purpose to be achieved, through their collective endeavours. It is therefore based on the duality of organisation and the society, with the boundary of an organisation interfacing with the society. It may also interface with other organisations. It is a social arrangement, pursuing collective goals and controlling its own performance.

It is a system consisting of integrated group to achieve the organisational goal. It therefore requires inputs, a process whereby the group is aligned, ultimately to achieve the pre-fixed goal and output in the form of products, services, etc. There may be incidental outcomes out of organised efforts in the form of jobs to workers, enhanced quality of life to customers or related ones. It gets feed-backs from the beneficiaries as well as from its environmental constituents like, society, government and so on.

Every organisation must not only acquire initially enough power, energy, and inspiration to start with, but it must also get similar energy input while functioning to keep it going and progressing.

Definitions

An organisation operates according to an overall purpose or mission, via an intentionally organised group of people, based on some values or priorities in the nature of how they carry out their activities. The values are the culture of an organisation. Organisations do have visions which indicates the minds about how it should be working and how it should appear when everything is going on well. Strategies and strategic goals decide the approaches of an organisation for its effective functioning. These normally work in the larger interests of society. That is why dacoits and burglar's organisations are not allowed to operate in any society.

Various definitions of an organisation have been suggested to define the organisation scientifically and in generalised terms. **Koontz and O'Donnell** [3] give two different definitions for organisations. In one it is defined as :

"The process of bringing together, uniting and managing a group of people for achieving some common goal or objective".

Here the emphasis is on the dynamic nature of the organisation. In the second **"It is the structural arrangement for deciding the interrelationship of individuals in a group formed to achieve some common objective".**

Here the emphasis is on the structure of an organisation. The dynamic nature and the structure, both, are important in understanding organisations.

Organisations have the freedom and are capable of deciding their own structure, style of functioning, interrelationship with the rest of the society and other organisations and so on, within the legal provisions under which it is formed. Since the membership of an organisation is purely voluntary, any participant being not happy with the methodology, has an option to leave it and join, if desired, any other similar organisation, generally in a democratic set-up. This is also in the interest of keeping organisations fit and active. Governmental organisations may be exceptions in this respect.

This is the reason why organisation has also been defined as:

"An art and science of keeping together and motivating a group of people for achieving certain higher objective for the benefit of the society at large".

This definition is more in tune with charitable or national or such lofty non-profit making organisations.

John Argenti [1] goes a step further in defining an organisation. He thinks that since organisation operates in a society by taking something and, in terms of its objective, gives out something to the society at large, the definition should include the interrelationships of society and organisation. Therefore he says,

"An organisation is a group of people working together to yield a satisfactory benefit (objective) for its intended beneficiaries (participants) while causing no significant harm to any interest group or individual with whom it deals with directly or indirectly".

This is the definition more suited to commercial organisations or profit making organisations. Being a part of society, it is the moral and bounden duty of any organisation to see that, by its activities it does not hurt, damage or inflict loss on any individual or any group in the society beyond legitimate extent. It emphasises the ethical standards to be followed by organisations. The present day concept of ***corporate social responsibility*** (***CSR*** for short) has been evolved from such considerations only. This subject got impetus first from **Howard R. Bowen** [4].

Organisations are formed in the larger interest of the organisationality and therefore it should make sure that it does not damage this larger organisationality in any way. It is in fact meant to further consolidate this basic organisationality. This gives a basis for assessing organisational impact on the society or on international level. From this point of view the concept of ***social audit*** propounded by Bowen is catching increasing attention in the corporate world. In this respect matrix of controllers, leaders, managers, workers, stakeholders, product quality, economic performance, employee relationships, environment, resources, community welfare, government relations and even international implications may be developed to assess the performance of any organisation *vis-à-vis* the society. In a way this can also be considered as a modern definition of an organisation.

Ideal Organisation

Organised efforts have always been eulogised in Indian society since times immemorial. But these were more confined to family level and not much above. There are ***shlokas*** in Vedas which emphasise the importance of organised activities. In the schools of those days (*gurukul*) the teacher and the taught used to chant **sit, eat, think and work together**. While describing the message of Vedanta, **Swami Vivekananda** proclaims, **"to make great future India, the whole secret lies in organisation, accumulation of power and co-ordination of wills".**

In the typical Indian style anything and everything is described in its idealised form so that all efforts, by any one, are directed in the correct direction. For an organisation the idealised form put forth, by the Indian seers, was of human body. The various parts of body, with widely differing appearance and distinctly different individual functions, still work in perfect unison, devoid of any tension, in the form of the body as a whole, in achieving the objective of excellent body health and work out-puts. There is no conflict of interest or function amongst the individual parts. Likewise an organisation, with varied participants and their functions, must also work in an integrated way like a human body. There should be no tension whatsoever amongst the participants. The parts of the human body have only one and only one aim of keeping the body healthy and secured and, carry out all those activities in self interest. Similarly the organisation must also function as one integral unit with one and only aim, that is of organisation as a whole, alone. The parts do not have any volition.

This is called ***angangi bhava*** (the whole and the part behave in unison considering themselves to be the same and not different and that one working for the other) in the traditional Indian context. Proper understanding on the part of the individual parts of the body is responsible for the upkeeping of the body as an organisation of the various parts. These parts take care and sustain each other and thereby also the whole body. This is the idealised expectations from participants in any organisation. The modern organisations and their management systems have yet to reach this stage even conceptually, leave aside attempting to attain the same in reality. The minimum that is expected is at least to adopt this as an ideal for modern-day organisations. Once this is done the endeavours in developing management systems could be focussed upon accordingly. What is necessary is to adopt the Indian perception of any orderly arrangement or organisation of humans to be as close to the natural forms as is possible.

Organisational Structures

The process of organisation involves setting up of a structural arrangement wherein those picked up shall be placed for effective discharge of their contribution in achieving the common goal. **Four main structural formats** have been evolved. These are the **pyramidal or hierarchical, committees or juries, matrices and ecologies**.

The pyramidal structure is a common one wherein the leader perceives and decides how the others should act to achieve the organisational objective. It is very rigid in terms of responsibilities. The early organisations were of this type. Here the **Peter Principle** operates. It states that every one tends to rise to his level of incompetence

In big organisations, more so in governmental organisations or in university like organisations wherein large number of experts participate, the organisational functions are allotted to a small group, called committees, sub-committees or juries, who deliberate on the issue in detail and make way for final decisions. In general small groups or task-forces are formed for specific problems to be deliberated upon to suggest the final decisions to be taken in the larger interests of the organisation. This is to save time and energy and make use of expertise in narrow areas to arrive at correct decisions. Similarly cross functional teams are formed to achieve the same.

Sometimes the same job is assigned to more than one group and their final suggestions are cross examined to get the best of judgments. Many times a small group is assigned to more than one leader to cross fertilise the creativities in arriving at the correct judgment.

If may happen that some effective part of an organisation gets all the necessary inputs whereas the other not doing well may starve from getting anything in terms of 3-Ms. The ecology of organisation decides this pattern.

In social and political organised efforts the chaotic situation is often blended with systematic organised efforts to arrive at the right solutions. Such organised efforts have been referred to as ***chaordic***, combination of chaos and order, character of organisations.

There are formal as well as informal organisations and that their structures differ considerably.

Hierarchical Power Structure

Organisation is a hierarchical structure of participants in which superiors and seniors to the juniors and subordinates are readily discernible. There is in fact an up and down. As physical structures are stabilised by distribution of the loads and various forces, similarly in social structures like an organisation the hierarchy is maintained by distribution of power alone. This is the only way to stabilise the organised format. According to **Kenneth Galbraith,** the American Ambassador in India during the regime of President Kennedy [5], "**One of the striking characteristic of social reality is the phenomena of power. This makes submission of some to the will of others as inevitable even in modern society. Nothing whatsoever is accomplished without it. Power can be socially malign but it is equally essential".**

Any social hierarchical arrangement essentially stands on superior and inferior, lower and higher, more useful and less useful, more important and less important, with more power and less power and all such anti-socialistic or anti-equity qualities and principles. Even those who hated such disparities and inequalities from the bottom of their heart, the Marxists, endeavoured hard to construct societies eliminating these inequalities, could not, in reality, even reduce them in the social set-up they evolved for bringing equality in their societies, wherever they tried. In this context therefore Marxism is merely a human desire and nothing else. In fact no large enough society can be governed without forming varied organisations and which can not be created without creating the hierarchy of humans in some or the other form, howsoever flat they may be. It is inherent in it even if it is based on network formats.

Organisationality and organisations both, evolve common rules and procedures of behaviour for individuals to make the entire whole function effectively and efficiently. Discipline is achieved only through such organised formations. Therefore **Fritjof Capra** [6] says, **"In the long history of human civilization numerous forms of social organisations have been generated by the need to organise and distribute power and nothing else".**

Therefore society is nothing but a system of power relations. Whatever structural forms or groups are evolved in the society these have only one aim and Capra further puts it as, **"All such structures or social institutions are ultimately rules of behaviour that facilitate decision-making and embody relationships of power".**

Organisations are created to meet, at least broadly, some of the needs or selfish interests of participants. Hence participants have to accept the hierarchical arrangement and be happy with whatever power comes their way. Additionally they may try on to acquire more power in the same structure, in due course of time, if they so wish. In fact **some have to forego their power willingly, in favour of the others, for something material in return, to bring organisations into existence.** The act of foregoing power results in creation of authority which motivates the organisation to be active in meeting its aims. Power can be treated as a value in its own right and is also instrumental in realisation of other values.

It is humanly impossible not to use the power that is bestowed on any individual, the way one likes, at least to some extent. But there is slight distinction in using power, for the purpose for which it has been bestowed and, for some personal gains. When some willingly forego their power to others, in associating with an organisation, they expect that the power will be used only for the purpose for which it has been given to them, or in other words for achieving the objectives of the organisation. The line of demarcation between whether the power is being used for the very purpose for which it has been given or is being used for some other selfish motive is very thin and very difficult to demarcate. Moreover this demarcation is fairly subjective. Human tendency is not only to use the power for the purpose for which it has been given but also for some selfish motives as well. The selfish use of power in an organisation is surely exterior to organisational objectives. It results in exploitation of those who have willingly surrendered their power. The fraction of power so used for ulterior motives is referred to as ***surplus power*** by **Alvin Toffler** [7]. It commonly happens in almost all organised efforts.

The same thing happens in evolved structures like villages, society or nation. There also, some get more power than the others. Those who get extra power by virtue of the social developments, in a way, also get a chance to exploit those getting less power. This is how it was exploited in India by the so-called high caste people. The exploitation of the society by the democratically elected politicians, as commonly seen and more particularly in India is yet another typical example to illustrate the point in this respect. Therefore it is of prime interest to understand how power has been acquired and is being exercised and, what provisions are made to control it and to what extent?

Ideal View

In any society all are not equal in terms of their abilities, intelligence, social upbringing and so on. But the hierarchical social structure should not result in exploitation of the have-nots or those relatively inferior. No ideal social structure has yet been evolved any where in the world where no-exploitation is guaranteed or was practiced. It is believed that the nearest ideal social structure did exist, long ago in India in the ***Sat-Yug*** as described earlier in Chapter 4. All were living as per Dharma (not religion but rule of law), sustaining the society in its ideal form and were thereby enjoying fully secured and happy life-styles. At that time, required discipline was perhaps enforced in the family itself informally and hence there was no need to enforce it through governance of, whatever little kingdoms then existed.

The social psychology required for such social sustenance was developed through enculturation which emphasised the spirit as

> ***tyajedekam kulsyarthe, gramasyarthe kulam tyajet,***
> ***gramam janapadasyarthe, atmarthe prithivim tyajet***

Meaning thereby that when need arises, individual may be sacrificed for the safety and security of family, family for the village, village for the larger society and finally even larger society may be sacrificed for the benefit of the universe.

Similarly some enlightened in the society, though in minority, were cultured enough, to the extent that they could think as:

> ***na twaham kamaye rajyam, na swargam, napunarbhavam***
> ***kamaye dukhkhataptanam, praninamartinasham***

Meaning thereby that some at least, wished neither for kingdom and heaven; nor for material richness; they only wished to work to eliminate the miseries and pain of the down trodden. They were not worried about their own physical pleasures but wanted the society to be materially happy. They were selfless to the extreme extent. They had really realised the all pervading Brahma in every creation and hence behaved in this exceptional manner.

Such people did not wish to use the power they were bestowed upon for their own ends even remotely. They always wished to work for the betterment of those who had given them the power in the social hierarchy. This is the ideal that has been propounded in Indian society through ages and there were always some who practiced it in their own life and showed the path to others to follow. This tradition continues unabated till today. The real *rishis, sadhus* and *sanyasis,* who had absolutely no personal selfish interests, belonged to this tradition. They were primarily responsible for the sustenance of the Indian society, culture and civilization through ages till today. That is the reason why the Indian culture is the only one which flowed uninterruptedly to this day, withstanding all the ravages umpteen number of times and yet regenerated itself every time to last till today. This was and is the key to sustain societies. Societies and therefore organisations are not sustained on the basis of some narrow selfish ends or wealth alone. Those civilizations which once flourished but were later decimated must have been on account of such individual selfishness alone.

Great men like **Swami Vivekanand, Mahatma Gandhi, Dr. Ambedkar, Dr. Hedgewar** and many others in modern times belonged to this tradition. They created mighty organisations, as suited for modern day social development, not for any personal gains whatsoever, but for the well being of the society at large. They never used the extra power others bestowed on them, in their organisations, for any personal gains whatsoever. The sacrifice was not just in terms of monetary gains but in terms of mental and psychological satisfaction as well. This is how the modern organisations need to be built to last longer over long periods [8] and run to make them most effective and efficient, perhaps great, not just good, on any world bench-marks [9]

These are no doubt great names but such people are found in Hindu society everywhere, even on local levels, taking inspiration from such great men and working in their own narrow area of interests, perhaps not noticed by many. Whatever organisationality still exists in Indian society today, it is more due to the efforts of such selfless characters alone.

This is the description essentially of the ideal NPOs, wherein there are no monetary gains involved. There it may be possible. But how to bring it in organisations where the real motive is profit alone? **Collins** [8,9] has very aptly described that, it is possible to achieve it even in profit making organisations through proper perceptions and assiduous efforts. There the perceptions of corporate social responsibility or societal awareness may be helpful in moving in the above mentioned direction

Countervailing Power

After all power is distributed in reality amongst people who are not ideal. They do suffer from usual selfish interests and as a result tend to use surplus power. Modern democratic societies therefore evolve their social structures with multiple power centers countervailing each other, in contradistinction to autocratic rulers. The power in democratic set-up may be centered in legislatures, executive, government including opposition, in some key person like the nominal monarchy or the President/Chairman or the like. In case any one misuses the power there is powerful independent judiciary where the issue can be adjudicated and any one is punished, if found guilty. In some countries there are ***ombudsmen*** to supervise the misuse of power by any authority. There are even regulatory authorities, vigilance authorities and other constitutional authorities to minimize misuse of power. Above all there is the free media which can publish whatever is illegal that comes to their notice for enlightening the society and provide better choices as their rulers in elections, next time.

References

1. Argenti, John, *Your Organisation: What is it for?*, McGraw-Hill, London, (1993).
2. Adair, John, *Effective Leadership,* Pan Books, London, (1998).
3. Koontz, H and O'Donnell, C, *Principles of Management,* (2009), as quoted by Rege, P.V. in *Sangathan Shashtra,* (Marathi), Edited by Sahasrabuddhye, V., Rambhau Mhalgi Prabodhini, Mumbai, (1997).
4. Bowen, H.R., *Social Responsibilities of Businessmen,* Harper, N.Y.(1953).
5. Galbraith, J. K., *The Anatomy of Power,* Hanish Hamilton, London, (1984).
6. Capra, Fritjof, *Hidden Connections,* Flamingo, (2006).
7. Toffler, Alvin, *Power Shift,* Bantam, (1991).
8. Collins, Jim and Porras, Jerry, I., *Built to Last –Successful Habits of Visionary Companies,* Harper-Collins, N.Y. (1994).
9. Collins, Jim, *Good to Great,* Harper-Collins, N.Y. (2001).

CHAPTER 8

MODELS

CHAPTER STRUCTURE

- Organisationality
- Sustaining Force
- Idealisation
- Organisational
    - Relationship-based
    - Goal-based
- Systems Theory
- Systemic Model
- Open System
- Effects

Organisationality

Organisationality evolves out of natural evolution. It does not have any specific direction or specific prefixed format for evolution. It is therefore difficult to develop specific models for organisationality. In the evolutionary process the development of cortex, the rational seat of judgment and action, enabled organisationality to develop in the direction of becoming larger and broader. This may somewhat be due to the instinctual nature of human beings. In spite of humans, being selfish, it is inherently in human nature. Consequently it is seen that it developed from tribe to family to self-contained village to society to nation to international level. But this direction of progress suggests that it only takes into account the human population alone, that is, it considers only the development from oneself to the human society as one single unit or is anthropo-centric. It does not take in its fold the rest of the living world or the entire creation. There is a feeling of humans, being far superior, quite different and specifically evolved to enjoy nature. This is the western world view and has Biblical support.

From this point of view the Indian traditional concept of psychological evolution of one's own-self from one's own physical existence, to that of family or society around, to the flora and fauna in the form of nature, to finally the whole animate and inanimate universe as described before, is the ideal mode of evolution of organisationality. This is most appropriate direction of evolution of organisationality as yet thought of than merely thinking in terms of only human community. The present world-wide worry about the alarming environmental problems, which include the flora and the fauna as well, indicate the world-wide awareness in developing organisationality on wider scale. The appreciation of the extent of bio-diversity of the earth, particularly against the backdrop of deteriorating environment as a whole, is nothing but increasing the organisationality in the same direction as that propounded by the Indian seers earlier. The perception of deep ecology is made in tune with this thinking. The gap left is only about the acceptance of universal consciousness ***(chetna* or *permeshti in Indian parlance)*** to match it with the Indian concepts of total universal view. Who knows even this may be accepted in due course of time. In fact in the form of preservation of bio-diversity of this globe, this has already been indirectly included in the perception without calling it the same.

On this basis the extent to which any society has progressed in the direction of evolution of organisationality can be assessed. Alternatively how much of the proportion of population has mentally evolved in this correct direction can also be assessed. Some complex measure could be evolved to assess all this. Several such abstract concepts have recently been quantised for their quantitative measurements and comparison. This may not pose any serious problem in trying to evolve it on the same lines, like human happiness or corruption indices and so on. It may not be difficult to evolve some such an index for measuring the organisationality as well.

A peculiar example of organisationality being affected by aggressors can be found in India. The Islamic aggression resulted in breaking away a sizeable chunk of Indian population from its earlier organisationality, forming quite a separate organisationality, which ultimately resulted in the formation of a separate nation of the separated group. However the religious basis of considering organisationality did not last long and the newly formed Pakistan, broke into two parts, namely Pakistan and Bangla Desh, purely on the basis of civilization again. It is equally true that this act has definitely resulted in consolidating the organisationality of the remaining Indian society and consequently it could think of assimilating again, some part of this breakaway group later.

One of the simple but indirect measure of organisationality of any society is to assess as to how many, what different types and quality and, how much durable organisations have been formed in that society. This may also include as to what extent they have transformed the societal life into, all pervading civic sense, better social discipline; establishment of rule of law; equality before law; care for old, disabled, children, females, and all other *have-nots* and so on. Wherever these achievements are of high order their organisationality is seen as of high standard, like in the west or even in countries like Japan, Taiwan, South Korea, etc. This is how organisationality fundamentally helps in improving the social life, at large.

Organisationality does not have any other model except that of the Indian perception in the form of increasing one's own self from ***vyashti* to *samashti* to *srushti* to *permeshti*,** as described before.

Sustaining Force

In an organisation an individual participant is connected with the rest in a very characteristic way. This bond is the life source of sustaining any organisation. **Fritjof Capra** [1] calls it as the ***emergent structure*** of an organisation, which is entirely abstract in nature. It has been described earlier. This bond bestows on every one in the organisation some additional qualities and strength which are not felt readily while working in individual capacities. How this happens has already been explained earlier. Attempts are made, these days, to inculcate all these in organisations, through appropriate training programmes.

Since human behaviour cannot be predicted with certainty at any time, human behaviour has no cause and effect relationship. Man is not a robot to conform to such certainties. This becomes very clear by conducting a very simple and interesting experiment. Some persons are asked to sit one behind the other. A message is told to the first verbally and asked to pass it on one by one through the entire column. When the last person is asked as to what message he received, the message finally conveyed, surprisingly, has nothing to do with the original message given to the first person in the column. It gets distorted beyond imagination during such transfers. This happens purely because the same words do not convey the same meaning to every one. Whatever is heard is first understood and then the meaning derived is transformed in ones own words and then only it is conveyed. It is here where the distortion occurs. It is not true with only verbal messages but such distortions occur even in written messages, if asked to convey in one's own language, to a considerable extent. This is the reason why human psychology, history, economics, anthropology and all such social sciences and productivity science, technology and engineering form the basis of evolving the methodology of better and better management practices of organisations.

It is necessary to appreciate that the individual and the group existing as an organisation are two different things. The example of cricket is well akin to us. The role of captain and his personal play are two different things. The individual never really forgets his own identity in an organisation, in spite of the fact that he is working in a group. An individual works as an individual and simultaneously as well as a group. This is the reason why individuals do work for their own selfish interests even in an organisation while striving for the common organisational goal. Smooth functioning of an organisation will be possible only if these two do not clash. If they clash then there will be problems on one or the other front.

Idealisation

As per the Indian tradition, every individual is nothing but the universal spirit or soul itself as manifested in the form of life. Similarly the society also is believed to have its own life-sustaining spirit *(chetna)* or soul. The social organisations must therefore conform to the natural forms, as far as possible, to remain natural. Any deviation is bound to create related problems in its functioning. Since the best organised form of nature is human body, so the organisations must also conform as far as possible to this structure in principle.

Organisational

Organisations are formed to achieve some pre-fixed objective(s). In fact it is the very *reason d'etre'* of organisations. The structure of an organisation is so designed and manned and, its management is so planned that this objective is achieved most effectively and efficiently. The organisational model can therefore be depicted in different ways as per the perspective. These models are relationship-based, goal-based and system-based. These are described below.

Relationship-based

Many people work together in an organisation. It is bound to result in interactions amongst them. The interactions are very much subject to individual behaviour, aspirations, restraints and such other individual and group psychological forces. In other words their mutual relationships shall dominate in deciding their co-operation and co-ordination. What are the different types of relationships that are possible in a group? What does the picture of an organisation look like when considered as based on relationship amongst the participants?

In one of the concepts **every individual in an organisation is considered as a fraction and all such fractions put together should be equal to one whole.** To make it so, the organisation has to be well balanced in terms of its constituents, in the sense that they are not only committed to the objective of the organisation but are psychologically attuned to work together in a co-ordinated manner. If these are not well balanced, to that extent the organisation shall not become one whole. The organisation in this case is more cohesive and therefore committed for the cause for which it has been established. The individuals understand that on their own-self, they can not attain the goal but when put together they can realise the orgnaisational goal readily. Social organisations may conform to this model better.

In another model an organisation is considered to be a **conglomerate of individuals as the particles are present in a mass of sand.** In this case the individuals, in an organisation, do not have much to do with each other in terms of any human bond, as sand particles do not have any mutual bonding or emergent structures, because of the very neutral nature of particles in a mass of sand. The organisations exist practically for name's sake .The organisation is formed to serve very fragile and minor objectives. Typical examples of this are the organisations of scientists, literatures, players, professionals and so on. Many federations may belong to this category. The organisation in this case does not fulfill much of their selfish interests. Those can be met by themselves working alone. They get together to achieve some specific common and limited objectives as compared to their own individual achievements. It often works as a pressure group to ensure the participant's own selfish interests and safety.

In yet another model an organisation is assumed to be like **a living human being** and the members consider themselves like various parts of the organisational-body, akin to a human body. Here the individual does not have any independent existence in any way. But the individual's progress is guaranteed through organisational efforts alone. **'Not me but only organisation'** is the motto in such organisations. It was seen in organisations like the freedom movement in India or *Acharya-Kul* and may be true elsewhere. It may also be seen in religious organisations. This is the spirit that is consciously cultivated in organisations like the RSS or the *Sarvodaya*. This is cultivated in organisations wherein the members are totally committed to the organisational objective like military or even those of terrorist and of dacoits..

There is also a model looking basically like the family. This is combination of above mentioned two different models wherein the members consider themselves as fractions of the whole in the form of an organisation and also consider themselves like parts of an organisational body. Here the members are prepared to sacrifice for the sake of organisation and hence do not complain even if their selfish interests are not met in any way in the organisation. This is not possible in profit making organisations because those essentially work for meeting the individual's selfish interests. This may be possible in organisations set-up for some lofty cause like the freedom movement or presently the RSS. In fact individuals join such organisations, sacrificing their own self, for some larger good. There is a saying in Marathi ***(gharchya khawun lashkarachya bhajane)*** which means that you eat at home but go to the military camp to cook food for the soldiers, free of cost. This is befitting for such organisations. These organisations can be formed only when a very lofty and statesman-like leadership is available. People join such organisations taking inspiration from leadership with high moral stature.

It should be understood that when individuals join any organisation they are apparently presumed to agree with the objectives of the organisation. But this may not be completely true in commercial organisations wherein people join, at least to start with, to earn ones own living, and may even participate per force in the absence of any other alternative, for ones own sustenance.

Goal-based [2]

An organisation includes the tangible requirements for achieving the goal as generally referred to in the form of **3-Ms, as money, men and materials**. Like-wise it also includes intangibles like the structure, style, co-operation and co-ordinated work-culture, systems of communication, schemes of motivation, issues of happiness or miseries of the participants and so on. In fact an organisation consists of a complex web of these tangibles and intangibles. Organisation itself develops this web as per necessity and requirements to achieve the set-forth goal. The connectivity involved in this web is so complex and so multi-dimensional that it is bound to give rise to fundamental differences about the very path of achieving the goal and on the micro-level there may be hardly an area of agreement. Hence the ways and means of achieving the simple looking organisational goal appears to be too complicated in view of the expected organisational activities. A typical example of this confusion can be found in governmental activities in India. Even when, enough money, human resource, other material requirements, broad method of achieving the objectives, relevant activation and so on, are all available and still the organisational efforts seem to go astray or become atrophy. As a result the priorities of using human resource, choice of work and its methodology, avenues of expenses, etc. all take non-synchronous directions. In fact the desire in the form of the objective itself gets altered without stating so. This results in transformation of the objective of the governmental organised efforts, into selfish personal objectives of some or many. Alternatively it gets embroiled into organisational power-game or politics.

In fact the organisational execution very much depends on the value-system of the participants. In the absence of any such value-system in Indian governmental establishments, organisational work goes atrophy. Hence the simple looking objective of an organisation transforms itself into a very complex goal to be achieved in practice. It further gets complicated because of the external environment. All this complicates the matter making the object of developing the goal-model a difficult task. Besides it changes with different types of organisations.

Initially it was thought that it would be easy to develop such a goal-model because many abstract attributes of organisations were not known then. As these became evident, the limitations of this model became obvious. But while assessing organisational efficacy, on the basis of this model in those days, the assessor quickly jumped on the conclusive part as to whether the organisation achieved its objective or not. The criticism took the form of subjective assessment of the leadership. Question-mark was laid on, if the simple looking objective of an organisation was at all that simple? It however led to study the objective of an organisation in all its perspective. From this it became obvious that the simple looking objective is in fact not at all that simple. It is intimately related to the style of management, which varies from person to person.

But all this study led to appreciate the various requirements of an organisation to attain its stated objective. It was also observed that often the objective is never achieved. Does it mean that the organisation is of no use? And yet the organisation seems to be working satisfactorily. These earlier studies led to identify and appreciate various factors affecting the effectiveness of an organisation. All this coupled with the knowledge from many other branches of science finally led to appreciate that an organisation is a complex system, consisting of many tangible and intangible things and, needs to be studied as a system alone, to appreciate it and to evolve ways and means of its better and efficient management.

Systems Theory

The early attempts to develop the organisational model in terms of the goal miserably failed. By the middle of 19th century the science of thermodynamics had become fairly clear in terms of its three laws. Out of these the Third or the Entropy Law was variously applied to social systems as well, to better understand them. It was essentially an attempt at the unification of science and scientific analysis. It was sought to unify as much as possible a broader perspective for creative analysis. After Second World War it crystallized into the concept of systems, as set of elements in standing interaction. From there the concept of physical systems, along with its closed and open type varieties, became obvious. The same later on was further evolved for living organisms in the form of systems theory. It proved to be useful in organising knowledge about many social objects. Eventually it came to be applied in the field of social science as well.

Theory of systems was thus developed out of all such applications. It appears to be highly attractive from the standpoint of empirical research. It gives excellent opportunity for fusing micro and macro analyses into one. Thereby it helps to create theoretical constructs of any analysis It was evolved as a branch of science by **Fritjof Capra** [3,4]. **Accordingly the essential properties of any system are properties of the whole, which none of the parts possess.** They arise from interactions and relationships between the parts. These properties are destroyed when it is dissected. In the Newton-Cartesian era, no wonder, the attempts to know the world by studying its parts utterly failed. The individuality`is thus lost when things are put together in the form of an organised whole. The nature of the whole is quite different from that of the parts and is more than the parts put together. It is easily illustrated by the example of human body. A part thereof is not and can not be the body. The attributes of a part is quite different from the whole in the form of the body. According to **Fritjof Capra** [3]:

"Systems theory looks at the world (here organisation) in terms of interrelatedness and interdependence, and in this framework an integrated whole whose properties cannot be reduced to those of its parts, is called a system."

On this basis any organisation can be studied taking into account all the tangible and the intangible variables of an organisation, in an integrated fashion, in the form of a system. Although all these variables of organisation superficially appear as discreet and structured in a hierarchical manner, they are in fact interrelated and interdependent, to the extent, that they can not be studied in isolation fully and properly. It in fact forms a complicated network in an organisation. Systems approach makes it possible to study them in an integral manner. To understand the whole from the parts is Newton-Cartesian perception. Hence for holistic approach to be effective the ghost of Newton-Cartesian perceptions strangling our neck had to be first discarded against the backdrop of systemic **Einsteinian** world view in the form of its holistic nature and interconnectivity of everything in this world as a complex network. The modern deep ecological approach helps to appreciate the organisational systems much better. It is something more than mere holistic view primarily put forward first by **Einstein**.

Systemic Model

The above mentioned requirements for formation of an organisation appear as if these are distinct and discreet and therefore somewhat basic or fundamental requirements. But in reality it is not so. There is none more important than the other since all of them are intimately interconnected in the form of a network. Such an approach as everything being of equal importance in a system was first formalised in physics by **Geoffrey Chew** in his **Boot-strap** philosophy, denying anything as basic or fundamental. The organisational web of tangible and intangible factors is seen in systems theory as a dynamic web of interrelated events taking place in the form of activities of an organisation, accepting everything as of equal importance.

Systems thinking is always process thinking and hence any organisational thinking is about organisational processes and not of its discreet constituents. Every observation about an organisation in reality follows other earlier observations only. What is observed is in response to earlier questions, wishes and expectations. This systemic thinking originates always from thinking in terms of total organisation and not about its parts in isolation. It takes into account the organisation as a functional unit and an inalienable part of the larger world around. It must also take into account the social and the natural environment in which it exists.

In a system there exists a dynamic equilibrium between various variables, resulting from mutually opposing forces, which impart fair amount of dynamism and flexibility to the organisation. If any of these forces tries to assert itself in its own way, by making the system move in its preferred direction, then it automatically results in opposite forces acting against it, in trying to restore back the equilibrium. As a result no constituent is considered more important than any other. This is a network of all such variables and a small variation even by an apparently minor constituent may cause great upheaval in the entire network. All are therefore treated as equally important and dealt with accordingly. The internal co-operation, mutual help, understanding and co-ordination is considered to be the responsibility of all. This is the idealised state of management. But it is the responsibility of the controller, leader and the manager, individually and jointly, to see that the organisation tends to move in the idealised direction. This bears on all the participants to appreciate and imbibe the system approach in managing the organisation. It only means that the organisation has to be more open to anything and everything to move it in this idealised direction. Such a system always tries to establish equilibrium with the social environment as well. But it must be remembered that openness is against human nature because of his selfishness. From this point of view whether and, to what extent the organisational objective is being met, can be studied with respect to each one of the organisational variables, by assessment and by trial and error method, if needed.

No organisation is originally started to close it down, except the *ad-hoc* and the project organisations. But it is equally true that organisations do decay and finally close down. They may even merge with some others on account of their own selfish interests. Hence attempts are needed to keep them running and growing. This is possible only through managing the organisation assuming it as a system and then assessing the effect of each one of the variables on the growth of the organisation. It is therefore important to know more and more about the effect of individual variable on attainment of organisational objective. This gives leads as to how these factors need to be altered to make the organisation perform more effectively.

Open System

System model presumes an organisation to be an inalienable part of the society along with similar other organisations in the society and, hence the society and other organisations constitute the external environment of the organisation with which it interacts, when considered as an open system. It is also presumed to be working in a given natural environment. The effect of organisation on social and environmental aspects has acquired great importance in managing organisations now. Assessment of this aspect is possible only if the system model is presumed before such considerations. It is not only better but it is more efficient to assess the overall effect of organisation on the above aspects rather than considering the effect of each one or group of some variables of the organisation on the society and the environment. This is true even in the case of profit making organisations as well.

Under **Newton-Cartesian** influence, the profit making organisations were merely profit driven and hence disregarded not only the well being of those manning the organisation but its ill-effects on the society and the environment at large were also totally disregarded. Those were the days of exploitation of everything for making profit alone, by some influential and stronger ones. Those were the days when the management used the surplus power to the extent possible for their own selfish interests. Now the outlook is completely changed. The controller, leader or manager has to worry about the efficiency and effectiveness of human resource within the organisation because it makes the organisation more efficient and competitive. The general humanitarian considerations have now forced them to work for the benefit of society while making profit and take into account the environmental considerations, flouting of which is neither permitted to any one, nor by law. This is the net result of development and growth of international organisationality, reflected in increased awareness of welfare of the entire globe as such.

System approach allows ready flexibility in decreasing or increasing the extents of the organisation and the society, including the environment, for consideration, regarding any issue whatsoever. Hence as per requirements, the part or whole of an organisation and the relevant social environment can be taken together as a different system for consideration. This approach has therefore resulted in primarily integrating the organisations from within, with all their variables, and along with integrating it, with the overall security and betterment of society, including the environmental considerations. The organisation along with the whole earth (*srishti* in the Indian terminology) is now generally considered as a system for assessing the impact of organisational activities on the society on a short-term or long-term basis of considerations.

Effects

The system-approach has had tremendous beneficial effects on the society. Firstly, organisations came to be considered as an inalienable part of the social system and meant to develop society at large. As a result, they became more modern, in tune with time. The stability of organisations increased beyond expectation and as a result, not only their efficiency increased but their contribution to social welfare improved. Psychologically it became more normal for individuals to work in various organisations for serving the larger and varied social interests as well. It also resulted in integration of the society at large, in terms of production, distribution, sale, marketing of goods and services and also in terms of cultural evolution. Indirectly it improved the organisationality of the society and conferred even on earlier colony states more stable and sound nation-hoods. It proved a boon to improve the international organisationality as an extension of the social/national level, and thereby contribute to world peace and progress of humanity as a whole.

References

1. Capra, Fritjof, *The Hidden Connections*, Flamingo, (2003).
2. Etzioni, Amitai, *Modern Organisations*, Prentice Hall of India, N.Delhi, (1965).
3. Capra, Fritjof, *The Turning Point*, Flamingo, London, (1983).
4. Capra, Fritjof, *The Web of Life*, Flamingo, (1997).

CHAPTER 9

FREEDOM

CHAPTER STITUCTURE

- Western View
- Psychology of Individual vs. Group
- Indian View-point
- Existence at Large
- Comparison
- Proactivism
- Contract
- Indian Dilemma

Material things can be organised as per one's own desire. They will stay in the order in which they have been placed, unless disturbed thereafter. They have no mind of their own to think and alter themselves and therefore no freedom. The living world is however different. The flora cannot move from its place but the fauna has locomotion to alter their own positions, at least to some extent as per their desires and requirements. The animal world, if at all, has a much less evolved mind. But human being is quite different. He has a highly evolved mind, consciousness, etc. and because of which he has his own way of living and working. This is reflected in his instinctual freedom. Freedom presupposes availability of choice. If there is no choice of alternatives there is no freedom. But freedom is not absolute. It is conditioned by the society and ones own needs, to be met within the social constraints. The social evolution has evolved ethics and morality in individuals and groups, out of these constraints. Individual freedom generally manifests itself in the form of ethics and morality in the society. The question arises as to what is the psychological status of an individual in an organisation *vis-à-vis* that in smaller group within an organisation or the organisation as a whole?

It is of primary importance in managing organisations effectively and efficiently in achieving the organisational objectives. On the one hand there is the natural tendency to ensure one's own freedom as per one's own evolved ego, in the direction of self-actualization as suggested by **Maslow,** and on the other hand there is the tendency to make all alike to make organisations work smoothly in a co-operative and co-ordinated manner. This dilemma is always faced by the controllers, leaders and managers, on whom the responsibility of managing and developing the organisation depends. They have to find solutions with respect to such human psychological dichotomy within an organisation.

Western View

Every individual is born in this world with his own characteristic genome, which makes him unique *vis-à-vis* all others. Similarly individuals also grow under different family, social and cultural environments. All this results in evolution of a characteristic ego or personality of every individual. This is reflected in his temperament, his desires, his likes and dislikes, his affiliation, his attitudes, his choices and so on. It eventually results in one's own unique personality, with unique viewpoint on anything and everything in this world. This is described in Indian philosophy as ***pinde, pinde matirbhinnah*** (it means that every one is different in his understanding and approach). Notwithstanding this, psychologists do try to group them together to study human beings in more detail, as is done in any scientific study. However every individual has his own way of behaving and reacting in an organisation. This is the greatest of challenges before the management in any organisation.

Unless and until, all such varied individuals, are moulded into one organisationality or in **Capra's** perception into an emergent organisational structure, in any organisation, no organisation can function actively and efficiently. This is the inherent conflict or **internal dialectics** faced by every organisation. The European or western thinkers, in the last couple of centuries, along with many Japanese thinkers joining them in twentieth century, have thrown enough light on these apparent self contradictions. Of these the influences of **Karl Marx** and **Sigmund Freud** have been the dominant one. These two have acquired so great an importance that unless the views expressed by these two, in particular, are taken into consideration no socio-scientific discussion of any social phenomena can be complete.

The European thinkers always felt contradiction between the individual's natural instinctual freedom and the inherent requirement of socialising process to fit one into groups, organisations or organisationality of some kind. It was difficult for the freedom loving westerners to accept that some restriction in individual freedom was implicit in social life. This is how they felt the power game or exploitative behaviour between subordinates and super ordinates in any group activity, in any organisationality as well as in any organisation. This was the result of dominance of, particularly the **Newton-Cartesian** influence, which led to the development of tremendous tensions between individuals and organised activities. As a result individuals paid a heavy price for being a part of an organisation and thereby that of their society. Social scientist **Herbert Marcues** [1] saw it as: **"The result of historical social process of exploitation of individuals by groups".**

According to another social scientist **G.S. Mead** [2]

"It is suppression of natural desires and motivations of individuals. An individual's personality really never becomes a truly social one. Society somewhere always inflicts injustice on an individual".

Sigmund Freud [3] was more forthright in stating that:

"There is an irremediable antagonism between human individual and civilisation (group) and an unavoidable antagonism prevails between instinctual needs of the human organism and the requirements of civilizing process:.

He therefore considered suppression and exploitation of an individual as inevitable in developing social life.

Herbert Marcues felt that social progress made so far has been due to suppression and exploitation alone. The only question therefore remains whether the suppression and exploitation was justifiably tolerable or was it in excess? Justified suppression and exploitation is that which resulted in social progress or equitable distribution of life sustaining and supporting means. If this was not the outcome then the suppression and exploitation was nothing but dictatorship of some or a small group.

Many times scientific and technological progress has been achieved through such dictatorships but it is in fact a *by-product* and not the main aim. It means that instead of broad social progress, this suppression and exploitation finally leads to individual's miseries and sorrow. Individual's efforts and activism in this case is misused by the tyrants for their selfish ends, disregarding individual's well being.

Under the influence of **Newton-Cartesian** world view, existence of human beings was assumed to be limited to physical body-level alone and that mind was not even considered to have an independent existence. Hence human being was looked upon as if he was merely a bundle of desires to be met by production of required goods on required scale, aided by industrialisation, even disregarding social and human considerations. Since this was more readily and efficiently possible through organisations, people in a way were forced, to work in an organised fashion, in the western world, leaving no alternative to them for sustenance.

Psychology of Individual vs. Group

One of the important fall-outs of this influence was to assert that the individual's psychology was quite different from that of the group. With time however the westerners did realise the mental and psychological needs and also the intellectual needs of individual human beings. Hence slowly their view point pertaining to individual freedom and the socialising process did undergo several changes in balancing both the requirements at the optimum. The famous **French Revolution** resulted in emphasising the importance of individuality in the form of **freedom, liberty and equality** beyond any doubt. Socialising process therefore underwent some paradigm change since then. This paved the way to act against suppression and exploitation decisively, without affecting the material well being, achieved by organised industrialism. As a result anything that came in the way of individual freedom or personality was consciously avoided, to the extent possible, even in managing organisations and thereby the society at large. This was the driving force for the changes brought about in organisational management, particularly since the end of Second World War, in general and more particularly, in the last couple of decades. The systemic thinking has further strengthened the consolidation of individual freedom in organisational matters.

Indian View-point

In traditional thinking in India, no other aspect of human life has been dealt with in more detail than personal ego. It has been considered as one of the main obstacles in the progress of humans towards realisation of Brahma or salvation. The traditional literature is brimming with ways and means to subdue the personal ego. Once Moksha is considered to be the supreme goal of human life, it can not be achieved without transcending the personal ego, as is emphatically preached and practiced. In order to appreciate the ways and means of transcending personal ego, personal nature, individual freedom, societal obligations, including those of family, were also appreciated along with their intricacies. All this led to the development of thorough understanding of primarily the human nature, social existence, the natural surroundings and finally the entire animate and inanimate universe, to make one lead a happy, dominantly contented and pleasant life. This was essentially systemic thinking and nothing else and has been appreciated in the west no better than by **Fritjof Capra** [4].

From this, the four-tier traditional concept of *vyashti, samashti, srushti* and *permeshti* as described earlier was evolved. But this is too abstract for ordinary human beings to understand and follow it in one's own life. Therefore, an idealised individual life was designed and put forward, to be followed in real life, as far as possible on an individual and social level. Accordingly the human life was considered to be ideally of one hundred year's extent.

This was divided into four equal segments of twenty-five years each which was individually called as an ***Ashram***.

The first twenty five years (first eight years of childhood to be deducted from this) was called the ***Brahmacharyashram***, which was meant to learn and acquire everything required for sustaining the later married and family life in adulthood. One was expected to remain as bachelor in this period. The second twenty-five years, that is from age twenty-five to fifty, was meant to lead a normal family life, earn livelihood, get married, enjoy worldly pleasures, procreate to continue the human society and to sustain the rest of the family and also the rest of the society at large, along with the others in the three other stages of their personal lives. This was called the ***Grihasthashram***. This period is characterized for acquiring, collecting, storing, enjoying all material things and above all enjoying power, if any.

The third quarter of twenty-five years, that is from fifty to seventy-five years of age, was called the ***Vanaprasthashram*** in which one was expected to slowly renunciate every thing material in life, to the extent possible, so that the onward march on the path of Moksha, with total detachment of physical world, could be travelled at ease. This was meant to give up all possible material pleasures beyond sustenance, positions of honour, power and everything that was earned in the earlier *Grihasthashram*. Since nobody is to stay in this world for ever and since the stay here is too small as compared with the life of earth and even society, everyone must hand over his even hard earned wealth, honour, positions of power and every such worldly thing, claimed to be his own, to the next generation smoothly. This is the period of giving up, leaving, renunciating, detaching from material pleasures. ***Vanaprasthy psyche*** is the most unique characteristic of Hindu society, not thought of and hence not exhibited by any other in the world. It is the main sustenance of peaceful and progressive society. The alternative is to sustain the tensions arising out of and for accumulation of worldly wealth and power.

The last twenty-five year period was called the ***Sanyasashram*** which was not compulsory for all. Those who could stand the regours of hard life were expected to relinquish everything including his own family and migrate into jungle, away from the social life, to lead very ascetic life-style and meditate to achieve Moksha or Brahma.

The four-tier individual development of expanding ones own self and the four-tier individual social life-style was designed to transform human being into Narayana or set oneself on the path of Moksha or Brahma realisation. Hence the Indian *seers* never felt any dialectics or conflict between an individual existence and his socialising process. In fact the Indian seers always thought that an individual does not have any separate, distinct and discreet existence without the society, nature and the universe as a whole. The emphasis was therefore always more on social existence. Great thinker **M.S.**alias **Guruji Golwalkar** [5], the second chief of RSS always said,

"The thought of society *(samashti)* must not be allowed to get obscured even for a moment from the eyes in favour of individuality or instinctual selfishness", (he is emphasising here only the systemic thinking in the simplest form legible to common men).

This traditional spirit resulted in highly cultured and civilized social life in India for millennia. However Golwalkar's vision has been described as a terrifying vision by people like **Jyotirmaya Sharma** [6], when he was deputy editor of Hindu, the English daily published from several cities in India. We do not expect better understanding from such people who are Indians for names sake and by their upbringing in the west are more influenced by the western thought and culture, essentially based on dialectics. If the traditional Indian vision is a terrifying vision then why worry about society and the presently terrifying environmental degradation of the globe as a whole because it is the net result of instinctual freedom, opting for unlimited physical pleasures alone, disregarding the society and the nature?

There is another reference of extreme influence of the western thinking of physical pleasures on the basis of dialectics. It is a book written in Marathi ***(Majet Jagava Kasa)*** by **Shivraj Gorle** [7]. While discussing the mental confusion, at one stage in his own life, about whether to work for own-self or for the society/nation, Gorle claims to have opted for self enjoyment, in preference to social well being. This is again the case of conflict between individual instinctual freedom *vis-à-vis* the social needs and obligations. But the green movement now expects lots of restraint on the part of those who were once champions of individuality and, exploiters and suppressors of human beings under one or the other garb perhaps all over the world and that too for over few hundred years.

If one considers that the global environmental worries are left to individuals, assuming that they will take care of it as per the requirements, then it should have been solved long ago, since individually they would have acted as per the necessity in larger interests of the society. The history speaks far too otherwise. In fact why should the individuals, out of their instinctual freedom in its extreme, think about the society at all? Once one accepts personal instinctual pleasures, overriding and in disregard to collective well being, then suppression of individuality and exploitation of others, who are relatively weak, poor, illiterate and unorganised, directly or indirectly, is inescapably the outcome.

We are not living in an idealised society wherein everyone is conscious of his/her own obligations to behave in an idealised way. Such things are never solved by appeal to the individual conscience alone, there has got to be some kind of social awakening, pressure, movement and legislation of effective kind to make it more effective [8]. This is nothing but the same ***samashti*** and ***srushti*** perceptions of Indians. What else is it? Their worry of environmental degradation is nothing but indirect admittance of overriding importance of society in respect of individual instinctual freedom and nothing else.

The individualistic lifestyle is relatively far easier, in terms of work inputs. Universal identity expressed in the form of social consciousness requires far greater work inputs rather than when individual freedom is the sole aim. Many may be scared of accepting it, perhaps just for this reason.

The strong family-centralism in India, evolved over the extended agricultural era, has been instrumental in developing the societal obligation, the first step in socialising process, overriding the individual instinctual freedom in India.

Existence at Large

The famous case of **Midnapur** [9], quoted in social science text books, about two child girls that were carried off to a wolf camp, were developed as animals in their life styles, simply because they did not get the required social environment, during their upbringing in the early childhood. This is a typical example that emphasises the role of society in bringing up any individual to civilized state, unlike the animal world. The family is chiefly responsible for making an individual sociable. Civilization is not an individualistic concept; it is a quality of a larger human group. How can this be forgotten and kept on emphasising the individual freedom and attendant instinctual needs, against socialising influence? **How can individuality override the social needs and security?** Does not right social needs include the well being of an individual and his enlightenment to a level of universal consciousness? What is that society wherein the individuals feel unattended in attaining their legitimate individual needs? Is it even worth calling it a society?

As per Indian thinking, every individual exists and operates on all the four levels almost simultaneously, swinging from one to the other level as per the requirements. At times the existence appearing on any one level is merely an apparent illusion, at best. They saw the individual, with all his freedom and individuality as a level of existence which must transform into higher level of social existence, without any conflict between the two. Nature has evolved human beings to exist first as individuals and then as social indivisible parts. However it did not stop at that. Human being has to evolve further to identify himself as an inalienable part of nature because he cannot feel happy without the surrounding nature being conducive to him and, finally with that of entire universal existence or the cosmos.

Even the western thinkers lately accept multilevel existence in the form of structures of systems within systems. **Fritjof Capra** [10] asserts that every system is a whole with respect to its parts, while at the same time it is a part of a larger whole. Thus, **cells combine to form tissues, tissues to form organs, and organs to form organisms. These in turn exist within social systems and ecosystems.** Throughout the living world, living systems nests within other living systems. This view matches that of Indian thinkers, without accepting the perception of Brahma. It amounts to accepting the lower level as an inalienable part of the larger whole with unbreakable connection amongst them. Therefore organisational form is a totality of connections amongst the constituent systemic elements.

The individual instinctual freedom exists at the physical level of existence and if it is not curtailed, it would only lead to conflicts amongst individuals, amongst individuals and groups and amongst different groups and, eventually loss of peace in society all over. This is bound to tend to barbarianism as was seen in the stone-age, before social evolution, when might was right and nothing existed beyond the individual bodily pleasures. It also manifested in a naked style in colonial era, which was nothing but extension of the same stone-age spirit on the part of stronger organised societies in subjugating the relatively weak agricultural and stone-age societies elsewhere in the world.

If the social structure is such that it provides all the four-tier facilities for individuals to lead their lives, then there appears no suppression or exploitation of any one's freedom or individuality, by any one, for his own personal ends. It is true that while emphasising the human nature, the Indian seers went in-depth to understand it along with the ultimate goal of human being. This was not mechanically imposed on the individuals in some form of regimentation. Had it been so there would have been conflicts on this account as well? It was left to individuals to embark on this path to the extent possible individually, depending upon his/her personality. Those who led the society did stick to this path as guiding examples or model heroes for the rest.

They never thought of individual or the society in isolation, devoid of total existence, as the west did. However interactive contact between the thinkers of the west and the Indian thinkers bridged this gap to some extent in the twentieth century.

According to famous thinker of last century, **Will Durant** [11], **"the individual is as much a product of society as society is a product of the individual. A vast network of customs, manners, conventions, language and traditional ideas lie ready to pounce upon every new born child, to mould it into the image of the people among whom it has appeared".**

This is different from the antagonism seen by other earlier social thinkers and philosophers of the west. But it still reflects that the socialising process is nothing but dictatorial tendencies of the elders on the rest of the society. It was somewhat refined version in the light of understanding of the Indian social thinking.

In reality however it did preclude the Indians from studying the individual *vis-à-vis* the society as the west did, compartment-wise, for their better understanding. That is the reason why in the Indian traditional literature, no discussion is seen on the subject like study of comparative psychology of group *vs.* the individual, as is amply available in the western literature. The result of this comparative study has already been quoted above.

Comparison

In the current western thought, in the improvised version of the **Newton-Cartesian** period, human being is accepted to exist at three different physical levels and these are the bodily, mental and intellectual levels. Human efforts, individual or in the form of an organisation, are directed to meet the needs arising out of this existence. Now attempts are being made to minimise the suppression and exploitation of an individual by the group at any level. This requires, as a priority, ethical behaviour on the part of human beings. Why should an individual's behaviour be based on ethics? Does it lead to some kind of pleasure? Where will the ethics come from? It has to have some ethereal basis. **Jesus Christ** preached that one should love one's own neighbour as much as one loves oneself. At the physical level, the experience of one's owns existence distinctly separates one from the rest, say the neighbour. How can then anyone love the neighbour as one's own self?

Late **Swami Ranganathanand** [12], then Chief of Ramakrishna Mission, has explained it in terms of the four-tier Indian concept of happiness wherein he stresses that there is definitely the fourth level of happiness to be achieved by human beings. This fourth level is the spiritual level wherein the soul is considered to be a universal entity, though it appears to exist separately in every animate and inanimate existence. Once it is accepted as an universal entity, all encompassing, *omni-scient* and *omni-present*, the neighbour, though appearing as different entity, in fact, is not separate, it is the same as anybody's self, as far as the soul within is concerned. Hence it is the logical basis for any one to love his neighbour as he loves himself, because the two being, not different, but the same as universal entity. There is no alternative to this concept.

On this basis, the western approach and motivation for an individual, in the form of one's own physical attainments, no longer hold true. No one has that absolute freedom to enjoy one's own life, while living in a society. It is always bound by the society. The egoistic perception that *'I will gather this or that or become this or that'* and such other outwardly desires then become meaningless. Conquering nature, as was once thought, under the **Newton-Cartesian** influence, as the primary goal in the west, no longer holds true. All efforts of individuals, whether carried out individually or in groups, have to be directed to realise the ultimate reality. All efforts at co-operation, co-ordination, understanding, mutual communication and sustenance are all considered in Indian perception as Purusharthas (the four in the form of Dharma, Artha, Kama and Moksha) which is nothing but only that what is worth achieving in one's own life.

The Indian thinking therefore developed, unlike the western duality, in the form as non-dual or Advaita. There was no reason left for conflict between individual and the society or the nature or even entire existence. The well being of the society is seen as the objective of individual's life; the well being of nature is seen as the objective of the society, in turn of individuals and all these leading to well being of the entire universe. What else is required to sustain human beings in the form of organised units like the society at large?

Those who believed in all these perceptions lived in India all through the ages and are still seen living even today. Collective existence in the form of family or self-contained village or organisation in present day world was seen as exposition, above that of an individual, as merely higher level of existence and nothing else, the highest level being oneness with universal entity, called by different names like Brahma, Moksha, Nirvana, Arihant, and so on. The present day alarming calls about environmental degradation is nothing but expression on the same lines of universal oneness realised long ago by Indian seers. This is quite contrasting with the earlier thinking, in the west, under the influence of **Newton-Cartesian** world order that led to the development of exploitative industrialism. In this respect only the names seem to differ, the ecological awareness and the realisation of Brahma more or less appear alike. But there is lack of clarity in mere ecological awareness as compared to what the Indian seers thought as Brahma, in terms of the fundamental perception. The Indian perception stands on solid foundation as compared to the superficial ecological considerations, with certainty of achieving the desired results. It also amounts to that if the ecological considerations were not alarming they would go back to the stage of exploitation, which is worse.

Proactivism

Even after meeting all the essential and auxiliary requirements in forming an organisation, there is no guarantee that the organisation shall function effectively. All these facilities only indicate the capability of the organisation to function effectively. In reality organisations have to be managed properly to make them active for attaining the set-out goal. Management science has been fairly well developed to train the controllers, leaders and the managers so that they could manage the organisations in the direction of achieving the objective. This is done by the **five-point management techniques adopted universally and known as planning, organising, staffing, leading and controlling** of organisations. Mutual help and co-operation is not just enough in any organised effort. It is the co-ordination between human resource, finance and strategies, at the optimum, established by the manager, makes the organisations active in attaining its goal.

Co-ordination is the management of interdependence in an organisation. It is orderly synchronisation of fitting together of the interdependent efforts of individuals in attaining common objective. If a manager performs his functions of planning, organising, staffing, leading and controlling well, then co-ordination is automatically achieved. Without co-ordination, individuals and departments may begin to pursue their own individual or specialised interests, most often at the expense of the larger organisational goals. Co-ordination is meant to reconcile the individual differences in approach, efforts or interests of the individuals and departments by avoiding inconsistencies in their priorities, strategies, objectives and policies. Co-ordination harmonises the individual's and corporate goals by making individuals see how their job contributes to the overall goals of an organisation. For this the informal relations amongst the individuals play a crucial role. Individual freedom could be enjoyed within these limits of corporate life. This only emphasises the necessity of emergent structures in an organisation.

An organisation is formed of individuals with their own characteristic mental world, which remains intact even after joining an organisation and carrying work collectively. The collective mental world of the organisation as a whole, without killing the individuality, has to be developed consciously and without which it will not function uni-directionally in unison. This makes the organisation a living entity like any other individual. The diversity is in fact the strength of an organisation and it has to be properly harnessed for achieving the organisational goal.

An individual is an asset of strength in an organisation and every effort is made to harness it. But it should also be understood that it can also be the greatest hurdle in the progress of organisation if he is not mentally attuned to the organisation and thereby its goal. It is here that the manager's skills are needed to chanellise the individuals towards meeting the organisational objectives. Gone are the days when organisations were run bureaucratically wherein the top management would do most of the thinking and administration and order those down below to merely obey them and yet attain the organisational goals. Now everyone is expected to think, find ways and means and to co-ordinate every such effort, to the extent possible, in achieving the objective.

Contract

In the west individuality was very clearly perceived in the form of enjoying the life at all costs. But they could not perceive the society and its ultimate aim. They could not establish the mutual relationships amongst the constituents in the form of a society early. But people do come together and live collectively as society. How to account for this? In the absence of any other ethereal bond, because of not understanding the real nature and purpose of human beings, they understood human relations, as needed, in the form of contracts and nothing else, as a tool in achieving socialisation. Excessive emphasis on individuality prevented them from discovering the innate social relationships. The intense desire of keeping their individuality intact, as distinct from the others, had left no option of developing any other form of relationship between individuals, except that of a contract, which was later substantiated by legal provisions in the form of constitution of the nation. The same was then extended to international or human level. Even the marriages were considered by them as merely a contract. Their families are therefore breaking to the stage of single parent family by breaking the contract whenever it becomes untenable, due to dispute mostly over physical pleasures. Similarly they are not worried about the natural social relationships and obligations except those imposed by law.

Unless and until they overcome the contract theory and develop the human bonds, in terms of human nature, as the Indians did, the westerners shall always find the organisation of humans a great unsolvable challenge, in spite of their sincere efforts in that direction. All the challenges of organisation are not just of organisation, for some sectarian purpose, but for organisation of the society, neigh the entire human race, can be met successfully on the basis of Indian ethos as explained above. For this to be achieved some have to forego their individual freedom to the extent of even sacrificing their physical pleasures, some have to give up their mental pleasures in the form of power, some have to give up their intellectual pleasures and accept construction of a all-happy society as their sole creative and innovative mission of life. Such people can be the right leaders for management of the society at large. In India the enlightened ones behaved like this, as explained earlier in Chapter 2 and 3, and hence they sustained the society all through the challenges of times as and when necessary. The non-acceptability of the spirituality in the form of Brahma, God and the like (not religion) is the greatest of the stumbling blocks in the progress of western psychology in the right direction.

Indian Dilemma

Being only well versed in the western patterns and not knowing the eternal values and knowledge of Indian ethos, the so-called modern Indians are only blindly copying the western model of progress, in the form of their organisational models, for increasing the physical pleasures. The Indian psyche, being split between the two, stands at the cross road and does not know where to go. This does not mean that minimum sustenance need not be provided to all and particularly to those who do not yet get even that. Material progress to that extent is a must but freedom in the form of consumerism on the part of some is not permissible.

On the one hand it is presumed that progress means industrial production aided by information technology and that is the only way to ensure minimum sustenance to all. On the other hand the traditional Indian ethos, including the value system of the then agrarian order, emphasised as best by many, mistakenly assume that material progress is no panacea. What is good for any one may be left to the individual within the four fold requirements of human beings? Individual freedom has to be appreciated within these limits alone.

References

1. Marcues as quoted by Zeitlin, Irving, M., *Rethinking Sociology – A Critique of Contemporary Theory,* Rawat, N. Delhi, (1996).
2. Mead, G.S., *as quoted in Ref No. 1.*
3. Fried, S, *as quoted in Ref No. 1.*
4. Capra, Fritjof, Tao of Physics, Flamingo, London (1991).
5. Golwalkar, M. S. alias Guruji, *Guruji Samagra*, Compilation of his thought, Suruchi Prakashan, N.Delhi, (2006).
6. Sharma, Jyotirmaya, *Terrifying Vision* (M.S.Golwalkar, the RSS and India) Viking, (2007).
7. Gorle, Shivaraj, *Majet Jagawa Kasa*, Marathi.
8. Friedman, Thomas, L., *The World is Flat*, Penguin, London, (2006).
9. Harlambos, M. and Heald, R.M., *Sociology – Themes and Perspectives*, Oxford, Chaman Enterprise, N.Delhi, (2003).
10. Capra, Fritjof, *The Web of Life,* Flamingo, (1997).
11. Durant Will, *The Story of Civilization,* Vol 1, (our oriental heritage, section on India).
12. Ranganathanand Swami, *The Message of Upanishads*, Ram Krishna Math, Nagpur, (2006).

CHAPTER 10

PSYCHOLOGY

CHAPTER STRUCTURE

- Feudalism
- Psychological Extents
- Organisational Conflict
- Reality
- Industrial Feudal Progress
- Feudal Politics
- Professionalism
- Westernisation
- Disciple

Feudalism

Feudal mind-set is essentially based on the perception that some small minority is more equal than the others. As a result this minority has several privileges which others do not have. These have been available through generations and perhaps as God's grace and therefore the rest should not have any moral right to come in the way of them enjoying these rights. In fact the majority through their conscious efforts must see that these privileged ones get all the possible pleasures, even at times at their own costs. These gifted ones may enjoy these privileges without any hindrance from the rest. There are no limitations on their enjoyments. They may be gracious enough to throw some crumbs of these pleasures, after they are satisfied, to the rest as a matter of courtesy. The majority must obey the privileged ones without any argument or question, thinking that their orders are always in their own best interests. In other words all the necessary thinking, about everything of interest, will be done by the privileged ones. The group of society has just to follow their desires as dictates and nothing else. If such is the mind-set of the group or society then it may be classified as a feudal mind-set [1]. The general social framework and the mentality of majority conforming to it is ***feudalism***. By and large new philosophy and new way of life is unthinkable in such a society, in spite of changing times.

This mind-set was entrenched right since human beings were living in stone-age, in the tribal form, when the majority had to obey the stronger and more intelligent one amongst them, for getting sustenance and safety, which was otherwise not possible on individual basis. It got further rooted into the psyche through the family-life wherein the elders became the unquestionable guides and the younger ones had to obey them in almost all matters. In fact discipline was enforced in those days through family alone [2]. The development of kingdoms, in the next evolutionary step, led by the kings, consolidated this psyche. The prolonged stone-age and the agricultural period was responsible in getting it into the psyche of an average individual. This was more so in India because it had the longest agricultural era when compared to other societies in the world.

As long as social life was simple and was confined to small villages for most, it went on well due to this feudal psyche. But human being cannot be conditioned like this as his instinctual freedom would not allow him to remain so conditioned. As social life became more complex, the individual freedom became more dominant and had to be satisfied in terms of their desires and needs. The feudal conditioning had to be consciously uprooted in view of individuality and even by fighting against it, at times at the cost of even sacrifice, for upholding human values like equality, liberty and freedom. Those who did it eliminated the feudal mind-set and established equality through an all-pervading democratic order.

In India where the agricultural hang-over is so dominant that it still exists in spite of establishing *de-jure* democratic equality. The caste structure, whatever is the reasons for its evolution, but by virtue of its high and low perception, consolidated the feudal mind-set for ages, to the extent that it is seen even today after establishing the democratic set-up. The feudal psyche however did not come in the way of establishment of good organisations. The predominance of **Newton-Cartesian** perception and adoption of bureaucratic methods came in handy to aid formation of organisations under feudal mind-set readily.

Psychological Extents

The progress of realisation of one's own self from realising as an individual to family to society to nation and to the international level occurred in all societies in the world, to more or lesser extent but more specifically in the west. In India this progress occurred in the direction of individual to society to nation to international to nature to universe as described before. This has resulted in a paradigm change in the outlook of these two specific societies, that is the western and the Indian societies.

In order to describe this fundamental difference, **Deen Dayal Upadhyaya** and **D.B. Thengri** [3], the two famous ideologues of RSS, in the 20th century, took the help of one simple figure consisting of concentric circles and a spiral, which is described in **Fig. 10.1.** The concentric circles show the various levels of social evolution from individual to international level, each stage being represented by a circle larger than the previous one. The spiral shows the progressive identification and enlargement, starting from individual, to higher levels of evolution, with the larger and larger size circular part of the spiral. The western model is described by the concentric circles in which the stages of development are shown as discreet. One has to generally dissociate or break away from the earlier existence to become part of the next larger entity. This is the reason why they experienced conflict between these states of human existence particularly between, individual freedom and the socialising process, being contradictory in nature. This has already been discussed in detail in Chapter 9. This may also be the reason why the predominance of organisations resulting from industrial revolution, led to breaking of the families. Whereas in India the situation is as described by the spiral wherein there are no clear cut demarcation lines between one and the next level of existence. One slowly changes to the next level without noticing it distinctly.

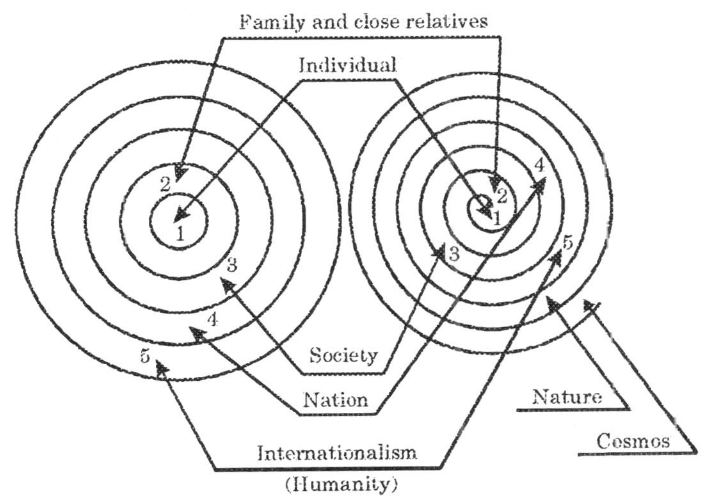

Fig. 10.1 : Schematic of western mind-set is depicted by (a) as concentric circles and of Hindu mind-set as by (b) in the form of a spiral to differentiate their fundamentally different perceptions.

Indian seers felt that human existence can not be compartmentalised in the form of an individual, family, society, nation, international level *(vasudhaiva kutumakam* in Indian terminology) and so on. There is some form of integrated existence between these levels since the focal point is ultimately an individual human being, whose existence is being investigated. The line of demarcation between these levels is diffused, so that an individual can move forward and backward as per the requirements and need of the time. It is also required that these movements occur without any upheavals and tensions in individual's life. This is possible in the four-tier, but integrated, Indian perception of existence. In fact it originates from the basic presumption that there was the universal ***atman*** or Brahma alone in the beginning and that it felt like becoming many ***(ekoham bahusyam)*** and this is how the universe was born.

It is therefore not correct to experience conflict between the various states of existence since everything is originating from the same source. One must understand conceptually that the social perception-models of the westerners and the Indians are quite different and hence there lies the basic difference between their concepts of society and an individual. In the absence of any specific connection between individual and the society, as per their perception, the westerners established it through social contracts as described before.

Organisational Conflict

Organisation is taken here to represent the corporate world meaning thereby that it is individually participative, mutually co-operative and action-wise it is a co-ordinated group in its general purpose. From the above it is clear that the Indian psyche is far more amenable to form organisations. It has also been stated in Indian philosophy, through **Shrimad Bhagvad Gita,** that every one should take up the social profession commensurate with his liking and innate nature while being active as a part of society. This is what is termed as the social discipline, expected from every individual. This is a very flexible social discipline.

In comparison, basic psychological change was required in individuals for social development in the west. One has to change himself to fit into the social set-up there. This is the beginning of the conflict between individual and the socialising process in the west. The formation of organisations therefore has to take the form of rigid social discipline which brings in attendant tensions and which are not very conducive to social progress. The historical processes that went into moulding the westerners in a way contributed to make their organisations more rigid. For all practical purposes of life, the Indians remained organised at the family level only. The family unit, under biological compulsions and under the influence as mentioned above, remained very informal in its discipline. This could also be the reason for the difference. The discussion of mental make-up in an organised state and at family level, as described above, is about what once existed in India and not about what exists today. The western psyche, in last almost a century, has also undergone some paradigm changes, in trying to understand organisations and their problems for making them more effective and efficient.

Reality

The picture depicted above is of the Indian society when it was a very simple agrarian society. It did not have the complexities as are witnessed in the present-day industrialised world. The basic perceptional theme as shown above might have worked on those small and simple village-level social structures. The present Indian society, neigh all societies in the world, have now become too complex and are far from the idealistic state described above. The all pervading social consciousness, as described above, is more or less missing from the present-day Indian society. This is the reason why and also because of the British influence, Indians are organising themselves through organisations on the lines of the western model only. But the social compulsions, as were experienced in the west, were almost absent in India and consequently it poses a great hurdle in developing the organisations that are needed to organise Indian society today on the western lines.

It is true that ordinary human beings readily understand the compartmentalised social structure. It is easy to appreciate that in order to become a part of an organisation. One has to discard, at least to some extent, the individuality to become a part of an organisation. For the sake of material requirements and pleasures the individuality is readily forsaken. But this is only an outwardly agreement. In reality human beings cannot readily set aside own individuality even after becoming a part of an organised structure, that's for certain.

Industrial Feudal Progress

Historically famous ***Magna Carta*** of Britain (1215 AD) that is much trumpeted and hailed as the greatest charter of human liberty, is in fact an attempt of feudal lords for freedom from the monarchy. It was not a declaration of rights for all citizens. It was these feudal lords mainly, from the then agrarian order, with their enterprising abilities, led to the early development of industries and related organisations when the industrial revolution occurred in Europe in general and in Britain in particular. The early enterprises and organisations thereat therefore came to be known as entities of these families. Similarly those who invented some technologies and started industries based on their inventions also came to be known by such individuals or families. But in due course of time they transformed these into professional organisations as per the requirements of time and as per their overall social understanding to develop them. Now except the exceptional ones (like say Ford Motor Co. of USA or Bosch of Germany), their organisations are not known by the families but by their **brand names** like AT &T, 3-Ms, IBM and so on. Even those known and owned by families are run professionally and with other's professional participation, rather than as ***family unit***.

Industrialisation started in India after the establishment of British Raj in India in the middle of nineteenth century. The early entrepreneurs like the **Birlas or Tatas or Godrejs or Mafatlals**, who started their industrial enterprises in those early days therefore, came to be known only by their families. But the picture has not changed much since then. The

Ambanis, the **Singhanias**, the **Jains**, the **Kirloskars**, the **Mahindras**, the **Bajajs** and hundreds of others, who started their enterprises much later, still continue to be known by their family name only. Some of them like the Tatas have truly converted themselves into professional organisations. But these are exceptions. Some like **INFOSYS** who started and aimed to be only professional organisation, right from its inception, are exceptional, in the Indian scenario. Most still continue to be run as family organisations, even with minority share-holding, when rest of the majority holding is of the public at large. The public holding being diffused does not get decisive say in running the organisation. There are many who still justify ***family control*** as superior to professional control even now because there have been many instances when the professional leadership has miserably failed for being selfish, to the detriment of public. The recent (2008 AD) economic recession and decimation of some big organisations in the west are solely and certainly due to the anti-social attitudes of some truly enlightened professionals, for certain. There is apprehension in the west if they have been producing only rascals through the well known management institutions. That gives weightage to family owned enterprises.

This is not just true of that sector, where money is to be invested and whoever puts in his money, in the beginning, retains his control, it is true with many others as well. Barring exceptions, organisations in India are mostly run by individuals and families, even in the field of charity, education, co-operative sector, social service and above all in political arena. There is no professionalism seen in such organisations.The peculiar part of all these is that these are *de-jure* democratic entities, as per the law of the land, but are *de-facto* run as family fiefdoms. The promoters continue to run such organisations, as their own, even after being duly constituted as legal entities. They do not find anybody beyond their progenies or the closest kins to whom they could hand over the mantle next. In fact when it comes to a choice between own but relatively inferior progeny against even the cousin, own progeny is chosen in preference to lead the organisation. Such is the reality in present-day India.

Feudal Politics

The most glaring example is found in the political organisations in India. Most of them, barring an exceptional one or two are known and run by individuals or their families as their personal or family fiefdoms. The largest, the oldest and the most influential one, which ruled India, the maximum number of years, since independence, is also run as a family fiefdom. The worst part is that those who participate in such organisations feel proud to work in such feudal setups in the name of democracy. All the decisions in such political organisations are taken by the individual or the family to whom it is supposed to belong to, camouflaged under camouflage of democratically wrapped cover. Nothing wrong is seen in all this. It is not exceptional that several close relatives from the same family get elected on behalf of these parties and they only occupy the ministerial berths in the name of democracy. It may also be same in many under-developed and newly liberated countries in the world. They became independent, not because of their strength and capacity to run their societies as independent nations, but because the Europeans, under various pressures, from within and without, could not continue to administer these colonies anymore.

It only means that in these societies general public did not understand the value of freedom, equality, liberty, fraternity and so on, what is essentially required to make a true democratic society. More than this the social leadership who ought to have realised this has also utterly failed in imbibing these liberal values. That is the reason why **Winston Churchill**, the then leader of opposition in British parliament, is on record to have opposed granting freedom to such colonies and more so to India, for being unfit to be administered as democratic nations. These societies continue their earlier feudal mind-set, only under the new garb of democratic structure, to which they are not truly akin in any way. This is what is being experienced in a way in India even after sixty years of independence.

Such is the perversion of democracy purely because of the feudal mind-set of the people in India [2]. Those who do not have faith in democracy, those who do not run their own party organisations democratically, swear in the name of democratic constitution to uphold democracy. What a travesty of truth? Who would believe it? Who can believe it? Even the democratic government is run by these feudal lords more or less as their personal fiefdoms, often disregarding national interests and under camouflage of democracy. They are only *de-jure* elected by democratic processes. In reality they empower the old feudal structure in their own constituency in the form of caste, region, language, religion and such basis, except the true pan-Indian democratic basis. A very critical comment on this has been made by Patrick French [4] who foresees that the Indian Parliament may get reduced to **'Vansh-Sabha'** rather than Loksabha soon.

But there are some exceptional ones who do not rely on any such parochial appeals for getting elected. When people get such choices and when they are sure that he/she will work for their progress, they do opt for such representatives disregarding the narrow sectarian considerations. But such choices are exceptions rather than a rule. Therefore it is yet to be commonly observed, particularly in India.

The political feudal set-up operates in two different ways. On the one hand the leaders behave like lords who throw away crumbs towards the followers, as their bounden duty to look after their welfare. Similarly the followers accept that they are at the mercy of their political lords. Wherever these psyches operate it is essentially a feudal system and nothing else [2].

However feudal mind-set is no obstacle in developing organisationality. It can be developed under feudal social set-up as was achieved in European nation-states. It had to be finally dispensed with in favour of liberty and equality purely because of their enlightened leadership. Organisationality can even be developed under the religious dominance as was achieved under Islam as well as Christianity. But it led to extreme feudal social set-up under the dominanace of the religious leaders. This organisationality is of its own type and will be discussed in greater detail later.

Professionalism

The sorry state of affairs, in India, is purely on account of lack of appropriate organisationality, at the social level, to suit the modern times. It could not be developed properly in the course of historical developments owing to various reasons, as explained before. Although some attempts were made to develop it in the pre-independence period, whatever was then achieved was destroyed in the post-independence era when mere subsistence came to be focused against the higher values in life. In democracy people get the government they deserve is after all true. If mere bread was the only consideration then British rulers were providing it equitably to the extent possible. Then why did we drive them out and become independent of their control?

True professionalism did not and has not developed in India, practically in any sphere of social life. It requires some values like equality entrenched in individual psychology. The social psyche is however practically that of slaves evolved and established through nearly twelve hundred years or even more of subjugation and still continues unabated. It is further fortified by the ***disciple-guru*** relationship evolved as part of the Indian social evolution all through the ages (it will be discussed in detail later). For the vast majority the only thing left in life to be achieved, is just to somehow sustain their lives. This pushes them back, almost to the same level, perhaps stone-age-cum-agricultural era, when social evolution had not occurred in the human society. How can such a situation allow real professional organisations to flourish in India in almost any sphere of social life? Those who understand this are in minority and they do not have much say in political management of the affairs.

Westernisation

Now organisations even in India are being formed on the western model only. The original Indian thought is practically forgotten. Since the life sustaining commercial world has adopted this approach, common man is left with no alternative but to adjust himself to this reality by falling in line. Hence the entire social life is tending to take the *western-style* shape, particularly after independence. Surprisingly in the pre-independence era the emphasis was on national identity in every aspect of life, with emphasis on traditional values, and now after independence, it is all forgotten and everything is being westernised to the extent possible in the name of progress and internationalism. The emphasis on traditional values in a way endorsed the original systemic thinking only. The same however has been lost in later-day industrialisation. Had they really imbibed the systemic thinking along with the recent globalisation the problems would have been reduced considerably? But in copying the western model Indians have copied the outdated **Newton-Cartesian** model of industrialisation. All the problems stem from this perception. That is why the social consciousness is practically absent in India. It was neither operative in **Newton-Cartesian** world either. As a result there is a crisis on the social front in India, in trying to adopt the western model of organisations.

Disciple

Modern organisations have changed so much from the **Newton-Cartesian** days, in their management style, that they no longer treat individuals as mere servants or disciples obeying orders from the top level of an organisation. To the extent and as far as is possible all are treated at par and taken into confidence while deciding the strategies and action plans of an organisation. This has definitely given dividends in terms of efficiency of functioning of an organisation [5,6]. The workers are now treated as co-workers in its true sense, as far as is possible in many flourishing organisations.

The Indian social psyche has been mainly feudal as discussed above. Coupled with this is the influence of religiosity, in terms of apparent efforts, even merely mechanical, for achieving Moksha, by becoming some *seer's* disciple. This aspect has a far overriding influence on Indian psyche as a whole, than any other factor. Indians therefore have a bent of mind which makes them easily a disciple of anybody. Even in organisations therefore this psyche plays its role in converting the participants into disciples of leaders/managers, rather than co-workers, even in the modern days. In the form of real co-workers they are treated at par and their say is treated with respect. Once one becomes a disciple, on his own one gives up independent thinking and follows the leader blindly. In that case he works more mechanically and thereby his energies are not fully used for organisational work. This is a kind of feudal mind-set and nothing else. It will be discussed at length again while discussing the religious organisations in detail.

Even in social organisations where attempts are consciously made to dispense with feudalism in its working, the ego of the leader never dies as it ought to. It is not easy either. The management intelligently and perhaps clandestinely ensures feudalism to prevail in the working of that organisation in subtle ways. True professionalism is not sought after in its management. It could be perhaps because the leaders do not know true professionalism. Leaders in such cases get followers purely because of their selfless character and may be on account of the high ideal put before. These qualities may be great in them but are not enough for following true professionalism in their management. That is the reason why such organisations continue to be active so long as such a leader is in command. The moment he disappears, by way of his death or otherwise, the organisation soon becomes defunct. The Gandhian institutions and many more typically illustrate this phenomenon.

References

1. Sharma, R.S., *Indian Feudalism*, McMillan, Delhi (2005).
2. Toffler, Alvin, *Power Shift*, Bantam, (1998).
3. Nene V.V., *Deen Dayal Upaddhaya Thoughts* (Marathi), Vol 1 Bharatiya Vichar Sadhana, Pune (1986).
4. Patrik French, *India a Portrait,* Attan Lane, N. Delhi, (2011.
5. Tom Peters and Robert H. Waterman Jr, *In search of Excellence*, Profile, (2003).
6. Tom Peters and Nancy Austin, *A Passion for Excellence,* Profile, (2003).

CHAPTER

11

PROCESS

CHAPTER STRUCTURE

- Instinctual Self
- Civilizational Progress
- Challenge and Response
- Cause and Effect
- Organised Efforts
- Leader
- Entropy Law
- Paradigm Change
- Information Technology
- Minority-majority
- Organisation
- Mechanical Bonding
- Liberalism
- Danger
- Law of Identity
- Fall-outs
- Experienced Guides
- Reactionary Approach
- Theory vs. Practice

Instinctual Self

It is natural instinct of all living beings to remain alive through own nourishment, by exerting oneself, to the extent possible. That is why those life-forms which have no locomotion must get the nourishment at their own place through the soil and the atmosphere. Those who have locomotion can move in search of nourishment to some extent, depending upon their capability. These are the challenges every life form faces as a matter of routine and meets them instinctually with suitable response in the form of its efforts. This is in-built in every life form. For humans many more things are needed for satisfying their instinctual self.

Civilizational Progress

Humans, being far superior and possessing extra-ordinary intellect, than any other life-form, will surely respond to such challenges in a much better way, for certain. That is how human beings have not only survived the ravages of times but have progressed from almost the animal level to the present-day's most enlightened social level. This has also resulted in flourished civilizations in various forms in various societies across the whole world. But it is equally true that this has not resulted in uniformly similar civilizational progress in all the societies all over the world. Why is it so?

Equally true is that many different civilizations fluorished on the earth in the past and have been decimated after some time. Some of their remains or literatary record only indicate that they once existed in some part on the earth. Whereas some civilizations have continued, from the time of their inception, till to-date, uninterruptedly, albeit with some minor alterations, keeping the essential paradigm the same. What is the reason for this differential state of affairs? Can it be explained in terms of group, organisational or social behaviour and their differential capabilities?

It is necessary to appreciate the process of formation of organised efforts and organisations. How these are nucleated and what factors favour the process of nucleation or what factors oppose this process? When the society was in tribal form or in early agricultural format the necessity for organised efforts or organisations did not arise, beyond the naturally evolved group-level activity. This necessity arose when society developed additional needs such that these could not be met by the evolved groups alone and division of labour in the society and barter of goods or services, amongst them, became imperative. In a way the challenges posed with time had to be met more intelligently with better alternatives such as more organised efforts.

Challenge and Response

One of the world-famous historians of twentieth century by name **Arnold Toynbee** of **Oxford University** studied this phenomenon in much greater depth than, perhaps any other historian of his or earlier times. He wrote down the account of all his observations, in the classical form of twelve big volumes as ***A Study of History.*** He has analysed how civilizations come into being, get nourished and flourish and are wiped out in due course of time. He has postulated a universal sociological theory called ***Challenge and Response Theory*** [1] to explain the phenomena of rise and fall of civilizations, meaning thereby the progress and decay of organised societies.

Every one faces problems and challenges in one's own life as a matter of routine and has to respond to them in order to survive and progress. Life is always full of challenges to which one must respond appropriately. Nobody prefers to commit suicide by totally succumbing before the challenges. Occasional suicides are exceptions and hence they, in fact, prove the above rule. When challenges are so big that one does not individually feel confident to face them, then an attempt is made to face them collectively by the family, if otherwise possible, by mutual co-ordination and supplementation of efforts. When the challenges are wide-spread and affect many more people at the same time, then, man being more intelligent and capable of understanding the strength of collective action, attempts to connect, co-ordinate and supplement each other's efforts, more intelligently, in a unidirectional way in the form of organisations of some or the society as a whole to respond to the challenge unitedly. **Human beings always have been and always will flock together to give life meaning and purpose by forming organic relationships with others**. They also want to believe that their efforts have a purpose and make a difference. The history of civilizations all over the world, since their inception is replete with examples to testify this truth.

A strong stimulus is required to get organised activities going. A weak stimulus in relation to the extents and gravity of the problem may even scuttle the stimulus right in the beginning itself, before any action commences. Appreciation of such requirements, in the light of the challenge before, does not dawn on everybody and anybody and at any time. There are always some gifted ones who understand the nature of the challenge and how it needs to be faced appropriately. Such people are not only intelligent but also possess sufficient creativity and innovativeness, along with many other rare human qualities, to evolve appropriate ways and means of responding the challenge. Toynbee [1] refers to such people as ***creative minority.*** But according to Toynbee the creative minority does not respond to the challenge on their own. They collect and organise the required lot from the remaining majority for effective action. They have to explain to the majority the impending challenge and ways and means of responding to it, without which the majority would not fall in line. The majority has to be activated into united action, under their own leadership, in response to the challenge. On the whole it is an organised effort taking co-workers from the majority. If the challenge is too difficult, the initial creative stimulus itself may be stifled before coming into existence as an organised effort, perhaps because it has fallen short of the requirements In that case somebody else or a group of some other creative persons, may be at some other time, try it again. This process goes on as a matter of routine in any society. But at some time the creativity overrides the challenge and is successful in organising the response, when other factors also are favourable.

Cause and Effect

Whether the response is successful or not depends on many other factors, including the strength of the response, overall environment and situational factors. In the history of mankind the way different societies responded to different challenges faced by them at varied times was totally different. That is the main reason why different societies developed and organised themselves in different ways. This has nothing to do with the ***cause and effect relationship*** as is applicable in the material world. **Toynbee**[1] therefore says:

"Challenge and response resembles cause and effect only in standing for a sequence of events. The character of the sequence is not the same. Unlike the effect of a cause, the response to challenge is not predetermined, is not necessarily uniform in all similar cases and is therefore intrinsically unpredictable".

This can be readily understood from a simple example. If somebody slaps a person for some reason, the response is not as per the cause and effects, the same everywhere. In one case the person may run away thinking that he is unable to retaliate. In another case the person may retaliate but get beaten further in the process. In yet another case the person may collect a few people around, convince them of the individual insult and motivate them to retaliate collectively since it is in their interest as well. This is precisely the **challenge and response theory**. It is responsible to a great extent in developing organisations or organised activities. This is equally well responsible for development of organisationality as described earlier.

Organised Efforts

Whether or not the response is successful in meeting the challenge is a different story, but organised efforts are not only possible but they are possible only through the joint efforts of creative minority activating the majority through their appropriate synchronised and organised efforts. All civilizations have come into being through successful responses of such organised endeavours, socially on a vast scale, at some point of time. Equally true is that all those civilizations which got decimated in due course of time were wiped out purely because similar organised efforts in responding the challenges under altered conditions afterwards, proved a failure. The creative minority in normal course becomes the controller-leader or manager of that organised activity.

Arnold Toynbee's theory of challenge and response is with reference to challenges to be faced by activities of a large group, perhaps in the form of societies. Any organised effort in the present day society for achieving anything for the benefit of society at large should also fit into this framework. In fact, it does.

Take the example of a co-operative housing society. The idea of possessing a house of one's own, strikes practically every one. Some float the idea and soon realise that it is not within their capacity to take the matter further. Some other collects a few, convinces them the necessity of obtaining such a house by some kind of a joint effort. But they soon realise that the hurdles in the way are insurmountable and finally give it up. While someone or few get convinced about the project, convince a few others about it, feel confident of surmounting all the hurdles in the way and get it going by taking many others in the fold. With the initiation of some and association of many others the challenge is responded adequately in getting one's own houses in the form of a co-operative housing society.

Leader

In any society and at any time, there are always some who belong to the creative minority or enlightened category, whereas the majority is not all that superior. The intellectual height or the level of enlightenment of such people may differ from society to society and also with respect to the time during their evolution. They visualise some useful activity for social development and who get the majority associated with them in the form of an organisation to carry out the specific job in response to the challenge. There is no specific format of organised effort in any such responses. It all depends on time, situation, place, society and so on. In the commercial field **promoters play the role of creative-minority**. They understand what product or service that is needed in the society and set up an organisation in the same way to cater to the social needs. The same thing happens in political and social arena where the creative minority forms organisations with the majority for meeting the challenge as per their perception. They automatically become the natural leaders of such organised efforts.

Entropy Law

There is the third law of thermodynamics which describes the status of order in any material system *vis-à-vis* its energy. This law is also applicable in general to establish the stability of any material thing in its environment. This has something to do with the energy property known as ***entropy.*** This is therefore called the ***Law of Entropy*** or the law of disorder or disintegration. Hence if metallic iron is left on its own in open air it is bound to degrade to its own oxide in due course of time. During the evolution, ever new life-forms were evolved through changes in some of the old ones, to better adapt to the natural surrounding. This process continues until it becomes impossible to sustain the life-form any more through minor changes. At such times the new life-form evolves by total mutation of some of the old ones giving rise to altogether new life-forms. This does not occur as per any pre-design. These are emergent life-forms coming up as per the evolutionary process to suit the emergent times.

With the passage of times as the external environment changes and as the aspirations of those who work in the organisations also change; it goes on becoming more and more difficult to meet the challenges posed on the way of meeting the organisational objective. The organisational leadership goes on making changes in the organisation itself and in the style of its management, to suit the altered conditions. But it should be remembered that no amount of changes can convert a bullock cart into a motor-car or a car into an aeroplane.The same holds true in the case of organisations. Minor changes as stated above may turn out to be helpful to some extent only.

Paradigm Change

But if the situation is pregnant with challenges such that minor changes in the existing organisations no longer produce the desired results then the only alternative left is either to destroy or replace the old order, if so required and/or design new forms of organisations to successfully meet the new challenges. The old order has to give way to a new one. In such a situation, mutation of organisations, like what occurs during natural evolution, may become necessary. The creative minority with adequate innovative capability may develop altogether new forms of organisations, or new styles of management to respond suitably the emerging challenges. This ability is manifested by only a few gifted, creative and innovative individuals with deep foresight. The entropy of the old organisations is so high that it no longer sustains itself. The new organisations have nothing in common with the previous ones. The *Independence Movement* led first by **B.G. Tilak** and later by **M. Gandhi** or the organisations started by **Dr. B.R. Ambedkar** or the RSS started by **Dr. K. B. Hedgewar** are some of the typical examples of such innovations in the field of broader social developments. These organisations were all unique in their own way and never thought of before in any form by any one else

The same has been the case with the organisationality in the past. That is the reason why it underwent so many mutations as discussed earlier, in evolving new forms of organisationality as per the need of the time.

Such mutations usually occur in the case of social, political, charitable, academic or even religious organisations. Such mutations did occur in all types of organisations, neigh in fact in the society/nation itself, when the first wave agricultural society started changing into second wave society because of the industrial revolution. The industrial revolution changed almost all the organisations either fundamentally or altogether new, unheard-of organisations were designed and formed to suit the challenges of industrialisation.

The patterns of centralised and concentrated hospitals, schools, colleges, recreation centers, libraries, charitable institutions, etc. were developed for the first time as a result of industrialisation. It changed completely the social lifestyles and had practically nothing common with the agricultural social pattern. The creative minority of industrial era met the challenges of industrialisation fairly adequately, all through the era, until the information technology revolution set in.

Information Technology

The organisational pattern once again underwent changes and in some cases mutation to suit the challenges of information technology onslaught. The earlier organisations fundamentally based on maximization, concentration, centralisation, synchronisation, standardisation and specialization, as revealed by **Alvin Toffler** [2[, started changing their pattern and alongwith, some altogether new ones came into existence like the new e-banks, new transport management systems of goods and passengers, new satellite based communication systems, new marketing and salesstyles in the form of malls, new manufacturing technologies to suit individual needs, distant and diffused education systems including the world-wide-web, new entertainment patterns catering to individuals or small groups, new organisations and their management patterns for sports and games on national, regional and international levels and so on.

The production technology underwent fundamental changes, using computerisation, to the maximum extent possible. The out-sourcing, off-shoring, and the vendor system completely changed the production and the distribution-styles of goods and services. All this required altogether new types of organisations and innovative management styles, unknown in industrial era.

Minority-majority

The meaning of creative minority and remaining majority as defined by **Toynbee** [1] has nothing to do with the social, religious or political minority/majority syndrome with respect to society, caste, religion, language, etc. It is purely related to the innovative and creative capability of individuals with respect to understanding the challenges before the individual, organisation or the society/nation. It is also based on individual nature of a challenge alone. For a given challenge whoever has the capacity to give adequate response to it is classified in the creative minority category and the rest in the majority. It does not entirely depend on the formal education or the individual wealth. This capability is related to one's own intelligence, curiosity, creativity, self-confidence, organisational ability, overall personality and leadership qualities and so on. This is not a fixed and permanent division. It depends purely subjectively on the quality, severity, extent and the timing of the particular challenge. It is possible that with reference to some challenge, one who is classified in the creative minority group may be classified as majority with respect to some other more severe challenge and *vice-a-versa*.

This division is not in mathematical terms in the form of some percentage. It is only an apparent division which depends on the individual challenge and the overall social environment alone. It cannot be decided in advance by taking some tests. It is all decided by the time and situation alone. Many times such responses get buried in the beginning itself for want of adequate creativity and helpful environment and other requirements for success.

Organisation

Organisation can not be formed in just two tiers, one of creative minority and the others as majority. In fact an organisation is more often a multi-tiered structure. Each of these tiers constitutes the sub-organisational level. There are several such sub-organisational levels to make up the overall organisation. At each such sub-organisational level the creative minority of appropriate ability joins with the corresponding majority to form that level in the form of a sub-organisation. The quality of creative minority leading each one of the sub-organisational level differ and therefore that of the majority also differs at that level. The quality of creative minority goes on increasing with higher and higher level in the organisational structure. It also means that the quality of majority also similarly goes up alongwith. It is highest at the top of the organisational structure. This will easily clarify that the creative minority and majority is often decided by the requirements of the level in an organisation. Organisations can not be formed merely by the creative minority or the majority on gross level. They are to be differentiated as per the requirements. The creative minority at each level is supposed to lead the team at that level. It is as per the requirements of the sub-levels in an organisation.

There is a saying in Marathi which states that intellectuals cannot be organised. This is because of the above reasoning. For organised efforts creative minority and majority have to join hands, there is no escape from this. If only intellectuals try to organise themselves, that is, if only leaders form an organisation alone, then intellectual exercise alone may take place without any action thereat. If only majority forms an organisation, then it may resemble the rudderless boat, knowing not where to go and therefore drifting in all stray directions, instead of in the direction of meeting the objective. There are number of instances in Indian society which substantiate the above facts.

In the Indian polity, there were intellectual stalwarts in the form of well known socialists. They criticised and fought each other and with the rest without attempting to get the majority along with for doing any concrete organisational work. In the other extreme is the republican group after the demise of **Dr. B. R. Ambedkar**, without any capable and creative leader and, as a result, is drifting in all possible directions as any majority would in the absence of a proper creative leader. On the contrary without many stalwarts, worth the name, the Congress has been able to form and run their organisation and contribute to social development by taking every effort to take the majority along with, particularly after independence. The **RSS pariwar** is a typical example wherein stress was laid to achieve the right mix of creative minority and majority to establish a mighty organisation.

Usually the proportion of minority to majority is around **1:9.** Generally about the same proportion is presumed in working out any modern management chart. One can generally guide and get work done properly from around 5-10 people directly and readily.

Mechanical Bonding

The compatibility of majority with the creative minority is generally activated in the organised form essentially mechanically only, said Toynbee [1]. This was more to explain the civilizational progress, essentially based on wars between kingdoms, wherein the required fighting force could be created in this way readily. Even now the same approach is adopted for raising the modern day army. Hence they are trained more mechanically.

These are the views expressed in the mid-nineteen-fifties or before when the organisations were run essentially bureaucratically, under Newton-Cartesian influence.

The science of organisation was not then all that developed as is today. In modern organisations, in general, the entire work force is expected to do at least some creative work, including the lower most levels as well, if otherwise possible. Earlier in a factory the manager was supposed to do the creative work and the workers were expected to follow merely the instructions flowing from the top. Even now organisations like the McDonald's are run in this fashion only, as has been discussed earlier. But in the evolving knowledge era, everybody is encouraged to contribute creatively, as is feasible, to the organised efforts, particularly where decisions are to be taken at various levels of the organisation. The work force is therefore trained accordingly, to fully exploit their creativity. The relative proportion of creative and mechanical work to be carried out by the different strata in a modern organisation is qualitatively shown in **Fig. 11.1** to indicate the modern approach.

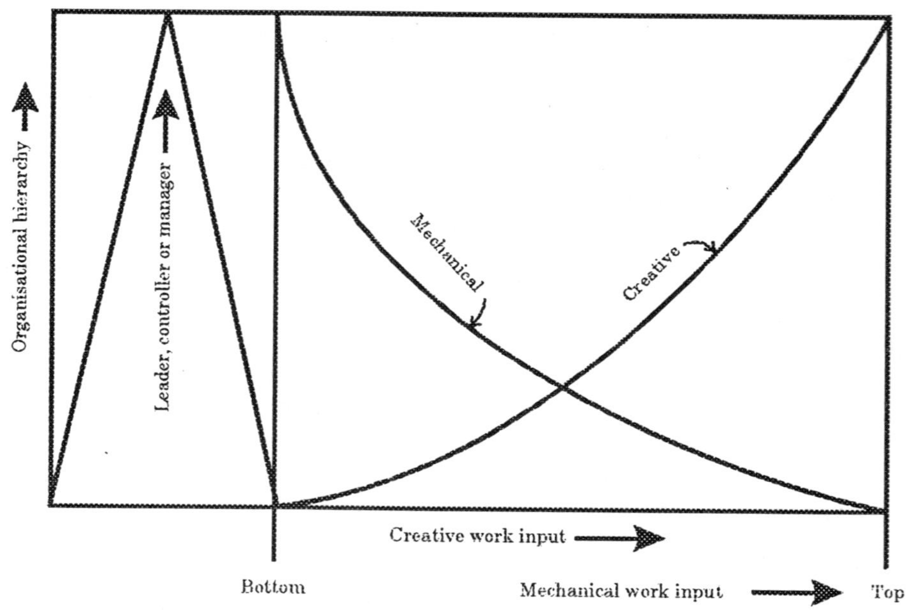

Fig. 11.1 : Shows qualitatively the proportion of creative work and mechanical work expected from various strata in an organisation

Liberalism

With all this for an organised effort relatively superior creative minority must be compatible with relatively inferior majority (in terms of creativity) so as to function smoothly and efficiently. The westerners, under their capitalist but liberal and open social system, provided to the creative minority the required atmosphere conducive to creating excellent organisations, as per their own capacity and by which they did and made tremendous material progress The majority in a way, for earning own livelihood, was forced to join the creative minority. But the society on the whole was benefited. These nations are rich nations of the world today. They are famous for their quality products, low prices on account of their high working efficiency. On the contrary, in the communist ruled nations, anybody was branded as creative minority and the majority was forced to work with them, almost per force. The net result was that communist nations, with socialist planning and execution, without exception were notorious for their inferior quality products, low efficiency and as a result they were very poor, by western standards. If by whatever reason incompetent minority is saddled with majority then the result is just the same as was seen in communist regimes. This is the reason why, China, notwithstanding their political communist regime, opened up their economy, as in the west and, progressed beyond imagination, within a very short duration, by allowing the real creative minority to liberally form required organisations. This is quite a different model of organised efforts, which has made wonders, and hence needs to be studied further.

The role of creative minority is like the engine in a train that resembles the creative minority. There is only one engine in a train while the rest are coaches, as if majority, with no self locomotion. This way it can achieve the objective of transportation readily. The train does not consist of all engines, neither of all coaches. In either case it is of no use. The organisational chariot runs on two wheels, one of creative minority and the other of majority. The westerners designed their organisations essentially on this principle and drove their organisational chariot with unprecedented speeds.

Danger

There is an inherent danger in this arrangement. The possibility of the creative minority usurping all the organisational power for personal gains does exists in this arrangement. Hitler and Mussolini were created this way only. That is why the modern democratic set-up has made such usurption more and more difficult. The free media can also provide some safeguard in this respect. Yet the possibility of usurption cannot be eliminated altogether. But it will be like preventing baby's birth just because of the fear that it may turn out to be a demon later. If one is really scared of this possibility, then how will the society continue, in the absence of any alternative? This is therefore a challenge and has to be responded to with boldness.

Nature has evolved human being in such a way that he/she can keep him/her alive merely through simple mechanical activities of the body. The rest of his/her energy is supposed to be used for creative activities and for which he/she has been provided with a powerful cortex brain. This is the reason why there is enough mechanicalness in human activities, if no creative work is done. The progress so far made by human beings has all been possible only through the creative abilities only. Unfortunately this has also involved a lot of them doing merely just the mechanical work. There is thus a danger of and also easier one for human beings to get more mechanical. The attraction of material pleasures are driving people to be more mechanical, since the path of creative work is becoming more and more arduous. The ultimate choice is left to an individual, either to opt for mechanical work or for creative work. In this tug of war let us not blame the rope, said Toynbee [1].

Law of Identity

In social and more particularly in the political arena it is often seen that the leadership, at least at the peak level, is usually exceptionally creative. The majority that joins them for whatever political/social activities often joins them essentially only mechanically as is propounded by Toynbee [1]. Firstly the organisation more often operates at the vast social/ national level. It may even be true at the international level as well. The example of India's independence movement, carried under the banner of Congress, can be studied in this respect. It gained momentum after **Mahatma Gandhi** assumed its leadership. He mobilised the masses by connecting them with the idea of gaining independence, through purely unrelated programmes, like spinning cotton by hand, taking out processions in every village, locality and streets, shouting related slogans, burning of foreign clothes and so on. Such acts had nothing directly to do with getting India's independence. Yet the entire society/ nation was in a way organised to fight for independence. It imbibed the right spirit of independence amongst the masses. These were purely mechanical acts of interlinking the creative minority with the vast majority, as propounded by Toynbee, and which finally culminated into a mighty organised force, before which the British Rulers had to give in and grant independence to India.

A still more vivid example is of RSS, started by **Dr. Hedgewar** [2]. He wanted to train people who would be ready to work ceaselessly for building the nation as per his own perceptions. What did he do for that? He started what was called as ***shakha*** (meaning a branch) wherein every day, people would collect and carry out some physical exercises, sing some patriotic songs and discuss the ills of the society. Through such mechanical activities he inspired thousands of people to work for the well-being of the Indian nation of his perception. There can be difference of opinion about his perception but he built a mighty organisation which, even after his death, continued to grow and has evolved into the mighty RSS-pariwar now, who could even rule India, for a while, through their Prime Minister.

Toynbee [1] himself describes the same by giving an example of a motor car. The car has four wheels and they rotate only around their own axis. But the car does not rotate around only. It can go forward or backward linearly. There is therefore no ***Law of Identity*** which dictates that the activities of a social organisation should have semblance with its objective. That is why the activities carried out by the Indian Independence Movement or those by the RSS branches had directly no semblance with their own objectives. Purely mechanical and unrelated activities can be used to achieve the larger social organisational objectives. The key lies in knowing the connection between the mechanical activities and the ultimate aim to be achieved.

This however may not hold true for profit making organisations. These have to either produce goods, distribute and sell them or to provide some kind of services to finally earn profit. Their every act therefore has something to do with their objective directly.

Fall-outs

Creative work is possible primarily through the use of mental and intellectual abilities and their exertion, whereas the mechanical work is more restricted to the physical level only. Hence creative work has the ability to raise human beings to higher levels above the mere physical level of existence. This way there is also a chance that one may get the glimpse of spirituality which may be just next to mental and intellectual levels. The comprehension of the dangerous effects of global environmental degradation on the very human existence, and ways and means of overcoming it, above the merely physical pleasures, is a creative work of high order. It comes closer to appreciation of the spirituality only.

It is the duty of creative minority to make human beings think more from heart rather than from mere body or mechanical level. This will be possible only by running the organisations in such a way that the organised efforts cultivate human values along with the production of physical goods for body level pleasures. With such lofty ideals in mind the creative minority is bound to develop right types of management styles of organisations.

Experienced Guides

In traditional Indian thinking, whenever there is confusion, as to how one should behave in a given situation, what **Bhishmacharya**, while lying on the arrow-bed, replied to **Yudhishtira**, in Mahabharata, be followed. Bhishmacharya said that let there be no doubt, one should look at great men *(meaning thereby intellectuals)* as to how they behaved in similar situations and just follow that ***(mahajano yen gatah sa panthaha)***. The importance of creative minority in organising social life dates back at least to that time. Similarly Bhishmacharya also said that whatever bad happens or wrong is done in any society let it be known that the responsibility of which squarely lies on the creative minority, for failing to guide the majority on right course. What his actual reply was, ***"raja kalasya karanam"*** meaning thereby that king alone and not the subjects are responsible for all ills in any society.

Reactionary Approach

Often many organised efforts are started in the form of purely a reaction to something that was not liked by some, for one or the other reason. Such efforts do not have proper positive foundation to stand on. The effectiveness and efficiency of such efforts always remain in doubt. These do not last long because the sharpness of the reaction and thereby the reactionary efforts fade-down with time and that leaves no ground for the efforts to continue for long. Organised efforts must therefore have some positive reason to start with to stand on proper foundation, with proper direction to move. Several such examples can be found in social and political life of a society wherein the attempts to organise as a reaction of something have failed to achieve any worthwhile result. At the same time and in spite of stiff resistance, organisations have progressed well purely because of their positive appeal.

Theory vs. Practice

The philosophical thinking that went on in the west was always more in the form of theoretical and abstract thinking, without its direct applications in real life. That is the reason why their sociological progress did not occur as per their philosophical thought but on its own pressure of change, as per the physical needs of the society. The second wave changes that occurred earlier and the third wave change that is taking pace in the western society are not due to any prior philosophical understanding. **Toffler** only decoded the changes later in the form of his famous wave theory [3[. Even now they are unable to design the future social structures that may be needed in due course of time. The exception is of **Karl Marx** who worked out the philosophy for generating directly the required social structures, in the best interests of the society. It failed in evolving the society of his dreams is quite besides the point.

On the contrary the Indian philosophical thinking was intimately related to its direct application in evolving the social structure and life-style for making the individual more happy and contented and the society, as a result, a better place to live in. This is the reason why the Upanishadic philosophy, the first of its type in the world, led in its applied form, the Indian society, which could stand the ravages of times, umpteen numbers of times and yet stay vibrant and assimilating everything from whatever corner came around till to-date. This is the fundamental approach which differentiates the Indian social organisations from those of the rest of the world.

References

1. Toynbee, Arnold, *A Study of History*, Abridged Edition, Oxford, (1972).
2. Palkar, N.H., *Dr. Hedgewar,(Biography in Marathi)*, Datey, Dr. Hedgewar Memorial Society, Pune, (1960).
3. Toffler, Alvin, *Third Wave*, Warner, (1995).

CHAPTER 12

LEADERSHIP

CHAPTER STRUCTURE

Controller, Leader and Manager

Currently three different terms are used in organisational management literature to describe those who guide, organise, plan, control and in general manage the affairs of any organisation. These three terms are controllers, leaders and managers. These are often used synonymously but they differ significantly in their roles. To start with, those who promote any organisation, usually assume the role of a ***controller***, in setting the broad aims, the guidelines and arranging the initial material resources including the finances to set up an organisation. Once the organisation gets going, they do not take part in the day-to-day functioning of the organisation, except to guide it in a general way so that it progresses on presumed track of achieving the objective. The ***leader*** is often the chief executive who runs the organisation and looks after the day-to-day working. In fact he manages the organisation and is directly responsible for all its day-to-day activities. He is usually a trained professional in management science. The leader is also referred to as manager if he leads an organised group. A leader can be a leader of a totally unorganised group like those seen in political or may be social activities. The terms that are generally used to describe a leader of an organised group are ***managing director, chief executive, executive director or manager.*** A manger must possess the qualities of leadership but the converse may not be true. The manager-cum-leader usually has clear cut authority and guidelines to run or more precisely manage the organisation. He is therefore, perhaps solely, responsible to motivate the man-power at his disposal to achieve the organisational objective. He may either create atmosphere conducive for progress or even damage it by his erroneous and perhaps selfish actions.

The roles of controller and the manager-leader often get blurred and this is the reason why the best organisational practices clearly differentiate these two roles, emphasises **John Argenti** [1]. Controller or governor is supposed to represent the interests of beneficiaries. Leader/manager is supposed to execute, achieve the expected results, through actions of the staff at various levels, like building factories, running machines, sweeping floors, posting letters, writing accounts and so on.

Governors define corporate aims and managers decide the means. Both are essential for effective organisation. When these two get overlapped or blurred only one of these shall dominate to the detriment of the other, finally reflected in organisational performance. Let us not forget that the modern world is characterised by specialisation to the extent possible. This has got to be recognised by one and all while working in an organisation. But it is not all that easy to achieve it in reality. It requires lot of training to make sure that people appreciate who specifically can meet their specific expectations.

There is no well defined science of leadership as such, though broad guidelines for effective and efficient leadership are well known. The technology of developing leadership has been evolved to a large extent through much of trial and error over a long time. Since the leader has to manage men, money and materials, his understanding of human psychology to handle men, financial appreciation to understand relevant economics and his understanding of logistics and pricing of materials of his interest, definitely does help him to manage the show in a better way. In all these three requirements, the handling of men is the most trying task and which more than any other factor decides the progress of any organisation. This is truer in the case of non-profit making organisations. With all possible psychological understanding of human behaviour, leadership is still mostly a matter of art or at best a craft and has to be learnt assiduously. In modern times some techniques have been developed to help manage organisations in better ways and these are taught in management courses at the university level. It has something to do with extracting extra-ordinary things from ordinary people, by motivation or perhaps often using some kind of allurements. The test lies in influencing people such that they will strive willingly and enthusiastically towards achievement of the organisational goal. The Indian philosophy is the only one that comes in handy for such things as will be discussed elsewhere. In short, the functions of a leader is policy determination, policy execution and policy control.

Importance

The basic three requirements as essential requirements for the formation of any organisation have been described in Chapter 7. But the auxiliary three are more related to running and managing the organisation. Out of these three auxiliary requirements the leadership is more important than the other two. An organisation without proper leader is like a rudderless boat not knowing the direction to go for achieving the objective. Many exceptionally good social organisations have been managed well without adequate finances and proper rules and regulations of behaviour, but never without proper leadership. Those who do not know how to do things fight with the tools, so goes the saying. Similarly those who do not know how to dance complain about the floor. In fact, real leaders create everything out of practically nothing. The same is depicted in one Sanskrit saying *(subhashit)* as

Kriyasiddhihi satve bhawati mahatan nopakarane

Meaning thereby that without even right and adequate tools, like men, money and materials, great work can be accomplished merely on the basis of the leadership qualities alone. They create required man-power by training whoever is available. Real leaders do not complain about absence of anything. They are confident enough to create their organisational world relying more on their own capabilities rather than on the tools. With all other things at their best, but poor leadership may make a mess out of it, is also a well established fact. If all the requirements are provided then a good leader can create an organisational heaven out of it, is also an equally established fact. This is truer in the case of NPOs as compared to the profit making organisations.

The leader is solely responsible for the growth or fall of any organisation. In a way he sits at the steering wheel of an organisation and from where, with his diligence and hard work, he can drive the organisation to its destination. He may even fail by his incompetence, perhaps catastrophically on the way. What Bhishmacharya said in Mahabharata, while lying on the arrow-bed, was absolutely right. He said,

"raja kalasya karanam"

Meaning thereby that it is the king or leader in the present context who fails, and not the associates.

What Makes a Leader?

A leader himself must be exemplary to the extent possible in all matters of interests to his subordinates. This may include his high morality, honesty and consistency in dealing with different people at different times, thoroughly objectively. Besides he should be able to communicate properly and in proper language what he wants to convey, in writing or orally. He has to conduct meetings regularly and hence he must possess the skill of conducting such meetings. He must definitely understand financial management in profit making organisations. These days he must also understand the external social and political environment, since it can affect his working, in spite of his best knowledge about the internal affairs of the organisation. In NPOs he must understand the social environment and requirements wherever the activities are being carried out and keep on assessing impact of his services on the beneficiaries.

A leader has the authority, but should be able to exercise it in a more responsible manner. He must bear in mind that the power given to him is for meeting the organisational goal rather than for exploitation of others for personal gains. He must also understand that human beings have different motivating forces at different times and under different circumstances and should still be able to inspire them for work. He must therefore have ability to inspire his subordinates at all times and under every possible circumstance. He should always act in such a way that it develops an atmosphere conducive to attaining the goal. It thus means that a leader must understand his power of authority, understand the people from whom he has to extract work, must inspire his subordinates and should possess working-style such that the atmosphere around is always encouraging and motivating for others. On the whole he must offer means of satisfying his co-workers, such that, while achieving the organisational goal, they should also feel that they are attaining their personal goals as well.

Several traits have been identified to assess anybody's ability for leadership. Often it is seen that many leaders possess many of these traits. But it is not clear which one and how many of these the leader should possess to become good leader. It is also claimed that leadership is only 15% inspiration, perhaps meaning thereby intelligence, and 85% perspiration in the form of toiling. It may be truer in the case of NPOs. Whenever such things are said they have a specific context.

Human beings have their own characteristic personality evolved on the basis of his genome, obtained at birth, and mode of upbringing, education, training and social surrounding. The net result is that he may dominantly possess a broad behaviour that may broadly be classified as autocratic, democratic or non-interfering type. When a person becomes a leader he may adopt one of these styles of functioning as his own style in leading, depending mainly on his behavioural traits. Each one of these dominantly broad behavioural traits may prove useful in leading an organisation of a particular nature or even at particular times. If a wrong choice is made chances are that he may not prove successful. Situationally he may have to adopt one or the other style as well and he should be able to cope up with that as well, in spite of his dominant trait. A failure in this respect may result in overall failure in achieving the objective.

Every organisation has its own characteristics and therefore a certain type of leadership only suits it most. It is better to choose the matching leader to run such an organisation. This argument holds true for commercial, charitable, academic and such organisations. But **for religious, political and social organisations leaders are not chosen, they happen to develop themselves as leaders** and lead the organisation of their own imagination and making. .

There are programmes meant for training leaders. This is possible for commercial organisations wherein efficiency is supreme consideration. It is found that definite improvement in leadership qualities does occur through such leadership training programmes. But it is highly a subjective outcome. The leadership qualities required to run political and social organisations is quite different. But even there some programmes are being conducted to improve the leadership skills. This is truer perhaps for middle level leaderships and not for top level leadership.

Basic Approach

Whatever the type, size and whatever the circumstances of starting the organisation the leader finally will have to lead it towards the objective and if possible further growth. These can only be achieved if the leader has insight as follows:

1. Realisation of the goal
2. Clarity of goal
3. Integration of all co-workers
4. Predominance of collectivity
5. Broadly democratic style of functioning
6. Awareness of reality inside and outside.
7. Continuity of prior capable leadership

And the leader has the following dominant qualities:

1. Flawless planning to make path of progress vivid
2. Stainless character to avoid selfish and sectarian interests
3. Organisation and empowerment of subordinates to the extent possible
4. No comprise with core values
5. Availability of required resources
6. HRD strategies and their retention

Break-through

As we look around we do find that there are people who just cannot be leaders, they are meant to be followers only. Whereas some people seem to be very capable of leading but they are not seen leading any organisation. The same holds true at the social or national level. Many appear to be capable of leading the society in one or the other sphere but do not get a chance to lead. Every leader needs a break-through or a chance to prove his leadership mettle, at any level. It is often seen that those who get the break-through prove their ability well, by way of results.

The case of **Narendra Modi**, the Chief Minister of Gujrat, for nearly ten years now, is a typical example to prove this point. Nobody, including the organisation to which he belongs to, ever knew that he was such super leadership material of the political arena. He was catapulted directly into the Chief Minister's chair without any prior experience of governance, even of the lower most strata like municipality or gram-panchayat. He has done wonders as far as the material progress of the state is concerned. He has been appreciated for his governance even by his dire opponents in the political field. **Kumar Mangalam Birla** was also catapulted at a very young and perhaps not enough matured age, to lead the family's commercial empire. He did well in taking the family business to greater heights. Still better example is that of **M.S.** Alias **Guruji Golwalkar**, who was made the RSS chief at just the thirty fourth year of his age, on the demise of the founder of RSS in 1940. He did wonders and as a result the RSS became synonymous with his name. Same is the case with **Deen Dayal Upaddhyaya** who built the then Bharatiya Jana Sangha when he was just thirty three years of age. Another example is of **D.B. Thengri** who built the mighty Bharatiya Majadur Sangha and achieved number one position against the traditional leftist's labour organisations. Such examples need to be studied in depth to understand the science of leadership, if any. Such examples point in the direction that leaders are more a born material than cultivated one. Is it really so? Who then becomes social or political leader? Is it by birth only? The answer can be found in the study of history.

It should not be ruled out that even after getting a break-through; a leadership material may not be successful because of many other situational and time-dependent factors. Should this then be called as a break-through at all? It could be a debatable issue. It can therefore be said that even for a leadership material, many factors have to converge to ultimately make one a successful leader.

Realisation of Objective

For anyone to become a leader in his own sphere of activity, he must be completely dedicated to the cause of the group which he leads. He must have single minded and unflinching devotion to the cause. The more is this devotion and dedication the more likelihood is that he will lead that organisation in right direction effectively and efficiently.

In fact the possibility of his becoming a leader is directly proportional to his devotion and dedication to the cause. This is how **Arya Chanakya, Adi Shankaracharya, Shivaji, Swami Vivekanand, Mahatma Gandhi, Dr. Ambedkar, Dr. Hedgewar, Guruji-Golwalkar**, not only developed their own organisations, to fulfill their own dreams, but led them to a fair bit of success. The only common thing in all of them is the above mentioned fact. With such dedication and devotion, almost all the rest of the qualities, required to make one a good leader, perhaps automatically dawn on such leaders. Can it be said that when such leadership qualities already exists in any one that in turn develops in him the dedication and devotion for some cause of his liking anyway?

If the master key of leadership is known then it may be translated into making leaders as per requirements. Here is the real hitch. Dedication and devotion to a cause cannot be easily cultivated, much less in short duration of training programmes. In this respect the British example is worth noting. When someone asked about how England produced series of good Prime Ministers, one after the other, who led Britain from one to the still higher glory? In answer it was said that they were produced at the play fields of **Eton** and **Harrow**, the then well known English schools. What was so special about these schools? The only specialty of those schools was and still is their overall endeavours to cultivate in their students dedication and devotion to the glory of British nation and its supreme importance in the well being of the entire British society, right from childhood. The children get imbibed with these ideas and accordingly their personalities are evolved. But it is equally true that not all the students there finally become such great leaders. Those who have the natural traits pick up the thread there and become even prime ministers to lead their nation.

This can be cultivated through teaching correct and inspiring history, to start with. It is meant to draw correct lessons from history, of great achievements and of failures, but with the reasons thereof. **Nothing in future can be created without active connection with the past and consciousness of the present**. It is meant to raise the individual as nothing but a part of the society/nation. It is cultivated through developing consciousness about the organic unity of the society/nation, rising above any other parochial interests. It is cultivated through making the students realise their ultimate goal in life as being for the welfare of the society and not for individual selfishness. When the upcoming generation goes through such training, in the formative years of their upbringing, every individual realises his own goal in life in tune only with social/national interests. The instinctual freedom of own physical enjoyment then become secondary.

Finally in whatever field they end up in individual life, they all accept the challenges standing before and respond them with all their might, with devotion and dedication, taking others along within an organised manner, to achieve success. The innermost victorious mood ultimately ends up in success and only success. Such people prove to be the leaders, wherever they go and work, with whomsoever they work, in whatever circumstances they work, with whatever tools they work, without complaining about anything, they set an example of their own as to how ideally one should work for a given cause. **Victory comes without asking, to such people**. They are the real leaders. This is the arduous path that needs to be followed to make anyone a leader. Such examples are not just of only known great men as mentioned above, but even ordinary men and women, when ignited with the cause or mission, put up exemplary leadership qualities in their own narrow field of operation. In the words of India's ex-president and great scientist of repute, **APJ Abdul Kalam** [2], **"such ignited minds are capable of doing wonders wherever they work"** Exceptional qualities perhaps automatically arise in such ignited people. The intellectual ability in such cases becomes secondary, not primary, to the dedication and devotion. Leader has to be a creator of thought. He must also use thought and must act as catalyst of thought.

Clarity of Vision

To cultivate such unstinted dedication and devotion, the objective must be very clearly defined and spelt out. It must also be for a lofty cause and not for some purely petty personal gains. If the objective itself is vague, then such thing cannot be cultivated. The ignited minds are capable of igniting others, in a similar way as a lamp can light up another lamp. In the pre-independence era, the objective of making the country free from British Rule was crystal clear to everyone and, that is the reason why great leaders were therefore produced for the cause, befitting the challenge. They also inspired others to work in the same fashion readily. But after independence the objective of building the nation was not properly spelt out in legible form to average people. The leaders also got embroiled in petty selfish political interests to enjoy the power, not experienced before. There was no focused objective, as was visible in the pre-independence era. It was fairly a diffused objective, without any clarity of the nation of their imagination, which they wanted to build. Almost anybody's any act could be shown as in the interests of nation building, under disguised manner.

Adoption of socialism as a state policy conveyed to the masses that everything is going to be done by the leaders from the capital-seat and that public need not do anything. All they are required is to vote and elect them by putting their vote every five years. The gullible masses believed in this rhetoric as true. No leader worth the name ever told the public that they have to work hard in co-operative and co-ordinated manner for the building of a strong, united and prosperous nation.

The net result was that the leaders also became less focused and hence the deterioration that has set in has gone beyond anybody's control now. It has now become a *liazus faire* affair.

Foresight

Another important quality required of a leader is the foresight into the future. A leader has to lead the others into the future which is unknown to the rest. But the leader has a deep insight such that he should be able to see the future to a large extent and therefore he is able to lead the others in the direction of his vision. The same is often referred to as statesman-like quality in the field of politics. This differentiates the usual leaders from the visionary statesmen.

"The visionary leaders do not do many different things, they do things differently", in the words of **Shiv Khera** [3].

The names of the leaders cited above were statesmen in their own spheres. The statesmen are more by birth than merely by cultivation. But usual leaders for usual purposes can be cultivated by suitable training. These are generally confined to the middle level ranks in any organisation.

This is the reason why these days corporate sector lays heavy stress in training leaders for their own organisational managements. Leadership training has thus acquired an important part of human resource development in most of the medium and large enterprises in business. The same to some extent is true of social and political arena as well. There are such organisations where leaders are trained for better performance.

A lucid description of how enterprises acquire their own direction and how essentially leadership steers such enterprises to visionary organisations is given by **Jim Collins** [4,5]. He emphasizes that the leader must have in his vision the total architecture as to how the enterprise is going to shape up in future over an extended period, in spite of ups and downs on its way. This is the only sure way of progress for any organisation and it all depends only on the right leadership.

Laws of Leadership

It is rather difficult to predict beforehand as to who is capable of becoming a leader of a given category. It is also impossible to judge if anybody is a leadership material by birth. All types of processing, training, circumstances luck (in the form of sum total of all unknown factors) and all such variables are seen to make leaders of different organisations and societies at different times. In historical perspective, perhaps the above mentioned Modi-syndrome seems to be a common feature. If it was wholly a training affair, then leaders of repute would have been produced as per requirements. But it is not seen to hold true.

Lord Rama and **Lord Krishna** were definitely men of exceptional abilities and therefore both of them are now revered as gods. But they did live as human beings once on earth and led very powerful movements of their times. There has been no second similar one again on this earth. In fact all such great leaders are produced once only. Their second version does not come again. **Every time a new great man may come but not the copy of the old one.** Each one leads in his own characteristic way, since the situation every time is characteristically a different one, perhaps fundamentally different from the previous ones. There is no logic to predict the birth of such great men again either. However for general purposes, to carry out definite and predetermined tasks, people with sufficient intelligence, are trained to become leaders.

J.C. Maxwell [6] has enumerated **21 irrefutable laws of leadership** which control leading. Some of the important ones are described below.

Only visionaries become ultimately the leaders. Confusion in perception will not make anyone a leader. One who has clarity of path only becomes a leader. A leader always gets people inferior to him as his subordinates, because otherwise the situation will be the other way round. He must therefore evolve his style of working taking this fact into account. He must himself be confident about his strategy and approach, so as to inspire enthusiasm in his subordinates to work along the given guide lines. **It is human weakness to readily become person-centric in all activities rather than be mission-centric**. The subjective strategy appears to work only initially. But it proves disastrous in the long run. This is particularly important in NPOs where people often get inspiration from someone's personality. They get disappointed or frustrated when such a person disappears from the scene, for whatever reasons. Hence people must be trained to develop focus around the cause rather than on the personalities. There are umpteen examples to suggest that the fundamentally person-centric nature of Indians have often landed them in trouble, beyond repair.

Goal Orientation

A leader must be psychologically oriented to focus on the goal rather than working for some personal aggrandisement or for some false notions like sacrifice, chivalry and the like. **Shivaji** was exceptionally focused in achieving the goal by whatever means without eulogising gallantry, valour or false sense of greatness as the Rajput Sardars often revealed. **Lord Krishna** did all sorts of cunning things but was focused to ultimately establish the just cause for the good of the rest. On the contrary **Mahatma Gandhi** emphasised the purity of means more than the final success. **Whether to weigh the purity of means more against the final victory, by whatever means, has always been a point of debate and shall perhaps continue till eternity.** Some stress one aspect more than the other. The saintly leaders opt for purity of means and the usual leaders opt for final success, as is seen to hold. One should make his choice as best as it suits him. Many times circumstances dictate which one to prefer against the other. One thing is certain that the leader must not divert his attention even for a moment from the goal.

Real vs. Pseudo

These are the days of advertisement and media hype about anything. The image rather than the reality has acquired great importance. False images of greatness can be created using media. Similarly a great leader can be degraded through persistent use of media in wrong ways. The leader should not take the credit of success and attribute discredit to the followers or the subordinates. The best alternative is to give credit of success to all those who participated in the work and accept all the discredit as leader's own failure. Such is the graciousness of real leaders. Those who always take the whole organisation with them, in times of crisis and in success or in failure, as a solid single unit, prove to be finally better leaders. It reflects in projecting that all achievements made are by using media techniques. This is more relevant for leaders of the NPOs. It may also lead to success if attempts are made unitedly and not by any individual's specific qualities.

Core Values

There must be some core values to be adhered to while managing an organisation. They may vary as per the nature of the organisation. These give the leader additional strength and ability to get right co-workers for getting the job done. These may include honesty, discipline, fair deal with every one, giving what is of government to the government and keeping only what is of owner with the owner. It also means caring for the society around and at large as a priority. In the social affairs leaders prove to be great if they exhibit some generally acceptable core values and beliefs.

Core values can be evolved consciously against the backdrop of long range perception and planning with some lofty ideals to be achieved through organisational activities.

Unique Role

It is the leader who steers the organisation through good or bad times. The organisation either produces goods or provides services through their own participants. In broader sense it is true with every organisation. This is referred to as the **'inside'** of an organisation by **Peter Drukker** [7]. These goods or services are sold/provided to the outside social world on local, regional, national or even on international level. This is called as the **'outside'**. Those working inside an organization know mostly the inside and those who work outside know mostly the outside. The unique person is only the Chief Executive Officer (CEO) or Managing Director (MD) who is supposed to know both sides very well and his **main job is to connect the inside with the outside** so that in tune with the outside forces, the inside is managed and thereby the objective of the organisation is met. This is the unique job and the unique role of any CEO/MD. **Drukker** therefore puts it,

"The CEO is the "link between the inside that is the 'organisation' and the outside as the society, economy, technology, markets and customers. Inside there are only inputs or costs. Results are only on the outside" [7].

In the parlance of management everybody inside is a *producer* and everybody outside is the *customer,* irrespective of the type of an organisation. The products/services generated from inside is sold or marketed or provided to the outside. The CEO must be able to define the outside very well so that the customer's needs are fulfilled.

CEO therefore must know what the aim is and what are definitely not the aims of his organisation. He has always to establish balance between the present and the future. It may include expanding of organisational role or even closing down a part considered as an unnecessary load, in terms of efficiency and effectiveness, in relation to the aim set forth by the controller. Continuity of leadership is essential in any organisation to grow on a long term basis. This is the part of the balancing act of CEO. Similarly he has to shape the values and standards of his organisation as meaningful outside and relevant for the present and future. He is chiefly responsible for setting up the values, the standards and the ethics of his organisation. In ultimate analysis it means to lead the change for survival and growth on the long-term basis.

HRD and Retention

Every task requires building a team in the form of an organisation with people of varieties of skills, capabilities including intelligence and creativity. Such people are not normally readily available. They are trained to suit the organised attempt. They should be retained for sufficiently long duration in the interest of the organisation. These days people easily leave one job for another normally for the sake of higher remuneration and/or power. That is the reason why their retention is a big headache. The leader should be able to retain them longer by making them feel that, that is the best place for work than working elsewhere.

Types of Leaders

Depending upon the personality, as evolved by birth and by social upbringing, a person may be basically classified as democratic or co-operative and group-friendly. Alternatively he may be autocratic in nature dictating every time his own terms and exerting himself so that group activities are carried out as per his own perceptions alone. In some cases one may be very docile to the extent of not exercising any authority or his own desires while working in a group. **Leaders of the same basic three types are generally found around.** Each style is useful to lead a certain type of organisation better than the other types.

The assertive, autocratic, egoistic leaders were alright for running organisations prior to the Second World War, because the organisational structure and operation was then predominantly bureaucratic in nature. It worked well in those days when colonialism of Europe dominated almost all over the world. There was no competition even amongst organisations working apparently in the same field of interest. This was so because every organisation had its own niche area of operation where there was no competition from even similar organisations. But soon after the end of Second World War and of colonialism along with it, severe competition started amongst the organisations operating in the same field. Organisational efficiency came to the centre stage for organisations to operate effectively for their own survival. Now the area of competition has enlarged still more with similar organisations from the newly liberated nations arising on the horizon.

The upper most consideration in any organised effort now is its efficiency of operation. It means that the inputs and the outputs have to be weighed, finally in terms of monetary values, to decide whether the organised effort should continue or be sold/amalgamated or disbanded. Every responsible parameter which improves efficiency is encouraged, supported, stressed, applauded, awarded and every parameter which reduces the efficiency has to be suppressed, eliminated or killed to the extent possible. All the above activities fall in the jurisdiction of the leader of an organisation. It has all led to develop understanding of leaders, their types, their categories, their groups and their individual characteristics and the assessment of how to fit them in the best possible manner, wherever required.

Basically therefore three different types of leaderships have been identified. These are:

1. **Democratic**
2. **Autocratic**
3. **Non-assertive**

Each one is useful in certain types of organisations, where it fits in well. In most profit making organisations the days of usefulness of autocratic leadership are practically over. Democratic leadership, taking and seeking co-operation from all sections, even in deciding the path of progress, has now become essential. Gone are the days when some individual, claiming to possess all the know-how, would be able to run organisations towards its goal.

Models

According to **Allan Keith**, authority on leadership development," **leadership is ultimately about creating a way for people to contribute to making something extraordinary happen"**. This is possible either by following someone in his footsteps, without questioning or by listening, seeing, understanding the leader and acting accordingly.

There are therefore basically two models of leaderships. These are:

1. **Follow-me or copy-me model**
2. **Do-as-I-say model**

In the Follow-me model the leader is supposed to be the hero whom the others are expected to follow, as an example, in all respects. The followers are supposed to copy the leader, to the extent possible, in their own life to ensure right performance. The leader is presumed to be the ideal in this case, worth following and copying. The wonder-making leadership, particularly on social fronts comes in this category. The religious leaderships or leaders of charitable organisations may also fall in this category.

In the Do-as-I-Say model the leader brings forth the right path to be followed by the followers. It is in a way intellectually-guiding and telling one what is the right thing to do, without perhaps himself obeying the same. A medical doctor may tell his patient that tobacco is injurious to the health while himself smoking a cigarette or chewing a tobacco-pan. He is telling the truth, which is in the best interest of the patient. He is guiding the patient correctly. He does not expect the patient to consider him as a role-model or hero and follow him in his actions. But in social, political or religious organisations, people often follow the leader's life-style in toto. At least attempt is made to do so. There the Do-as-I-Say model cannot be active. If the leader wants the followers to do something or to behave in a certain way then he himself has to set an example of his own so that the others can follow it in their lives. At least in part, the follow-me model is always actively in action. The followers tend to copy at least some things the way leader acts and behaves. Many social organisations carry their work essentially on the basis of follow-me model.

Theories of Leadership

It is often believed that leadership has relevance with respect to period, places and people, which are critical factors with varying impacts. But the purpose remains an overriding consideration. The required qualities also differ with respect to cultures and geographies as well. Hence leadership is a time, situation, geography and culture related dynamic phenomenon.

There are many theories proposed to explain the leadership phenomenon. The **Great-Man Theory** assumes it by birth. The **Behavioural Theory**, on the contrary emphasises that they are made by proper education, training and upbringing. The **Trait Theory** suggests that only few people are born with the qualities that make finally the leaders. The **Contingency Theory** however focuses on the relational aspects with others, that may change from time to time, that make the leader, depending upon the situation or environment. The **Participative Theory** is based on the involvement of all in the group effort. The **Relational or Transformational Theory** is more in terms of relations between the leader and the followers. Every theory must accept that it is the purpose, dedication and commitment that make a leader in the ultimate analysis. Whatever be the case a leader must lead and not get led by the followers as is often found in the Indian political scenario. If the leader is led by the followers then no progress is perhaps possible. This is what is seen in present day political scenario in India.

Indian Psyche

In India social life is still governed by the high morality personified by the lives of **Lord Rama** and **Lord Krishna** depicted in the two great epics, **Ramayana** and the **Mahabharata** respectively. They are considered as the direct incarnation of God Vishnu. These two great men still guide how one should behave in a particular situation, by looking at the way they reacted in their own times. This is because these two great men, are believed to have behaved ideally in their own life and in their own times, and it is expected from every one to try to behave the same way in their own situations. One expects such ideal behaviour from even the present-day mortals. In the absence, he finds them worth dumping or discarding. But life is always far from ideal. The average Indian does not seem to realise it readily. For him only the black or the white colour exists. He does not readily realise that there are innumerable grey shades in between.

For him any **one is either Rama or Ravana and not a mixture of the two.** For him, otherwise, any one is **either Krishna or Kansa/Duryodhana and no mixture of the two**. In the real world one may find a combination of Rama and Ravana or Krishna and Kansa/Duryodhana in all possible proportions, that is zero to hundred percent in either case. One has to deal and work with such imperfect individuals in real life. The leader should understand such varied grey shades in people with whom he has to work and yet achieve the objective. A leader therefore must look for some good or worth while qualities in everyone and make the best use of it and, see that as far as possible the bad or undesirable things do not come in the way of his achieving the objective. The required quality is to get people going alongwith, to do the expected. This in particular requires the development of a work-culture conducive for everyone to put in his best and most.

Experience vs. Creativity

While selecting any manager, experience is often taken into consideration before selection. In the agricultural era the social and individual life style did not change very much. In fact it appeared as if there was no perceptible change in practically anything in one's own life time. Under those conditions the experience gained in responding the challenges in the past helped to respond, and perhaps successfully, nearly similar situations when they arose again next time. Therefore experience does help if the challenges are somewhat similar to the one faced before. In the present information technological world everything is changing so rapidly that the emerging situation seems to have no semblance with the prior situations in any field of activity. The earlier experience therefore does not count much in tackling such altogether different situations. The **new challenges have to be faced with creative solutions** and not in the same old style in the past. Managers have to be basically creative to respond challenges as and when they emerge and not rely much on earlier experiences because they have their own limitations. When mangers are to be selected to lead any organisation, it is not the experience but his creativity that needs to be judged and in general a creative one should be preferred against the experienced one. This is not to underrate experience in solving problems. It does help, but in the emerging world to a limited extent only, and that too in some specified circumstances, elsewhere creativity counts much more.

In the agricultural world creativity was unknown. It came to be known somewhat after industrial revolution. But it is a trait of information technology era, let it be understood.

The emergence of ever newer challenges also requires in a way an ability to tackle the adverse and unknown conditions. This is very special faculty expected from leaders. Modern era always brings forth challenging situations and leaders are expected to stand up to such adverse situations and come out triumphant.

References

1. Argenti, John, *Your Organisation, What is it for?* McGraw-Hill, N.Delhi, (1993).
2. Kalam, Abdul, A.P.J., *Ignited Minds*.
3. Shiv Khera, *Your Can Win*, Shiv Khera, (2002).
4. Collins, Jim, *Good to Great*, Harper-Collins, N.Y. (2001).
5. Collins, Jim and Porras, Jerry, I., *Built to Last*, Harper-Collins, N.Y. (2002).
6. Maxwell, J.C., *21-Irrefutable Laws of Leadership*, Magna, Mumbai, (1999).
7. Drukker, Peter, as quoted by Lafley, A.G. in *Harward Business Review South Asia,* (2008), May, p. 34.

CHAPTER

13 STRUCTURAL-TYPES

CHAPTER STRUCTURE

- Pyramid-flat Range
- McDonald's History
- McDonald's Syndrome
- Pyramidal Model
- R and D Model
- In-between
- Organisational Culture
- Freedom at Individual Level

Pyramid-flat Range

The way various organisations are structured and managed depends on their type and size, the product and service they provide, geographical area of their operation and so on. On the whole it depends on how much of the individual's freedom is to be curtailed in an organisation and sacrificed for the co-operative working required in an organisation. It varies right from almost no individual freedom to almost total individual freedom. There is a wide spectrum of such varieties. At the one end is the organisation typically represented by McDonalds and at the other end those of the professional, artists, literatures and so on. It may be surprising to note that the military or the defense organisations, including all its types, in reality do not represent the extreme end, though it is fairly close to the extreme end. These are often referred to as ***bureaucratic*** **or** ***pyramidal*** organisations wherein the orders from top have to be followed without much of application of one's own mind. It will be seen in greater details below.

Similarly organisations like the NASA, ISRO, DRDO, AEE and such other basically research and development organisations, where plenty of freedom is given to all levels to work out their own plan of actions at lower levels, do not represent the other end either. Though it comes closer to the other extreme end. Such organisations are often called in recent times as ***flat*** organisations. It is illustrated in **Fig. 13.1**. This also will be dealt with in greater details below.

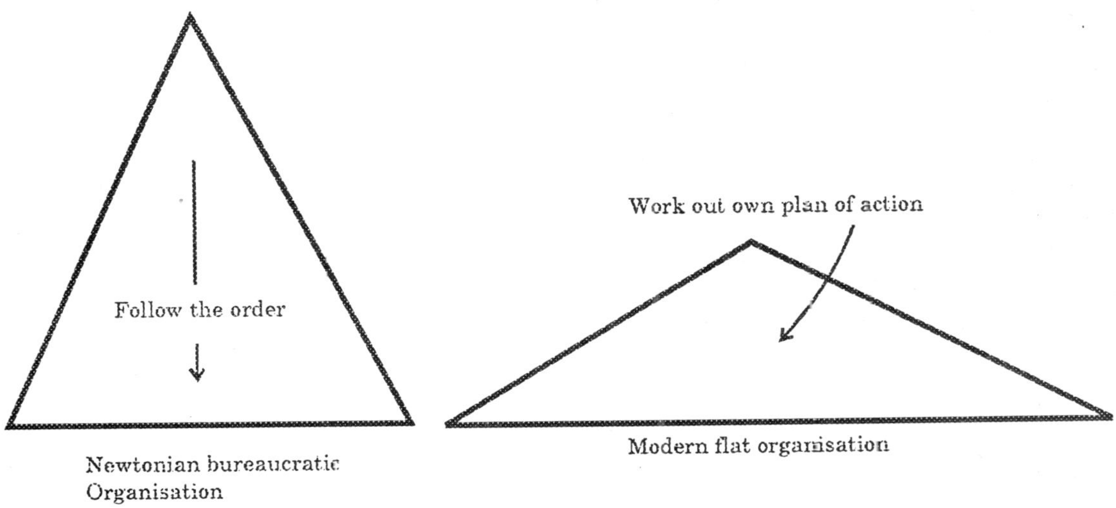

Fig. 13.1 : Schematic representation of bureaucratic and flat organisations.

What does the above ***organisational structural spectrum*** with two extreme ends as mentioned above manifest? The two ends basically manifest two diametrically opposite conditions, mind-sets and hierarchical patterns in managing the organisations. It is often referred to as ***bureaucratic*** at one end to ***flat*** at the other. The net result of such perception decides how flat or pyramidal they will be in their organisational structural character. The military is pyramidal to the extent possible. Creative minority is strictly compatible with the majority in the organisation and more mechanical to the extent possible. The majority is not expected to think much creatively and contribute at every stage of operation. The thinking, creative and innovative part is left to the minority or the leaders at the top only. The R and D organisations are such that almost every individual has lot of freedom to think creatively and contribute to the developmental programmes that are going on. The leader expects such contributions from the lower-most strata of the organisation as well, if possible. In the organisations of professionals, literatures, artists and so on everybody keeps his own freedom practically intact while being in the organisation, to the maximum possible extent.

Between these two extreme ends of the structural spectrum lie all the rest of organisations of all hues with respect to their structures. It depends on the type of leadership available, type of organisation, other organisational and the environmental constraints. In commercial organisations, meant to make profit as their primary objective, may choose their own place on this spectrum accordingly.

McDonald's History

McDonald's example is often quoted in management literature, on commercial organisations, to illustrate how a streamlined and extremely pyramidal management can be.

The first McDonald restaurant was started in 1955 to provide fast food with four specific characteristics. It offered very limited menu, with high quality, at moderate price, under best possible conditions of cleanliness and extremely efficient service. The promoters designed the system; the equipments required therefor and planned how their other objectives will be met. The product, its handling, cooking procedures, kitchen layouts and man-power requirements were all standardised and strictly enforced. Finding it to be a resounding success right in the beginning, they opened up similar restaurants afterwards elsewhere, one after the other. Then they started offering part share holding locally, or full franchises, to be run as per their strict guidelines, without any deviation. If any additional intellectual inputs, by way of any alterations in the prescribed practices were required, these were considered by the apex body, and if found suitable, were introduced everywhere, to make all operate strictly under the prescribed operational conditions. Very soon they were able to standardise it all over to the customer satisfaction. By 1983 it had in USA more than 6000 such restaurants in operation.

It was then expanded by opening the same in different countries under the same brand-name and similar conditions of operation, with some unavoidable changes in the food types and tastes, as per the local requirements. Even these were okayed from the top management after thorough local market research. By 2002 the number of restaurants increased to 24000 and expanded in 120 different countries. By now it is in the range of

30000 and in nearly 150 countries. Thereby they achieved their dream of being the major player in food services. No wonder they are very popular all over the world for their above mentioned characteristics. Seeing McDonald's success, Burger King then came up to compete with them to serve the same range of food.

Seeing their success other such food chains opened and operated on similar pattern of management like the **Burger King, Pizza-Hut or the Kentucky Fried Chicken** and so on, from USA alone. Other countries also copied such things on smaller or larger extent. In India this has inspired the Udupies to start their own style restaurants everywhere, based on similar objectives, but quite independently. The Kamat's hotel is another example. Several such, on small scale, exists everywhere.

McDonald has therefore become a pronoun for such types in management literature and taught as a model. It is in a way the ***McDonald Syndrome.*** What does it mean in terms of organisational science? This is the pertinent point that needs discussion here.

McDonald Syndrome

McDonald has now come to mean a certain type of managerial practices, which are taught to business management students, in the form a basic theory. Every organisation has a number of tiers of management, depending upon its size, type and outlook. The question as to how much freedom is to be given at every level for effective and efficient management to meet one's own objective becomes the key management decision. The McDonald style is possible only if a laid down practice is to be obeyed strictly to obtain desired results. It is also applied wherein practically no creative response is expected from anybody at the lower levels; they have to simply stick to the designed practice. The policy decisions, innovation and changes if any, are all accordingly left to the top one or two levels. This is the typical case of ***'follow the order, do not apply your brain and the results shall follow automatically'***. This is practically the military strategy of *'not to question why, but to do or die'*. It means perception of one or a few to be followed by the rest in commercial world, almost mechanically. Such a system works in the case of some simplified products or services with equally simplified plan of production, marketing and sale. It also works only if there are practically no alternative products to compete. If these conditions are not met this pattern is likely to fail.

This is like a small factory producing certain simple product(s) with assured market. It can be run with an innovative or creative manager and the rest practically carrying out the job as per the designed practice. This was possible in the early part of industrial revolution in any society. It can go on merrily until somebody offers a better and a cheaper product, produced by alternative innovative route. Alternative fast foods, in the form of fried chicken or pizza and the like have in fact duplicated the McDonald managerial practices and nothing else, with only change of precise product to be produced and sold. They are not really the competitors because their products are different, though one may choose one for the other at times. Burger King is the real competitor since it also sells exactly the same product. They are also doing well on the same lines. Burger King is also following the same style of management as originally evolved by McDonalds. But they have not been able to displace the number one position of McDonalds. It has also not been possible to substitute burger by any alternative form so far as the choice of food is concerned, to challenge the McDonalds.

Pyramidal Model

The early organisations, which were managed more under the **Newton-Cartesian** perception of world model, were pyramidal in structure and management, as has been already indicated earlier. The McDonald model is quite different from those pyramidal organisations. As far as typical pyramidal model is concerned, the military represents it more ideally than anything else. The basic difference is that the McDonald does not have many tier-management, whereas military definitely has. McDonald essentially has just few tiers, viz the top management, marketing in between, perhaps the central and the regional ones, because of its vast expansion, and finally the franchise holder. The franchise has to follow the design in toto to deliver the goods. If the design is followed in toto then product of the right quality at best possible service and economy is assured. The franchise need not bother about the public awareness. The top management of McDonald has brought to the notice of public at large, through appropriate advertisements, what they are out to offer, through their outlets. As long as people get the assured service, quality and cleanliness and at appropriate price, there is no problem on the sale front. The McDonald's top management keeps watch on their functioning. Anybody can complain if there is any deviation from the assured services by any franchise holder. There is therefore not much of policing required until complaints are received.

Essentially the same models are now used in running the chain of departmental stores. If the prescribed standards are not followed by the franchise then the contract is straightaway cancelled. They can afford this, on local level by changing the franchise, without loosing overall business to any greater extent. Hence it is not strictly a pyramidal structure in the classical sense because for pyramidal structure there has to be more tiers of administration. Therefore it is not under the Newton-Cartesian influence in the classical sense. It has acquired its own style of management and hence it is a syndrome of its own type in toto, without question. The work force at franchise or own outlet are trained initially fully to imbibe the spirit of McDonald's for which it stands. They are not supposed to innovate the existing system by applying their own mind at any stage, while running the franchise. They are to mechanically follow the instructions from top, and if strictly adhered to, then the results are assured to follow. Who would bother to change anything if expected results are even otherwise met by merely following the pattern?

R and D Model

The management style at the other extreme is manifested generally by the organisations of professionals, artists, literatures and so on. The members in such organisations are themselves enlightened enough to be creative, innovative and self supporting. They are not there to produce a product or service out of their common and co-ordinated efforts. In fact they form associations to serve some common interests like getting some governmental concessions or conduction of some joint public programmes and the like. Such organisations are in fact essentially get-togethers of such people for some simple common interests or to work as pressure groups to extract something from the powers that be or even to project one through organised efforts. These can also be called social groups or clubs instead, rather than strictly organisations. But since these are also registered like any other organisation with some broad aims, they are grouped likewise. Herein every participant practically retains his own independence and gets something more in return for joining the organisation. Hence this represents the other end of the spectrum. These organisations are not just flat but are practically only a ***horizontal-line*** with pyramidal peak just discernible, perhaps through microscope only. The federations also fall in this category because the constituents therein would also like to retain their independence, to the extent possible. The management in such cases is totally responsible to the constituents and stays there at the mercy of the constituents. Hence it does not take any independent decisions to impose on the rest. It in fact takes the opinions of the constituents and acts as majority would like to.

In research and development organisations like the American NASA and similar ones in the western world and ISRO, DRDO, BARC and similar organisations in India, lot of freedom needs to be given even to the most lower levels so that even that can contribute innovatively to the total efforts. Bright ideas can strike serendipitously to any one, even at lower levels and that is precisely made use of for meeting the organisational objective. **In such organisations there is no specific product to be continuously produced and marketed.** Every time the product is to be designed anew for a special application. There is no standard method of production for such products. Every time even the methodology of production has also to be evolved to suit the product. Under such working conditions, no standard conditions, rules and regulations can be formulated and laid down to carry out the job at the lower levels. All the levels have to be given utmost independence to think, try, if failure occurs, then modify and finally complete the job as per requirements. At times it may also need informal assistance/guidance from outside, and for which the particular level or individual there needs independence of authority to act in best interests of the organisation.

Such an organisation can be managed with least possible pyramidal structure. It however needs overall centralised planning and organising. The execution can be left to the lower levels as per their perception. It must be as flat as is possible. It is here that individuals or groups of just a few are considered to be project organisations, for the job at hand and are allowed required freedom, with the sole aim of meeting the local as well as the overall objective. These are termed as ***atomised organisations*** by Deal, Kennedy and Allen [1]. These also are in a way strategic business groups. Such organisations are very flat in their management structure. Those who allow such freedom at the level of individuals or groups or the level as a whole seem to progress well and achieve their objectives more effectively and efficiently.

In-between

Most of the organisations, whether NPOs or profit making or otherwise, fall between these two extreme ends of the structural and management styles spectrum. The actual proportion of top-control and freedom at the lower levels is a matter of subjective choice of the management. There is no mathematical formula which can be taken as a guide in such cases. Having experienced the limitations of pyramidal structure in organisations, attempts are being made now to decrease the pyramidal structure, everywhere and to increase initiatives at all lower levels, to the extent possible. There may even be instances wherein the reversal of some pyramidal form might have been necessary. It is all highly individual and particular time-centric considerations.

In common parlance decreasing the pyramidal structure and increasing the lower level initiatives is often referred to as ***flattening*** of the organisations because the structural height of the pyramidal arrangement decreases in the altered set-up. To what extent the pyramidal height is to be reduced depends on the extent the lower levels are capable of initiative and creative inputs and in reality give out-put as per organisational expectations. There is therefore always a dilemma at the top management level as to how much freedom is to be allowed at any given lower level for effective working style. This dilemma is shown in **Fig. 13.2** which indicates the inverse relationship of bureaucracy and personal creativity in an organisation. Every product or service to be produced and marketed needs a certain amount of lower level initiatives and creativity and partly the traditional bureaucracy, to make use of the elders experience and judgments, to produce it optimally, in relation to its cost of production and the price it fetches. Hence it is the controller's judgment to opt for appropriate mix of the two and review it sustainingly to improve the organisational efficiency, in view of the actual experiences. This is what is depicted in **Fig. 13.2**.

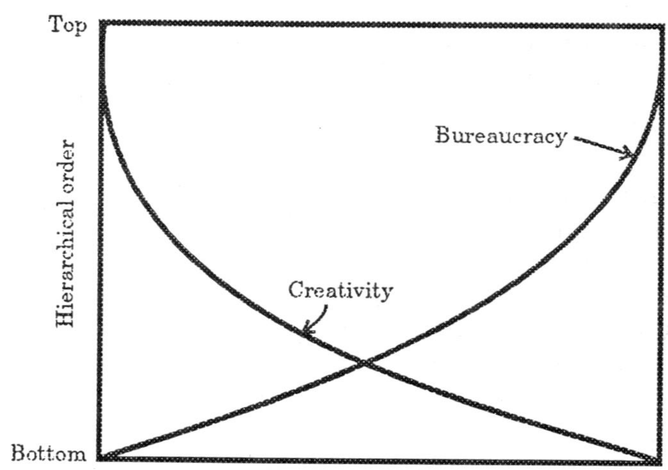

Fig.13.2 : Depicts the qualitative inverse relationship of bureaucracy, pyramidal arrangement and the flattening and increasing lower level initiatives.

The right combination of bureaucracy and individual or lower-level freedom is a matter of continuous evaluation and upgradation to see that the effectiveness and efficiency keep on improving. It will be reflected in better profits in any profit making organisation. Equally it will reflect in more efficient NPOs. The general atmosphere of working will become more pleasing to all at large. Those dealing with the organisation from outside, shall feel improvement, like those dealing with governmental organisations. People would be happy to deal with such organisations.

Oganisational Culture

In general, the credit for developing the concept of flattening the organisational structures along with many other innovations to achieve excellence in management goes to **Tom Peters** and **R.H.Waterman Jr** [2] and **Austin Nancy** [3]. That is the reason why management has come up to review the existing management practices and to innovate them further in the direction of flattening or even otherwise for achieving excellence. In this respect concept of organisational culture has recently come up. Organisational culture has been defined as a general pattern of behaviour, shared beliefs, values, and such other things that are common to members of an organisation. Culture in an organisation is a collective behaviour of a group. In an organisation individual thinking, behaviour, reaction to anything, learning, transmitting knowledge, industry, commitment and such things over a long period constitute the culture. It can be a stable one or a changing and unpredictable one in an organisation. The mission statement and adherence to it in a way gives an indication of the culture of any organisation. Slogans adopted can also be an indication, at least of the management, about the culture they have built up or aim to build up.

The role of leader is of supreme importance in this respect. Example is better than precept, so goes the saying. Basically the right attitude and initiative of the leader are most essential in developing a right culture in any organisation.

Freedom at Individual Level

Although a certain type of structure can be chosen for an organisation as per its needs it does not decide the freedom available to an individual at any level in the organisational hierarchies. This has to be decided and assiduously cultivated in any organisation. This is of utmost importance at the highest level where finally decisions are taken for their implementation. At that level full freedom must be available for each one to express his views without hesitation so that all possible facets of the problem are revealed to all for their honest reactions and final decision in the best interests of an organisation. The same thing must hold true at all levels to the extent possible.

The chief characteristic that transforms good organisation into a great one over a time is the availability of such freedom and sportsman spirit of understanding at the top level, according to **Collins** [4]. As long as the top team has the right passion to make their organisation great, through conformation to their core ideology [5], all open and frank discussions finally help in making right decisions. The same spirit can be rigorously cultivated at all the levels over a time.

Freedom is a double edged weapon. It can also be used to unnecessarily defame individuals in subtle ways. Due care needs to be exercised to see that the freedom that is allowed is utilised for the benefit of an organisation.

References

1. Deal, T., Kennedy, E.and Allan, A., *Corporate Cultures (The Rites and Rituals of Corporate Life)*, Perseus, Cambridge, Mass, (1982).
2. Tom Peters and Robert H. Waterman Jr, *In search of Excellence*, Profile, (2003).
3. Tom Peters and Nancy Austin, *A Passion for Excellence,* Profile, (2003).
4. Collins, Jim, *Good to Great,* Harper-Collins, N.Y. (2001).
5. Collins, Jim and Porras, Jerry, I., *Built to Last,* Harper-Collins, N.Y. (1994).

CHAPTER 14

FORMATION

CHAPTER STRUCTURE

- Governmental Control
- Nucleation of An Idea
- Endeavours
- Prior Assessment
- Project Report
- Promoter
- Initial Approach
    - Purpose or Mission
    - Objective or Goal
    - Policies and Strategies
    - Procedures
    - Rules
    - Budgets
    - Timings
- Commencement
- Environmental Compulsions

How does an organisation actually form? Even if it is the interlinking of the creative minority or intellectuals with the majority, how does it actually take place in real life to finally result in an organisation? What are all the activities that go in before any organisation is formed to start its functioning?

Governmental Control

Now in any society/nation almost everything, except perhaps the spiritual activities, directly or indirectly, is controlled by the state, be it through whatever form, perhaps more through appropriate legislations. Even those who value individual freedom upper most do not lag behind any one in this respect. This is primarily because almost all activities except the spirituality are measured in terms of money, directly or indirectly and nothing else. This has been the net result of industrialisation, for sure. Money is as yet the only parameter invented to measure any thing [1]. It then becomes shear economics and nothing else. No wonder humane feelings and considerations have been the victim of such thinking. It is the primary tool for meeting varieties of needs of people. Economics is the basic reason of conflicts amongst individuals, groups, societies and nations. It is also a matter of competition and therefore to maintain law and order within and to ensure security against the outsiders, the state as a representative of the society must ensure, as far as is possible, smooth economic progress of their own society. It translates into the state, controlling all the economic activities of the society, through appropriate legislations, even while giving adequate freedom for such efforts. Even those areas where economics may not be involved, similar situation may arise. The state therefore prescribes the methodology of formation of organisations in every social field of activity.

Under such a situation if any one wants to start an organisation then it is imperative to bring the relevant organisation into existence, under the prescribed legal framework. There is always a legal process prescribed for this and the relevant rules and regulations have to be followed in not only formation but running and even finally closing down any organisation, as and when required.

There are organisations like the co-operative housing societies, co-operative banks or the credit co-operative societies wherein public finance is either involved or there is considerable financial involvement, by way of borrowing, from governmental or semi-governmental organisations. Such organisations are to be formed with tight legal control, within a prescribed legal framework, and very minor scope for private play, by way of bye-laws is allowed, for the sake of financial safety. Such organisations can be formed by a group but only as prescribed by relevant law or laws. There is not much of scope left for its innovative management. **They look more like the McDonald-management under the government.** Hence they are readily formed and strictly run as per laid down guideline. In spite of such controls when the organisers flout the legal provisions in taking decisions, then it must be dealt with as per the legal provisions. When they are allowed to flout, it is done only with political patronage. The responsibility lies on those who avoid behaving as enlightened ones.

Only religious organisations are exceptions since these are not formed under any law. It is purely an inter-relationship between man and God. However when tangible things, like property, finance, purchase, sale, etc. are involved, even in these organisations, they have to be carried out under the banner of legally formed organisations only and are subject to the same laws like any other charitable organisation.

There are organisations meant for nation-wide lofty causes which are invariably started first as some form of movements and thereafter they achieve, if at all, regular forms of organisations. These are not formed as per any state legislation. Some individual with dedication and selfless devotion for a lofty cause starts walking on the path and in due course of time, people join it so that it becomes an organisation. The ***Indian Independence Movement*** is a typical example of this category. It was not formed formally under any specific legislation. Most social reform organisations fall in this category and quite often are not registered bodies either. Still better example is that of RSS. It has acquired the number one status in relation to non-governmental organisations, in terms of its size and area of operation. But it has stoutly refused to get registered under Indian Society's Act of 1860, under which all other charitable organisations are otherwise registered. It does not consider itself as a charitable organisation. It does not consider itself as religious one either. It is more akin to political organisations, but it does not take part in democratic processes like elections, and therefore is not required to be registered with the Election Commission of India, the chief statutory body that looks after such matters. It is of its own type and by comparing it with any other existing organisations it cannot be understood fully. Can such a thing exist in a society that is dominated by the western organisational model?

An organisation is fundamentally formed on the basis of duality of organisation and the rest of the society. The RSS does not consider itself as based on this duality because it is not meant to organise some specific segment and sphere of the national society [2]. It proclaims that it is meant to organise the entire national society as per its own perceptions, into a form of its own perception of traditional organisationality. Is it not a challenge to sociologists and managers to study such an organisation to understand better the science of such an organisation?

Nucleation of An Idea

As a result of social appreciation and enterprising ability one may get an idea of some need of the society in the form of some goods or some services. The goods and services here mean anything and everything required in a society for individuals, groups or society as a whole. One who gets such an idea discusses it with some of his relatives, friends and acquaintances to assess if his appreciation is valid or not in the prevailing social circumstances. He may consult suitable advisors or consultants in this respect. From such discussions if one is convinced that his basic idea is in fact in the best interests of the society, often also in his own personal interests or at least not conflicting with the interests of the society, he may start thinking in terms of starting the relevant project in the form of an organisation.

In the case of profit making organisations there are many who think in such terms, primarily because of their overall background of economics related activities. In the case of social, academic and such other fields, such a basic discussion is a common feature of general social interaction in the form of chat, gossip, speeches, seminars or media discussion and similar exchanges. The same does not hold true in the case of religious organisations. It will be discussed separately in more detail later. In political field it is always a matter of debate in small groups. In media it is their normal duty to discuss the impending necessities of social/national life and to suggest the requirements of possible future organisations, directly or indirectly. On the international level the participating governments always discuss the necessity of some more organisations for better co-operation and for finding solutions to existing problems, beyond national limits.

Endeavours

This has already been discussed to some extent in Chapter 11 under section on organised efforts. Formation of any organisation is often preceded by number of abortive attempts, made by those who ventured to form organisations but retracted after some time, thinking that it was not their grain of salt. In social, political or charitable fields of activities this is fairly a common experience. In commercial activities such examples do exists but are less common.

In some cases the attempts are made in right earnest and with due consideration but somehow the circumstances change in such a way or the assessment falls so short of reality that the attempts have to be wound up, in-way between. Starting a new organisation is a challenge and needs to be responded with proper response, to make it successful. If the response falls short of requirements it ends up as only an abortive attempt and nothing else.

Prior Assessment

Before starting any organisation, knowledge of relevant laws under which it is to be legally established must be understood properly. This includes the knowledge of the government departments which deal with such matters, along with their specific requirements.

Before deciding to venture into formation of an organisation the overall social environment, with respect to all possible activities of an organisation, needs to be assessed properly. This may include the availability of raw materials, man-power and transport and so on for a commercial organisation venturing for productive activities. Similarly if any tax concessions are available or whether there is any social unrest and prior information of such types is relevant before starting commercial organisations. Many times transport facilities and related economics are of utmost importance before deciding to set up any activity at a given place.

For starting a political party the knowledge of social mood is one single component that may need assessment. At times it may be formed as a breakaway unit from some other organisation. Some other times it may be formed out of amalgamation of people or groups from many different political segments on account of some compulsions. For starting academic institutions the local need may be a dominant consideration. Some may consider it as money-making proposition and camouflage it under the pretence of social service. But it is not considered here. For starting a charitable organisation the specific social needs must be assessed beyond any doubt.

Project Report

For starting any organisation such preliminary studies, assessment and final judgment therefrom is always necessarily taken before hand. It may also prepare or get prepared some assessment and judgment in the form of a project report of that proposed activity, before any decision is taken for its formation. For charitable, social and such organisations the project report may even be in the form of some considered opinion of some well known personality. But if it involves good amount of investment and if it is to come form some commercial establishments, directly or indirectly, then a written project report becomes a must, and often by a reputed establishment of chartered accountants or cost accountants, capable of doing such work.

The project report generally consists of the actual needs of the society at large in the form of organisational objective; the basic requirements to achieve the objective; the financial out-lays; the human resource requirements, its availability in the local region, their alternative sources; real estate, buildings and plants required for the project; financers available; market where the product/service is going to be sold/provided; the likely profit margins for commercial organisations or likely benefits that would be accrued by the society in the case of NPOs and so on.

Generally the basic project is first prepared for its general evaluation and assessment. A detailed project-planning and operational-execution report is also later prepared, once a decision is taken to start the organisation, with all necessary additional details of its execution.

Promoter

On all these accounts, if formation of an additional or a new organisation is considered necessary then it can take up the matter a step further. At this stage somebody individually or in the form of a small group decide to float the relevant organisation. Such an individual or a group, as the case may be, is known as the ***promoter*** who starts the preliminary work of the organisation by getting the preliminary project report prepared. This group itself gets the detailed project report prepared once the decision to start it is taken, after understanding the full implications therein.

The preliminary assessment before deciding to start any organisation varies considerably depending upon the type and size of organisation to be set up. This distinction is very clear between profit making and NPOs. But even in NPOs it varies considerably with respect to the proposed activities.

Anybody cannot become a promoter, of any organisation and at any time. The promoter must be known in the field of activities of the proposed organisation, wherein the organisation is to be created. He must have beforehand the confidence of majority, in the same field, by way of his capability. If this is lacking then it can create hurdles in setting up an organisation to the same extent.

Taking up the same example as taken earlier as of a co-operative housing society, the promoter will get support and encouragement from others around only if they have confidence in him or the few who propose to start it. In the case of medium or large industry the promoter of the company must be a known personality to enthuse confidence in public to purchase its shares and even join it as its active members. One who wants to start a new college/school, it is better that he is known to the locals as an academician or a social worker of some repute. For charitable organisations often one who is prepared to spend money can get it going readily, without many hindrances. He can hire the required people to carry out the activity if he has enough finances to put in. Others have to work to some extent before hand to establish their credentials.

Initial Approach

In modern management science this comes under what is known as planning. But planning can start only after the decision has been taken to start a particular organisation. But a lot of activities goes in before the stage comes in for planning. Profit-making organisations have a fairly standard pattern of their formation. The purpose or mission is earning of profit and nothing else, at least to start with. It is not at all so in NPOs. A lot of thinking and preparation go in before any charitable organisation can be started. In the case of the NPOs the considerations are much different. Planning consists of defining as *a priori* the following:

Purpose or Mission

An organisation operates according to an overall purpose or mission. Hence the purpose or a mission is a **'condition-precedent'** for any organisation. It may be spelt out in the form of a statement or may even be in the mind of the promotors. It must always be in the best interest of the society at large. In the case of commercial organisations, though they are meant to make profit as their ultimate goal they may still have a lofty ideal of some social service as their guiding principle for any action. In a way **it is the self-assigned task by the society to them in the form of an organisation.** For a business organisation the assigned task is to produce certain goods or services; for university it is the teaching, research and such services; for a political party it is to fight election and if voted by majority to govern and the like.

It is considered by many to articulate the mission statement very carefully to indicate what precisely the promoters would like to do. For example for a university the mission could be, to produce graduates with world-wide acceptability.

It essentially indicates how the organisation should be working and how it should appear when it gets going well. The members of an organisation often have in their minds the image of their organisation in the form of its purpose or mission.

It should not be mistaken as the philosophical foundation of any organisation. It also can change as per the need of the time and the exigencies. For example in times of need the university may produce graduates in large numbers, even without bothering much of their quality as a temporary necessity. Similarly sometimes goods are produced and marketed as per the need without looking much for their quality. Philosophical foundation of any organisation is quite different and it develops out of the social ethos.

Objectives or Goals

These are the ends to be reached with best quality standards with minimum inputs. Merely earning profit even in a commercial organisation, at any cost, can not be an objective, in the present humanitarian environment. It has to have some lofty social or humanitarian objective. Mere profit earning cannot be a motivating force for subordinates to work for long in any organisation. Lofty social ideals can only motivate people to strive hard and that too for long. Everything of an organisation is attuned to this end in mind. These include short-term and long-term perspectives as well. These are verifiable as per the activities of the organisation. The members work towards their mission while striving on the basis of their day-to-day activities to achieve their goals.

Policies and Strategies

These are overall general approaches to achieve the set goal. These are broad guidelines and paths to be followed by all in an organisation to enable the organisation to achieve its goal. Any time if any doubt arises as to how to react to a particular situation or to deal with an individual or a group, the policy statement can act as a guide to respond such a situation. Policy is not any document that is made right in the beginning as a sacrosanct document to be made applicable thereafter for ever. It is neither philosophy nor point of faith and beliefs not to undergo changes , once formulated. It is made essentially incrementally and radically and is always under scrutiny and revision against experiences. It is essentially meant for making the organisation more effective and efficient for achieving its goal. It is changed only by the top level management. Only care that is necessary is not to interpret some stray emergency decisions or other acts as policies of the organisation. It is the broad framework within which everybody is expected to act while striving to achieve the objective, lest any issue becomes a problem for unnecessary involvement of the top controllers/managers for guidance. Policies can be laid down with respect to anything related to the organisational activities and its long and short-term management, like recruitment, sale, finance, advertisement and almost everything or in the case of charitable organisations in the form of methodology of providing the services.

It should normally be the policy, right from the beginning, not to invent the wheel again or, again and again. Whatever is available, within the reach, should be adopted as it is and proceeded further thereafter to achieve the rest. Policies are generally made incrementally and not radically. It should also be the policy; right from the beginning, to take everybody into confidence, as far as is permissible, so that right culture evolves inside the organisation.

Procedures

These establish the methodology of working in the organisation on all fronts. These are normally very brief statements to start with but are expanded along with the developments in organisational working as per the needs. These may be formal statements as a broad framework to work within. But there are number of informal practices which are allowed to evolve so that very free discussion takes place at every level and all possible alternatives are brought forth to choose the best for organisational progress.

Rules

These are detailed procedures which can not be flouted under any circumstances. These are decisions to be followed by the concerned persons. These do not allow any discretion to managers. If any change is to be made in them in view of the experience then the decision has to be taken at the higher levels and accordingly the rules are modified. This also goes on as a routine activity at the top level as a routine management practice.

Budgets

To start with some provision has to be made for expenses for setting up and get going the organisation. A tentative budget is necessary in the beginning. But detailed budget has to be made in due course of time. It focuses its attention, in the beginning, with cash requirements and its sources so that the work is not hampered at any stage of the progress, in view of all possible variables and eventualities.

Timings

For commercial organisations the timings of starting the organisation and commencing the production of goods or services is always very critical. The histogram of activities is worked out to indicate the starting point with all possible foreseeable hurdles in its implementation. In case of NPOs it is not all that critical and hence it may go on course correcting till almost the end of preliminary work.

Commencement

Organisation may announce its formation after completing most of the above requirements at a suitable or pre-determined date with a bang like inauguration function, advertisements in print and electronic media or may just start producing the goods or the services on some particular day without much noise and fanfare, thinking that its products are bound to catch attention of the public, because of the promotors brand name.. Whatever is the chosen mode, it has to somehow announce to the interested public or the proposed beneficiaries that the organisation has been formed and is now due for full scale functioning as indicated earlier.

Organisations for a very lofty social cause are started probably by an individual, with or without few others, often remain unnoticed even after its commencement because it is too small, at the beginning, to be noticed by others. When it acquires some size and importance, in the public eye, then only others feel that it has started functioning. Thereafter many more may join it and as a result it gets going rapidly.

Environmental Compulsions

Organisations can get formed, at times, out of compulsions in the social environment. Similarly in spite of everything in order, organisations do not get formed simply because of hostile social environment. Hence the origin of organisations does lie in the nature of social environment. Some times the challenges posed are such that organisations get formed readily, for example at times of external aggression or natural calamity or accident, etc. Some times different people unknowingly long for some common things or their selfish interests coincide and when such people come to know of each other's such common needs, organisation is readily formed amongst them.

Organisations can not be formed just because participants are available. They need to agree on leadership so that the necessary hierarchical structure can be formed for creating an organisation. Usually some kind of promoter fulfills this need, at least at the beginning. It is also observed that leaders, out of their charming and capable personality, somehow collect people to form organisations, though it takes little time to form such organisations. Typical examples of such organisations are those created by **Dr. Ambedkar** or **Mahatma Gandhi**. The best example is of **Dr. Hedgewar** who created the mighty organisation known as RSS starting from himself alone and that too against all possible odds.

Panthic, denominational or *sampradaya* organisations (religious) are formed, knowingly or unknowingly, by the seer who has realised the ultimate reality. Even if he does not want to form an organisation, at times, people on their own collect around him and many times that takes eventually the shape of an organisation.

It is now common practice to form organisations facilitated by required legislation by governments. In this respect the democratic governments are usually very keen to organise society through such autonomous organisations. This is the dominant form of organising any society since the present size and the complexity of social life cannot be administered through direct governmental management of all affairs alone. The failed communist experiment has more than proved this. Local initiatives in forming fairly autonomous organisations, aided by suitable legislation, are now order of the day. The final control required to be used in emergency however, rests with the government.

References

1. Argenti, John, *Your Organisation: What is it for?*, McGraw-Hill, London, (1993).
2. Palkar, N.H., *Dr. Hedgewar, (Biograpy in Marathi)*, Datey, Dr. Hedgewar Memorial Society, Pune, (1960).

CHAPTER 15

RELIGIOUS ORGANISATIONS

CHAPTER STRUCTURE

- Abstraction
- Origin
- Different Religions
- Mode of Organisation
- Christianity
    - Origin
    - Early Progress
    - Spread in Europe
    - Divisions
    - World-wide Spread
    - Religion and Nationality
    - Secular Christian Nations
    - Finance
    - Degradation
    - Social Reconstruction
    - Natural Limitations
- Islam
    - Personal Law
    - Spread
    - Binding Force
    - Local Organisationality
    - Finance
    - Social Reconstruction
- Hinduism
    - Who is Hindu?
    - Philosophy
    - Social Manifestation
    - Dharma vs. Religion
    - Limitations of Religions
    - Social Reconstruction

Abstraction

As has already been discussed earlier with contextual reference that the religious organisations are its own types and they differ from other organisations even in some fundamental respects. This is the reason why these are being dealt with separately, in contradistinction with other organisations. In the word religion, ***re*** means again and ***ligo*** means connecting, building, meeting, etc. It therefore means again connecting, perhaps with from where one has come – the other world.

Notwithstanding the sole and common aim of making one realise the super- natural power, or seek salvation, that lie beyond the human senses, there is hardly any semblance between any two present-day religions in their preaching and practices. Besides this their historical record is far too different and antagonistic to each other. This is perhaps because there is no agreement between any of these religions, even in defining their perception of the supreme power. Each one has its own perception of the supreme consciousness. This has been highly subjective with reference to the originator of each religion. There is therefore not even a common scientific definition available by which a religion can be defined to the satisfaction of all concerned on universal basis, except saying that it is related to the other world beyond human senses. There are various terms used to describe the methodology of worshipping or uniting with or realising the supreme power like religion, denomination, sect, cult, Dharma and Sampradaya in the Indian context, and so on. One more striking difference between all the major religions is the extent to which, their activities are carried out in organised forms. Attendant advantages and problems with each one therefore differ fundamentally from one another. There are therefore many fundamental difficulties in trying to understand the common underlying principles governing various religious organisations.

With all these limitations and contradictions the average human being is deeply interested in religion to bring fulfillment to his own day-to-day life. The great historian of the previous century, **Arnold Toynbee** [1], has very aptly stated the importance of religion in human life as:

"In religion the whole of human being's personality is involved, the emotional, moral and intellectual facets. It is not limited to that part of it which is not accessible to the human senses. Every human being finds that he has been born into a world which is mysterious because the part that is accessible, intelligible and manageable is not self contained and not self explanatory, and is therefore apparently a fragment of some inaccessible larger whole. The key to understand the whole lies in understanding the inaccessible part as well"

The profound desire of human beings to get the glimpse of the inaccessible part of the whole world has been exploited, in general by so many, through organised efforts, to the extent of even letting appreciable bloodshed in the process. Whom to blame for such inhuman atrocities, carried out not just in history but also being currently continued? Who will deny that the study of science of such a tremendously effective force in the form of religious organisations is not imperative in the present day world that is heading for peace and integrating itself as one single family?

The desire to know the inaccessible part of the world has been observed to be very intense in a vast majority of human population throughout the ages, perhaps since man evolved in his present form, notwithstanding the onslaught of very vocal atheist minority, residing quite in juxtaposition with religious community. The atheist cannot or may not understand that catering to this need of the vast majority helps them lead a more peaceful, meaningful and contented life-style. There is the feeling of comfort being religious, in the form of cosmic existence. It also leads in general to increase the morality or moral life-styles that are liked almost by one and all. Equally, the religious beliefs do have capacity to lay the moral foundations required for freedom, a key to all pleasing democratic lifestyles, to a large extent. It will be possible to use it for such useful end only if it is understood in proper perspective and practiced towards that end.

The study of religions in the present context is **not to know their theologies and *inter se* merits and demerits**. The present interest is confined as to what extent effective organisations are formed in various religions as per the conditions laid down earlier in Chapter 7, and to decipher to what extent that influences their organised activities. From the standpoint of understanding the science of religious organisations it is necessary to see to what extent the essential requirements for the formation of any organisation are met in any religious activity. If these are met, at least to some extent, then there should be no hurdle in the formation of organisations in any religion. At the same time the extent to which the auxiliary requirements are met, shall decide how stable, effective and efficient such organisations shall be. This is what has been discussed in the present chapter.

Origin

It must be clearly understood that like the Toynbee's creative minority in civilizational upheavals, there is also the enlightened ones or the creative minority, in general, in the field of religion as well, who perhaps realise the nature of the supreme power and would like the majority to understand the same by joining hands with them in the form of co-operative and organised efforts. This is perhaps the origin of formation of religious organisations. The study of religious organisations is equally pertinent because some have consciously organised themselves well to carry crusade of conversion on that basis, using force and allurements both, as compared to others. Their objective is to bring the entire human race under their own fold by conversion, without hesitation. This is possible only through organised efforts by ever increasing number. This helps form religious organisations readily.

It has been done in the past and presently it causes unnecessary tensions in societies and in a way instigating those to form their own organisations to take on the crusades of the basically organised religions and secure safety of their own religion. This is yet another origin of formation of religious organisations, if they do not already exist. The psychology of use of force in propagating one's own religion also helps form religious organisations.

To understand all these nuances in religious organisations let us therefore first understand what all the different religions in the present-day world are, how they evolved and what constitutes their organised existence and behaviour? Let us also see how they behave in the organised form.

Different Religions

There are nine major religions in the present day world. Out of these the Hindu, Buddha, Jain, Shikh were originated in India; Judah, Christian, Islam were originated in west-Asia; Confucian was originated in China and Zoroastrian was originated in Persia or today's Iran. Out of these some are classified as pagan, meaning thereby that they are either idolaters or they existed before the organised religions came into being. Out of these the Confucian is more a philosophy than religion and lays more stress on how kings and kingdoms should behave. Zoroastrian was once a religion of a sizable population but it is no more so. It is the religion of mainly the leftover Parsis in India. These are the descendents of those who fled from Iran and took shelter in India when Iran was overrun by Islamic zealots after 8-9th century AD. Judaism is the religion of the Jews, the predecessors of Christians. They are also an insignificant minority, but fairly powerful by way of their wealth and intelligence. Einstein was a Jew and had to flee Germany and take shelter in USA. The whole world worships him as a great scientist of twentieth century. The Buddha, Sikh and Jain are essentially off-shoots of Hinduism, as those who have broken away from the Vedic traditions for one or the other reason, and they essentially concentrate distinctly on their own modes of worship. The Hindu Code Bill, which depicts the civil law in India for Hindus, is also applicable to them without exceptions because they do not have any separate personal civil law like the Muslims. Hence dominant religions are considered to be only Hindu, Christian and Islam, with their own characteristic religious identity. Much of the world's population is covered by them.

Christianity is supposed to be originated by Jesus Christ who himself was a Jew. The earlier holy book of Jews was **Old Testament.** Jesus' teachings contradicted the traditional teachings of Jews, given in Old Testament and hence they were compiled and later came to be known as the **New Testament.** It also contains the life sketch of Jesus Christ and is now popularly known as the **Bible**, to distinguish it from the holy book of the Jews. After his death the followers of Jesus Christ came to be known as Christians and their teachings as Christianity as distinct from the Jew's Judaism. One has to believe in Jesus, the son of God, and his teachings in the form of the Bible, to be a true Christian. The present universally adopted calendar or the **Gregorian** calendar, as is known, is supposed to be started with the birth of Jesus Christ. It means Christianity is now more than 2000 years old.

Islam was started by **Muhammad Paigambar** in the seventh century AD in Arabastan or present Arabia. His teachings are compiled in the *Koran*. One has to believe in Allah the only God, Muhammad the last Prophet and his teachings in the form of the **Koran,** the holy book, to be a follower of Islam, known as Muslims.

The time of origin, the originator and the codified teachings given in the form of a holy book are clearly known with respect to Islam and Christianity. It is also similarly known for Buddhaism, Jainism and Sikhism, to a large extent as well. But it is not known in the case of Hindism. There is no specific originator of Hinduism. There are so many great men who have contributed in the evolution of Hinduism. It is essentially a life style with dominance of culture and civilization but mixed with some religion. Hence the time of its origin cannot be told with certainty. Similarly there is no specific book of teachings of Hinduism. There are many but amongst the important ones are the ***Vedas, Upanishads, Brahmans and Shrimad Bhagwad Gita***. It is therefore more a lifestyle than any specific codified system of worship or religion, like the Islam. Hindu therefore cannot be strictly defined like a Christian or a Muslim or, even a Buddhist, a Jain or a Sikh. Even the name Hindu has been of recent origin and given by the outsiders to the people residing in the land known as India, Bharat, Aryavarta and so on at that time.

A Hindu can be somewhat identified in terms of some characteristics alone. He is assumed to believe in the all pervading cosmic power in the form of Bramha or any other similar conception, which is eternal and manifests itself in the ever changing forms called as Maya. Brahma is formless, qualityless, propertyless, all pervading and omniscient ***(nirguna)*** and omnipresent according to Hindus, but it can also exist as in some form, property, quality and so on ***(saguna),*** at the same time. It is depicted by various names. Therefore it is more a lifestyle than merely a set of worship of God in some specific form. In reality Hindu is the name of culture and civilization and not any religion. There is nothing like a Hindu religion and therefore Hinduism. A religion must have certain definite characteristics or codified form, like specific form of God, specific book of teachings and, specific form of worship, for being classified as a religion. These criteria do not apply to Hinduism for being called a religion. Yet in the common media parlance it is classified without any hesitation as religion, in juxtaposition to Christianity and Islam.

In fact under the Hindufold there are varieties of such religions, called as ***sampradayas*** by the Hindus, wherein there is a definite originator, definite set of teachings, generally in the form of some book, and broadly a definite mode of worship. This is the reason why Hindus equate their sampradayas with religions like Christianity or Islam. But there is much more than mere mode of worship in Islam and in Christianity, which is missing in Hindu sampradayas. There are some deviations in both Islam and Christianity, wherein they differ from their very original form. They believe in the same God and the holy book alright but there are some other differences. These are called as denominations of the main original religion. In Christianity there are Eastern orthodox, Roman Catholic, Protestants, Anglicans, Mormons, Seventh Day Adventists, Baptists and several others. In Islam these are Sunni, Shiya, Ahmedia, Wahabi and such others. There is a lot of animosity amongst them, in spite of the fact that their Prophet and the holy book is just the same. These denominations have crystalized into separate organisations. But much of their work remains similar to the original one.

A sect is a still narrower group separated from the original religion to assert its dogmas more emphatically with harshly strict discipline. There are various sects in Hindus like Ganapatya, worshippers of Ganesha only, Shakta, worshippers of Power only and very many others on much smaller scale. There are some such in Islam and Christianity as well, for example the Ku Klux Clan and so on.

Mode of Organisation

The modes of religious organisations are typically characteristic of the religion itself and it has much to do with its early history of progress. Christianity is well organised in the form of churches and pastors of various grades, under various denominations, with their international chiefs. They do not have a clear-cut religious civil law to guide the individual and his social life as a true Christian. But it does guide the society through organised Sunday-church worship of Jesus. Islam is organised through their mullah-moulavis, as religious teachers and interpreters of their teachings, whenever required in case of disputes and the masjid/mosque is the place of worship. Besides organising the worship of Allah it would also like to regulate entirely the individual and social life through the Islamic civil law, known as ***Shariya-Law.*** The Hindus developed their philosophy to ideally guide the individual and social lifestyle and expect the individual to follow the same to the extent possible, with no compulsions whatsoever. There are many who do not believe even in the basic tenets and yet are classified as Hindus only, perhaps not because they do not belong to any other religion but because the term Hindu includes even such people on the basis of their ancestral residence and fundamentally common cultural heritage.

Mahatma Gandhi is on record to have said that there is, **in Hindu society, enough room for Jesus, Muhammad, Zoroaster, Moses** and all such great men because it does not differentiate human population on the basis of their mode of worship of the Almighty. That is the reason why Toynbee [1] has pleaded that all other religions of the world accept and adopt the model of Indian religions. After getting independent Israel, the Jews compiled the story of where and to what extent Jews were ill treated in almost eighteen hundred years of their nation in exile. It is mentioned therein as an exception that they did not face any discrimination in India all through their stay. Those who decided to stay on in India even after formation of Israel find no discrimination at all even now.

There are six basic traditional philosophies of Hindus and three out of them are almost atheist in character. Even Sikh, Buddha and Jain religions are strictly inclined more towards atheism. Hence Hindu includes all shades of opinions under its umbrella. In fact it is not a religion at all; it is culture in which religion may be small part if one so wishes. It is not an organised religious society as a whole in any form. It is definitely a culturally organised society with some broad agreement on values.

Let us therefore see how these religions have organised themselves since their inception.

Christianity

Origin

Islam, Christianity and Judaism, because of their area of origin are also called as Semitic religions. This is because they believe that they are all originated from ***Sem*** or ***Sam***. The history of these three religions is responsible for their developments in an organised form. Out of these Islam and Christianity grew all over the world through their organised efforts in converting the local populations. Judaism remained confined to its own area of origin because it did not resort to conversion like the other two.

Christianity started after the demise of Jesus who preached something different from the traditional degenerated Judaism of the Jews, at that time, though he was born as a Jew and lived amongst the Jews. Those who did not change themselves in following the new tenets remained confined mostly to today's Israel as Jews. Religious faith is a very powerful motivation to go to any extent in defending it against any threat, more so from other religions, assuming them to be competitors. Religion was a powerful force everywhere in agricultural era. This proved to be true on preaching Christianity, at the beginning. It may be seen to be equally true today when the Islamic Jihadis go on rampage and vandalism in the name of Islam against the others. Obviously it led to clashes between those who changed into followers of Jesus on the one hand and those who continued the old practice of Judaism. The pity is that these conflicts even reached the stage of shedding each other's blood. Although Jesus himself preached only peace and love amongst all, until his death, the adherents on either side, being more dogmatic and perhaps not understanding the real message of Jesus came to blows, during the time of Jesus itself. It eventually resulted in crucification of Jesus himself by the Jews, on the cross. This must have added more fuel to the fire of their conflicts. The conflicts did not allow the growth of Christianity to any significant extent during the life-time of Jesus. But his crucification resulted in a permanent feud between Christians and the Jews. It must have motivated the followers of Jesus to carry on the crusade, perhaps with vengeance and it still continues till to date.

Early Progress

As is natural, the disciples of Jesus became more determined to spread his message after his death. The early twelve apostles in fact spread Christianity soon after Jesus. This is how Christianity started. It is also the prime reason why the Christians started organising themselves as a group and a force, for which the church, the place of worship, came in handy. But the faith in Jesus' teachings provided the necessary individual initiatives and, common agreed aim or object for co-operative action amongst the followers. Hence the three basic requirements were met readily to consolidate them as an organisation. There had to be a chief of church to not only continue the preaching of Jesus, with almost equal authority, but to organise and acquire enough strength to stand the onslaught from the pagan Jews. That is how they developed a church-centric hierarchical structure of preachers and the followers of Christianity right from almost the early days. The establishment of hierarchical social structure right in the beginning paved the way for Christian organisation to evolve and consolidate in due course of time.

When a few such churches were formed, it required to have an organiser-in-chief to manage the affairs of all the churches as an organisation. As a result the chief of Christian churches had to be nominated to manage the increasing spread of Christianity. Consequently the supreme chief, named as Pope, something like president in today's organisational parlance, was installed as early as in 142 AD, to look after the entire affairs of Christianity, including its spread, all over the region. It later became the post to be occupied by the organiser-in-chief, an undisputed leader, in the form of Pope. Whoever became the Pope became the philosopher, guide and organiser-in-chief of Christianity thereafter till to-date, for all practical purposes. This resulted in whole hierarchy of pastors with seniors and juniors, in between, with Pope at the zenith. This is how the Christian organisation came into being. The security considerations also demanded that the church had some defense arrangement, including eventually some form of army. The essential requirements for the formation of Christian organisation were not all available right in the beginning itself. They slowly got organised over some years or perhaps decades.

It may not be out of place to mention that the same mental make-up led the East India Companies to keep their own defense forces to safeguard their trade and other related interests, wherever they went, and which finally culminated in enslaving various societies around the globe using the same defense forces [2]

This is how the conditions were just ripe for Christianity as a whole to organise themselves against the rest. The ***us and they*** syndrome, as essential, for the formation of organisation as suggested earlier (Chapter 3), developed in place, in Christianity, almost right in the beginning. That became their very nature in due course of time. It also hardened their attitude to the extent that theirs was the only true religion and the rest were all pagans, at least in the then area occupied by the Jews, worth conversion into Christianity for their salvation. Christians had to resort to conversion of the Jews right in the beginning, on ever increasing proportion to ensure their own safety. It is normal human psychology to develop feeling of superiority, over the rest, in such a situation. Christianity started its conversion crusade with the feeling of superiority over the rest right from the beginning because of the historical necessity of survival. As discussed earlier such feeling eventually results in formation of organisation. This is how the early conditions led to consolidate Christian organisations based on church and its pastors, when it was confined to just a small area around its origin. The later historical processes favoured it to consolidate it as an organised religious force on world-wide scale, particularly after the Roman kings accepted it as their state religion.

Spread in Europe

It did not spread much in spite of all such favourable conditions like the creation of early zealots and their highly organised structure for some time. But in the 4th century the mighty **Roman Emperor Constantine** became Christian and accorded Christianity the status of a state-religion. Those were the days of early agricultural era in southern Europe with the king dominating in all walks of life. Hence the subjects had no option but to follow the king and embrace Christianity without question. At that time even otherwise Europe did have neither any single acceptable and formal religion of their own nor any other form of wide-spread social structure. It came in handy for Christianity to spread very rapidly over entire Europe without much opposition. Rome the capital of Roman Empire then became the seat of Pope as well, from where he used to control the Christian organisation of pastors and all their activities, to the extent they had spread. It also resulted in domination of religion in every sphere of life, including the material life as well. This further strengthened the Christian organisationality and organisation.

After the fall of Roman Empire in 5th century AD there was no, worth the name king, left in Europe to govern the European society at large. The European society was fairly divided in terms of regions, customs and perhaps language as well. The Christian religiosity, in the form of organisationality that was developed by then over almost the entire Europe came in handy for Pope to rule Europe by maintaining even an army of his own. Pope had an army until 1860 AD when it was finally disbanded by the Italian government in view of the formation of modern nation-states all over Europe. The seat of the Pope and his little kingdom in the form of Vatican in the city of Rome still continues even today and is recognised as a state by most nations of the world. This recognition is obvious as ambassadors of various nations are deputed there, as if it is still a separate nation like many others.

Divisions

The monopoly of Pope reigning as supreme leader of all Christians, with a huge hierarchy of pastors and Bishops in between, ended in 11th century when the Eastern Orthodox Church first separated itself from the main Christian body ruled by Pope. However the remaining part came to be known as Roman Catholic, with Pope as their head and Rome as the centre and seat of power. As a reaction to Pope's domination and virtual autocracy, eventually in 16th century, the Protestants led by Martin Luther in Germany, separated themselves from the control of Pope and formed a separate denomination called Protestants. Thereafter in due course, some more denominations separated from the main Roman Catholic Church and declared their independence. But all these believe in Jesus the son of God and his teachings in the form of Bible and the prime desire to convert the entire world into kingdom of Jesus, but in their own denominational order. These groups are however still smaller as compared to the Roman Catholics. The Roman Catholics are the largest and most organised, in the form of their tight hierarchical structure, with Pope as their proclaimed and undisputed leader. This does not mean that the organisation of Christians, as a whole, disintegrated beyond repair. These varied denominations do co-operate with each other when it comes to dealing with non-Christians, world-over. The tight organisational format has been restricted to every denomination separately. But they have still their organisationality as Christians intact when it comes to dealing with the non-Christians because conversion of the entire human race to Christianity remains their sole and common aim.

World-wide Spread

Pope and his organisation, together with support from other denominations, played a key role in converting almost the entire societies in the colonies of European nations, particularly in Africa, both north and south Americas, Australia and many other isolated places in the world, under the pretext that they were pagans and that they did not have any other religion of their own. The same argument is made particularly about the *adivasis* in India by the Christian pastors, without understanding the concept of Dharma/ religion in India. That is how the Christians acquired the largest following in the present day world.

They tried the same trick in India as well but it did not cut much ice because of well entrenched Hindu lifestyles in India. The war of independence fought under the leadership of **Tatya Tope**, in 1857, taught the Britishers a lesson, that if they tried to interfere with the religious affairs of Hindus, in the form of their social perception, it would make them difficult to rule the country. That is the reason why it did not spread in India much, in spite of British rule for over a century. They however started many charitable institutions to provide services mainly in the field of health-care and education in India. The evangelical programme was carried out clandestinely under the new garb of humanitarian service in such poor and illiterate societies.

Even after the end of colonialism after the Second World War, the western governments in Europe and in America provide plenty of funds to various Christian denominations for their conversion activities. Pope has already declared publicly the present millennia as one for converting entire Asia into a Christian kingdom. All this is possible only through well organised efforts, greatly guided by Pope and his or similar other Christian organisations, with equally strong financial support.

All Christians in the world do not form only one organisation firstly because it is too big and secondly because there are many denominations amongst them and which compete to bring anybody and everybody into their own fold, even from amongst themselves. They do not see much eye to eye. But it has acquired its own organisationality at the international level, with Pope being their sole exponent. Though Pope is only head of Roman Catholics, he is still regarded as if he is head of all Christians in the world, or exponent of Christianity by the non-Christians..

The evangelical programmes in India are going on with extreme vigour after independence, taking advantage of constitutional provisions of fundamental rights for propagation of one's own religion in what was a part of Indian traditional belief that the path of reaching God can be a purely individual choice, with no compulsions from anywhere, and therefore provided in the constitution, as fundamental right and supported with additional clause for protection of religious minorities, is hereby misused in its extreme interpretation and perhaps to the extent of its anti-national perception. This is helping them to consolidate their organisation. The of-shoot of the organised strength finally led to the demand of Christian majority Nagaland to be made a separate nation, like the Muslims who demanded and got away with Pakistan in 1947. What havoc organised religious population of illiterate and poor faithful can lead to, in the form of partition of traditional nations, is for all to see and deduce their own conclusions. Is it not therefore worth studying as science of organisation?

Religion and Nationality

It is true that the organisationality developed by Christianity, particularly in Europe, when Christian organisation, with Pope as their head, was a dominant force, did not lead to evolve Europe into only one nation-state. The religious force proved to be too weak in this respect. The local organisationality, aided by language, culture and customs and on the basis of governance in the form of small kingdoms, fought wars after wars leading to even world wars, just to prevent any other's domination. It ultimately led to evolution of their own identity, as distinctly different from just the common religion, into a number of nation-states in Europe that we witness today.

Secular Christian Nations

The scientific and technological developments, in the form of industrial revolution, was mainly the reaction of Pope's autocracy, perhaps dictatorship, in controlling entirely the social life, from 5th to nearly 15th century. It evolved into search of universal truths based on ones own experience and on experimentation rather than relying on the version of Pope based on something in Bible or otherwise. The net result was their conflict with religion manifested by Pope. This ultimately led to confine Christianity to a very narrow area in their individual and social life. The nation-states confined themselves to secular or worldly interests only, leaving the religious or other-worldly part to individual's discretion. Similarly they disregarded Pope's directive in governing the state, which was run as per their own secular constitutions.

But there is a catch in this, which is not readily discernible. All these western nations, being still essentially Christian by faith, at least in some small segment of life do identify themselves as Christians alone, whenever the question of religion comes in. They would be quite happy if all humanity was to embrace Christianity, in the form of a religion. As a result and as a part of larger Christian society they do support the evangelical activities of Pope or any other Christian sects clandestinely. On the governmental level, though professing secularism for their subjects, they use it as a tool to help convert the remaining non-Christian population elsewhere into Christianity, by providing finances and otherwise helping them organisationally. Many trans-national commercial organisations, interested in only material progress still financially support Pope and his activities. Strange, isn't it, but true? They help them financially under the garb that Christian organisations carry out social service activities. But it is not entirely service. It is coupled with proselytisation as well for sure. No wonder it worked as fifth column, during particularly the Second World War and, thereafter is currently working as somewhat the same in the under-developed countries. (For more read a recent book "The Armies of God: A Study in Militant Christianity" by British born, Malaysia based academic, Iain Buchanan)

Finance

It is true that many Christians do donate a lot of money to the church regularly at their Sunday meetings or for any of their special service project to the needy ones around the globe, as a matter of charity. But the main finance comes from the MNCs and basically the nominally Christian governments.

With the heavy financial support hundreds of thousands of converted Christians are recruited, as paid workers, in third world countries to carry on the evangelical work, under the garb of charitable organisations, with the sole aim of conversion, using the enormous finance available at hand. The poor and the illiterate are allured into their fold with a variety of material benefits or tricks out of this money-power.

That is how Christianity is the most well organised religious force in the world today, supported financially by most western secular national governments and their dominant multi-national companies. As a result they find no dearth of finances for their organised evangelical activities.

Surprisingly however, in spite of their well organised religious activities it is loosing its hold on the western population very rapidly. The irony is that many of them are more interested in Indian philosophy and life-styles rather than in the Christian way of life. This also needs to be understood more intelligently.

Degradation

It may be of interest to read the data submitted at the **'Leadership Summit'** of Christian pastors held at Barrington, Illinois, USA, in 2009, where the speakers included, **Carly Fiorina, Bono, Tony Blair** (ex-prime minister of U.K.), **Jessica Jackey** and others. The whole idea was to make Christian organisations to work more effectively and efficiently [3]. What do the data submitted there tell?

Since 1990, the Americans who claim no religious affiliation have nearly doubled in 2006, which has now quadrupled in 2009 **(according to 2009 American religious identification Survey).**

The same survey reveals that two-thirds of Americans believe religion's influence is waning and that those who think religion can offer solutions to today's problems has come down to only 48%, a historic low.

Those who attended Sunday church have dwindled from 20.4% of population in 1990 to 17.5% in 2005 and are projected to be only 13-14% in 2020. The reasons quoted are related to consumer driven material-oriented enjoyment life-styles.

In spite of such a pathetic situation on the religious front and, instead of spending the church energy in orienting essentially the westerners back into the church fold, since many right thinking people over there still think it has a purpose, the Christian organisations have concentrated their whole attention and energy in converting the poor and the illiterate of the third world. Why is it so? There cannot be any other reason but to believe that there must be a clandestine objective behind the whole game-plan.

Their governments have withdrawn from the religious sphere and confined themselves to only the secular part of life to be run essentially on the basis of their constitutions with liberty, equality and fraternity as the guiding principles. They refrain from doing anything in religious affairs, even if the population is loosing interest in their churches and its activities. They have left it truly to individual choice. But they would still like the poor and the illiterate from the third world countries to be converted to Christianity to increase the western social influence, all over the world, through activities that they finance clandestinely. Perhaps they may be doing it since it may be of some help in increasing the western social influence along with some possible help in their intelligence activities around the globe.

To quote again from the above mentioned Leadership Summit [3], it is stated that the problem before the Christian churches is not that they are too religious but they are too rigid in their organisational set-up, with all its attendant problems of deterioration and decay. In stead of cultivating the moral foundation of their society at large, for making it more suitable as a democratic society, they are out to rule other societies, as Pope ruled in 5-15th century Europe, in the name of Jesus and nothing else. Once such a motive becomes the policy of an organised effort, it automatically leads to making societies just slaves under the influence of religious opium and nothing else, which is possible only amongst the poor and illiterate of the third world, where they are presently concentrating all their energies and spending all their finances.

This is how the organised Christian churches are playing havoc all over the third world countries. Should not therefore freedom loving and truly spiritual individuals understand the science of religious organisations as well? It will be commented upon further later after dealing with the other two major religions.

Most of the Christians, who are well educated and occupy reasonable positions in their societies, have turned themselves as secular like the average Europeans. They are not much interested in sectarian Christian activities. The newly converted in the third world mainly carry out such activities, using the finance of western world, channeled through mainly Pope and such other Christian organisations. They work under the garb of charitable organisations catering for education and health. It is neither charity not philanthropy; else they would not have bothered to concentrate on evangelism. That is also why their activities go on in remote forest areas amongst the so-called original tribes who are extremely poor and illiterate. Every attempt is made to maintain their identity as distinct from the main national body of population, in the name of religion. This helps the cunning pastors to organise them on the basis of religion for political bargaining. The basic aim is not to cultivate the ideals of Jesus in the form of love, service, compassion and brotherhood. The original approach has long been given up by them almost everywhere in the world. It is being used to consolidate mechanically the Christian population as a bargaining force in such democratic nations like India to the detriment of the nation at large. What havoc the Christian religious organisations are playing, particularly in the north-east provinces of

India, must now be clear. The so called democracy-loving western and essentially secular nations are financing such activities. How to explain this dichotomy?

Social Reconstruction

Original Christianity is essentially to teach love, compassion, service and fraternity to all. It did not elaborate any alternative to the then traditional Jewish social structure even in the times of Jesus. It does not suggest one even today. That is the reason why even today their emphasis, more outwardly, is on service in some or the other form. But this can lead to a more pious society and therefore organisationality. It is more a mode of worship of Lord Jesus for salvation. Unlike Islam, there was never and there is no Christian programme or philosophy of social reorganisation even today, based essentially on teachings in the form of Bible, besides devotional worship of Jesus Christ, through weekly church services and other service activities to the needy ones. This is essentially a religion like many religions in India, otherwise in its perception and operation.

Natural Limitations

It has already been mentioned earlier that acquiring power for one's own mental satisfaction is a natural trait. If power comes without much of efforts there is every chance that it may enter the head for its misuse. Christian religious organisation readily bestowed fair bit of power in the pastors. There may be some who used it solely for spread of Christianity. But it is likely that some others misused it for personal gains. It has been used by many for sexual abuse all along in their history and that continues even today. The same power was misused by a number of Popes almost over a millennium, using even military power when needed, to rule ruthlesslessly all over Europe in the period 5th to 15th century. That is the reason why its reaction erupted in the form of rational and scientific thinking almost all over Europe. The more is the religious monopoly the more are the chances of misuse of that power.

The same psychology is manifested, particularly in third world countries, to grab political power through religious organisations and under the garb of service.

Islam

Islam was the result of enlightenment received by ***Muhammad Paigambar*** in seventh century AD directly from the messenger of God, in Arabastan or Arabia. He was claimed to be in regular contact with **Gabriel**, the messenger of ***Allah***, the supreme power or God, who revealed, through Gabriel, how humans must behave ideally in this world. What Muhammed heard in his trance and told to his contemporaries afterwards, were later on, after his death, compiled as his teachings, in the form of what is now known as **Koran**, the holy book of Islam, like what is Bible for the Christians. The followers with belief in Allah as the only God, in the holy Koran as containing Allah's final revelations, through ***Allah's last Paigambar*** as Muhammed, are called Muslims. There will not be any more of any

Paigambar and therefore no other Koran thereafter. That is the reason why the Koran as a guide, is final for all the ages to come, for ideal human behaviour or for organising the society, as they believe. **Without the acceptance of these three conditions one can not be a Muslim**. The conditions are rigid and do not allow any deviation with time, no matter whatever else changes in this world with time.

It is faithfully believed that Allah's words, through Gabriel, were heard by Muhammed in the period 612 to 632 A.D. As Mohammed started getting Allah's commands he started preaching the same. Those were the days of worshipping God through varieties of images in Arabia since they were basically idolaters. What Mohammed started preaching was worship of formless and shapeless God by the name Allah and no one else and not in any other form of image? Hence his teachings were directly in conflict with the then prevailing mode of worship in Arabia. By that time even Christianity also had spread to some extent in Arabia. Muhammed's teachings were in conflict with Christianity as well. As it happened between the Jews and the followers of Jesus earlier, because of his non-traditional preaching, the same psychology perhaps created conflicts in Arabia between the pagans and Christians on the one hand and the followers of Muhammed on the other. It also resulted in blood-shed on either side. Muhammed had to flee from Mecca to Medina to save his own life from the onslaught of the pagans/Christians. In Medina he did not face that stiff resistance from such people. He was successful in converting many into his mode of worship and thereby he created an army of his own followers and then, with sufficient strength, invaded Mecca with full military might. He defeated those who had earlier defeated him and compelled him to flee, and then he established the kingdom of Muslims at Mecca. Except one all other idols there were destroyed. What remains is now known as **Kaaba** today. The governing or so to say the military power of the superior group was then available with him for enforcing the Muslim way of life as was revealed to him by Allah through Gabriel. The place of worship in Mecca, now famous as Kaaba, became their holy place, to the extent that it later became the centre, or the holiest of all places on earth, where every Muslim must go and visit, at least once in his lifetime. Initial order in Muslim society was established using military power. Ordinary folks cannot stand such onslaught. They succumb and just fall in line. This is how order was established in Muslim society right from the beginning using force and not persuasion.

After the death of Muhammed, many felt the necessity to have a leader to lead the Muslim society in all aspects of sociological, political and religious affairs. This gave rise to the institution of ***Caliph*** as their supreme leader. The differences on who should be the Caliph finally led to the evolution of ***Sunni*** and ***Shia*** sects amongst the Muslims. The entire life sketch of Muhammed with many details was later on compiled into what is called the ***Hadiths*** to guide the Muslim society in their day-to-day problems. Their sociological laws were codified in the form of ***Shariya-Law*** for effective implementation of Islamic order. The Shia and the Sunni have their different perceptions about it as well. These two books are the sole guide whenever or wherever there is a doubt to decide what is right or wrong for any Muslim, at any time thereafter. In that also, if there appears to be a conflict between guidance from the two, then Koran's version shall be taken as final. All this constituted fixed and unchangeable cultural patterns, beliefs, moral values and social norms for the Islamic society to sustain and grow. This was propagated as originating from Allah himself and hence eternal and, not exhibited by any one except by the Muslims. It reflected in their social expressions of morality, interrelationships, inter-personal communication as well as ethical acts. It led to build a kind of togetherness and common identity. To that extent it was definitely the advanced version of social order vis-à-vis the traditional one prevailing there. It therefore opposed ethical philosophy and rational human approach in anything. In short it killed the individuality or individual freedom as distinct from that as propagated by the Muslim holy books. This was very effective in organising the Muslim society. It is true even today.

Many feel that the verses in Koran before Muhammed fled Mecca preach Islam with tolerance to all others and their different faiths. Whereas those verses which are from the period after he fled to Medina, indicate more intolerance to other faiths. This seems to be rational because there are some verses which teach tolerance whereas some others preach intolerance while dealing with the non-Muslims, including interpretation of ***jihad.*** But this is beyond the scope of the present book. Many quote the acceptable one to defend Islam, whenever and wherever necessity arises. But that leaves confusion in the minds of others as to what is the correct perception of Islam at present.

Fact remains that even Muhammed had to use military power, to annihilate the unfaithful, to establish his religion, for whatever reasons. This perhaps paved the way to eliminate the unfaithful and establish the social order of Islam. Like Christianity, Islam also aims in converting the entire human race to the Islamic way of life. According to them there is no place for alternative faith in this world.

What is an ideal Muslim like? According to them the ideal Muslim is one who converts others into the Islamic faith. Such a crusader of Islam shall get a place in heaven where he will have all the pleasures and enjoyments of life. There is therefore no need to bother for pleasures on earth in the present life. There seems to be hardly any spirituality, as is commonly understood, in all this.

It only means the life on this earth is trivial as compared to that available in heaven. It also amounts to treating life on this earth as sacrificial for converting others into Islamic faith. Why so many Jihadis are seen to sacrifice themselves as human-bombs these days may now be clear. It may also be clear why the godfathers of Jihadis are readily able to train them into such suicidal acts, without any sympathy for even the innocents who get killed in their Jihadi terrorist acts. Herein lies the basic requirement for the formation of organisationality and regional organisations of Muslims in the form of ***us*** against the rest of the local population as ***they*** with superiority of us beyond any doubt. The use of organised military force is permissible in Islam to maintain the Islamic order. At the beginning of agricultural revolution the stone-age nomads tried to destroy the agricultural social order using brutal physical force to enforce their own order. It failed because they could not organise themselves on a larger scale. It is the same thing in principle enforcing the population as a whole to live in a prescribed way. But Islam was established by building sufficient organised strength to start with itself, in spite of its brutality.

Whenever there is any deviation the rebels are normally in small minority, at least to start with. If they revolt against the established practices it is permitted to be crushed with military might, as was done by the founder himself. No wonder the Jihadis use force to establish the Islamic order even in the present day world. If anywhere the existing government does not provide protection against the Islamic zealots then common individuals have no defense against the onslaught of vindictive, cruel and organised Islamic strength, for certain.

Their approach is such that it forbids critical thinking, moral reasoning, freedom of will, self-examination, introspection, creative imagination, aesthetic creation, humour, artistic expressions of the infinite for intellectual and emotional satisfaction as human beings. They consider it as complete philosophy for humans for all the time to come and hence there is no need to spend any more energy in seeking the truth by way of thinking and experimentation. Similarly they consider that the moral principles of non-Muslims are inferior to theirs' and hence worth decimation. The final truth has already been revealed in Koran. Hence it decimated even their traditional philosophical thinking in whatever form it existed before Muhammed. The masses were in reality reduced to almost robots to behave as per their brain programming, initially enforced under duress and later as their habit and superiority complex. Consequently the Islamic societies in general remained illiterate and under the influence of their mullah-moulavis. It proved to be a most useful situation to remain organised as if under the Newtonian-Cartesian bureaucratic influence.

The Shariya-law does not allow behaviourial norms based on individual conscience. Hence moral duties as prescribed in Shariya-law, suited to those times are considered as Islamic moral duties. Islam does not allow moral decision-making if it conflicts with that of Koran or Hadiths. It therefore forbids situational ethics. The Islamic system as a whole is the most effective tool in developing highly a bureaucratic organisational order, without even high hierarchical order. The system has well defined aim, lot of followers interested in the teachings and highly co-operative approach to spread Islam. This is almost ideal situation for organisations to flourish in Islam.

Personal Law

Unlike Christianity, Islam elaborates how individuals should lead their normal social life as an ideal Muslims, by following what is called the Shariya-Law which prescribes how societies and in that families and individuals should behave for a peaceful and contented life. Islamic societies are governed not by the modern day constitutions of nations but by this civil law. The advice given in Shariya originated with reference to the social conditions prevailing in Arabia at the time of Prophet that is seventh century AD. Enforcement of Shariya-Law required governmental might for its effective implementation. It therefore became the habit of Islam to develop Islamic social order using state-power. In a way Islam was propagated and enforced everywhere in the world through kings and their organised military-power and now by the Shariya-based constitution of various nations in modern times. The Jihad is just to establish this order. The terrorists have this single aim as can be seen from the present-day conditions in Pakistan. In modern times no Islamic society, contrary to their claims, is governed entirely by Shariya-Law anywhere in the world. Yet it is peculiar to note that the Jihadis aim to establish this order. Their vigorous pursuits are due to this commitment.

Spread

Those were the days of conquering other kingdoms through one's own superior military power and organising capability. The religious vigour, coupled with sacrificial motivation, proved to be highly a motivating force for such religio-military adventures. The kingdoms of the semi-nomadic and semi-agricultural kings, in western, central and north-central Asia did never have any specific organised religion of their own, except in the case of Persia or modern day Iran. They all readily succumbed to early Islamic order imposed through military power. Upon their conversion into Islamic states, they themselves started crusades for the spread of Islam through more organised armies with extreme vigour and cruelty. The crusades also aimed to loot and plunder the wealth and women wherever they went. Spread of Islam by such forces came in handy for their material lusts. They were more barbarians in such acts and Islam has been spread predominantly by such forces. Those who claim to know real Islam have never criticised these acts of their co-religionists. The history of India is full of such stories. In this endeavour they reached even up to Spain in the west and up to Indonesia in the east. Many of these kingdoms felt pride in declaring themselves as Islamic states and being administered through Shariya-Law, under the military threat. The dissenting voices were either forced to convert or were butchered. This is how the Parsis in Iran had to flee to save themselves. Now no Parsi is left in Iran. Finally the whole of middle-east, much of central Asia and Iran, Afghanistan were entirely converted to Islamic order.

High cultural order is no guarantee of safety and security. All these regions which succumbed to Islam were then agricultural societies organised on local levels only and had never before faced such organised invasions sustainingly on such a large scale. Even if the Islamic zealots were defeated initially they had to give-in to their sustained and persistent invasions on an ever increasing scale. The religious motivation of such organised barbaric forces proved to be much superior against the local strength. It cultivated a sort of victory spirit and superiority complex in consolidating the Islamic order wherever they went with their swords coupled with high sacrificial spirit.

There is however a paradox in how Islam was spread. On the one hand the followers were brain programmed to consider life on earth as sacrificial but on the other the military strength that was used to spread Islam was motivated by lust for wealth, power and above all women. That is the reason why some say that Islam was spread not by the real followers of Muhammed but by the barbarians under the guise of Islam. But the real ones do not express regret for such barbaric acts. Who is correct then?

They faced stiff resistance in India and were successful only in partly converting the population into followers of Islam. This lot finally created Pakistan as their Islamic state and nearly eliminated most of the non-Muslims from there. There is a tussle going on in

Pakistan between those who would like to enforce Shariya-Law and those who are opposed to it. In India Muslims have a different personal law based on Shariya-Law as different from the Hindu Code Bill meant for the majority Hindus, including the Sikhs, Buddhists and the Jains.

Much of the elite Muslim population then existing in India migrated to their dreamland as Pakistan, around the time of independence in 1947. Those who could not go were essentially the poor and illiterate amongst them. They are now mostly under the controls of the local mullah-moulavis, with nearby masjid as the organisational and controlling centre.

Binding Force

As Christianity proved to be a weak binding force amongst the European societies, similarly Islam did not prove to be a binding force between the west-Pakistanis and the Bengalis of the east. The Bengalis broke away from the west Pakistanis in 1971 to form a separate nation called Bangla Desh. It only proves that in the absence of anything else, the religious bond may manifest itself in safeguarding Islam. But when it comes to deeper cultural bonding Islam also does not prove as strong enough an overriding bond to keep the people together as one society. This is also the reason why there are many dissentions even in Islamic nations. Iran and Iraq, though adjoining and Islamic nations don't see eye to eye.

Islamic bonding is manifest only with reference to non-Muslims. This is also obvious since the different denominations in Islam often take each others blood, on just minor issues. The Christian bonding also manifests with reference to non-Christians only. The organisationality of all as Muslims is not very strong. That is why there are so many Muslim nations, even adjoining ones, run essentially on the basis of Shariya-Law, but distinctly based on ones own regional cultures and some feudal dominance. They do not mind fighting to decimate each other to save their own culture, civilization and feudal power. Fact remains that on the whole this worldly selfish interests dominate more than the other worldly interests even in Islamic societies. Yet a sizable section of Islamic societies everywhere are motivated to convert the non-Muslims to their fold at any cost, including own sacrifice. In fact the organisationality as shown earlier (Chapter 3) is more a result of common history rather than merely the conversion into some form of religion, more perhaps at the point of the sword. But with regional common history, culture and civilization, coupled with central governmental administrative power, religion helps in consolidating the organisationality, that's for certain. The illustrative example is of Jammu and Kashmir State, wherein the Muslims would like to develop Islamic state based on Kashmiriat which is nothing but the culture and civilization of Kashmir, claimed to be different from that of the rest of India.

Local Organisationality

There is no pan Islamic organisation, like the Roman Catholic Church with the Pope as its supreme commander and all levels of hierarchical structure, to look after the interests of Muslims all over the world. They have now evolved some kind of organisationality at the international level, by way of getting together occasionally, to work out some common strategies, in view of existing problems and possible threats to Islam at large. This is the reason why if anything as per their own perception is seen as against Islam's basic tenets, then they all raise their voice against it (for example publishing of Satanic Verses by Salman Rushdie or picture of their Prophet by some journalist in Holland sometime back). The individual Islamic society, based on their own national boundaries, have become too conscious of organising themselves on the basis of Islamic identity, but distinctly of their own, helped by the governmental unified administrative order. Again they have several sects and they do not see eye to eye readily, but when it comes to non-Muslims, they get united in their approach and action. The ***us and they*** model of organisation then comes into effect readily.

By far the Muslims are relatively poor and definitely illiterate by any world standards, except some population of the oil-rich nations. Those who are well off are often seen becoming more secular, observing Islam in a limited sense, just like the Christian westerners. But the poor and the illiterate ones are being used as a force for religious chauvinism by the mullahs, carrying out their activities from the places of worships, more or less unhindered under the garb of religious freedom [4]. Gathering of Muslims several times everyday, in the nearby masjid, offering prayers in an exemplary manner, helps the mullahs to propagate readily whatever is required to a sizable Muslim population. This is the easiest way of organising Muslim population in the form of local cells. No such thing is possible in any other religion or even societies. The disciplined way in which the Muslims attend the prayer in local masjid is certainly worthy of praise. But that only breeds the Jihadi spirit in such a gullible lot. The organised strength of Islam in such localised areas grows purely because of negligence of others, even from amongst themselves.

Every attempt is made to maintain their identity as distinct as possible and Islamic in character, based on the ***us and they*** syndrome. Hence wherever they are in minorities they try to keep their identity separate from the national mainstream under one or the other garb. This helps the mullahs to organise them on the basis of religion. Unlike the Christian attempts of only mechanical conversion, Islamic efforts are serious in cultivating their own ideals, based on Shariya-Law and Koran, albeit forcing the society to the thirteen hundred years old social customs.

Finance

Christianity's spread requires considerable financial support since their work is carried out through several service oriented projects. No such thing exists in Islam. Every Muslim is taught to contribute a certain fraction of his legitimate income for religious activities. This is used to sustain their mullah-moulavis and the mosque. Lately however liberal finance is available from the oil-rich Islamic nations of west-Asia for spreading Islam wherever possible.

Social Reconstruction

Unlike Christianity Islam is not only methodology of worship of Allah or a pattern of good social behaviour like the Christians, but it is a complete social structure of organising the Muslim society, based on tenets of Islam, as depicted in Koran, Hadiths and Shariya. This is the way the devote Muslims would like to reorganise their societies, on the basis of principles propounded in seventh century social environment, even in modern times without any hesitation. Even those Muslims who otherwise lead a secular lifestyle, as the general Europeans lead, would be happy to see the Shariya order established in the society around, because of their innate affinity for Islam deep in their heart. This is the reason why they are well organised as Muslims and behave as far as possible as Muslims. Their psyche is essentially Islamic in character.

Hinduism

Hinduism, Hindutva, Hindu culture, Hindu civilization and such terms are used to describe in some way the society and its lifestyle in the land known as Aryavarta, Hindusthan, Bharat and now India. The terms that correctly describe this society are Hindu Society, Hindu Culture and Hindu Dharma. There is nothing like Hinduism, since it smells as a codified way of life or religion. It indicates the social lifestyle, traditional value system and broader individual and collective life-aim to help sustain the universe and not any segment of population, even in India. It is therefore essentially a perception of life, on universal level, and is applicable to all human beings, no matter what part of the world they reside and how they would like to achieve salvation. It is all encompassing in its meaning.

One more term has been added to denote Hindus in juxtaposition to others, particularly in reference to Muslims and Christians. This was introduced by the revolutionary **V.D. Sawarkar** (Andaman fame), in the form of **Hindutva** [5], as different from Hindu Dharma. The problem with this is that it codifies the perception of Hindus and brings them at par with Islam and Christianity. Hindutva gives a definite and codified framework and therefore defines Hindus in the form of basically religion, which many would like now that way to identify them as distinct from Christians and Muslims. But it is quite likely that many Hindus may fall out of this framework, being not qualified. This has created a lot of confusion about Hindus, Hinduism and their lifestyles. The more correct term would be **Hindu-ness** than Hinduism to denote the qualities of this group of people, plurality being the chief one.

Who is a Hindu?

So far no body has been able to define Hindus as was readily possible in the case of followers of other religions to the satisfaction of all concerned. The original name of this group of people was just ***humanist*** (*Manava Dharma*). But the outsiders named them as Hindus, perverted from Sindhus, particularly to distinguish them from outsiders.

Freedom fighter **Lokmanya Bal Gangadhar Tilak** considered only those of *vedic traditions* as Hindus. The Buddhists, Jains and Sikhs were not considered by him as Hindus.

V.D. Sawarkar defined Hindus as those whose religious traditions originated in India. Hence it included, amongst the Hindufold, all those left out by Tilak. **Dr. Hedgewar, who started RSS for organising the Hindu society, did not bother to define Hindu**. All those, including the Christians, Parsis and the Muslims, who considered this land as their motherland were considered by him as Hindus. **For him Hindus have to be defined exactly as French are for France, English for England, Germans for Germany or Americans for America and so on.** Hence all those for Hindusthan are Hindus, indicating only cultural traditions and not by any mode of worship. Dr. Ambedkar while piloting the Hindu Code Bill in parliament as Law Minister defined indirectly the Hindus as was defined by Dr. Hedgewar. As has already been mentioned that Mahatma Gandhi had a very wide and all encompassing definition of Hindus, without putting it in words clearly. His devotional songs indicated his approach in this respect.

For an average person it creates lot of confusion because he is unable to understand the nuances between the various terms and definitions. Worshipping God as per one's own style is just a minor part of Hinduness and is left entirely to the individual's choice, if considered necessary.

One thing is very obvious that the various groups, now being identified on the basis of cast and sub-castes, language and region in India, are apparently very diverse, in their outwardly habits and living styles and yet have an innate unity from within. Those who see just the outwardly appearance mistake it as many nationalities, in India, and those who study it in depth realise the innate unity or organisationality of Indians amongst all the apparently different groups. Here the general term Hindu or Indian is used to denote the society living in India that is Bharat for the sake of clarity and simplicity in juxtaposition to the Muslims or the Christians. Even the Supreme Court of India has commented that the meaning of the term Hindu becomes apparent only against the context and not otherwise.

Philosophy

The Hindu philosophy was developed essentially by studying nature along with human beings in all its possible facets and depths, like the very nature, purpose and objective of human beings on earth. **It is basically the science of existence of human beings.** So many philosophers, over the entire length and breadth of this land and over a long period, contributed their own individual perception to evolve the Hindu or the Indian philosophy. This was evolved long ago and, perhaps 5-7000 years B.C., into a full fledged outlook of life. No single individual or any society elsewhere in the world has come even closer to these ideas, in their wider and deeper perception. No single individual can be attributed the credit for evolving this total perception. All such individual perceptions were taken into account in evolving the philosophical consensus of Hinduness. Similarly the exact date of its formulation can not be stated with accuracy like in the case of Christianity or Islam or some other religions in India.

Social Manifestation

The Indians did not stop at only developing the philosophical perception of the world because for an average man it does not mean anything, directly related to his own life. Hence those thinkers evolved the methodology for an average person to lead such a life so that each one may be able to understand the deeper underlying philosophical meaning. This led them to conclude the concept of atman or Brahma as discussed earlier (Chapter No.2) and the lifestyle in accordance with the overall philosophical base.

The four tier, increasingly expanding, individual identification with the reality, is the corner stone of Hinduness. The perception of *vyashti, samasthi, srusthi* and *permesthi* is already described before (Chapter 3). The fourfold objectives to be achieved by an individual, in the form of *dharma, artha, kama* and *moksha*, has also been described earlier. This was translated into actual life style in the form of four *ashramas* on the basis of division of required lifestyles as it varies with ones own age, as *brahamacharyashram, grihasthashram, vanprasthashram* and *sanyasashram*, has also been dealt with earlier. The simple social lifestyle in the form of self-contained villages, in that agricultural era, was based on division of labour in the form of four *Vernas* as *Brahman, Kshatriya, Vaishya* and *Shudra*. This simple division was essentially meant to suit the simple self-contained village lifestyle of early agricultural era. This was not supposed to be a permanent social order. It was a social order which had to be in tune with time and circumstances, in the form of ***Yug-Dharma*** (see details in next section) of the time. In fact it should have been continuously improved with changing times to suit the emerging needs, as is done in modern organisations to keep them going. But since no changes were made in that, in relation to increased division of work in the society, commensurate with changing times, the system degenerated into the obnoxious caste and sub-caste system, as is seen today, is besides the point. It must be scrapped lock, stock and barrel, for certain, without any delay, in the best interests of all. It did create the worst type of stratified society, that's for certain. But this is not the present point of discussion.

Dharma vs. Religion

When the English people came in contact with Indians and when they compared the lifestyles of Indians with that of theirs they called the Indian lifestyle as some kind of religion, since they did not know what true Dharma was meant in India. By equating Indian Dharma with religion, Indian socialstyle can not be understood. The meaning of ***dharmashala*** (free lodging for travellers), ***dharmic dispensary*** (free social health care), ***dharmic pan-poi*** (free water provision during summer), connotes the true meaning of Dharma in India. In the Indian parliament it is boldly depicted as ***dharma chakra pravartanaya,*** which does not have any religious connotation either. There is no religion involved in these phrases. The duties are variously described here as Dharma which is the sustaining force for social order. There is therefore no religion like Hindu, it is the name of a lifestyle or culture or civilization alone, which may include the mode of worship of some God, if one desires. It is purely a perception of reality and methodology to live happily as an individual, as a society and as humanity at large and at the same time.

The term Dharma means all those rules, regulation and duties of individuals and the society at large, which maintains balance between nature and the human being for his joyful sustenance and safety, individually and socially. The Dharma is therefore defined here as the force of sustenance of the society, neigh the entire universe, and includes all the attendant activities, individually and organisationally, in tune with time. That is the reason why the Indian society sustained all the ravages of times in its entire history and still kept going till to-date. This was made possible by evolving families, as a social unit, on very sound foundations. All the activities, including the economics-related ones, were family-centric in India through the ages. It did not require any professional organisational order higher than that for sustaining the society. However it could do wonders even on that basis.

It led to develop two basic characteristic concepts, one in the form of ***Yug-dharma*** and the other as the ***shasvat* or *eternal dharma*.** The eternal dharma means all those principles that are universally valid at all times, like the acceptance of universal consciousness in the form of Bramha, unity in diversity, worshipping of God or realisation of Brahma, through either the formless, shapeless spirit or in the form of some image of its incarnation, realisation of Moksha through all worldly activities guided by the limits of true Dharma and so on. The ***Yug-dharma*** was meant as the social order in tune with time. It goes on changing and must change with time.

Indian or Hindu philosophy and its practical manifestation in the evolution of societal order did lead into its organisation on a very sound footing and because of which only Hindu society has been immortal through ages, albeit by accepting whatever worth emulating that came its way and by transforming it to suit the Hindu lifestyle. It is therefore described like the river Ganga that remains Ganga in spite of so many other streams, including river Yamuna, joining it on its way. It is however also a fact that the Yug-dharma was not followed later to change the social structure to suit the requirements of time and hence the decadence. But with even that decadence the original spirit is still evident in the society, somewhere and sometimes.

Limitations of Religions

Christianity and Islam confined themselves to increasing their number mechanically all through the ages to develop organised society. They were contented with their followers worshipping their lord in the prescribed style. It could be done through rigid organised efforts only. But that proved to be a hindrance in the evolution of a socially sustainable order as per requirements of times. As every organised effort is essentially based on the ***us and they*** concept (as described in Chapter 3), with pride and superiority complex in ***'us'***, it is bound to be exclusive. This is indeed their character.

That is why those who believe in Christianity are called ***faithfuls*** whereas those who do not are called ***unfaithful*** *(or heathen or pagan)* and that it laid on the faithful to convert all the unfaithfuls into faithful. Similarly in Islam those who have opted for Islam are considered as belonging to ***dar-ul-Islam*** and those outside are considered as ***dar-ul-harab*** and it has been dictated as the bound duty of every one in ***dar-ul-Islam*** to convert those in ***dar-ul-harab*** into their fold. These conversion acts are considered as most superior acts of an individual and for that, one will be duly paid in return by way of his superior and enjoyable position in heaven. Use of every possible means for such conversion was accepted. No wonder they organised themselves very well to carry out this dictate. It was logical to use physical might for such a sacred act, when needed. Islam and Christianity are both exclusive in this sense and their protagonists have caused immense atrocities and huge amount of human bloodshed in the name of their religions in history and are causing the same even now. This in fact is the darkest spot in human history.

The Indian viewpoint is altogether different. The spiritual experience is to understand oneself and it is only the attitude while leading the normal life. It can be experienced throughout, without interruptions, even while working, eating, sleeping and doing all the daily routines. One has to learn only the art to achieve it. Since every individual is characteristically of one's own type, everyone has to be trained to develop his own attitude on individual basis alone. It cannot be done mechanically, and commonly for all, in an organised way. This is the reason why Hindus have not organised their society to cater to this need and instead they have developed the philosophy and the required flexible social order for attaining bliss on individual basis.

To help average individuals to realise the inaccessible part of the existence some religion with minimum organisational structure along with maximum possible scope for individuality, was also designed in India. But it was not made compulsory for all in the form of dictates, enforced through dictates of the priests. There is no rigidity on any front in Hindu society. They have only shown them the direction and motivated them to march on this path to the extent possible within the fourfold ideals of achievement based on *dharma, artha, kama and moksha*. Those who confine themselves at the level of physical pleasures, they are allowed that freedom to enjoy that as well. That is the reason why they have not dissected the human population on the basis of any faith. They believe that every human is essentially divine in himself and all that is needed is to remove the veil of ignorance, covering the individual's perception, to enable one to realise one's own universal character of oneness with the cosmos or the Brahma. The essence lies in conquering own-self rather than others or nature.

Wherever the Hindus went in the world they went with this message and tried to raise the spiritual standard of the local population, to the extent possible, rather than inflicting atrocities, conquering and looting them for own physical pleasures. Those who had wealth and/or power were never worshipped as heroes in India. Comparatively those who did not have wealth but were enlightened enough by conquering themselves, by way of their material needs, by renunciating all their wealth and lived as sanyasis, were the most revered ones. They proved to be the backbone of sustenance of society and its peaceful progress as a whole. The Indian society progressed not only to achieve the status of a ***golden-land*** but the status as ***spiritual world-guru*** as well. The family-centric lifestyle proved adequate for all this. It did not organise itself further on professional levels at all. But because of its long existence as a society, sustained on these lines and not taking note of the changing times *vis-à-vis* the evolution of other societies in the world, it had its own aberrations, by way of rigid caste structure, developed in due course of time.

As it happens with all man-made organisations, the Indian organisational structure also degenerated to a very loathsome level. But this does not discredit the fundamental approach, as being unique and capable of reorganising the society once again in the light of even the changed scenario.

Social Reconstruction

The Indian philosophy has essentially been evolved to understand the nature and role of human beings in the universe. Having understood the central theme to make human beings happy and happy all through one's own life, they evolved suitable social systems so that everybody could march on the path of seeking happiness or even bliss. Hence it is not just theoretical philosophy but is essentially an organised social structure, evolved for that purpose, through which the philosophy would manifest. It did suit the early agricultural era of those days and as a result a healthy society lived here for ages. But it lost its dynamism and got stuck in the rigidity of the path rather than focusing on the objective of attaining bliss. The problem with Hindu society is not that they are too philosophical but they have become too rigid in their old outdated structure, mistaking it to be eternal. The thinkers in Hindu society could not differentiate between *shashvat* and *Yug-dharma,* with time as was expected. Those who were entrusted to guide the masses on this path lost their creativity to make suitable changes in the system to suit the emerging social needs. **What was taught as simplified methodology for ordinary humans for achieving the ultimate truth, got degenerated with time into merely rituals and mechanicalness, dictated by the later generations of the so-called custodians, who turned out to be totally ignorant of this great philosophy.**

It went on degenerating into a system that lost completely any semblance with the original design. It has now come to the stage worth being discarded lock, stock and barrel. But the social customs and traditions have become so rigid that not many are able to transform it now to suit the modern industrial and informational technological world, keeping the essence intact. This is the hangover of that agricultural era, so ingrained in a vast majority of Hindus that it refuses to leave. As a result the society as a whole got subjugated for more than thousand years and so many Hindus succumbed and got converted into Islam and Christianity. The Hindu society is under besiege and almost at the brink of decimation. But the so-called custodians of the Hindu way of life are unable to appreciate the danger and continue only mechanically and rigidly to march on the illusory path of salvation, which will not be achieved this way anyway. This is the chief reason why the Hindu society has been unable to organize itself in tune with time.

The Hindu society got organised not on the basis of worship of some God but on the basis of developing right environment for everybody to march on the path of salvation, with enough individual freedom to choose one's own way.

Why do religions degenerate into such rigid and mechanical state? What is the way out? Is there a way out for resurrecting the old spirit of Upanishdic days for organising the Indian society?

The more the religions insist on the behavioural system, the more it will be mechanical and consequently more tightly organised. The more it insists on deliberate and definite indoctrination, the more they become rigid and try to fit all into straight jackets. The more some feel elitism by being a part of any religion, the more they become organisational zealots. As compared to Christianity and Islam the Hindu society had all these things at the minimum and hence it did not organise on religious lines.

References

1. Cogley, John, *Preface by Arnold Toynbee on Religion*, Encyclopedia Britanica, page 441.
2. Robins, Nick, *The Corporation that Changed the World*, Orient Longman, Hyderabad, (2006).
3. Hamel, Gary, *Blog – Organsed Religion's Management Problems,* (2009).
4. Frawley, David and Rajaram, navaratna,S., *Islam in Today's World - The Myth and the Truth,* Nimisha research Foundation Publication, Banglore, (2000).
5. Sawarkar, V.D., *Hindutva,* (Compiled by V.V. Kelkar), (Original in English) Nagpur (1923), Translated in Marathi by N.D. Sawarkar in 1926-27.

CHAPTER

16

DISCIPLE - SYNDROME

CHAPTER STRUCTURE

- Christian Perception
- Islamic Perception
- Indian Scenario
- Salvation Paths
- Origin of Hindu Sampradayas
- Fall-outs
- Devotion
- Progress

Christian Perception

In the case of Christianity the initiator Jesus did not want to start a new religion by replacing the earlier Judaism. All he tried was to teach love, compassion, service and such human qualities par-excellence, to make social life far better in the then existing religious chaos. But the followers changed the emphasis to building an organisation of the followers for cultivating these qualities. As a result it crystallised into a new organised religion with Jesus as its prophet, Bible as the holy guide and Church as the organising centre with the self proclaimed leadership of pastors who preached, in their own way, what Jesus wanted to convey, but that did undergo changes with time since then until today.

This is how the monopoly of pastors with Pope as their head was established, in deciphering what Christianity meant, should any controversy arise. Everybody had to simply obey them, with no alternative to go to. It is just human to misuse such absolute power. Through the power of church they inflicted plenty of atrocities even on the general public in Europe. All those who believed in religion and were afraid of God's curse had no alternative but to fall in line with the church as their disciples, willingly or unwillingly. Disorganised individuals could not stand the strength of the organised religious force with military strength. With the passage of time the original design of Jesus got extremely perverted. The pastors were able to brain programme the gullible masses as per their own religious design in evolving their organised strength which then could be, at times, used for their own personal whims. It has not improved in any way thereafter until today.

This is precisely the surplus power used by the so-called custodians of Christianity. Those enlightened ones who understood this surplus-power game got rid of it in many different ways. The so-called Protestants who criticised the monopoly of Pope finally developed their own monopoly over the breakaway group. There are still enough gullible followers left who meekly submit to the traditional religious monarchy, as they find it difficult to come out of the religious fold, lest god's curse befall them.

The rational and right thinking Christians are worried about the state of affairs of churches all over the world. They would like religion to play its role in moulding morality, cultivating value of freedom and such desirable values, in their followers, in tune with time and social democratic requirements. But in the absence of any such attempt, and insistence on the old dogmatic style of functioning, their appeal in their own land is continuously falling, particularly when the average public is getting more enlightened in such matters. Those who do not want to sever their relationship with the church, find themselves as helpless spectators before the pastor's rigid and age-old style of functioning. This type of rigidity in the organisation, insisting on being the sole custodian and interpreter of what Jesus originally meant, is the main obstacle in the progress of church. This is the opinion of many enlightened Christians around the world, including the ones quoted in previous Chapter No. 15 as the report of Leadership Summit, 2009, organised at Barrington, Illinois [1]. This is essentially the ***devotional syndrome*** to start with but gets transformed into ***disciple syndrome*** in due course of time. It is characterised by disciples following blindly the religious leader without question and rational enquiry. The problem is not that they are too religious but they are too organised in age-old rigid form which is not at all suitable to present day social conditions. God-fearing average masses are thus exploited for personal whims, in the name of religion. A way out is needed to maintain it in a more useful form for the society or to those who need it specifically. What's the way out is the big question?

Islamic Perception

In the case of Islam, the Prophet himself eliminated the pagans, in the beginning by peaceful conversion, but later on using military might, to establish the new social order under religious decree of Islam around Mecca. It was later extended to increasing area around. In this process of expansion many essentially barbarian societies got converted to Islam. It is these barbaric zealots who spread Islam more using barbaric methods, based on use of superior military power, atrocities and cruelty perhaps under the garb that they were following the same style adopted by the Prophet himself while establishing the Islamic order in his own days. Islam did not spread over much of the Asian and European regions by peaceful persuasion as it ought to have been.

With all that they could not build a world Islamic organisation on the style of Christianity. The local level organisations were supposed to be *masjid-centric* operating under the leadership of mullah-moulavis, as the most knowledgeable and capable person as social guide, and in case of dispute, for interpretation of Koran and Shariya, in final analysis of Islam, even through use of force, whenever needed. The society was in a way forced to Islamic order using state power. It did not allow any individual deviating from the dictates of the mullahs. If somebody dared, he was dealt with brute, organised and intimidating force.

In the agricultural era itself they established the social order such that all the Muslims became uncomplaining disciples of Islam via the mullahs. The brain programming of such poor and illiterate lot was so perfect that they behaved as per the dictates of the local mullah. Plenty of surplus power was used in establishing this order. Such gullible and God-fearing masses had no option but to fall in line against the organised power of the so-called custodians of their religion. It still continues in the less literate and poor masses.

As a result Islamic societies have been generally backward all over the world. The rest of the world is trying to cope up with impacts of industrial and information technology revolutions, through modernisation and education. The Islamic society however is still harping on to go back to the seventh century social order as an unalterable choice, since it was prescribed by the Prophet himself, as an eternal order. Even the enlightened ones and the right thinking Muslims, being in minority, find it difficult to change it because of the dominance of the mullah and maulavis and their grip over the masses. The poor, ignorant and gullible masses come in handy as an organised force for the mullahs to enforce the order, should any revolt occur anywhere to the extent of even disregarding the modern governmental administration. This is the ***disciple syndrome*** in Islam like the same in Christianity. Even the right thinking non-Muslims of the world would like them to change, in tune with time. But they also find themselves helpless in front of the rigid organised strength behind the Muslim religious leaders. The present situation in Pakistan illustrates it well.

This is how both Christianity and Islam brain programmed their own followers, into a religious force of Christians and Muslims respectively, with the dominance of ***us and they*** syndrome making everybody to be uncomplaining and unrepenting disciples of the respective faiths. Fact remains that in every religion the real spirit slowly dies down after the demise of its originator, may it be even stalwarts like Jesus or Muhammed, giving rise to unwanted rigidity and mechanicalness in the style of worship, finally resulting in ***disciple syndrome*** in its ultimate analysis. The main problem again is not that they are too religious but they become very rigidly organised and vast majority of gullible masses are with them in harping the age-old dictates, without understanding the modern day world.

The situation is somewhat similar and in someway different in India because of altogether different perception of human being and God and the mission of the human being on earth along with that of society at large.

Indian Scenario

In India at the beginning itself and much before anywhere else, the enlightened ones realised the true nature of man and nature, their interrelationship and the purpose of human existence on the earth. The perception was not the result of any individual's divine perception. It was the net result of perceptions of many such great thinkers and intellectuals amalgamated into one. It was not mere intellectual acrobatics either. Those thinkers were more concerned about the well being of all individuals, without exception and the society at large and hence translated their unified philosophy into social organisation such that everybody could march on the path of realisation of one's own true purpose, which is realisation of Brahma. No single individual could therefore become the central focus of such organised society at large. Instead of being individual-centric it became path-centric or philosophy-centric. It had to be based on rational thinking of many after mutual cross checking. Since the perception was not at all rigid in its implementation, masses could not be initially brain programmed into it mechanically. The thinkers had to appeal to the intellect of the masses, at least initially, for their acceptance. But those who were supposed to be the custodians of such freedom later brain programmed the masses much in the same way as was done in Islam and Christianity. Although force was never used for its spread, the gullible masses were brain programmed fairly perfectly to fall in line.

Salvation Paths

Taking into account the various perceptions over a long duration and the varied nature of human beings, three distinct paths were identified for salvation as the extract of their total and overall perceptions. These were the, ***gyan-marg,*** the path of knowledge, the ***karma-marg,*** the path of social activities and the ***bhakti-marg,*** the path of devotion. Every one was free to choose any one of these three as per his inherent nature and liking and proceed ahead. The three were not totally discreet with nothing to do with each other, but were only apparently differentiated for choosing any one of them as the dominant one. Routine lifestyle was such that after choosing any such dominant path the other two would also be followed to some extent anyway.

The *gyan-marg* was rather difficult, since it involved deep study, thinking and analysis and so on as it was more philosophical in its approach. The Upanishadic ***rishis*** represented this category. It was followed thereafter by many like Maharshi Vyasa or Patanjai or Adi Shankaracharya or the Acharya tradition of southern India and so on. In recent times it was followed by Ramadas Swami, Swami Vivekanand, Arbindo, Dayanand and the like. Its nearest equivalent in modern times, in general, would be the philosophers and natural scientists. It was not and it is still not everybody's grain. This is meant for only select intellectuals, who would then be the guides for the rest of the society in such abstract matters. One very overriding thing about this path was that whoever and at whatever time followed this path, it resulted in giving upto-date direction to the social reorganisation. This is the only reason why the culture uninterruptedly came down to the present time and in the form suited to the time.

The *karma-marg* requires persistent efforts, with hard work and dedication for some social cause. It requires a certain mind-set such that one does not bother about the fruits of his efforts, but simply continues in spite of success or failure. Only some comprehend it to be within their reach. It was adopted by Lord Rama, Lord Krishna, the Pandav brothers, Arya Chanakya and so on in earlier days and in recent times by Shivaji, some Peshvas, Guru Govind Singh and the like. In the twentieth century it was followed by Mahatma Gandhi, Pandit Nehru, Dr.Rajendra Prasad, Subhash Chandra Bose, Dr. Ambedkar, Dr. Hedgewar and Guruji Golwalkar and so on. The identifying thing about this path is that a continuous series of such people lived here from times immemorial to guide the society and saved it from disintegration and ultimate decimation like other cultures and civilizations.

For the common man both of these were rather difficult to follow. Hence for the common man, a more simple and easy to follow path, in the form of *bhakti-marg* had to be designed appropriately. Since it is not easy for the common man to realise the formless and shapeless Brahma in the form of *nirguna*-God, the *bhakti-marg* was invented to worship the almighty through some image, to realise the same more easily. This is known as *saguna* devotion. It was apparently devotion of some individual or some inanimate image in the form of God. The devotion style was not any specific one but it varied as per the individuals preaching the same. But through it the *nirguna*-God had to be realised, by persistent practice in due course of time. It therefore became readily acceptable to a vast majority. Many having realised God or at least claim to have got some glimpse of Him, preached the methodology of devotion in their own personal style to suit common folks from times immemorial till to-date. This was also translated into daily worship styles, in some form, at home as well. The idea is to make everyone conscious of the supreme spirit every moment and in every routine activity, accepting that it is only God who is acting through him or her. These styles were purely subjective in nature and as a result innumerable devotion styles were developed in the Hindufold since ages and many of them continue to be practiced even today.

This is how the salvation was visualised and practiced by the common folks in varied ways and forms in India.

Origin of Hindu Sampradayas

In the case of Hindus, it is a ***condition-precedent*** that the individual must first have the urge for realisation of God. It can not be forced on anybody by any one, howsoever a great enlightened soul may be available to preach. Such things are purely one's own sweet will and it depends on one's own overall personality. Unlike the Christians or the Muslims, the Hindus did not impose any religion on any one. They only made him aware of his mission, as a human being, on the earth. The question of organising Hindu society on the basis of religion therefore did not arise at all at any time and that nobody ever attempted to do so. Hindus devised, individual and social lifestyles, to suit every individual, as per one's own liking and perception so that he/she may ultimately realise God in due course of time and, if not in the present birth, in some other birth thereafter. They therefore preached spirituality in all its aspects in relation to individual and social happiness, with motivation to march on the right path, to the extent possible.

There have been many who either claimed themselves to or others thought that they have realised God in some or the other form, since times immemorial. In west Asia, Jesus and Muhammed Paigambar have been acclaimed by their followers, as exceptions, to have realised and that they were in contact with God during their lifetimes. But it has been a very routine matter in India, in that many claimed to have realised God. This is seen even today to hold good. It is a matter of ones belief and other's faith, after all, since it has not been and cannot be proved by any universally acceptable scientific manner as yet.

Many such enlightened ones in India, who even after realising God, did not bother to come in contact with common folks and, instead preferred to stay away in forests on their own, practicing their path for realisation of the supreme all the time. Sometimes by chance the common folks would get some glimpse of their enlightenment, as a rare event. But on getting some such information or hearing about them, many common folks would try to locate such people and insist on following one or the other and his path, whatever that be, for realisation of God. There have also been some who, having realised God in some form, as per their claim, would also like the common folks to realise God like themselves. In that case they would collect people and prescribe the details of the methodology to be followed by the otherwise ignorant folks, to march on the path of realisation of God likewise.

In the Hindu pantheon the description of the way of realising God, is not just a sermon or an intellectual lecture or a trick or some such thing to be told by the enlightened ones and to be followed by the followers thereafter purely mechanically. That is why there is no conversion programme in Hindu culture. In reality it involves the most difficult of the tasks of control of mind and for which one's own body has to be disciplined rigourously to begin with. In order to discipline the body, some discipline in the form of some rituals, yogas and exercises, perhaps apparently mechanical to look at, but to just make one more attuned, have to be strictly followed and practiced for a sufficiently long duration, in the form of leading very ascetic life, known as ***sadhana*** in the Indian parlance. Those interested and prepared to follow the rigours or the ascetics would accept the rituals with full faith and follow them with due diligence and earnestness. Some, having embarked on this path, as only enthusiastic beginners, may leave it in between, thinking that it was not their grain any more. In the *bhakti-marg* this was simplified to most minimum.

When it comes to rituals, no matter what religion is prescribing it, there is always some kind of mechanicalness in it. The Indian religions have a marked difference from others in that they do not confine to the mechanicalness only; they are supposed to venture on further as per some capable one's directions. When the body is toned up mechanically sufficiently, then only perhaps they are told the inner intricate secrets of control of mind and further sadhana for realisation of God. One has to kill his own ego and surrender himself to the guru completely to realise God, as is the belief in Indian parlance. This is in principle the devotional path for realisation of God in the Indian system, by following any one of the many alternative devotional systems. This is precisely the reason why the foremost belief of Hindus is

Ekam sat vipra bahuda vadanti

Meaning thereby that truth is one, learned men describe it variously. No one can be Hindu without this conviction.

All such devotional paths have had one common influence on the masses. Most of them became religious for some time of the day, carrying out some rituals in the hope of realisation of the supreme, usually at home itself. This finally evolved into a lifestyle of several such daily and periodic rituals, to be followed without questioning. It did brain programme the masses no doubt. But it was never organised into some kind of strength by those who guided these rituals. The social structure in the form of four Vernas however slowly led to establish the hegemony of the Brahmin class over the masses, in the form of a conduit for realisation of Brahma, through such mechanical rituals. Much of the society could be mechanically oriented in search of Brahma and as a consequence it could be cast into a fairly rigid organised form which later culminated into the obnoxious caste structure.

The process is not all that rigorous in Islam or in Christianity. Mere acceptance of Jesus or Muhammed as God and follow their teachings and the suggested simple lifestyles would do. Conversion of non-Muslims and non-Christians into their respective fold was and is even now considered more important than practicing an ascetic and honest lifestyle, with love, compassion and service as the basis and conducive to existing times, on individual level.

Religious organisation under Hindu life style is formed when people collect together around willing guru in the form of some enlightened soul, with the objective of salvation. Since every guru will have his own characteristic style of devotion and sadhana, the organisation shall take its characteristic shape accordingly. There are therefore innumerable such religions and their respective organisations in India. These are fairly loose as compared to the Christian or the Islamic organisations.

The basic essential three requirements as depicted in Chapter 7 for the formation of any organisation are thus fully met. The objective of salvation is genuinely accepted by all. They are prepared to work under the guidance of guru who may guide them individually or together. Whether this organisation will be a balanced one, so that it can function and progress well, shall depend on whether these requirements are in proper synergy or not. The situation in the case of religious organisation is shown in **Fig. 16.1.**

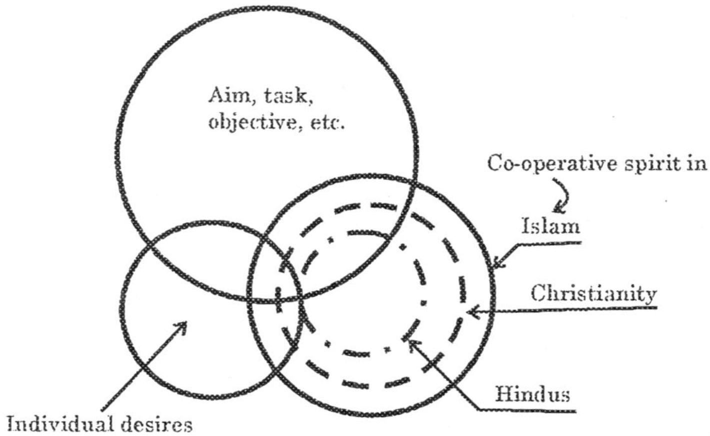

Fig. 16.1 : The three circle model of organisation as applicable to religious organisations, indicate here the minor role of mutual co-operation. The circle of co-operation in the case of Hindus is very small, that in the case of Christianity is bigger and that in the case of Islam is almost equal to that of the other two, making it a more balanced organisation.

Herein one circle shows the objective as realisation of God, that is unanimously agreed by one and all, and that all participants are very serious about it, at least to start with. The second circle shows the individual's selfish interest, in joining the group, to learn from the guru, in the form of agreement with the objective of realisation of God. The third circle of co-operation is not of much importance because the activities have more to do with the guru and not with fellow participants. It is therefore too small as mutual co-operation is not required to any appreciable extent in day-to-day functioning, except on some rare occasions, when the group as a whole would like to give a public programme of some kind.

In Islam and in Christianity the third circle is equally large because of mutual co-operation in religious activities, indicating that their organisation is much stronger than those of the Hindus. In that also the Islamic organisation is stronger than the Christian one. The organizational part is dominant because they are interested in conversion of others to their fold.

There have been and there are even today a large number of such religious organisations in India amongst the Hindus. To name a few the Gayatri Pariwar, the Pariwars of many saints like the Shankaracharya, Madhva and so on are typical examples of organisations in the Hindufold. There are many small ones even on local levels. All such religions in ultimate analysis have to programme their follower's brains onto the path of salvation, characteristic of their own. These are commonly referred to as ***sampradayas*** and not religions in the Hindu parlance.

The story of Gautam Buddha or Mahavir Jain or Guru Nanak is just similar in principle as far as the formation of their own group of followers is concerned. They have a very large following even now. Traditionally they have been sampradayas within the Hindufold only. In all these cases it eventually led to the formation of their own organisations known by their own names, as distinct from each other's.

The Hindus however still do not claim Hindu to be a religion in that sense at all. Unfortunately wherever somebody has to put his religion in writing, it is easier for Christians and Muslims to put it as their religions. Strictly speaking Hindus must put their sub-denominational religion under that column. But some how in juxtaposition to Christianity and Islam, Hindus put Hindu for such purposes and degrade their culture to religion, and basically the perception, erroneously and unknowingly.

The name Hindu signifies culture, civilization, life style and some shade of religion for those who practice it, all mixed into one. It is rather difficult to examine these in isolation without taking the others into account. There has been totally atheist amongst the Hindus as well, since faith in Brahma is not the pre-condition for being a Hindu. Maharshi Charvak typically represented this category, who believed that it is all materialism and nothing else in this world and hence enjoy the human existence, to the extent possible without any botheration of realisation of God or any such thing. Once the body is burnt nothing is left, was his *mantra*.

Fall-outs

Spirituality is not everybody's grain. It requires something more. But the devotional path, being simple, motivates a large number to join and embark on the path of realisation. In effect many disciples pick up merely the mechanical part of the process rather than the inner essential spirit which has something to do with the mind and ego. It also requires an equally competent guru to guide those interested seriously. If the guru falls short or if the disciples fall short, in either case the march gets affected adversely. It is rather difficult, since there are no criteria, to compare the religious organisations as to how much any one is effective as compared to the other. This in effect results in some peculiar characteristics in the participants. This is more pertinent to the present study because these are reflected in one's social behaviour.

Religion is supposed to develop human personality more conducive to the society at large. One is expected to become morally more strong, more selfless and open for social cause and, is prepared to sustain best possible and timely social order, rather than working for just self. In other words religion should train and cultivate individuals in the direction of better human culture and social life of the group, in tune with time. The history of devotional appeal in Islam and in Christianity does not stand anywhere on this test. It has created more blindness in their poor and illiterate followers and in general has prevented their social progress, as is understood in the present day world. They care two hoots for the rest of human race that is out of their fold is another serious anti-social matter worth probing.

The Christian uprising in the tribal belts of India bears testimony to this fact. On the whole they are more interested in influencing the politics than the morals of individuals. Some of them want to breakaway from Indian union into separate nation as Muslims have done in recent past purely on the basis of their religion.

The Muslims pleaded themselves as separate nation on religious basis and got away with Pakistan and openly proclaim to annex some more parts of India into Pakistan, in spite of the fact that they own the same culture and civilization as the Hindus. Those who are left in India always appear to plead their separate cultural identity, which in fact in their minds is only religious identity, under one or the other pretext. They seemed to be not interested in evolving a national society, except on the basis of Islam.

The Jihadi activities going on in increasing proportion in India and elsewhere bear testimony to the basic Islamic outlook. Many Muslims and even non-Muslims side-track this behaviour as aberration of few misguided and illiterate persons, emphasising that the Muslim society at large is very peace-loving and pious. Firstly these aberrated individuals are not an exceptional few; it is a sizable mass of organised lot with all possible financial and other resources at hand. Secondly many of them are well educated and well versed in modern-day technological world affairs. Thirdly anybody from any corner appears all of a sudden as a Jihadi without any specific reason legible to others. It all creates an impression that anyone may become Jihadi in the prevailing circumstances any time. There is no way to identify the possible culprits at all. Equally true is that there is no point in branding all Muslims as Jehadis. Even otherwise they certainly are not all Jehadis. By so branding they are unnecessarily being pushed to the unwanted side, must be borne in mind.

An average Muslim, who is prepared to come out on the street for any of their own sectarian cause, is totally silent on the killing of the innocents and destruction of properties under the Jihadi onslaughts. They are blindly bound by their religious leadership in the form of mullah-moulavis who appear not much worried about these atrocities, as it is seen merely as an extension of their historical approaches, right from the days of their Prophet. The disciples, being bound to them by constant brain programming, of their superiority and universality, convince themselves either in agreement or as just helpless. They have to obey their religious leadership and are not supposed to override them, as has been taught to them since the days of their Prophet, disregarding their own conscience.

It is true that in spite of such religious pressures some individuals, who are trained in modern life styles, do sincerely condemn the Jihadi activities occasionally. They are also scared about the possible physical onslaught on themselves, from the Jihadis, who any way, do not care about human lives.

On the whole the leaders of organised religions are always out to increase their number, even mere mechanically, to increase their strength, through their propaganda, more amongst the poor and the illiterates. Their poverty or illiteracy does not bother them. They are more interested in retaining their traditional Islamic character, instead. They have no value for human freedom. They have no value for women as equals in the modern society. The religious considerations, as depicted by the mullahs, remain overriding against any circumstances. This is how true devotees always behave as pawns in somebody else's hands and help consolidate the religious organisations

Devotion

Devotion in every religion is always blind, in its final analysis, and results in mental programming of human beings into organised human machines, described as animal farms by **George Orwell**. The appeal is always emotional since it does not stand rational scrutiny. It is related to the human limbic system and cortex has practically no role to play in devotion. The most precious gift of nature in the form of cortex to human beings is thus left unused in religion. The codified system in which one has to live in religion, converts humans into robots who can be readily organised and put into whatever action required, without bothering about one's own life. Consequently such a human machine or fanatic force can only be run by the leaders as per their sweet wills, as the *on-off* button rests with them.

In organised religions the followers are made to believe in a certain rigid framework that explains the origin and existence of an individual on the earth along with what shall befall him after death. Belief is nothing but a state, an internal representation that governs behaviour. These beliefs guide in unfolding to him the meaning and direction in life. These beliefs work as pre-arranged organised filters to one's own perceptions of everything in the world around. The brain simply does what it is told to do. These are thus commands to the brain to decipher what is occurring around in a pre-fixed way, to the extent that it defies understanding in any alternative way. There is always a place or situation where such beliefs do not replicate and yet religion teaches them as all pervading truths.

Anthony Robbins [2] therefore concludes that human history is history of beliefs and nothing else. The religious leaders have contributed the most in developing our beliefs, individually and collectively. To change the existing beliefs we have to start with our own beliefs, through our own understanding of the world around.

In Europe due to scientific developments they have been successful in overthrowing the brain programming of church and evolve scientific temper even in common citizens. Christianity has therefore no control on masses now in the western world. Being helpless in Europe or the western world, they are now trying it amongst the poor of Asia. But Muslims of Arabia or any such countries could not modernise to this extent yet except perhaps in some exceptional places like Turkey and in parts of some other countries.

The case in Indian religions or sampradayas is no different with respect to mechanicalness in the practice of worship or devotion. But there are some fundamental differences. Let's see what it is and how it operates.

Progress

The way the religious organisations are formed within the Hindufold is like in any other religion but the progress therein is quite different from the way the other two major religious organisations have progressed. People essentially collect around some enlightened individual, in whom they have faith that he would direct the others on the path of salvation and that they are prepared to follow him. So long as the enlightened soul is alive there is no problem with respect to guidance for individuals to march on the real path of individual salvation, without causing any harm in any way to others. The basic difference is that innumerable such choices are available in Hindu society and Hindu way of life, unlike the organised religions.

As the size of the denominational organisation increases it becomes imperative to have lower level guides to guide the lot at the initiation level with overall supervision by the guru. Many get well trained in the mechanical part of the process to act as the guides at the initiation. It is rather difficult to know as to how far an individual has progressed in controlling his mind and concentrating on realisation. Outwardly one who is mechanically up and devotes more time for sadhana appears to be better, but which may not be true.

After the demise of the original guru, either immediately thereafter or in due course of time after one or more gurus in succession, at some point of time, it is most likely that the organisation may not get an equally enlightened person as the guru. Even otherwise with the passage of time emphasis on mechanicalness goes on increasing until eventually even the later guru himself along with the followers, practice only the mechanical part of the process told by the original guru, since no one is any more enlightened, in real sense, to understand the deeper underlying meaning of the path of their salvation. The objective of salvation then gets transformed into path of routines, and even the routines get transformed into a blind alley with nothing to go on further. The leader is also transformed into spawns with no specific direction to go. The training then becomes a second, third or higher order hand with all originality lost once and for all.

This always happens in every religious organisation sooner or later after the demise of the original guru. It has happened in Christianity and in Islam as well. The original guru is enlightened with respect to the objective and hence is innovative enough for overcoming the obstacles in the path of salvation for all. It does not hold true with later gurus. Then it is only an organisation carrying out mechanical exercises with theoretical preaching as told originally without any personal experience of realisation of God. People however still continue to be part of the organisation with the hope of realisation of God. Sometimes one becomes a member of such organisation just because of family environment and practice right from childhood, without understanding any deeper meaning therein.

Under Indian conditions such sampradayas have even been reduced to what are called ***maths*** (equivalent of monasteries) which becomes just the sustenance source of living for those who have been historically living there, by generations. People do contribute monetarily, as in the past with faith, devotion and piousness and the show goes on at material level, without having anything to do with salvation. It cannot be said that this is absent in Islam or Christianity. The general atmosphere in Hindu society, being broadly spirituality oriented, is such that there is motivation to go on like this, with the hope that some day realisation may occur. Many times the so-called later leaders of such denominations show one face in the public and are quite different in reality. Some of the maths or monasteries become dens and centers of all sorts of unwanted activities going on there clandestinely and yet there will be blind followers of such maths as well. Such is the level of brain programming that is possible via religious teachings even in the Hindufold.

The redeeming features of religions in the Hindufold, unlike Islamic and Christian's organisations are that there is not one but many such alternative religions available in the Hindufold for any one to join. There is no competition amongst them. These do not prescribe any other social order, other than the common traditional one, broadly described as the Hindu social system at large, and as a result their brain programming is limited to the individuals rather than become a social phenomenon at large, particularly like the Muslims. Even if anyone does not join any specific sampradaya, the general lifestyle as a Hindu does contain some nature-tuned rituals that are enough for one's own practice for salvation. None of them long for increasing their number merely mechanically. They get impressed more by quality than by quantity. One can readily leave one and join the other religion, if impressed by the other, without anybody's any hindrance. Nobody is compelled to be a part of any religion. Everybody is free to practice the religion to the extent possible, without any compulsion. The ***Charwakians*** did not join any religion. Even today the ***anti-faith*** and ***anti-blind devotion (andhha shraddha nirmulan)*** groups do not join any religion and lead a normal life in Hindu society. The beauty of Hindu society is that there is scope for all such varieties without any quarrels and loss of peace in the society. One can practice pure spirituality on individual basis, with individual guru, if possible and if needed, without getting entangled in any religion, practicing it at home, as a purely private affair or a general lifestyle as a Hindu.

Although all religions have the same characteristics, irrespective of their names, those in the Hindu fold did not develop into a mighty and fanatic religious force because of the reasons mentioned above. Had it developed like that with only one specific religion for propagation, then there is every reason to believe that it would have swept the whole world and cast it into a monolithic long ago. The success of Buddhism in spreading itself almost all over south-east Asia, using even the state power as Ashoka did, indicates the possibility of success in this direction. This was however an exception. But Buddhism lost ground in India itself afterwards against the traditional tenets of plurality in Hinduism. That traditional influence is still there. But it is equally true that just because of this shortcoming, in the form of extreme religious liberalism, it fell easy prey to other non-tolerant and exclusive religions later, because of not understanding their real motive. Hindus took them as one like the many in their fold and that is where they made a blunder and are paying a heavy price for it in return.

It is natural, that even religious human beings may fall from their earlier high moral levels with time, on account of many reasons. Even if the leader in question so falls, his religious following still remains intact due to the devotional bond developed earlier. That is how this bond gets translated into various social organisations and they continue to operate even if the organisations go atrophy. Let us see what this bond is like?

References

1. Hamel, Gary, *Blog - Organised Religion's Management and Problems*, (2009).
2. Robbins, Anthony, *Unlimited Power,* Simon and Schuster, London (1986).

CHAPTER 17

HINDU SOCIAL SYNDROME

CHAPTER STRUCTURE

- Devotion Centralism
- Devotion-centric Society
- Sectarian Consolidation
- Social Organisational Psyche
- Basic Fault
- Commercial Organisations
- Conservatism
- Human Nature
- Way-out
- Modern-day Challenge

Devotion Centralism

As described earlier the devotional path of salvation amongst Hindus was developed for common folks. **Devotion essentially means negation of rationalism.** It is belief in someone accepted as divine and therefore beyond rationale. It has since been very commonly adopted in India by a vast majority of population, all through ages, as part of their overall social set-up. The secured, peaceful and prolonged agricultural era has been very helpful for such development. The family, in the form of dominant social structure, showing respect to elders and faithfully looking for their guidance in almost every affair was no less responsible in shaping the devotional character. The feudal set-up characteristic of prolonged agricultural era, contributed equally towards the development of devotional character of an average Hindu. The long and almost continuous tradition of ***saints, acharyas, sanyasis*** **and *gurus***, emphasising the devotional life pattern helped people to adopt this style for marching on the so-called path of salvation, generation after generation, till to date. Whatever was lacking in society, in this respect, was completed by the family environment generally attuned solely to salvation. In return the devotional path helped create people in the form of saints, gurus, acharyas and sanyasis. The required leadership to provide guidance, whenever needed was developed with mutual help and sustenance. It stabilised itself, and has been very dominant in shaping the psyche of average Indians through ages.

But this has had one great detrimental effect on the psyche of the average Hindus. They do not become devotional to a spiritual guru, for just transcendental achievement, but they tended and even in present times, tend to be devotional to the creative minority or leadership in almost every other field of social activities like social, political, charitable and so on. Rather than applying their own rational thinking about such activities they associate with these activities willingly as their devotees. **There is every reason to believe that the devotional nature has entered the genetic code of average Hindus**. It has thus become his second nature. The devotional character is characterised by the dominant use of the emotion-centric amygdala circuit of the limbic system, rather than using cortex, the characteristic of rational human beings.

The devotion-centralism is the entire basis for developing the Christian and the Islamic societies. Although the westerners, on the whole now, have rejected it in favour of scientific or rational thinking, it remains dominant in Islamic society, even amongst the so called western educated Muslims, to a large extent.

Devotion-centric Society

If there is a towering personality in any other activity of his liking, an average Hindu may join its leader and become its blind follower without going into the pros and cons of that activity as a whole, in depth. That is the reason why the political parties are run by individuals with unquestioning devotees as their workers. This is the reason why commercial activities of some such individuals are seen with mere devotion, disregarding their any other faults. This is how individual social workers of established credentials get plenty of blind following, without many efforts, and irrespective of their other faults. This is how an individual with no organisation, like Anna Hazare gets good impromptu following in organising his activities from place to place, in Maharashtra. In fact rather than assessing the activity, with all its right and wrongs, pros and cons, they go only after the personality blindly, thinking that the leader is going to guide them almost ideally and that thereby they are going to contribute for the welfare of the society and perhaps thereby attain salvation. This is highly subjective orientation of average Hindus. In such cases the leader's line is towed in toto and unquestioningly, even at times irrationally. But on the demise of such personality or his quitting the scene for one or the other reason, the followers get confused whether to continue or to desert the organisation. Such is the individual-devotion-centric social lifestyle of an average Indian even in present day India.

Can it be considered as a proof of the rule propounded by the historian Toynbee [1], with respect to the creative minority mechanically taking along the majority for united action in response to the challenge posed before the society, perhaps more dominantly in India than anywhere else?

The western style education, introduced by the Britishers in India, and essentially based on rationalism has not made much difference, in general, in this respect. The leader is considered to be the personification of ideals, while the followers consider themselves as mere mechanical pawns with no intellectual power of their own. This in a way reduces the human beings to mere machines and thereby the society leaving their immense creative power unused.

Sometimes people are seen to be very rational in some sphere of life, but at the same time very devotional in some other. Else how can you explain research workers in material sciences being very devout and perhaps blind followers of something, at home or in society elsewhere? How do the two co-exist? .Most of the Indians divide their life into two distinct compartments of spirituality and the material world. Perhaps they open or close any one like one opens or closes a drawer of an almirah, as and when required as described by Pawan Verma [2].

The only redeeming feature about such social psyche is that it has not become devotees of any one single individual any time in the long history in perpetuation. There have been many such individuals whom different groups followed as their devotees, at different times. No single one dominated as superior over the others any time, since they were never compared with each other. Each one was considered to be great and unique in his own ways and style. The choice was left to the individuals and as a result many had somewhat similar reputation and pretty good following. Such plurality helped to keep the issue of spirituality alive in discussion for the creative minority all through the ages. Therefore it did not lead to making the society a homogeneous society blindly following only one path like the Muslims or the Christians. It remained plural all through, which is also the strength of its own type.

The worst fallout of this is the sectarian social awareness, limited to their own devotee group at best. Notwithstanding lack of any dominant animosity amongst them, it did not lead to consolidation of the entire society at large, into a pan-Indian organisationality throughout the long history. That is also the reason why several kingdoms co-existed in India throughout the ages and not understanding the importance of, and perhaps hindering the emergence of, a central governing authority, in spite of scientific and technological developments, and attendant increased transport and communications, extending all over India and even on international level. The net result has been lack of any organised, co-ordinated and centralised single response to any challenge before the society, like the external invasions, which came in against the Indians at large and not against the isolated small kingdoms. As a result the invaders were dealt with, on the basis of generally the individual kingdoms, and not on the basis of India as a whole. They were successful if the individual king was superior to the invaders. But if the individual proved inferior and was defeated, it was not just the individual's defeat; it proved disastrous, even for the rest. **That is how the Indians were defeated on local levels to finally end up in India's slavery as a whole.** Hence in spite of being scientifically and technologically advanced, and consequently wealthy, the plunderers looted this land bit by bit over a long period, ultimately reducing it to a pauper nation [3]. This is also the reason why the Indian society, as a whole, never understood the implications of organised strength of invaders and the necessity of consolidating Indian organisationality for its rebuttal to ensure its own security and sustenance at large.

There are two glaring instances in the history of India, one from the Muslim and the other form the British invasion periods, cited here as mere illustrations. It is recorded in History that one Muslim *sardar* with hardly a hundred soldiers ran amok right from Delhi to Kolkata (then Calcutta), destroying property, molesting women, grabbing wealth without facing any joint resistance from the local Indians anywhere. Everywhere everybody, without exception, felt that he was alone and how he could resist such organised attack? Nobody could develop an organised resistance. What a contrast for the society which was cultivated to think in terms of ***samashti-bhava*** and which believed in advaita philosophy and eternal nature of soul.

Similarly in 1757 when the Nawab of Plassy in Bengal province was defeated, the triumphant British Governor General **Robert Clive,** marched through the city with only a hundred British soldiers, accompanied by a few hundreds of Indian mercenary soldiers. There was a huge crowd to watch this scene, as they had never seen any thing like the marching army of soldiers before. Had each one in the crowd hurled a stone at Clive, he would have run away to Britain, for not to return again any time thereafter [4]. But this did not happen and it paved the way for establishment of the British Empire in India in another just one hundred years only. It is the Indians who destroyed whatever little organisation it had built and hence it is the Indians who enslaved India. No wonder the Indians are treated merely as servants who would serve anybody for sustenance disregarding his national affiliation. In that they are too devout to the master as he was earlier to his spiritual guru. **Service to master is again in his genetic code**. It is the same disciple-syndrome.

This is to emphasise what has already been discussed earlier as the necessity of developing first the organisationality of the society as a **condition-precedent** for its eventual evolution as a nation. The homogeneous society formed by the dictates of Islam, in spite of its other shortcomings, proved to be superior, in their organised strength, to the traditional Indian society, notwithstanding its high philosophical ideals. Even the material-oriented western societies, being better organised, also proved superior in this respect, in their later invasions.

Sectarian Consolidation

The classical examples of deterioration of lofty devotional idealism into rigid sectarianism can be seen in Indian context readily. There are many such examples. Let us see some of them.

Guru Nanak Deo started his devotional path, by combining some good things of Islam and amalgamating them with the traditional devotional path of Hindus. He as usual got a fair bit of following and his teachings were later compiled as Guru Grantha Sahiba, for his followers to follow. After Guru Nanak Deo there were in all ten gurus who continued the devotional preaching in the form of a sampradaya within the broad Hindufold. In the time of, particularly Aurangzeb, even their gurus were executed for refusing to embrace Islam. The reaction was obviously very sharp. Until then they were not outwardly discernible from the rest of Hindu society in any way. For retaliating against the atrocities of Aurangzeb, **Guru Govind Singh,** the tenth guru raised an army to protect the Hindu society in general and their group in particular. The soldiers were asked to wear five things such as a **specific underwear, grow hair all over the body, a turban on the head, keep a dagger all the time and put a *kada*** (metal ring) **around the wrist**, so that they were discernible as soldier-cum-martyrs. Every Hindu family was expected to offer one young boy to become a disciple in the form of a soldier of Guru Govind Singh for this purpose. He thereby raised a huge army and fought successfully against the Muslim atrocities and saved Hindus from being converted to Islam, to a large extent. The same army later fought the Britishers also very well under the leadership of **Maharaja Ranjit Singh** in the early nineteenth century

The nomenclature of disciple in Indian language is ***Shishya*** (in Devanagari script) which got perverted into the term ***Sikh*** (***sha*** being replaced by ***kha***) in due course of time and because of their distinctly different outwardly appearance the group came to be known as ***Sikhs***. Until recently there used to be a Sikh member in many a Hindu families discernible with some of his five outwardly characteristics, such as turban, beard and so on. But slowly the original oneness of the group with the Hindu society at large faded and the group identified themselves as a separate group as distinct from the rest of the Hindu society, initially because of their outwardly appearance and later as an independent religion, because of their distinctly different mode of worship and their insistence on being recognised as a separate entity, as is natural perhaps for political mileage. Herd instinct had its way. Rather than being a part of larger whole as Hindu society they now prefer to be identified as separate religion with nothing to do with Hindus.

The inter-marriages of Sikhs in otherwise beardless Hindu families were a common practice until recently. It stopped thereafter. The system of Hindu families making one of their members a disciple or a Sikh also stopped in due course of time thereafter. Now it has been recognised as a separate religion for all practical purposes and is categorised as minority religion in India, in juxtaposition to even the Hindu. Where has the original aim and purpose gone? The later followers have conveniently transformed it into a rigid devotional organisation for self maintenance, forgetting the original larger objective. The disciples have in a way turned against their own ancestors. What kind of disciple-syndrome can it be called? This is the disciple-syndrome in larger social perspective.

The desire to have a separate identification is innate in humans and is based on ***us* vs. *they*** syndrome. Any slight possibility of crystallizing out as ***us*** on any basis, against the larger ***they***, acts as a trigger in this respect. It has also been seen even amongst the Christians and the Muslims as well in the form of their many denominations.

The other example is of *Lingayats*, a powerful, forward-looking and dominant caste amongst Hindus in Karnataka. Where and how did it originate? It is an interesting story. It has its origin in **Guru Basaweshwara,** a stalwart of his times and with statesmanlike qualities. He was very upset seeing the division of Hindu society on the basis of castes and sub-castes and wanted to unite the Hindu society into a mighty organised social force. Being enlightened, he decided to eliminate all such caste differences and make the Hindu society a homogeneous one. He worked out a very simple process for achieving his objective, so that it could be readily followed by one and all, without any hesitation. He declared that one who wears a ***Linga*** (symbol of God Shankara) on his chest and worships God Shankara, shall have declared himself as Hindu with no caste. Since the right thinking people were also worried about the state of affairs in Hindu society, like Basaweshwara, but not knowing what to do, picked up the idea of Basaweshwara, very rapidly and a large number became his followers or his devotees on this basis.

It continued even after his demise with equal zeal for some time. But slowly it converted itself into a group wearing linga and worshipping God- Shankara. Eventually they all forgot what Guru Basaweshawara had in mind and how he wanted to consolidate the disintegrated Hindu society by a very simple methodology, through wearing of the Linga. They became mere mechanical followers by way of wearing the Linga, as per the laid down practice, as a mark of devotion to Guru Basaweshwara. It paved the way to become ***us,*** as wearing ***Lingas,*** against the rest of the Hindu society as ***they***. The group slowly crystallized into a caste by itself, what is presently known as the **Lingayat** community in Karantaka. It perhaps stems from natural herd instinct fulfilling essentially the safety of the group. It takes conscious cultivation to be a part of a large organised whole and to feel happy and safe.

How a devotional practice gets transformed into a mechanical one, devoid of its original intent, is typically seen in both of these examples. This is also how the Hindu society got divided into various distinct groups over time. This is nothing but the disciple-syndrome in operation in larger social perspective.

Social Organisational Psyche

Where are the original Gandhian institutions of pre-independence days, in spite of being established directly or by the blessings of the great Mahatma? Originally they were meant to inculcate the spirit of self reliance, simple living, brotherhood, and so on leading into a pious society like the one in the days of Ramayana in the form of **Ramrajya**. That was the ideal placed before them by **M. Gandhi,** since it was readily understood by one and all. It was full of vigour while Gandhi was alive. But after his sudden demise and in spite of profuse governmental financial help, all these institutions have been reduced to mere skeletons and are now generally shown as museum pieces to visitors in and around Wardha, the ***Karmabhumi*** (place of work) of Gandhi.

They were started on the basis of devotion to Gandhian ideals, but perhaps more to Gandhi himself. Hence after him, within a very short duration, they were reduced to mere mechanical routines, in the form of outwardly Gandhian values, and now even that has been abandoned. It is astonishing to note that not even one could imbibe Gandhi's spirits, to continue the work on the same lines and recreating them to suit the changing times. The devotion to Gandhi did not allow the followers to change its format, as it was tantamount to disrespect to Gandhi himself. This is how devotion to and becoming a disciple of somebody turns the followers into mechanical units devoid of any relationship with changing times in India, as has been seen through ages. Sound financial support to all such organisations could not sustain them in their original spirit, since everybody had become devotee and not even few could become the creative minority required to keep it going, in right spirit. When common men join any such activity as a devotional act, without bothering about its intricacies and underlying meaning, it is bound to forget the underlying principles and get into the rut of its mechanicalness. Can it be called the same disciple-syndrome?

The same is the story of those who claim to be followers of **Samartha Ramdas Swami**, who was the chief architect in transforming the public opinion in favour of forming his own empire, in the form of Shivaji's kingdom, against the invincible Mughals, some three hundred years ago. He devised a novel organisational system wherein every village was organised to suit the requirements of time. There is every reason to believe that he did copy some good things from the organised Muslim society to consolidate the Hindu society. It was all overrun later by the Britishers in establishing their colony. But there is a group who still tries to propagate the same ideals in Ramdas's name even after three hundred years, when the social background has undergone a paradigm change. It is now reduced to a set of rigid mechanical rituals in token of propagating Swami's teachings in the present and totally different social environment. It is nothing but typically a disciple- syndrome.

The organisation which has grown to the stature of the biggest NGO in the world, the RSS, is no exception in this respect in its basic aspects. Its founder Dr. Hedgewar started what he called as *shakhas* (literally meaning branches) as a means of achieving his objective of a unified, system-integrated cultural and civilizational Hindu nation. He used to say that Hindu society was fortunate to have come in contact with an aggressor like the

Britishers. He wanted to inculcate many of their qualities and in particular their better organisational skills and group-nature, amongst the Hindus. That is how he was able to create innumerable great personalities including organisers, thinkers and philosophers through this system, who in turn were able to create eventually the present-day ***Sangha Pariwar.*** Howsoever one may dislike their ideology it still remains the fact that they have been able to build a mighty NGO. The original design was nothing but some physical and mental exercises carried out daily for an hour, without fail, but had a deeper invisible meaning of establishing the organisationality of pan-Indian or pan-national society at large, based on its traditional universal outlook. The emphasis however, in practice, and in due course of time, turned out to be more on making everybody a disciple rather than a thinker or a co-worker, in tune with the traditional Hindu psyche. It took the regimes of the founder and two more such chiefs before it started becoming rigidly mechanical in its practices.

The average participant in their branches now, being from the same traditional Hindu devotional mould, did not and still do not understand fully the true meaning and spirit of this routine, in spite of the founder's rigorous attempts, by way of their training in that direction. Those who understood carried the message further even after the demise of the founder. But the organisational routine went on becoming more and more rigid and unchanging, and out of tune with time, as it did not undergo much of a solid change, since its inception. It took two more such enlightened leaders(chiefs) before it gave way, as the rate of change in the social environment, in this long run, could not be matched by the changes from within fully, particularly with respect to the originally prescribed routines of *shakhas*.

The transformation of pure RSS into RSS-pariwar did help to carry the same spirit further in tune with time, because the pariwar organisations are more in tune with changing times. But the traditional routines, being retained the same, made the average participant in the RSS activities even more mechanical in participation, even in the outgrown sangha-pariwar. The original system has now almost reduced itself to a mechanical routine without any more creativity. Those attending the branches are mostly doing it as a matter or rituals rather than as an instrument of creation. The RSS would have faced the same fate as that of many such devotional systems but for the fact that diverse activities in diverse fields, needed to cater to the overall objective, in tune with time, were started with required creativity, and because of which only that the sangha-pariwar grew and still keeps going. Time is the best healer as well as killer, so goes the saying. The original ***shakha-system*** has been killed by the time-factor and transformed into a lifeless mechanical routine only. The deterioration in shakha-system has been more than that in the pariwar. It has resulted in the pariwar becoming stronger than the parent RSS. But even in the pariwar organisations routines are fast over-taking creativity and making them more rigid. It would be worth knowing any counter argument from *RSS* that it is not the disciple syndrome working underneath its *shakha-system?*

In 1925, when RSS was started, it was quite natural to collect people and carry out their parades in uniform and that it attracted many readily. The attraction for ordinary people to join RSS was mainly because no such thing was known to Indians before and that the strength of the Britishers was mistaken to be in the form of their marching soldiers, as that was their outwardly appearance. They never realised that the strength of Britishers was not essentially in the parading soldiers but in the intellect, creativity and the spirit of eternal glory of their society, manifested in their organised form, military being only one of its outwardly manifestation (recollect what **Churchill** said and quoted earlier on page 33). This was understood by Dr Hedgewar very well and hence he started to organise the society, using not just the military format but also in cultivating the same spirit in the form of Hindu cultural nationalism. Many intellectual and creative people, understanding the same, joined him and this creative minority alone afterwards led RSS to grow to the extent of today's mighty sangha-Pariwar

But in their initial zeal to increase their outwardly strength, and not knowing who belonged to what category, they allowed many ordinary people, with basically the same traditional devotional disciple-syndrome mentally in tact, to join the organisation. Obviously this number was far larger than the creative and intelligent ones and always outnumbered the creative minority.

The times have changed since then beyond imagination. The military format of exercises is no more a point of attraction to even ordinary majoritarian Hindus, much less to intelligentsia, in independent India. But RSS refuses to change its course as it has become second nature to the followers, as it normally happens in any organisation with time. Many of the followers are far elder and experienced in the routines, and still believe that it is the only path of salvation for the nation of their perception, as was given to understand in their own lives. It has become second nature to them. After eighty-five years of its existence and having seen few leaders one after the other, no contemporary RSS controller/leader is now in a position to override the followers, to change its style of functioning, as it happens in almost every such organisation. The problem is not that the RSS is too organised in the form of sangha-pariwar, but as RSS, it has become too rigid in its approach in spite of changed times. The situation is too analogous to Christian churches in the enlightened western societies. Their old rigid format does not attract people any more and as a result its strength is continuously falling. The right thinking sympathisers of RSS would like it to flourish and contribute good many workers for national reconstruction in the form of the sangha-pariwar. But like the western Christian churches it has become too rigid to change with time.

It may not be out of place to understand why the almost ideal society developed in the simple agricultural Upanishadic period did not change with changed times and degenerated into a hierarchical and mechanically ritualistic present-day society, loosing its basic perception of ***samashti-bhava*** almost beyond repair. The degeneration has been almost complete to the extent that a majority now feels that all those high ideals are also worth throwing, lock, stock and barrel. This is nothing but disciple-syndrome. Nothing on social front remains good or best with time. It has a tendency to get rigid and therefore must change with time to suit the changed social scenario.

The story is no different with the so-called Marxist or socialist. They have become too rigid in their approach to adapt to the changing times and be the carrier of progress. In spite of total failures they refuse to accept that they have to change to achieve their objectives. This is also the same disciple-syndrome in operation, without them agreeing to it.

The story is the same with respect to many activities in the field of charity, social upliftment, politics, academics and almost everything else in India. In politics Hindu Maha Sabha exhibits similar fossilised and calcified behaviour limited to few devoute individuals here and there, posing as true disciples of the founder of the Hindu Maha Sabha, **Vir Sawarkar,** but not doing anything of his imagination any more either, in the light of changed times in post independent bifurcated India.

It should be understood, once and for all, that the basic organisational models, because they are not eternal, would not last for ever, even if it had proved successful initially. While keeping the core ideologies or mission intact the models must change with time in spite of their earlier successes. In reality the rate of success always drops after some time in any organisation, unless changes are made to suit the changed times. The leader should be able to discern it from even the success that is coming and alarm bells for suitable changes should ring in his perception. Appropriate changes are a must for every organisation and all along. That will only enable them to grow from good to great and not merely continue in same old rote style. Roteness is a sure path of decay. Nature has been continuously evolving to suit the current times. This is the quality of nature. So organisations must also evolve, through appropriate changes, to suit the emerging times.

Basic Fault

The Hindu society basically has been evolved with some peculiar characteristics. All through the ages, the lifestyles were extremely family-centric with no exposure to any higher level corporate social world. It did not have even corporate religious exposure as the Christians or the Muslims had, because of its very liberal outlook with reference to salvation. The Hindu way for salvation was highly individual-centric and diverse in its approach. In the field of economics, all the production, distribution and sales and related activities were either purely family-centric or were diffused social-centric. The religious congregations at various places all over India attracted huge populations in natural course, for some religious purpose, which incidentally acted as the market for sale of goods, without any advertisement, to help the overall economics of the society, but without any more organisational or corporate requirements of higher level [5]

Being agricultural society for a very prolonged duration, it helped consolidate the family. The individual behaviour was conditioned to accept the advice of elders, being more experienced, whenever necessity arose. There was not much of perceptible change in one's own life in agricultural society and challenges faced any time were more or less similar in character as before. In such a situation the effective response to the challenges, based on experience of elders, proved adequate. But as the pace of social change increased with time, as a result of more and more division of work, and more so particularly with industrialisation in recent times, the challenges appeared to be quite new and had to be responded with more creativity and in a far better organised way only. But the absence of exposure to larger corporate thinking and working proved as the greatest of the obstacles on this path.

The social structure was such that the ***sanyasis***, who had renunciated everything material in life, had allotted unto themselves the duty of modernising and guiding the society than anybody else, purely because of their selfless moral character than any other quality. The selflessness was considered to be the key characteristic for reforms and progress of the society. They were known for their knowledge of the path of salvation, if at all. But they were also presumed to be equally capable of knowing solutions of the material-worldly problems as well, just because of devotion to them. How can basically the other worldly people understand the material worldly challenges? It was based on the presumption that a selfless and other worldly person is more capable of guiding the material-world better than even the intelligent and creative ones interested in only the material world. It unnecessarily stifled creativity in the material world, which is the backbone for responding to arising situations. The social structure therefore became more ***sanyasi-centric*** rather than ***intellect-centric***. Such conditioning, being more prone to individual whims, is more prone to rigidity as well.

The excessive emphasis on salvation in relation to material welfare, and therefore on rituals thereat, made common man less interested in worldly affairs and attendant hard work required thereat. Entire society became ritual-centric in its daily routine lives. The creative minority failed to differentiate between importance of rituals and the spirit of social order with attendant material welfare.

An example can be cited as typical of that state of affairs. At one time the so-called intellectuals in the south were more worried about whether the sacred thread ceremony of **Saint Dynaneshwar**, son of supposed to be an earlier sanyasi, was tenable as per the scripture or not, while in the north, the Mughal emperors were inflicting all sorts of atrocities on Hindus and were converting them to their fold. The so-called creative minority of south was blind folded to this reality.

The society as a whole disregarded the role of governance in maintenance of the social order and as a result lost interest in who rules and governs the society. All this proved to be antithesis of consolidation of entire society into an organised and harmonious social system, on pan-Indian basis, with its increasing size. The impact of invaders, their intention of destroying even the lifestyles, could not be understood by the society in its proper perspective of larger corporate social interests. This is how the Indian psyche got evolved over time in at least the recent history. The intellectuals or the creative minority in Indian society totally failed on this front and the society had to undergo slavery for nearly twelve hundred years. All this was just the result of excessive emphasis on salvation and consequently ritualistic and rigid social lifestyles, under the illusion of salvation, rather than on giving creative response to the emerging challenges before the society for making it materially strong. Unfortunately even after all the miseries in the long history; the basic ailment is yet to be understood, leave alone its redressal, to transform the society to face the challenges of the present day world. **The problem is not mere rituals but too much of them with utter disregard for the larger organisational order of the society required in the present.** This is nothing but the devotional syndrome.

Commercial Organisations

The above mentioned observations are not only true with respect to the religious, social or political organisations alone. It seems to hold true even in commercial organisations or NPOs as well. Even NPOs have to have some daily routines which have to be at least in part as mechanical or ritualistic. But some amount of creativity also must accompany them to keep the organisations going. If the routines dominate so much that the creativity is practically stifled then the system slowly gets used to the routine more than anything new or creative.

The net result is that the original mission of the organisation goes on getting blurred and may even get substituted by mere strategies. Slowly the strategies are spelt out more and more in detail such that it gets codified into policies. If it is continued unabatedly then they generate spawns of practices, rigid enough and sacrosanct enough such that they become second nature or habits of the work force. The work force almost gets transformed into disciples of the manager rather than an intellectual and creative lot as his co-workers. This is the path of dooms-day for a commercial organisation, for certain. This is also the way how the social order was codified and finally calcified in India over the time. As a result the individuals become ritual-centric loosing their creativity altogether.

The possible dangers and danger zones in running an organisation over time must be understood by the promotors of the organisation or the controller, leader and managers very well. If the possible dangers are to be avoided. then from almost day one the planning, organising, staffing, leading and controlling of the organisation has to be carried out, taking into account all these possible future lapses, atrophies, compulsions and what not that may befall any time later.

To keep organisations going, the rate of change of external environment and the rate of change of psychology of work force with time, which mostly cannot be prevented, has to be matched with matching rate of change of internal methodology of working. **Any moment it should appear as if, that the organisation has just started to meet the specific social requirements with required planning, organising, staffing, leading and controlling.** Status-quo should be seen as the beginning of cancerous growth of organisations. It generates organisational inertia which deccelerates the progress. Organisations will have to be made more adaptable to any and every situations through appropriate changes. That should be the second nature of all in the organisation.

It must be understood that the organisations either progress or decay, they do not stay still, because they have to compete with others, in this dynamic world. Everything in relation to the individual and the society is changing and changing so fast that, unless updated, by whatever way it is possible, it is bound to go obsolete. The organisations of any form are no exceptions, to this general rule. The mantra is to change and change with time as per the need, as the nature has always undergone changes to adapt itself, to any diverse condition not seen before.

Although it is the common story of societies and organisations all over the world in all spheres of life, it is fundamentally the result of ***status-quoists*** religious influence on individuals and groups that gets manifested in this way in most of the society's world over. The basic religious attitude cultivated through dedication to ritualistic lifestyle, and insulated from any other thought, is sure path to such out-datedness in other spheres of life. In this context the religious leaders, through their organised strength and almost untenable belief-systems, are doing great disservice to the humanity by withholding the progress, of individuals and of societies, that otherwise would have taken place. Problems before humanity can be solved by facing them squarely rather than by turning a blind eye to them, under some untenable ideologies.

Every organised effort has some kind of mechanical routines and some kind of ethereal thinking in the form of mental and intellectual activities. Any extra emphasis on routines is bound to obscure the ethereal part and tend to make the organisation a rigid one. On the contrary any disregard to routines may result in confusion about the things to be done by the common workers. A right balance is therefore required to keep the organisation going and progressing. This is easily said than done and that is the real problem. It is fundamentally understanding the disciple-syndrome and acting against it.

Conservatism

The influence of prolonged agricultural era and the disciple-syndrome has resulted in making the Indian society extremely conservative and reluctant to any change, thinking that ***old is all gold***. This nature was further substantiated by the adoption of socialism as the developmental model after independence, wherein the social development, for enjoying the fruits of industrialisation, was supposed to be carried out by the initiative of the state or the government and not on the basis of the individual's creativity and innovativeness as in the west, in open, free and competitive spirit cultivated in that society. As a result, under the socialistic pattern, innumerable organisations were evolved in various fields to cater to this need in the form of closed systems.

Industrialisation does not mean mere enjoyment of industrial products in making one's own life more trouble-free. It's an open system and requires adopting an attitude involving creativity in actions, innovativeness in dealing with changes, risk taking to face competition, vigour and dynamism to stand all possible odds, hard work for its returns in terms of physical enjoyment and so on. None of these qualities could be cultivated in Indians to face industrialism in adopting socialism as a model of progress. Monthly income was guaranteed against no commitment; leave aside hard work and facing competition. The result was ineffectiveness and inefficiency on all fronts in social and individual life, resulting in economic crisis of unprecedented extent at the national level. It had to be solved ultimately by liberalising and globalising the economy, which now requires that individuals cultivate all the above mentioned qualities *per force.*

But those organisations which were started under socialistic development still continue, more so at the governmental level. Political expediency does not allow them to be disbanded and liberalised for open competition. Those involved are scared to face the competition in open socio-economy. One must learn that life is full of changes and challenges to be faced, if progress is to be made. Status-quo is human nature in the form of path of least resistance. But it is detrimental to human progress, for certain. In a way better organised society in tune with time and reality is what is needed.

Human Nature

As seen religion provides the most fertile ground for cultivation of disciple-syndrome. What has been described above is what is likely to happen in most organisations and not only in religious ones. It is true that in some societies a very large number live under substantial religious influence, where the disciple-syndrome originates and operates readily and becomes second nature of individuals, to be reflected elsewhere as well, as is the case in India. It is far more influential in the Islamic society than any other. The same is true with Christian society, but they have been able to come out of this syndrome at least in the west by confining religion to a very small corner of an individual's life and totally rejecting it on social and administrative level, in its reorganisation, as a result of scientific and technological developments. The problems are far more serious in Islamic society than anywhere else. How these are withholding their progress has been aptly described by **Thomas Friedman** in his best seller 'Hot, Flat and crowded' [6]. Since they do not want to modernise their society and since they would like to revive the original Shariya structure, they do not face the problems arising out of devotional disciple-syndrome. They are happy to continue in that order. The dilemma and tensions between the traditional Islamic society and the modernising pressure is evident in Turkey, which would like to modernise itself as in the west.

But the experience of many a modern organisations in the west, where the religious influence is almost negligible, also suggests growing rigidity in attitudes, resembling disciple-syndrome, with time. If the individuals are under the religious syndrome, it may get to that stage more readily and surely. It could in fact basically be a human psychological problem of lack of persistent industry and creative work. It turns out to be essentially out of lack of persistent motivation for innovative work.

Way-out

As seen earlier persistent motivation can come only from objectives worth living and striving for. Culturally the society must therefore develop an atmosphere of welcoming creativity in all walks of life, rather than sticking to some traditional path, even if it had been found to be excellent before. The same holds true for organisation as well.

The best way to adopt change is to first adopt it by way of change in the leadership to suit the requirements. It may appear as if it resembles the dictatorial regimes, which are changed by changing the leadership alone. It could be a death-bed experience. Alternatively the leaders must first chip off the calcified layers of routines and venture into the realm of creativity by rediscovering their own mission afresh in the changed circumstances. In fact passion for greatness is what is required. It can only be created with dedication to the core ideology, if any. It only means that you should go on asking the question everyday, what ails your organisation or why it is not progressing as per expectations. What can be done to get rid of the ailments and meet increasing expectations? If this is followed in every organisation the society as a whole shall automatically be created anew with time and every time.

It is in our earnestness to see that the religious syndrome should not get replicated elsewhere for the good of all and the society at large. One cannot have a split personality wherein the behaviour at one place has nothing to do with the behaviour at the other. When the disciple-syndrome is in operation in the religious reference, it is bound to reflect in other social systems as well as for that group. As a result the society loses on many accounts, but the chief concern being that the society has to pay for this loss, directly or indirectly. The progress gets unnecessarily adversely affected, affecting the society adversely at large. Only the rate of calcification may vary from organisation to organisation. What is the way out?

There is neither a standard nor a permanent solution available for avoiding the rigidity and calcification in any organisation as it is related to human nature. These have to be invented afresh every time. Let us not wish to search for ideal leadership because being human they also have the same inherent limitations. Let more people doubt the leader rationally and let the leader satisfy all of them so that he can establish his leadership properly. People are often so afraid of failures, and the system may also make him so, such that they do not dare to try anything and in such a situation how could a proper solution be found out Organisational culture of accepting even failures as a first step in the direction of progress needs wider acceptability, specifically in this context.

On the social front, before setting up any organisation care should be taken not to make it individual-centric but rather to make it purely objective oriented. The only organisation that has followed this practice rigorously is RSS. It has kept the saffron flag as its guru and not any individual, not even the founder. They think and talk of glory to motherland or nation and not of any individual, howsoever great he may be. Only an enlightened leader can think in this way and act accordingly. It may be partly achievable through lectures, write-ups, seminar and the like. But it is most effectively done by presenting almost ideal or near ideal role-models. Whoever are able to do it, their organisations, to that extent, are freer from easy calcification.

It is true that organisations flourish through effective leaderships. But it is also true that the leadership ego itself later becomes so strong that it becomes the very *reason d'etre'* for it getting rigid. It is a natural phenomenon and controllers have to be aware of it. It finally becomes a matter of trial and error to make the organisation work and is a matter of subjective satisfaction alone .The best possible way out therefore is to cultivate the social direction of progress in which individuals have to expand their identification from individuality to society to nature to the cosmos, as originally propounded by the Hindus in their ideal format, for the good of all in perpetuation.

Modern-day Challenge

The world has come so close together that human rights often override any other considerations. The United Nations Organisations is keen to establish harmony world-over amongst different religious groups and avoid bloodshed, in the name of religion at all costs. There have been attempts to understand each other's religion with open mind so that organisationality on the basis of human race shall get the required boost. The exclusiveness of Islam in the form of ***Dar-ul-Islam*** and ***Dar-ul-Harab*** and of Christianity in the form of ***faithfuls*** and the ***heathens*** is proving to be greatest of the obstacles. Their exhaustive efforts in trying to convert the rest into their own fold is causing unnecessary tensions every where.

Arnold Toynbee had earlier suggested the way out of this historical need. He had then emphasised [7] that, **"The spirit of mutual goodwill, esteem and veritable love that is striking today amongst the adherents of all religions is the traditional spirit of the religions of Indian family. This is one of India's gifts to the world. No gift could be greater and none is more timely in the atomic age."**

References

1. Toynbee, Arnold, *A study of History*, Abridged Edition, Oxford, (1972).
2. Verma, Pawan, *Being Indian*, penguin (India), (2005).
3. Robins, Nick, *The Corporation That Changed the World*, Orient Longman, (2006).
4. Shourie, A., *Individuals, Institutions and Processes*, Viking (1990).
5. Tupkary R.H., *Marathi Book on Organisation,* Mangesh Prakashan, Nagpur (2008).
6. Thomas L., Friedman, Hot, Flat and Crowded, Penguin (Allen Lane), Delhi, (2008).
7. Cogley, John, *Preface by Arnold Toynbee on Religion*, Encyclopedia Britanica, Micropaedia, page 441.

CHAPTER 18

NEO-RELIGIOUS SYNDROME

CHAPTER STRUCTURE

- Marxism
- Socialism
- Fascism
- Nazism
- Social systems
- Industrial Fall-out
- Rate of Reorganisation

Religion is characterized by few things like, belief in some enlightened person who is presumed to be gifted and to have realised God in some form, full faith in him to the extent that he/she can successfully lead others into the inaccessible world, strict adherence to the prescribed ritualistic methodology for salvation, belief in the path being the only right path for one's salvation and such other things. People are earnestly desirous of seeking salvation and thereby fulfill their desire of knowing the world completely and therefore are prepared to fall in line in the prescribed discipline of religion, by becoming its followers. The followers have to accept it unquestioningly to remain in any religious organisation. After the demise of the originator the followers are made to believe that the originator has once and for all the time revealed the secret of realisation and that path cannot be changed thereafter, by any one, under any circumstances. It eventually gets organised as a religious organisation.

There is no scope for rationality in any religion, it is a matter of faith and no scope exists for any changes therein. In other words it is a closed system, not amenable to any logic or is not affected by any ideas in the external social environment anytime thereafter. Often one joins it unknowingly, without knowing anything or understanding it, as a matter of family tradition, from childhood itself and continues throughout his life thereafter. This is what has been described earlier as the religious-syndrome. In other words religion is a kind of **dogma** or ***ism.***

The subsequent leaders and their followers are so convinced about the truthfulness of their path, with no alternative, that they would like the entire human race to follow the same. Some use force or even allurement to achieve this objective. Some others like to pursue and peacefully convince the others, but the aim is the same in either case. Whether one falls in line with this thinking willingly or under duress or by allurement is besides the point.

More than what has been said in any religion, the present book is more interested in the religious systems and their methodology of organisation. In terms of scientific understanding, anything that is characterised like religious systems must also be classified as only a kind of religion. Religion by tradition has been seen as a path of salvation. It is related to the meta-physical world. But a religious system is quite this worldly. Why should the system be classified as specifically for religions only? The same system can be used for achieving even the material pleasures in this world. The economic system of achieving the material pleasures can like-wise be equally dogmatic and intending that the entire human race should follow the same path. The proponents may emphasise that theirs is the only economic system worth following and that the rest are of no use; since the others are incapable of delivering the physical needs to the have-nots. It can also be claimed that it is perfect and need no changes whatsoever for its universal application anywhere and any time. Can then this be categorised as something like religion or say ***neo-religion?***

The same arguments can be made about some political or social systems, provided they have the same characteristics.

There have been some movements, originated in different societies around the world, to reshape the society, as per their own perception like the Marxism, Socialism, Nazism, Fascism and some others on a smaller scale. Although they are basically economic systems they do have political and social overtones underlying them. All these are highly organised systems with their own specific characteristics. Their followers do not believe in any deviation from the original text. They also would like to cast the entire human race in their own formats without any dissention from any quarter. These are nothing but **dogmas** and ***isms***. Even some other social reform movements are also equally dogmatic. Just like any religion, these are ***isms*** only or perhaps at best ***neo-religions*** and nothing else.

These are invariably totally materialistic in their outlook and do not believe in the other world that is inaccessible to human senses. But their formats and activities typically resemble those of religions. Basically these ***isms*** divide the human population into two clear-cut divisions, *viz* **those who agree and those who do not agree with them.** Dividing the human population in only two simple groups is characteristic of agricultural mind-set. This resembles the typical religious character of the organised religions. Every attempt, including physical power in the form of dictatorship, is used for converting those who do not agree into unquestioning followers. Hence these have been classified in the present book as ***neo-religions***.

On the basis of the above mentioned qualifying conditions for being classified as religion, let us judge these ***isms,*** whether they fall in the category of neo-religions and, if at all, then to what extent? These are specifically organised and in fact very highly organised activities. They have a highly pyramidal management structure resembling as of Newton-Cartesian era. Hence, these must also be included in the knowledge-body of science of organisation and need intelligent appreciation.

Marxism

Karl Marx is perhaps the only philosopher and social scientist who codified completely how the future societies should be reshaped to make human beings happy for ever. He was very disturbed by the exploitation of humans in general and small children in particular by the industries that had come up as a result of industrial revolution in 18th and 19th century, especially in north-western European countries like England, Germany, France and so on. He was aghast to see how so much labour had to be put-in by so many just to earn a material living, while the owner was enjoying the benefits without much hard physical work. This was attributed to the stratified society with class of capitalists or owner of the means of production and the rest as workers or labourers. Being a philosopher he worked out a social model to free the society from any such stratification and exploitation once and for all time to come. He also believed in pure materialism and considered religion as opium, worth discarding it for ever. His entire approach was basically in the form of a reaction, rather than going positively into the depth of human purpose as the Indian ***seers*** approached the problem ages ago. He acted reactively against something rather than proactively for something great.

He was searching for a single irreducible unit in economics – like the basic unit of the universal machine in the form of an atom of the Newtonian world-based on which social reconstruction could be carried out avoiding all the ills of the then society. He was basically under the influence of Newton-Cartesian perceptions of the world. He did not realise that the Newton-Cartesian model believed in a closed system, whereas the society is an open system and shall always remain so.

He published his thesis in the form of a book titled ***Das Capital*** which gives the blueprint of the future society of his imagination and how it would be established. He believed that the societal structure is the result of economic system alone and that the rest like religion, entertainment, arts, culture, laws, values and everything else, without exception, gets evolved in the form of super-structure on this basic economic pattern. Hence when economic structure is changed the society shall automatically change. He therefore designed a new economic structure to reconstruct the society in the form which came to be known after him as **Marxism**. The disparity and stratified class structure of the society, he believed, was reflection fundamentally determined by economics alone. Hence his essential suggestions are all related to economics alone. Many individually and as governments were so allured by his thesis that they became devout Marxist and tried to reconstruct society based on his ideas. They are all known as **Marxists**. In its applied form it was no less different than any religious dogma. Everybody was forced to fit into the organized structure set up by the state. They even thought of setting up communes to replace the families.

He forgot that economic system in any society is decided by available raw materials, level of education, scientific and technological progress, cultural and religious taboos, environmental considerations and vice versa. Then what is more fundamental? Does economics possess such an overriding role? The **post-Marxists** still consider all the above factors as reflections of classes alone. Marx could not appreciate that no social structure can be constructed or changed using only one force of change. There are many such forces that contribute to change. The change does depend partially on chance and many other indeterminable parameters, often called as chance or luck. It also includes human efforts to have its own role in social construction or change. Economics does get affected by the changes in science and technology.

According to him exploitation was possible because the means of production and sale of goods were in private hands or capitalists, who had no sympathy for workers. These few capitalists exploited the vast number of workers to the extent possible to earn profit and nothing else. His panacea was basically in the form of a reaction to these conditions and insisted that all the means of production should be owned by the state in the form of owner of all wealth, the production of which must be organised by the state as their representative. This would be possible only by establishing a state with dictatorship of the proletariat in whom all the powers shall be centralised. It could only be achieved through use of force and revolution for overthrowing the capitalists system.

Accordingly, **Czar's** feudal order in Russia was overthrown in 1917 AD by revolution led by **Lenin** to establish the **Marxist's social model**. Lenin himself was basically liberal in outlook. Since it was of universal applicability it was extended in the form of international commintorn by the later leaders of this revolution. The next generation of leaders was intolerant and enforced the Marxist's order through force alone. It also came to be known as communist regime or communist social order. Everything was nationalised and converted into state property. This could be done through dictatorship proclaimed to be of proletariat. In reality it was not at all so. Entire society was forced to obey the state dictates on all matters. They not only killed their associates but even butchered millions of those who opposed the system to establish order. It was practically reduced to an animal farm. Detailed instructions were issued by the state machinery to manage the society even on micro level. It had all the similarities with Catholic Christian or Islamic religious systems wherein force was readily used to make everybody fall in line. **Though it loathed religion as opium it had all the attributes of a religion.** The only difference was that it was about the physical world directly accessible to senses. Vigorous attempts were made to establish it all over the world in the form of international commintorn.

It can be classified as a neo-religion by its attributes. It is a closed system not amenable to any deviation from what was said by Marx several decades ago. In fact those who deviated were butchered in cold blood. An organised system in which individual freedom is eliminated cannot last long because of the inherent desire for freedom and association. Ultimately it proved totally useless and was thrown out lock, stock and barrel in all the countries that had once opted for it. They all changed to capitalistic system for economic development. In fact what was adopted was post-industrial or information technological pattern. But the adherents of Marxism still harp on it as the only panacea for progress of underdeveloped societies and the have-nots, in the same way as adherents of any religions believe.

Although the governments who adopted this system for reorganisation of their societies have discarded it, the adherents of this system still continue to believe in it and try to propagate it as their life mission. Those of stoneage mental make-up have now clandestinely taken to arms to re-establish the same in the name of Naxal, Mao or Marxist-movements of various types.

They have a rigid organisational set up, as a pre-condition, to enforce the Marxist's order like the Islamic order.

Socialism

Those who were humanitarian and valued individual freedom most were disturbed by the dictatorial communist regimes. They were all for emancipation of economic slavery of have-nots but without losing freedom. An alternative in the form of socialism was worked out wherein the individual freedom was maintained by maintaining democratic governance, based on open and free elections. It also considered nationalisation of economic activities as the only feasible alternative. It had all the attributes of original communist system except that the government would be elected periodically. Because of centralised economic control practically the same people got elected and the regimes acquired practically all the ills of communist regimes. Slowly the socialist systems also degenerated everywhere into very inefficient economic systems. They failed to appreciate that economic slavery finally converts the political freedom into political slavery as well. It also turned out to be a dogmatic system killing individual's all initiatives, not just in economic activities but, as a result, in all other spheres of life as well. The dynamism of society was thus lost in practically all spheres of life reducing it to a mere mechanical machine, capable of obeying superior's instructions, without any creative initiative. When wealth is not generated through economic activities how would it be available to all, particularly the downtrodden? Only minority was benefited by way of state largesse. They developed vested interests in this system which had to exploit the have-nots, may be indirectly. The most inefficient Indian scenario until the open system was adopted in 1991 AD is ample proof to prove the point. It has been finally overthrown almost everywhere in the world in favour of so-called capitalism.

This is another *ism* or dogma wherein the individual was converted into a robot to act as per instructions from the above, without applying his conscience. It had to be an organised human machine, developed through brain programming, and hence possessed most of the attributes of any other organised religion. It is nothing but only a neo-religion.

Fascism

It is a combination of political, economic and social perception of a society. It outright rejects democracy, liberalism and capitalism. There are both right and left politico-economical influences on fascist perception. Like Marxism it believed that all elements in a society should be unified through corporatism to form an organic state. Attempts were made by **Benito Mussolini** in Italy to establish fascist order just before the Second World War. State was considered to be a means to an end. It was a kind of hyper-nationalism based on citizen-nation relationship with state as an embodiment of collective will with people's community as its operating structure. It is essentially based on the assumption that only some understand what is good for the society to progress and the rest should simply follow their dictates for a happy life. In principle it resembles the creative minority and majority perception of Toynbee. This was another version of dictatorial regimes to enforce their writ on all the population under the garb of economic progress and authority. No dissention was tolerated in this set-up. It was possible through brain programming alone under the duress of state military power. It had all the attributes of organised religion. Hence it is classified here as neo-religion. It is now treated as an abuse to be called as fascist.

Nazism

This was known as **National Socialism** and it flourished in Germany, under the leadership of **Adolf Hitler**. It was born more out of the economic depression and hardships of 1930's. It was also the result of power craze of human beings to cast society as per their dictates. It is totalitarian ideology like the perception of Marx. It considered as primary duty of state to provide livelihood to its citizens. It was based on anti-parliamentarian, pan-Germanic and racist outlook. It reflected a conglomeration of collectivism, anti-semiticism, anti-communism and anti-liberalism in economics. It was a third way as different from communism and capitalism. It was developed as the ideology of **National Socialist German Worker's Party** in politics which ruled Germany and led it into Second World War. It propounded the superiority of the German race over all others and therefore had the desire to rule the world. It believed in cleansing the national statism through paramilitarism to develop a classless society. It was developed into a rigid social system with tight governmental control and exterminated the Jews in millions in cold blood to make way for new organic and pure race. Hitler preached that it was his true and master religion. Luckily it was defeated in the Second World War by the allied forces. It was another organised religion-like force that tried to enforce its writ with force even beyond its national frontiers. The initial organisation was developed through near perfect brain programming, later came to be known as **Goebel's techniques**. It is now seen with all possible contempt. In fact it is now an abuse to be called a **Nazi.**

Social Systems

There are many social systems which operate more or less like any organised religious systems. They have superior perceptions of their own to the exclusion of all others. These are closed systems, at the mental level, and not amenable to any changes readily. They believe that the truth, once and for all time, has been revealed by the originator and that it can not be changed thereafter like in any religion. The operation is equally like any other organised religion with extreme emphasis on their regular ritualistic routines for developing the cadre for furthering their cause. These may also be classified as neo-religions because of their common attributes with organised religions.

There was a time, particularly in the agriculture era, when some thinkers used to think that they would like to reorganise the society as per their perception. The first ever attempt in this direction was made by the **Upanishadic thinkers** in India and it proved successful in establishing some social order that was suited to that agricultural era. Since then no further attempt has ever been made until recently. The western society was never consciously organised on any pre-conceived principles or designs. It evolved from stoneage to information technology-based form with inputs from all possible corners and even common men, as and when needed. It in fact evolved with time along with ideas as they evolved. The **Marxist** or the **Nazi's** or the **Fascist's** attempts were the first ones to organise the societies with some preconceived designs and ideas, in the form of absolute truths as per their beliefs. These however more or less and on the whole failed.

There have been some such attempts in India in recent times in the form of Marxist movement to establish new social order. The Marxists have failed in India to establish it through democratic means and instead they have been divided in various groups who abuse each other as deviationists from the original Marxism. The same is now being tried through the clandestine terrorist attempts like Naxal or the Mao movements. Several attempts in the form of one or the other social reform movements have also been tried in India, but without much success.

Another large scale attempt is being made by the RSS through its *parivar* organisation and is going on with vigour without any discernible impact on the society even after eighty-five years of their strenuous efforts. In spite of such colossal inputs from thousands or even lacs of people, to organise the Hindu society, it has not borne out to be successful. In fact the Hindu society now is more divided than it was eighty-five years ago when RSS was started to reorganise it. However their efforts in the form of RSS-parivar are more wide-spread than any other attempt made so far by any social force. Their study is far more pertinent to better understand the science of organisation and also the limitations of organised efforts in reorganising the society/nation particularly when information revolution is sweeping the international community at an unprecedented rate.

All of these attempts have ultimately led to the development of disciple-syndrome amongst their followers, finally losing the initial vigour. Any such system requires strong organisation as a pre-condition for enforcement of the order of their perception. Such an organisation can only be built by brain programming alone and which as a rule is amenable eventually to disciple-syndrome and nothing else. The organisation in due course becomes too rigid to carry out their task any further, as has been observed almost universally. This is the only reason why even the then laudable Upanishdic-era attempts finally culminated into rigid and worst type of social stratification and exploitation in India.

Industrial Fall-out

The attempts to organise society as per some pre-conceived ideas succeeded in agricultural era because the system was simple enough to be applicable on a small scale then. Even Ram-Rajya succeeded in some isolated corner but could not be duplicated again, much less on a larger scale. The same approach to consciously reorganise societies appeared to succeed in the industrial era, perhaps because it was the era of organisations, something better than the agricultural set-up to put the enlarging society in order. But it was not at all as per any pre-conceived ideological plan. It got evolved with progress in industrialisation. Ultimately even the so organised industrial life became too unstable to continue and had to give-in before informational era. This phenomenon of change-over of organised forms has now acquired such a rapid rate that in all likelihood the organisational forms shall be changing continuously hereafter to suit the times, social conditions and the requirements.

Rate of Reorganisation

It was alright to think of an ideal model for reconstruction of society as per some pre-conceived design in the nearly stagnant agricultural society. That is why it worked successfully in the Upanishdic period and thereafter for some time in India. But it ultimately suffered from the **disciple-syndrome** and degenerated into an obnoxious caste-system. Now the longer the attempt takes to reorganise any society as per some pre-conceived design the more likelihood is that it will acquire **disciple-syndrome** and become rigid and untenable with changing time as the religious organisations have become rigid and out of tune in the present day world, in spite of so many intensely longing for, through it, the glimpse of the inaccessible world.

Even the Marxist's design of social reconstruction was so rigid in its approach that it could not keep pace with industrial growth and finally had to give in when the information era stabilized.

Smilarly even the Upanishadic early agricultural social structure in India could not change with changing social needs arising out of increased division of work and hence degenerated in to rigid caste structure.

The information technology based industrial lifestyles have reverted the process of organisation introduced and established earlier by the industrial revolution. Overall social life is becoming far too complex to be designed and organised by some or few in the form of an initiator of any prior design. The rate of change is so fast that by the time some design is worked out, it becomes obsolete by the time it is to be implemented. That is also the reason why every existing organisation with enough vitality and vision is continuously undergoing changes in tune with experience and requirements. Now decentralisation is the key principle of organisation in any sphere of social activity. The mind-set is fast changing into developing the style of *ad-hoc* organisations which are active only for the time being as per the demand and compulsions to suit the changing times. This is the reason why even the large scale attempt by RSS is not bearing the expected reorganisation of Hindu society.

References

Much of the material in this chapter has its origin at different places available on the internet.

CHAPTER 19

GROWTH

CHAPTER STRUCTURE

- Meaning
- Organisationality
- Organisations
- Principles
- Clarity of Objective/aim/task
- Surplus
- Approaches
  - Communication
  - Awareness
  - Disciple-role
  - Identification
- Controller-leader Separation
- Leadership Qualities
- Individual vs. Group
- Diversification
- Rigidity
- Success
- Creativity
- Dynamism
  - Built to Perpetuate
- SWOT and TOWS Analysis

The growth of organised forms has to be considered with reference to two concepts, viz the organisationality and the organisations. The perceptions of their growth are quite different. But growth in both is essential since they help grow each other mutually. Let us first see the growth of organisationality and later on organisations.

Meaning

The term growth in reference to organisation and its working means many different things to different people. For the controller, leader or manager of a commercial organisation it means rise in profit. To an average worker in such an organisation rise in emoluments of workers may appear as growth. To a leftist thinker it may mean rise in actual employment in any establishment. With reference to national thinking growth may mean percentage rise in gross national output. For an academic institution it may mean more number of students qualifying in first class or more number passing some examination. It may also mean development in buildings, laboratories, infra-structural facilities and the like. For a newspaper it may mean increased sale. For a social service organisation it may mean more number of people being served.

This creates problems in assessing the situation when in a commercial organisation profit is decreased but the number of employees has increased. It is also likely that profit may increase but the activities of an organisation has contributed in degrading the environment or has degraded the health of its employees. Hence growth parameter has to be worked out properly taking into account all such related parameters.

Organisationality

Human needs lead to develop organisationality and along with that increase in organisations, as division of labour is increasingly required. As has been earlier discussed, good organisations can be set up to the extent of existence of organisationality at the foundational base. Formation and operations of organisations help improve the organisationality. They always have a mutually accelerating effect on each other. Hence one simple way for growth of organisationality is to form and run varied and more organisations. In this process some may be decimated but others help improve the organisationality

For improving organisationality it is not necessary for participants to physically come together. All that is needed is to be mentally cohesive and united on the basis of some common beneficial ideas and concepts for liking each other. Whatever is beneficial to all in this respect shall automatically result in improving the organisationality. For example, any natural calamity, at even a distant place, resulting in perhaps somebody's death, is sure to result in the compassional feelings which in turn helps raise the organisationality.

But since it is a matter related to mental faculty, all that gives mental satisfaction aids in improving the organisationality. It could be music, art, cinema, literature, crafts, games, sports, culture and so on. In the parlance of present day international diplomacy, the interaction on such basis, are often referred to as ***soft diplomacy***. Similarly the attraction for scientific knowledge and technological advancements for creative contributions in such fields, all help improve organisationality, because all such knowledge becomes known to many others and is appreciated by others. It leads to the development of a mental make-up which appreciates other's achievements and a feeling of sharing one's own knowledge with others, without not even coming in contact with each other. It develops co-operative and caring mental make-up, which is very helpful for improving organisationality.

Earlier, under the influence of Newton-Cartesian perceptions, the westerners did not believe in the existence of independent mind, but now they have accepted the existence of mind as well as intellect besides the physical body, as an inalienable part of human existence. They have also slowly accepted, under the influence of systemic perceptions, that the body is no longer a mere physical machine but an integrated whole in the form of body, mind and intellect. However they have yet to accept the existence of soul, in some form, as believed by most religions. But even within the limited extension of agreement, of west with the Indian perception, leaving aside the model of universe in the form of discreet parts, they have now accepted the systemic perception of universe as inter-relationships of everything in nature. That is the reason why they take a system approach in understanding nature. That is also the reason why they are now worried about the impact of degradation of environment which encompasses everything in nature including the semi-physical existence, that is, mind and intellect.

The organisationality concept of the western world has definitely expanded from the earlier horizon to reach out that far but not as far as the Hindus have evolved, in seeing the entire existence, both animate and inanimate, as essentially one whole. For Hindus anything and everything have to be considered with reference to the universal wholeness in the form of their advaita philosophy or as per the Brahma-Maya model of their perception. General human intellect has yet to expand their vision to reach this level. Hence the limit of expanding the organisationality level seems to be up to the level of advaita. Ideal organisations can be visualised as built on the foundation of the organisationality concept of Hindus. These organisations will also grow in the direction such that the organisationality shall expand towards this end.

Organisationality cannot be readily increased artificially by any specific activity. It is related to only the mental level, which is very subtle and ever changing. It's an evolving process. It is also a historical process and sufficient time has to be given for its evolution. The least what is expected is that the individuals do not deliberately act in such a way as to stifle the process of its evolution. It is in the interest of humanity, and its continued existence as a whole on earth, to aim for organisationality improvement in the direction imagined by Hindus.

It needs to be understood that organisationality does not mean similarity at all and that too, secured under duress. In fact it basically means unity in diversity as it is quite natural. Any attempt in making the humans similar on the basis of religion, complexion, race, economic developments and such things will ultimately be not in the interest of improving organisationality at all. Life shall be too boring that way. Nature abhors such symmetry and similarity as is evident from the simple natural pedestrian track being always anything but straight and symmetrical in line. Any attempt to secure such organisationality, on the basis of common religion, has in the past resulted only in bloodshed and animosity. Organisationality means integration of human beings first on mental and then on intellectual level, which cannot be obtained by force and allurement of whatever kind. It may be possible by sustained brain-programming right from childhood, but that is tantamount to converting humans, with god-gifted creativity, into machines.

Some things may aid its growth, like the inculcation of spirit of co-operative working. Forming more and more organisations, with increasing size and extending over larger areas and social groups, helps in building up definitely the organisationality.

Organisations

Growth or progress of an organisation is a very complex phenomenon since it involves extracting work from group of human beings in a co-ordinated manner. It is not easy to predict how an individual, individually or in any group form, shall behave at a given time, in given circumstances and in given surroundings. The complexity increases further when some material and financial arrangements are to be interfaced with the group, in order to achieve some pre-set aim. It requires understanding of human psychology of individuals as well as of groups. It also requires understanding of finance, related material's world, processes and so on .It in turn requires understanding, in addition to psychology, of sociology, economics, politics, history and so on to understand individuals and their groups and make them work in the desired direction. All these therefore form part of basic organisational science and in its applied part as management.

Principles

The prime purpose of all organisations is not just survival but growth and that no organisation in the history of civilization has ever been formed in order to just survive. Organisations are founded to contribute something useful to the society at large and thereby grow. The organisations of terrorists or dacoits are exceptions. There is no point in allowing formation of organisations which do not serve, directly or indirectly, any social interests. Organisations may either grow or decay, but not stay on with time as has been discussed earlier.

Earlier business management practices and the way of development of present management courses at the university level are mainly geared to train the students for just not running the organisations but for their growth, against all possible odds that may befall them while in operation. The essentials of management in the form of five basic paradigms as planning, organising, staffing, leading and controlling are all fundamentally geared for the growth and progress of organisations. Those who fail in carrying out these tasks are considered as inferior managers to the extent of their shortfalls. Hence all the underlying principles of the above outlook in right directions shall automatically result in growth of an organisation. This is the simplest form of putting forward the growth parameters. But it is the most complex of human endeavour that can be thought of. It is also the reason why the management practices have always been under constant scrutiny for improvements. Several models, including the mathematical ones have been developed to help manage organisations on more sound, quantitative and scientific footing. Yet it still remains more as an art in its ultimate analysis, though all these help in evolving finally the art of management.

Clarity of Objective/aim/task

For growth, the aim or objective or task of an organisation, should be explicit so that all efforts can be directed for its achievement. But there are disagreements even on this issue amongst the experts in management. According to **Peter Drukker,** the doyen of management science, organisation may have more than one aim and should be considered as normal [1]. Should there be a principal one and the rest being secondary, is not clear from his proposition. Whereas according to **John Argenti** [2], another management guru of repute, organisation must have one single and clear-cut aim so that all endeavours are directed in achieving it. Whether there can be secondary aims or not is not clear from **Argenti's** assertion either. In his opinion if you have more than one declared aim, then it becomes impossible to assess the progress. It becomes impossible to compare the performance of one organisation with similar ones, as one of the two may be doing well in some respect, while the other may be doing well in some other respect and as a result no basis is available for comparison of their relative efficiencies.

When the aim is a single and focused one, the intended beneficiaries, for whom the organisation is supposed to primarily work, becomes quite apparent. Everyone in the organisation likewise gets clarity about group's purpose, which helps-evolve methodology of approach unambiguously. The work force knows what they are supposed to achieve. If there are many objectives there appears unnecessary confusion as to where the attention is to be focused and as a result there can be incoherency in collective organisational efforts. Hence to have one single focused aim is the pre-condition for any organisation to function effectively and, if possible grow.

Quite often multiple aims only indicate that the strategies and tactics have been mixed up in stating the aim, according to **Argenti**. It may be the result of lack of clarity about the vision and the mission of the group. It should not be the case for achieving smooth growth of an organisation. Argenti quotes many examples in support of his argument. He gives an example of a jail. What is the aim of a Jail? Is it to have more and more culprits and their training and so on? No, the aim should be to see how the jail has been instrumental in improving the culprits, during their stay in the jail, to enable them to live more normal life, after completing their term of punishment. Hence the single aim becomes very clear.

Similarly what is the aim of a school? Is it to cater to the needs of parents, society or even the suppliers of the school, along with imparting teaching? No, the aim of the school is only one and it is to teach and enlighten the students as per the laid down curricula.

Can any one ask the police force as to what else they can do for the society? No. In fact, it is the other way round. All the related ones should ask the main body as to what and how they can contribute in making them more successful in their primary task.

In the case of a university there can be confusion, whether its purpose is to produce graduates, carry out research or guide the society in various ways? Firstly are all these aims all that different and discreet from one another? On deeper insight it becomes clear that all these are only facets of the same single aim. The aim of the university must therefore be to generate knowledge by way of excellence in training, research and guidance of the society at large. If you do not teach or carry out research how would knowledge be generated? If you do not interact with the society at large, how will social needs be known in isolation? Hence even the single focused aim may at times be projected in its various facets and that may confuse the issue.

Besides the only declared aim, some incidental benefits may be accrued by others related to the organisation, but it is just the incidental by-product and not the aim of an organisation.

The organisational understanding has come a long way since the early days of industrialisation and colonialism, when the only motive in most organisations was to earn maximum profit and power, disregarding anything else whatsoever. It is no more so because the organisations have now realised their social and environmental obligations. They have to be conscious of social needs and problems vis-à-vis their organisational activities. Best course is to be physically and mentally in tune with the society around so that the organisational operations are welcomed by the society and effective interaction is possible. The concept of ***corporate social responsibility*** **(CSR)** and ***social awareness*** stems from this understanding alone.

Surplus

Although by surplus it was meant as the net gain over the expenditure, once upon a time, the term is now used in more generalised ways, in terms of achievements as envisaged in the objective. For commercial organisations it may be the profit. It may be giving service to the needy in the case of charitable organisation; it may be giving good governance in the case of political organisations; it may be achieving excellence in something; it may be performing the expected duty (for example security service or accounting, etc.) and so on. It means that with minimum input of money, men and materials and, with least amount of personal dissatisfaction, the objective is achieved, to the extent possible, by any organisation.

Creation of surplus is also the social objective in a generalised sense because by creating such surplus in any form, the society is directly or indirectly benefited. It is in a way a reflection of growth of an organisation. It is in the broader social interests that organisations function effectively and efficiently to generate surpluses to the maximum extent possible. Wealthy society is beneficial to all the constituents, definitely so in emergencies.

Approaches

An organisation involves people working together, with material, financial and intellectual inputs, in some specific social environment, to meet specifically the selfish motives of perhaps some, but at the same time indirectly helping to meet selfish interests of others, to the extent possible. This is an activity within the society as well as an inalienable part of the society. It is related to the selfish interests of others as well. It is related to human nature and it's aspirations, so also of the society as well. Hence the running of an organisation involves mainly inter-personal activities by way of communications between persons and groups, between organisation and society at large and between person and nature for required materials, if any. For all these functions to be more efficient, inputs by way of understanding of human psychology as of individuals and groups, social evolutionary history and social environment, scientific and technological developments, political environment, aspirations of individuals and groups, and such other things, are all essential. **It is a complex web of basically the mental, intellectual and material forces manifested in the form of individuals, groups, society and their aspirations.** These are human resources and their psyche, materials and finance, the legal framework and many ethereal things that have to be managed by the leader so that the work force works effectively and efficiently in achieving the objective, against the larger context of social interests.

Once it is accepted as a web then it becomes clear that a disturbance anywhere in this web, by way of clash of interests of individuals or groups or the society at large, may result in it's echoes in an organisation at places and in such a way as often unforeseen, unimagined and at times in resonance, such that the efficiency of organisation may be adversely affected. Although it is desirable not to get such disturbances for effective working, it is almost impossible to achieve such a situation in any organisation. For growth, the manager has to tackle all this and keep the disturbances within limits, so that the effectiveness and efficiency of working is conducive to attainment of the pre-set goal.

Being a complex web, equally complex set of theories have been put forward over the years, including the mathematical and behavioural ones, to understand the underlying phenomena and to work out ways and means of overcoming the disturbances, based on relevant tools, in order to manage the organisations. Each one of the theories emphasise one or the other aspect as overriding or as possible chief obstacle in management and hence attempts to explain how organisations may be managed to achieve the desired results. All the theories may not be applicable everywhere and under any situation. The assumption is that some may be more suitable to appreciate problems of some specific nature, in some specific areas and help evolve strategies of action thereat. These have therefore led to evolve varied management approaches to tackle the problems.

These are:

1. Empirical or case approach, based on trial and error
2. Managerial roles approach, based on inter-personal, informational and decision roles

3. Contingency approach based on standard solutions for standard problems expressed out of historical experiences
4. Mathematical approach based more on logic expressed in equation forms
5. Decision theory approach based on the science of making decisions
6. Re-engineering approach is based on re-thinking afresh about everything related to the problems.
7. Systems approach based on taking all parameters as one integrated whole and considering it against the environment or any variable from inside.
8. Socio-technical approach based on social relations and technologies
9. Co-operative social approach based on group working styles
10. Group behaviour approach based on sociology and psychology of groups
11. Inter-personal behaviour approach based on fundamentals of mutual inter-actions
12. McKinsey's 6-S approach based on strategy, structure, systems, style, staff, shared values and skills.
13. Total quality management approach based on total quality of products or services to satisfy customers
14. Operational process approach based on wider R and D efforts, assuming that organised knowledge, pertinent to management is available, in the form of a science.

Based on these approaches some models have been constructed to explain the functioning and therefore managing an organisation. The details of all of these approaches can be seen in standard management textbooks.

Whatever the theory and whatever the approach, a few things remain overriding for organisational progress and these are described below.

Communication

Proper and effective communication system between various levels on the basis of levels or between individuals of different levels and between individuals at the same level is necessary for working out the nature of the problems before hand and effective solutions thereat. Communication is a two-way tool and it is not complete unless the message is understood by the sender as well as the receiver and is responded to properly. In religious organisations it is often one-way only and hence it may be classified as dictation. This has been very aptly put by **Arun Shouri** [1] in his book titled ***'Individuals, Institutions and Processes'*** and shown that **in the absence of proper communication, the organisations invariably decay. Communication helps to bring out the hidden perceptions and thereby helps organisational growth.**

While describing how excellent organisations can be built, **Tom Peters** [2] emphasises that communication is life blood of an organisation. It is vital, not just a matter of good human relation.

"If no other parallel channel is provided for communication and if short circuiting of communication is not allowed to desired and controlled extent, the complexity of problem and multifaceted solution therefor cannot be provided, then there is no way to detect and correct possible errors and atrophies."

Awareness

Everybody is made aware that each one of them counts equally necessary and responsible for achieving the organisational objective and that organisational objective will not be achieved without effective participation of all.

Everybody should understand that even their selfish contribution is just not in their own selfish interests but it is also in larger social, national or international or even humanitarian interests. Organisational work is in a way their contribution to the larger cause. Everybody be made known that the success or achievement is due to the efforts of all, whereas the failures are due to the shortfalls of the leader, in not properly directing the rest.

Disciple-role

Development of leader-disciple relationship is on the whole detrimental to organisational progress, even in religious organisations. Human weakness tends to exploit it for either personal gains or it gets used for personal whims; both are equally detrimental. It kills the creativity of those working on lower levels and thereby does not use the full available potential of the work force. Hence relationship based on equity, equality and co-operation, as far as is possible, is the only way for growth of any organisation.

Identification

Everybody must be psychologically trained to think that the work they do in the organisation is nothing less than their own personal work, what they do for themselves or for their families, so that it will be carried out with expected diligence. For this to happen an individual has to be assimilated fully in the group, physically, mentally and intellectually. If any one is physically present for work but is not mentally satisfied or not engaged in the current work, for one or the other reason, then he may not put in his intellect in doing the work at hand. What kind of efficiency can be expected from such a split personality at work? Hence either one who has an integrated personality is selected and shall prove to be an asset to the organisation or in the alternative everyone is developed by proper training, into an integrated personality, to be more effective in their contributions.

Controller-leader Separation

It is generally necessary to keep the controller and the leader as separate entities to demarcate their functions of governance and execution quite clearly [3]. The controller is supposed to decide the minimum and maximum limits of objectives to be achieved through proper execution. Besides, the controller is to see that the organisation works in the direction of achieving the set objective primarily for the benefit of intended beneficiaries, while causing minimum damage to all other related ones. It is also supposed to provide the required finances, other special needs, etc. to the executive leader so that the execution can be carried out without resource restraints. The executive leader has to carry out the essential functions of day-to-day management, with all its details, in order to make the organisation work towards achieving its goal.

Sometimes these two may be amalgamated into one. In that case and particularly in commercial organisations, there are chances that the real financial picture may not come out before the stake-holders. There are chances of financial embezzlement. **Argenti** [3] therefore insists on separation of governance from execution. He also expects that they do not trespass each others area of authority which is readily possible in commercial organisations. But it is not at all possible in the case of political and religious organisations, wherein the two often exist as two-in-one. That is the reason why whether they are growing or not does not become clear so readily. But as an exception in pre-independence movement **M. Gandhi** was the controller and **Nehru-Patel** and some others were the executive leaders of Congress. Similarly in RSS this division is very clear-cut. **Dr. Ambedkar** was two in one in his Republican organisation, during his life time and the same model is followed by many of his followers. The choice is therefore fairly subjective.

But if the two are separate and their authority and area of operations are well defined it is bound to help make the organisation function smoothly towards growth. Growth depends mainly on these two being a single integrated and effective unit for activating everybody in the organisation towards attaining the objective. They individually and together, in unison, act like what an engine does in driving a train. This is what is management and administration in the parlance of organisational science.

Often the controller is the promoter, financer, facilitator and so on and the leader is the university trained paid management expert. The controller is not necessarily an individual but may be a group with a more dominant one as the chairman. Similarly the leader need not be an individual but a group with the chief being the managing director, chief executive, chief manager or the like. **The controller is supposed to work off-line, whereas the executive leader is supposed to work on-line** to keep the day-to-day functioning going.

The executive leaders may be chosen in terms of product-types, activities, regions and the like, if the organisation is too big to be handled by one single executive unit for effective progress. There is no standard organisational structural methodology that has to be followed for progress and growth. It is one's own subjective choice, based on one's own nature and experience. All types are seen in actual operation and producing expected results under certain set of conditions. The style is under constant experimentation and evolution, based on experiences.

Leadership Qualities

It is not the structural shape of an organisation that decides the progress; it is the quality of leadership that primarily decides the progress of any organisation. The leadership potentials have already been explained in Chapter 12 while discussing leadership. Here let us see the precise qualities required of a leader. The curriculum of management courses at the university level lay down good amount of stress on leadership qualities, because such university trained human resource is to ultimately lead organisations at required levels, in practice.

A leader is primarily supposed to be of victorious nature. He should possess self-confidence without any hesitation, honesty without compromise on core values, enough industry without shirking the responsibility, high risk taking ability without a tinge of *hara-kiri*, persistence in action without losing tempo, personal initiatives surpassing anybody else, loving nature towards one and all without discrimination, caring for other's difficulties and compulsions as if his own, not losing confidence in the light of even repeated failures, prepared to try it again and again with victorious psyche, co-operative working style by nature, inclusive of all without discrimination, attributing success to all others but taking the blame of failures on own self, very strict towards self but soft towards co-workers, encouraging others in spite of their failures, disciplinarian with understanding, dedicated to superiors and their cause, strong decision-making power without being obstinate, prepared to learn anything and everything from anybody and any corner, open in transferring own knowledge to subordinates, equally open in receiving it from even juniors, and such other innumerable excellent qualities.

Nobody in reality possesses all these qualities at their best. It is possible that all such qualities may be present together in only exceptional cases. Such people are great, perhaps by birth itself, and they march on new social developmental paths, of their own creation, in tune with time, in the form of their vision in action. The names like **M.Gandhi, Dr. Ambedkar, Jawaharlal Nehru, Swami Vivekanand, Dr. Hedgewar, Guruji Golwalkar** and such are the typical examples of this category. They are always few and seen only from time to time, may be as per Lord Krishna's guarantee that God reincarnates in such forms as and when the society is befallen on the path of decay, to set it right again and again.

But in the case of ordinary mortals, if not all, many such leadership qualities may be present in some who become the leader and see that organisations grow and progress. Some organisations are always lucky to get some such leader of vision and who can put that in action, in the form of well developed and progressive organisations. There have been and there are many known management experts who have been acclaimed capable of turning around a sinking commercial establishment into a flourishing one. The names like **Lee Iacocca of Crysler Motors, Fumino Mitarai of Cannon Xerox, Herbert Keileher of Southwest Airlines, Vasant Pandit of City Group, Arun Sarin of Vodafone** and such others fall in this category. Such a galaxy is not however found in social, political, charitable and such organisations so readily. There each one has to cultivate one's own path to establish one's own characteristic organisation. These leaders can not be transferred from one to the other organisations like in commercial organisations.

Every event in this world is neither predetermined nor creation of somebody's efforts alone. It is a result of mixture of the above plus a chance factor and luck, which means all the unknown factors put together. Some get the chance and are able to grow and make their organisations prosper thereby get classified as top class leaders. Whereas some do not get such a chance to prove their mettle and are classified as poor leaders in comparison. Great leaders are known after their work only. It cannot be predicted on the basis of some parameters in advance. There are also some who prove their excellent leadership qualities at one place but turn out to be a failure at some other place. This is an inexplicable phenomenon in the field of leadership. What factors favoured him to be successful in one place and what factors prevented him from becoming a good leader elsewhere can only be guessed, but not with certainty. Hence growth of an organisation is subjectively related to leadership personalities and circumstances when put together with so many ifs and buts.

Individual vs. Group

Although individuals together make up the group, the behaviour of an individual as an individual and in the form of a group is found to be quite different by the psychologists. It is also the general experience. All good and otherwise well behaved students from cultured families may behave like rowdies when in groups. Why is it so? It is because their psychologies are quite different in these two different existences. This fact was long recognised in the west through psychological studies. Hence while selecting human resources for manning an organisation; individual interviews are supplemented by interviews in groups, for selecting right individuals.

In Indian philosophy, no topic is discussed more in detail than an individual's ego. This was because personal ego was considered to be the main obstacle in one's own march towards salvation. Hence ways and means have been suggested to kill one's ego so that the difficulties on the path of salvation are minimised. Practically no attention was paid to understand the group ego or group behaviour in India. In fact it was not understood as two different entities at all. Hence it has been the common belief in India that once individuals are cultured properly there will be no problem left in the society to be solved for peaceful co-existence for progress of all.

Going back again as to what are the basic characteristics and desires of human beings, it would reveal that humans cannot be cast in one common mould. There will always be varieties of human beings exhibiting far different behaviours through their differential desires. They can never be made similar, perhaps even good. There will be good, bad and all such types. The same will be reflected in any organisation.

It has to be understood that all individuals will never be transformed into such ideal individuals, or even reasonable individuals. It is perhaps against the very nature of humans. Firstly because goodness is a subjective parameter of assessment. One may appear good to someone and at the same time he does not appear to be so good to others. Then whose judgment is right? Secondly it is not in human nature to be so uniform. Thirdly even if it is presumed that all individuals are somehow so transformed, there is no guarantee that they together, will behave nicely as per expectation. Hence good and bad is no judgment at all. However all through the ages attempts have been made in India to cultivate individuals, leaving aside the consideration of groups. The lack of proper orgaisationality has been its first victim.

The religious discourses in the form of ***katha-kirtanas*** in temples, what was very effective social communication and educational system once, also emphasised only to get individuals cultured. Even now those who are very popular in giving discourses and for whom thousands collect to listen to their narratives, or even those whose discourses are telecast daily, the emphasis is still on cultivating individuals, without even mentioning the necessity of behaving properly in groups or in organisations. Therefore teaching and training individuals and the groups to behave better as groups rather than as individuals did not arise. The individuality is so ingrained in Indian psyche that the necessity or superiority of group behaviour for social welfare does not have any appeal. That is why the Indians are worried about personal hygiene inside the house but least worried about public hygiene. Indians have no shame in degrading the public hygiene. Group, social or corporate awareness is practically nil in India. No wonder, insurmountable problems are faced in running and growing organisations in India. What is the way out? There is no alternative but to cultivate Indians for co-operative working styles, through whatever means available. This was realised no better than **Dr. Hedgewar** [4] and for cultivating the same basic spirit he started primarily the activities of RSS, as is claimed. This is in essence what RSS is even today, as is claimed by their adherents.

The importance of collective working can be taught through lectures, training programmes, using mass media and so on, but to some extent only. This has to be cultivated from school days, right through university education, if possible. But even this may not turn out to be very effective. It is no specific theory to be taught in exact mathematical terms. Example is always better than precept, so goes the saying. The controller, leader and manager will have to take note of the existing social reality and chalk out programmes and along with that set their own examples so that right psyche for collective working, thinking and living is persistently cultivated as a top priority in respect of growth and progress in an organisation. There is no short-cut to this. Else ineffective and inefficient organisational functioning will have to be tolerated. It pays, even in terms of monetary gains, to cultivate collective awareness in an organisation. That is where the modern concept of developing organisational culture comes into play. Hence there is the emphasis on developing such culture with due care and diligence [5]. What precisely helps in developing such culture in any organisation is a matter of subjective choice. But leader's character as an overriding consideration in this respect is generally agreed upon. **Shivaji** was so successful in establishing his own kingdom against heavy odds, perhaps because of his sterling character alone. It is equally true of Mahatma Gandhi. It is truer of Dr. Hedgewar, Guruji Golwalkar and other chiefs of RSS.

Rethinking on centralisation versus decentralisation, organisational hierarchies versus the general empowerment or vertical versus the horizontal structures and such things appear to be necessary to achieve right collectivity [2]. This is the third wave approach according to **Toffler** [6], which involves also the concepts of social-audit, personal or group ethics, rights, justice and so on. Since organisation is essentially a human group, it will function better if it is based on trust, ethical behaviour and human dignity. It means integrity, loyalty, caring, keeping promises by one and all in the affairs of organisation. All these help achieve collectivity and organisational awareness and as a result growth and progress

The management approach based on the well known five basic principles of planning, organising, staffing, leading and controlling needs to be geared essentially to cultivate the collectiveness in organisational working for its growth and progress, rather than trying to understand 'the management theory' as some put it. But it is all easily said than done. Human nature comes in the way as the main obstacle.

In short all those parameters that are considered helpful in developing a cultured society are all useful in developing a progressive organisation.

Diversification

It is often seen time and again when the internal as well as the external environment becomes such that the organisation seems to come to either standstill or even starts degressing. Nothing seems to work to make it move forward. Even change of leadership also does not give desired results. Should the organisation then be closed or merged with some more efficient one? Many do choose such a path.

But there are always some leaders who do not lose courage, heart and confidence even against such apparently insurmountable odds. They choose the path of diversification as a way out of this impasse courageously. In commercial organisations the range of products or the services are diversified in such a situation. It cannot be done just at the eleventh hour. Usually the planning is done routinely in such a way as to take into account any such eventuality. If it has been done this way then diversification does not pose to be any insurmountable problem. But if no prior thinking and preparation is kept ready, then it may result in catastrophe under such emergency.

In social organisations such problems do arise and alternative paths are chosen for the organisation to function and even grow. One of the best examples of this type can be seen and worth studying is that of RSS. Against the backdrop of changed scenario after getting independence, followed by Gandhi's murder and consequent ban on RSS for its alleged involvement, for almost one and a half year, the organisation had nearly collapsed to the stage of decimation, even after the ban was later lifted unconditionally. At that crucial juncture their leaders decided to diversify their activities, by starting organisations in varied areas of social interest like, labour, education, media, charity, politics, healthcare in forest areas and so on [7]. All these organisations have now acquired number one stature in national social life which eventually led to the formation of what the media commonly refers to as **RSS- Pariwar.** In about fifty years time they could get their own prime minister to rule the country, in the form of **Atal Bihari Vajpeyee**.

Howsoever one may disagree with their ideology and working style, but is it not worth studying from the point of view of understanding science of organisation or organisational growth phenomena through diversification?

It is always important to study all organised efforts and more so those of terrorists, as to why and how they are able to form organisations for inflicting destruction and miseries on the society at large, even at the cost of sacrificing themselves. How do they diversify their activities is also a matter of curiosity?

Rigidity

It is also in the nature of organisations that, over the time, their original visions become strategies, pre-set strategies get more codified into policies, and then policies spawn routine unalterable practices till finally the practices become habits. The result is that workers become blind and faithful disciples of the manager rather than creative co-workers. That is as per the Second Law of Thermodynamics as applicable to organisations, in the same way as was propounded originally for physical systems. For growth it must be avoided at every stage and state.

The alternative is to continuously change with time so that the hierarchies do not encrust into top-heavy bureaucracies, in the form of calcified layers, manifesting only in the form of highly specialised role and reflexive routines.

Most of the organisations understand the basic managerial approaches in the form of planning, organising, staffing, leading and controlling only mechanically. **This may be due to their very simplified appreciation of organisational working.** They treat planning as simply an exercise based on some past and future figures as an entire relevant base-information; organisational structure itself as simply an organisation; staffing as merely filling of vacancies; leading as simply issuing instructions and controlling only in the form of collection of some performance data and issuing further instructions. This essentially stems from assuming organisation as merely some structural form without any mind of its own. That is sure to transform organisation into a bundle of rigid policies, blind faiths and beliefs. No wonder the mortality rate of organisations, particularly in the commercial world is extremely high. Many financially lose even fortunes, in such catastrophes.

The Christian church in the western world has become so rigid and out of tune with their social advancements that it is continuously losing its appeal as has been described earlier. Some do suggest them to regain their old dynamism by undertaking suitable changes, by way of regaining the same old values of love, kindness, empathy, caring and compassion to anyone as human being. But it is becoming too difficult for the pastors, their guardians, to revive it in practice. As a result they have grown too rigid in their outlook over the years to the extent that even their overall decay does not awaken them to the reality. Same is the story of Hindu society and the rituals that are carried out as a means of attaining salvation. It has become too rigid a system of merely mechanical activities. The essence of all has already been lost.

Avoiding rigidity at all costs has also been the key to sustain and improve the organisationality of any society. The Indians seems to have failed to recognise it in any way and hence the deterioration and degeneration in their societal structure that is witnessed today.

Success

In the case of a religious organisation it may be a unique problem like onslaught of materialism, atheism, skepticism or relativism that might make it rigid in the form of natural reaction of defense. But for other organisations getting rigid is pure and simple institutional inertia not coping with the external changes in the environment by appropriate changes inside the organisation. In the words of **Peter Drukker** the *inside* is out of tune with *outside.* The mortality rate of organisations of all types, NPOs and non-NPOs alike, without exception has been very high and is increasing with time. This is because most organisations get shackled to one form, for having been successful once and thinking that it will be the sure path of success for ever in future. This does not come true because future is no extension or extrapolation of the past by any means. Those leaders who did wonders in organisational progress should only be seen as source of inspiration but not the one to be copied for future progress.

Progress is not a one time phenomena that it will keep on repeating without conscious and innovative efforts. Success has to be always a self-correcting phenomenon rather than a hard die in which anything could be cast as per requirements. Hence skill lies in not inventing but in reinventing brilliant strategies as per needs to adapt to emerging needs, by taking the evolutionary advantage to prevent organisations from getting rigid. That's why some are able to innovate into new forms more suitable to the timely needs, whereas the others find it difficult or even impossible to change. They have to give way to the more timely ones. That's just pure and simple nature.

For over 150 crore years the life-forms have been evolving to suit the changes in the natural surroundings. The organisations are no exceptions to stagnate by being conservative. They too have to evolve by changing their hierarchical nature and style of functioning by paving the way to up-to-date power distribution, for the simple reason that the power distribution is the key to functioning of any organisation. It should be the mantra of the time, as far as the organisations are concerned. Making organisations more flat has thus acquired the status of mantra in this respect [8,9].

Creativity

It is the job of the controller, leader or manager to regularly re-establish the required equilibrium for the organisation to progress on its scheduled path. In profit making organisations this is done almost continuously through assessment of the market, changing the strategies and tactics accordingly and by restructuring the organisation. Training of the staff, in tune with the changing requirements can also be another key area of change. The planning and organising of such organisations, in reality, should take into account all this initially and keep on updating the same with time, or at least periodically. It is not all that easy for other social or religious organisations to do it that quickly. Hence they have to do it at least periodically. In governmental and political organisations the assessment is continuous but bringing back the equilibrium is not all that simple because neither the workers can be replaced readily nor can their psychology be changed readily through training. It is here that the leadership is tested for sustaining the progress against such odds.

Such a situation is aptly described by the world famous management guru **Peter Drukker** [10] as:

"Human beings by nature, habit and practice are used to a way of working. Any change that is envisaged ushers in a sense of insecurity simultaneously with the change-process.

The management must therefore assure that the change is not going to affect the work force adversely in any way .Changes are necessary in every organisation with time and therefore he further says.

"The value of openness, trust, autonomy, proactivity and experimentation will have to be made the way of life in an organisation if the process of change is to be harnessed for organisational good".

Out of these trust [11] is perhaps most important. The required changes have to be brought in the organisation through very subtle means with great ingenuity. This is the expected skill of the controller, leader or manager. It is here that the Indian polity, as a whole, appears to have failed miserably in the post-independence era in tackling such challenges that came across them in reorganising India. The leaders in fact were led by the masses rather than they leading the masses. It is a case of majority leading the creative minority, a prefect upside down structure. No wonder not much of progress is seen in such a situation. It has become more and more difficult for all such organisations, to bring about the required changes in the man-power to suit the external environment. Most of them are succumbing before the existing man-power helplessly. The deterioration in the organised Indian polity, in the post-independence era, is the result of inabilities of the leaderships on this front, for certain.

Dynamism

Growth and progress fundamentally stem from dynamism of an organisation. Dynamism means the ability of an organisation to cope-up with any change in the external environment as well as problems arising out of internal changes caused by changes in the psychology of the work force or the changes in management style. Systemic behaviour is best exhibited by organisms and therein they not only maintain but grow in spite of changes in external environment. The same is expected of organisations vis-à-vis the external environment. It also means the liveliness, dedication and determination of the work force be maintained to face the challenges posed by the external environment. **The responsibility of keeping up the required dynamism essentially rests on the leadership.** The leadership is expected to do all that, so that the organisational dynamism does not die down under any circumstances.

Universities like Oxford and Cambridge have been not only functioning but progressing for many centuries now. What has made them growing and progressing over such an extended period? They have maintained their dynamism in spite of profound changes in the British society, over the time. The leaderships over the time knew what they were meant for and drew inspiration from perennial source, like their great nationalism. They did not allow themselves to get rigid with respect to anything, without losing discipline. They have changed themselves to suit the times all along. The performance of Indian universities against this backdrop has generally been simply pathetic, in spite of enough financial support from the local and central governments after independence. For example, the Banaras Hindu University, started by **Pt. Madan Mohan Malaviya,** in 1916, flourished into a premier institution in just thirty years until the demise of the founder in 1946. Within a decade it started decaying and now it has been reduced to the stature of any other average university in India. Why did it decay so early and so readily? Why did it lose its dynamism? Same is the story of many other institutions. What is wrong with them?

In the popular Indian parlance the reason given for the decay is that it is all ***politics*** that has destroyed these institutions. What is after all politics? Politics is nothing but another name of selfish interests, resulting in exploitation of the organisation for selfish gains, with utter disregard to its high common ideals and objectives. The moment the leaders themselves lose sight of the objectives of an organisation, the fall is imminent. By contrast, even in the post-independence India, the **Indian Institute of Technologies and Managements,** or even some other institutions, perhaps by luck got leadership with right mission, and by keeping their vision in active action, they have been able to come to world standards like Oxford and Cambridge universities.

Those who directly or indirectly contribute in blurring the organisational vision also contribute in reducing the dynamism, which is sure to result in decay in due course of time.

At times public pressure in democracy either helps to maintain the dynamism of public institutions or even kill it, as the case may be. **Indian Hockey Federation** has become almost a dead institution, since it has lost its appeal and not many are interested in that game any more. Whereas the **Board of Cricket Control in India** (BCCI) is gaining more and more dynamism through ever increasing public support, for their ever innovative schemes like, first the one-day matches and now the T-20 matches. The IPL is still better and acceptable version with players from all over the world playing the matches. It is all the result of public interest and also its pressure to deliver goods.

Built to Perpetuate

Organisations of any type is supposed to grow with time. They are not meant to somehow just survive. Every society is in perpetual existence, in spite of the fact that the same human beings shall not be there for too long. Humans are born; they grow, carry out some activities and disappear from this earth some day. In terms of social existence the individual existence is negligibly small. Society is increasingly being sustained by organisations. For progress of society, these organisations must also continue perpetually. The alternative is that every time new organisations will have to be created and nourished to deliver the expected things to the society.

It is equally true that the products and services they provide eventually become obsolete. For maintenance of continuity they must go on changing their products and services so that no obsolescence will be faced. Similarly all those who manage the organisations have to quit after some finite contribution. For organisation to continue to serve the society they also need to be replaced after certain duration, commensurate with human life-span. Every organisation must therefore make way for new blood to be infused periodically so that new ideas, products and services are generated. For growth of an organisation all these are routine processes to be carried out regularly. Organisations therefore should not rely too much on some individuals alone, howsoever charismatic they may be.

Jim Collins [12,13] has analysed several commercial organisations to understand why some have survived over a very long time and grown while some others, in spite of making profit have not been able to grow to the same extent. He concludes that only those who had vision and felt that they had a mission to fulfill through their organisation have grown over such an extended period. In order to keep the continuity their mission was not just to make profit but to work for some core ideology that has a direct bearing on the welfare of the society.

Organisations should not be built around any charismatic leader, though such people are useful for temporary organisational growth and progress. These may be good organisations but aim should be to have great organisations; good is just not enough. For something to be great it must have an inbuilt style of management such that the organisations shall go on getting very capable leaders one after the other uninterruptedly. Study of RSS may be worth while in this respect. In other words they will not be just leaders but instead will be architects of organisations. It also requires concrete organisational mechanisms to stimulate not merely work culture but changes and improvements in tune with time. It is basically the perspective that keeps it going. In evolutionary natural process, better adaptable species have been evolved through mutation, selection and genetic changes.

Similar adaptability is expected of an organisation to suit it to evolving times. They must feel to serve the society through better products and services, continuously changing in tune with time.

The entire management process of planning, organising, staffing, controlling and leading will have to be geared such that there will always be dedication, commitment and enthusiasm for taking the organisation to still greater heights. Profit is no aim to motivate people in this direction. They have to be motivated for something much higher in life. Profit then automatically follows. The mission should be to see that human beings face fewer hardships and feel better comforts through their products and services.

This essentially requires core ideology for an organisation as the guiding star. This is quite different from culture, goals, strategies, tactics and the like. It is something for which the organisations are prepared to put everything at stake. The entire human resource is thereby aligned to the mission and vision of an organisation and not to mere profit. The subjectivity is thus eliminated and is replaced by total objectivity while working in an organisation. Whole of the organisation thereby gets motivated for doing better everyday than every yesterday. Long-term vision with respect to human resource, ideas, and technologies and so on comes to the centre stage of working.

It results in efficient management structure with right people at right places. They face the harsh facts and work out solutions accordingly. They have passion and endeavour for what best they can do within the given economic constraints. Every issue is deeply analysed with open exchange of views at all possible levels for right appreciation of the problem and decisions are taken accordingly. This is the sure path of growth and the alternative is path of decay, sooner or later.

SWOT Analysis and TOWS Matrix

One of the strikingly effective tool that has recently been invented, for making organisations very effective and efficient, is to carry out regularly the SWOT analysis of individuals, groups or the organisation as a whole. What is this SWOT analysis?

It consists of four-way analysis with respect to strength, weaknesses, opportunities and threats, the organization has or perceives. The four initial letters of these four parameters, the S, W, O and T constitutes the SWOT analysis. Out of these the first two, the strength and the weakness are related to internal state of affairs of the organisation or the inside and the other two, the opportunities and threats refer to the external environment or the outside. Strength means the overall capacity or ability of an organisation, in the form of material and human resources, to perform as per requirements. Weakness means the factors, in the form of lack of material, circumstantial and human resources that might come in the way of achieving the desired goal. Opportunity describes the multifarious avenues available for achieving organisational goal. Threats describe the possible obstacles by way of difficult competitors, lack of social requirements, external challenges and so on. In totality they give what is possible and what needs to be improved from within the organisation and what all prospect and obstacles may be faced in the outside world in getting the organisational objectives met. It is however a static analysis and the world is too dynamic to be entirely interpreted in terms of such static parameters. It is not possible to evolve alternative strategies based on merely such static analysis. But it does help in knowing the internal and the external state of affairs. It is the unique role of the CEO to keep proper balance between the inside (S and W) and outside (O and T).

Using the same four measures as above but putting them into a matrix in the form of interrelation of internal and the external situations in the form of TOWS matrix, gives a conceptual framework for systematic analysis that matches the internal and the external affairs in the form of four situations which can be best utilised to organisational advantage. It is shown in **Fig. 19.1.**

Internal factors → **External factors ↓**	**Strengths (S)**	**Weakness (W)**
Opportunities (O)	**SO – situation Max-max**	**WO - situation Mini-maxi**
Threats (T)	**ST – situation Max-mini**	**WT - Situation Mini-mini**

Fig. 19.1 : TOWS analysis for formulation of organisational strategies to face possible different situations.

It leads to four pairs of situations as below

1. Internal strength/External opportunities as SO strategy, as the best one that could be exploited to organisational advantage in time.
2. Internal weakness/External threats as WT strategy, as the worst situation, either to be avoided or faced with courage, or even the organisation may be sold or disbanded if faced by a blind alley.
3. Internal weakness/External opportunities as WO strategy as medium in its potential which can be suitably made use of.
4. Internal strength/External threats as ST strategy as also medium in its potential to be suitably exploited to advantage.

One can react to the available combination by taking maximum advantage of the SO situation, by way of either improving the internal situation to manage the WO and improving the external situation to manage the ST situation and, can even think of selling the business or winding up the organisation when under the serious enough WT situation.

The same analysis can be made about the projected situation after some specific time to evaluate the future situation and to find out the best possible favourable situation for growth and progress. It will be possible to forecast the growth in future under specified conditions or time lapse for such favouable situations can be predicted.

As mentioned above an organisation may grow if the relevant factors like increasing vigour of participants, their creativity, hard work inputs, co-operation and co-ordination and such factors, along with favourable external opportunities and minimum threats exists. If the situation is contrary then it may slow down the growth and perhaps set-in even decay. This is dealt with again while discussing decay later.

References

1. Shourie, A. *Individuals, Institutions and Processes,* Viking, (1990).
2. Tom Peters and Nancy, Austin, *A passion for Excellence*, Profile, London, (2003).
3. Argenti, John, *Your Organisation: What is it For?* McGraw Hill, London, (1993).
4. Palkar, N.H., *Dr. Hedgewar, (Biography),* Dr. Hedgewar Memorial Soc. Pune (1960).
5. Deal, T., Kennedy, E. and Allan, A., *Corporate Cultures (The Rites and Rituals of Corporate Life)*, Perseus, Cambridge, Mass, (1982).
6. Toffler, Alvin, *The Third Wave*, Warner, (1985).
7. Sheshadri, H.V., RSS- *A Vision in Action*, Jagran, Banglore, (1988).
8. Tom Peters and Robert H. Waterman Jr, *In search of Excellence*, Profile, (2003).
9. Tom Peters and Nancy Austin, *A Passion for Excellence,* Profile, (2003).
10. Drukker, Peter, as quoted by Vasant Desai, *Dynamics of Entreprenurial Development and Management,* Himalaya, Mumbai, (2004).
11. Covey Stephen, R., *The Speed of Trust*, Free Press, N.Y. (2006).
12. Collins, Jim and Porras, Jerry, I., *Built to Last*, Harper-Collins, N.Y. (1994).
13. Collins, Jim, *Good to Great,* Harper-Collins, N.Y. (2001).

CHAPTER 20

INSPIRATION

CHAPTER STRUCTURE

- Human Factors
- Motivation
- Theories of Motivation
    - Theory x and Y
    - Maslow's Hierarchy of Needs Theory
    - Hertzberg's Motivation-hygiene Theory
    - Expectancy Theory
    - Equity Theory
    - Goal Setting Theory
    - Skinner's Reinforcement Theory
    - McClelland's Needs Theory
    - Motivational Techniques
- Inspiration
- Organisational Strategies

Human Factors

The main consideration in managing and growth of an organisation is the management of human resources, since managing the materials and finances is relatively easy. It is related to the bahavioural science, and the individual behaviour is least predictable. It essentially requires understanding of roles of humans in a given situation. This in turn is related to the individuality and the personality of a person.

After all what makes a human being to carry out various activities? Is it just for physical sustenance of one's self or at best of his family? This is true to a certain extent only. Humans do have physical desires but along with that they do have mental as well as intellectual desires as well. The proportion of dominance of each one of them varies from person to person. Does one work, to the extent possible, to meet them? Yes one does, but again to the extent determined by many factors related to himself and to the environment. At least some do have additionally spiritual needs as well and for which they really strive. But then why does the human being at times help others to achieve the same material pleasures? Whereas some other time he tries to oppose, out of jealousy to see that the others do not get the same? Sometimes one goes to the extent of even damaging the chances of others so that they do not get their needs met at all. At times he only shows that he is striving hard but in reality he is only evading the work; he only poses to show that he is working. Some such and many more types of complex and paradoxical behaviours are observed, depending upon the situation, person, time, surrounding environment, work-types and so on. How would one commence or continue to work even in adverse conditions, hostile surroundings, with somewhat unpleasant and disliked co-workers, under a loathsome boss, for unrewarding situations and so on?

With reference to an individual such problems are to be faced by an individual alone. But they affect all other related ones when faced in an organisation. Many such questions often crop up while working in an organisation. It has a direct bearing on human effectiveness and efficiency in carrying out a certain task. A manager has to face these problems with respect to his subordinates and co-workers and yet see that they work as per his expectations in finally attempting to achieve the objective. For an effective and efficient manager it is therefore necessary to understand what factors decrease the efficiency of an individual while working in a group, what factors motivate one to work or work hard and what factors inspire anyone to embark on work with full vigour and capability irrespective of any other consideration?

Motivation

It is rather difficult to define what is motivation? It often means all those drives, desires, needs, wishes and all such psychological forces that make individuals strive for something in a given situation. These either make one work in the desired direction, if present at sufficient potential or, make him shirk the work, if these are at their opposite. **Anthony Robbins** [1] calls these as value hierarchies as these are characteristically individualistic in nature. Additionally these vary with circumstances. What motivates one may not motivate the other. This is the greatest of the challenges to be faced by the managers. Hence a manager has to motivate his subordinates, in favourable and unfavourable circumstances, to act suitably as per his requirements in finally meeting the organisational objectives.

The manager himself must feel motivated to the utmost to start with. But for that he must learn to handle his own frustration, rejection if any, financial and other pressures, and above all complacency to start with. Then only he will be able to motivate his subordinates into actions as per his expectations. The more it is done on individualistic basis the better. Motivation is therefore that force which is induced by someone else in others with some ulterior intention or selfishness.

Considering the above mentioned basic human nature, a manager has to motivate every individual independently as well as in groups. There is nothing like an average human being, they are all unique in their own way, with respect to their desires, attitudes, potentials, ambitions, knowledge levels, skills, responsibilities, expectations and so on. Each one feels his own dignity in his own style and expects to be dealt with due dignity by anyone, even superiors. Above all each one responds in his own characteristic style in a given environment to whatever is put before him. His mood is dependent on so many variables that it is difficult to predict it beforehand with certainty.

Theories of Motivation

There are many different theories of motivation such as described below in very brief:

Theory X and Y

It was suggested by **Douglas McGregor** [2]. It describes the inherent nature of human beings in qualitative terms as theory-X like the natural dislike for work, effect of coercion/subjugation/pressure, fear of punishment, shirking characteristics and so on.

In the form of theory-Y it is the effect of allurement, threat, commitment, appeal to conscience, curiosity, imagination and creativity, described in Indian tradition as ***sama***(appeal) , ***dama***(monetary payment), ***danda***(threat with dire consequences) and ***bheda*** (pitting one against the other).

It is only qualitatively conceptualised to evaluate different strategies for being effective in different situations. It helps in selecting most appropriate approach in a given situation, being more effective than the other, in order to motivate someone to work, based on experience only.

Maslow's Hierarchy of Needs Theory

It has already been described earlier (Chapter 2). It has been disputed that human needs can not be classified in the form of such hierarchical needs at all. Human being is too complex to fit into such a simple straight jacket. But such needs do exist and humans do endeavour to achieve them or one can be motivated to work to achieve these.

Hertzberg's Motivation-hygiene Theory

According to Hertzberg it is possible to express some needs as satisfiers and some as dissatisfiers to human nature. The dissatisfiers such as mere maintenance, hygiene or job-contextual factors like usual working conditions do not motivate people to put in their best. But the satisfiers such as recognition, promotion, monetary benefits, etc. motivate individuals to put in their best in the scheme of organisational efforts.

Expectancy Theory

This was put forward by psychologist **Victor H. Vroom** [3]. According to him people work if they feel that it is worth as per their own assessment, in the sense that it will accrue something to meet their needs. He defined motivation as force obtained in the form of a product of anticipated worth of his inputs and the chance of it being successful in the form

Force = valence x expectancy

Where force is the strength of ones motivation, valence is proportion of his effort being successful and expectancy is the possibility of it being successful. Depending upon the output of this complex relationship, as per one's own assessment, one will get motivated for an expected action. The effort-performance-reward-satisfaction system can be integrated in the overall organisational strategy of management. It also throws light on what will be the result of a given direction to the work force.

Equity Theory

It is in human nature to compare him with others so that he is not taxed by way of additional work-burden as compared to others unnecessarily. A person also sees that he is not denied the same benefits in relation to others in similar situations. It is one's own subjective judgment of fairness of rewards. Those who feel that they are not discriminated would turn satisfied with the system and get motivated in work and *vice-a-versa.*

Goal Setting Theory

It is essentially management by objective **(MBO)** based on systems model of organisations. It requires that the objective should be very clearly defined and made understood to one and all. It motivates all to strive, if entire management is focused in achieving it.

Skinner's Reinforcement Theory

It is based on the assumption that workers can be motivated by providing proper design of work and environment. It is to say that organisation must be structured and managed properly for everyone to get motivated to work. It includes trouble-shooting in the areas where problems are faced during implementation.

McClelland's Needs Theory

It assumes that everyone longs for power, affiliation and achievement while working in a group. If these are provided appropriately one may get motivated to work. It perhaps holds true more for managers than for the lower level workers.

Motivational Techniques

The carrot of monetary gains is very commonly used for motivating individuals to work in an organisation. It may also mean as power as well, for some to work for. It works up to a certain limit in almost every case. Soon after getting additional monetary gains, one thinks that it is his normal due and nothing extra has been given to him by way of motivation for him to work. Hence he needs to be paid more for getting motivated to work. Hence there is always a limit up to which monetary motivation may work. There is usually no end to the expectation. It may result in unethical behaviour, perhaps in due course, creating other problems.

Promotional avenues are opened to motivate people into work. It may also result in the same situation as in the case of monetary gains.

Better quality of working conditions, by way of participation, job enrichment and so on are also used as motivators, often with reasonable results.

In short there is no single way and sure-shot path of motivating people for work. It is more a trial and improvement method for continuous review and action thereat without a specific end-solution.

Inspiration

Quite in contrast to motivation, inspiration is more or less a personal phenomenon, indicating almost in independent terms; one's own drives, wishes, desires and so on for doing certain things. One may get inspired by someone or a group, by circumstances, by environment, by cultivation and so on for doing a certain thing, irrespective of any other's any type of behaviour. Often people are inspired by certain lofty individuals and their works and achievements, for the good of others. Any selfish act of someone does not inspire anyone at all, except to become selfish likewise. One may try to motivate people, as mentioned above, but still individuals will have to get inspiration from within to march on the path of endeavours as per expectation. In ultimate analysis **motivation has to stir one's conscience so that he gets inspired from within** to work. This is the reason why monetary and authority allurements, though inspiring temporarily, do not last long as inspiring criteria.

The theories of motivation as explained above are more mechanistic in nature and hence cannot explain the phenomena of inspiration satisfactorily. It is not possible to account inspiration in terms of any causal principles. Inspiration appears as a sudden flash of solution to a problem or direction of endeavours to embark on. There is no ambiguity of conviction and hence it results in motivation. The source of such inspiration is beyond conscious and systematic algorithm that leads to such flashes and understanding of any thing. It is a sudden revelation without any awareners of intermediate logical steps. It has something to do with the phenomena of consciousness itself which so far has eluded any logical understanding. In fact it falls in the realm of spirituality.

In commercial profit making organisations monetary and power allurements or possibilities, can motivate people only to the extent of meeting, their similar selfish interests and no more. Alternatively coercion and threats, in the form of withdrawal of such benefits, can also be used for motivation. But in social, political, charitable academic and religious organisations, it is often not selfish but larger social and humanitarian interests that inspire people to be active, even to the extent of, disregarding their own selfish interests. Hence here leaders are often compared with a lamp which can light others to illuminate the space around, by becoming leaders themselves. Fact remains that there has to be something more ethereal and of larger interest for people to get inspired for doing some work. In the absence of such a thing it is not easy to keep people inspired for long. Most people often get inspired by some individuals and there has to be such people around for them to be inspired for certain tasks to be achieved.

Organisational Strategies

The most haunting problem of motivation is not something that crops up only occasionally, it is a problem faced all along and without respite in almost every organisation. Tremendous competition amongst organisations across the globe requires that the work force is always motivated, particularly in commercial organisations. Every additional endeavour to motivate the work-force is bound to lead to additional tensions in the work-force, even at times to the extent of straining individuals to the point of even psychological break-downs. Although work-force empowerment has been tried extensively, no other factor has so far been found to be more effective than the monetary and power allurements by way of promotions, particularly in commercial organisation. Sometimes coercion does work. Monetary allurements however do not work in NPOs to any appreciable extent because of their very nature. Hence all organisations in general, but particularly the NPOs in the form of social, political, charitable and cultural organisations, and which predominantly decide the overall social structure, are now facing challenges, unimagined earlier in the industrial era. They may sustain themselves through drawing energy and inspiration in five different directions simultaneously. These are:

1. Transformations in the organisational set-up in tune with time to suit every emergency, as a matter of routine practice.
2. Managing organisations by improvements in scientific managements, as is currently being understood, rather than depending upon yesterday's used-to techniques.
3. Drawing inspiration and empowerment from cultural ethos of human race in general and of the specific society, in which it operates, in particular.

4. Persistent and consistent endeavour's towards victory or successful developments, without any accomplice for intermediate failures.
5. Persistent efforts to cultivate idealism so that whatever work is being carried out is considered as an attempt towards achievement of that ideal.

The twenty-first century will be characterised by liberalisation, globalization, openness, secularism, individual spiritualism in place of collective religion, environmental considerations, scientific temper, knowledge predominance, cultural plurality, humanism, human rights, all inclusiveness, sustainable consumption and production and such other concepts, leading to mental appreciation of world as one single village. The individuals and organisations world over will have to accommodate all these overriding virtues and characteristics to cope up with times so that they act in unison with the larger interests of the society and humanity as a whole. Those who can not cope up will have to face great tensions to continue to function in the modern day world.

References

1. Robbins, Anthony, *Unlimited Power*, Simon and Schuster, London (1998).
2. McGregor, Douglas, *The Human Side of Enterprise*, McGraw Hill, N.York, (2006).
3. Vroom, V.H., *Work and Motivation*, John Wiley, N.York, (1964).
4. Drukker, Peter, as quoted by Vasant Desai in, *Dynamics of Entrepreneurial Development and Management*, Himalaya, Mumbai (2004).
5. Covey Stephen, R., *The Speed of Trust,* Free Press, N.Y. (2006).

CHAPTER 21

PERCEPTION, JUDGMENT, DECISION AND IMPLEMENTATION

CHAPTER STRUCTURE

- Perception
- Intelligence
- Judgments
- Decision-making
- Long-term, Short-term
- Alternatives
- Sixth Sense
- Blink
- Types of Decision-making
- Blame-game
- Creativity and Innovation
- Crisis
- Social Revolution
- Experience vs. Creativity
- Character vs. Efficiency
- Knowledge as Commodity
- Disciple vs. Co-worker
- Individual Entrepreneurship in Systems
- Decentralisation
- Frustration
- Implementation

Perception

The composite of two major systems of the human brain, the limbic system and the cortex, characterise the human being from the rest of the living world. These help him to perceive things, both tangible and intangible. The limbic system is characterised by the fight or flight syndrome like in animals. It helps him to instantaneously perceive things and act immediately without any rational thinking about the pros and cons of the action. This ensures most often safety and security as has been seen in the evolution process. The cortex is the seat of rational thinking which has several parameters. That is the reason why it is slow and can be still slower as per demand and requirements. If perception and consequent judgment was left only to the cortex there is a possibility of utter confusion because of innumerable available options. But the limbic system comes in as an aid and the two jointly can come to judgment rather quickly by way of intelligent use of emotions.

The necessity to solve any problem requires perception of the same as a priori. Perception of anything is possible only to the extent of one's own personality. It can be made fast if so required. Since personality is typically an individual phenomenon, perception also is typically an individual affair. Even in organised activities perception is ultimately possible only on individual level alone, although the rest may help in perceiving better. Perception is motivated by the basic cognitive ability, meaning thereby one's own ability to observe, assimilate the observed facts, compare these with the previous related memories, understand the issue therefrom and then appreciation of the entire scenario. That is the reason why every individual's perception about the same thing differs considerably from those of other's. It would be expressed by different persons to different extents, depending upon one's own power of expression. Perception occurs at the mental and intellectual level of every one as per one's own cognitive power. All those factors that are responsible for the development of personality may all be responsible for total perception.

All those parameters which affect perception as a whole may come into play while perceiving anything and everything, if required. It means known people or groups of people, their level of understanding, their desires, material things and services, their relationships, social forces in general and all such tangible and intangible parameters affect one's own perception. Which one of these shall play its role, and to what extent, depends on the overall personality of an individual and the issue before. The actual process of perception is quite complex but the natural computer in the form of cortex brain, with all the earlier cultural soft-wares loaded on it; make it easier to appreciate, to the extent possible. The limbic system hastens this process to a great extent.

Life is all uncertain. It is neither deterministic nor an extension of the past. Everyone always faces different problems not faced before in the form of people, their behaviour and overall external environment. In the parlance of **Arnold Toynbee** [1] these constitute as challenges and every one has to respond them to live in this world. It is therefore imperative to perceive them before, attain proper understanding, draw proper judgments and then only respond them to the extent possible either individually or in the form of an organised effort, to one's own advantage. The process of judgment and response thereat entirely depends on the extent of correct perception.

Perception in general is improved by observation, education, training, reading, assimilation of knowledge, emotional attachment, dedication, persistence, interaction with enlightened ones and so on. The experience of others, friends or professional experts, their motivating efforts, co-operation and such things also aid in proper perception and therefore of judgment and decision-making.

The deeper and more extensive the issue the more and prolonged rational thinking may be required for its proper perception and decision-making thereat. It may take an equally long time as well. Help from friends and from experts may also be useful in this respect.

The problem of perception of individual's challenges, about most of the things, is relatively simple as compared to that of every organised effort. It becomes more and more serious with increasing size and activity of an organisation.

In profit making organisations, the process of perception about everything that can affect their profit is continuously kept in view and processed. Ideally they should not be **'caught unaware'** about anything pertaining to their business. They therefore always keep on carrying out futuristic assessment. It is also equally true with all other organised efforts to save time, energy and money.

The responsibility of proper perception rests more on the leader because based on his perception; decisions are taken for the organisation as a whole. Proper inputs in the direction of achieving the organisational objective from co-workers, directly depends on the perception, judgment and decision-making ability of the leaders.

Anybody's perception, in its ultimate analysis, is decided by his own system of beliefs and values. When these become congruous, persons may perceive, judge, decide and act accordingly. Individuals have different ideas in deciding values and accordingly different ways to judge and decide things in their own ways.

Intelligence

It is through appropriate intelligence alone that right perception, judgment and decision making and even implementation is possible. **Jean Piaget** has defined intelligence as," what you use when you don't know what to do". **Juan Huarte** has defined intelligence as the ability to learn, the ability to exercise judgment and the ability to be creative. This falls in the domain of self-management which when carried out goes through steps like goal formation, research, strategizing, tactics and creativity. This leads to appropriate perception, judgment and decision making about anything and finally its implementation. This is in a way a problem solving strategy which has three components unified into one. The first is own-self, second is the environment that includes related people and the third is the situation in which the problem has arisen.

The first is therefore an alert about the problem. It is the recognition whether what is being done may be causing the problem. What is therefore required is to change own-self through change of own behaviour and try to solve the problem. It may be that some others are causing the problem and I have to exert to make them change and help solve the problem. It may be that some features of the situation are causing the problem and the answer lies in changing the situation to help solve the problem. As a priori I should not be too rigid about myself and should be prepared to exert to change as per requirements. But at the same time I should also try to change the related others to help solve the problem, if necessary. Additionally I should also try to improve the situation to help solve the problem. It is a holistic solution and must be tackled on all these three fronts considering it to be an integral system. Any rigidity on any front may prevent from solving the problem to the extent it affects it. The efficiency of perception, judgment and decision-making shall depend on how efficiently all these three factors are handled in a holistic manner towards solution.

As the above strategy indicates solution to individual problem, the same strategy holds true for solving organisational problems as well. The only change with reference to organisational problems is that the self then becomes the group or inside of the organisation, the outside means the outside of the organisation and the situation may mean the instant environment that is creating the situation worth attention by the organisation.

Judgments

Judgments are one's own inferences about anything that comes across an individual. He/she has to judge related people, processes, material things, their right costs and qualities and even abstract things like possible governmental legislations, political interferences, social pressures and so on before any action can be initiated in view of achieving some objective. Similarly in the case of an organisation the manager, besides the above, has to judge co-workers, their capability to do certain assigned jobs, their mutual trust and co-operation while working together, availability of adequate material and financial resources and so on to lead the organisation to achieve its objective. Every time a manager has to assess the situation and the conditions to finalise his own judgment and then direct his co-workers into certain action, by way of his decisions. The co-workers also judge the manager's sincerity, enthusiasm, commitment to the organisational cause, and if judged as at least reasonable, good or excellent being the best, they may plunge into action as per the decisions or directives.

In human resource development, for either fresh recruitment or promotion from within, the manager has to judge people whether they are fit for recruitment or promotion in view of the job requirements as planned. They have also to judge whether they are worth the money being paid as remuneration/salary/perks and so on. It is difficult to judge an individual human being because of his inherent nature being unpredictable. It can never be predicted precisely before hand. But broadly some very broad indication can be had as to how anyone would behave or react in a particular situation, knowing him/her for some time. Alternatively conditions can be created such that one has to work, at least to some extent, per force, to his best abilities or as per expectations. Judgments are therefore necessary before any decision can be taken. Without judgment no decision is normally possible, except the ones taken at the blink of an eye as involuntary decisions, which may or may not prove right.

Decision-making

Even when individuals act in their own capacity, a lot of thinking and assessment of the overall situation goes in before embarking on the actual action, so that the objective may be achieved with reasonable certainty and within the permissible costs, if pertinent. Nobody acts without any objective. There is always some objective in initiating any action whatsoever. In the case of group activities it is normally imperative to rationally judge the situation form all possible angles in a futuristic assessment-style before making any decision for the group to act in an expected way. The TOWS analysis, described earlier, comes in handy at such times.

Decision-making on the part of the leader has therefore acquired key importance in managing organisations. In ultimate analysis, it is his judgment that decides the course of action. He is at the steering wheel of an organisation. He has to steer clear towards the goal without any catastrophe on the way. Decision-making has been defined as selection of a certain path of action from amongst the varied and alternative available courses. It has direct bearing on achievement, and more so, on the involved efficiency, in achieving the objective of an organisation. The group theory postulates that decision-making is the end product of the activities of the leader.

Decision-making is to be distinguished from policy making. Policy making refers to broad perspective that would enable proper decision-making as and when required. Policy making refers to a collectivity of intersecting decisions. Policies embody instructions concerning conduct of power process. Decision-making is confined to making a choice from the available alternatives for effective action. Unless one has the required power no decision can be taken. Hence power is also defined as participation in making decisions. Decision-making analysis is thus capable of dealing with dynamic situations. The efficiency of an organisation is measured in terms of its capacity to take decisions that are widely accepted.

The process of decision-making goes through several stages before arriving at the correct decision, viz identification of the issue, why it has cropped up, where it is relevant, appraisal of juniors and co-workers about the issue, recommendation if any, previous relevant historical record, decision-makers own assessment, alternatives available and prescription of specific recommendation and so on. In management process power is effective participation in decision-making.

Once decision is taken it should be communicated for appropriate action and compliance for its overall impact and gains or loss, if any. It includes review and reassessment, if required and its termination if found to be disadvantageous.

In general decision-making involves following seven steps:

1. Problem identification and search for related information
2. Formulation of the alternatives for making the choice
3. Choice of the preferred alternative

4. Enforcement of the decision taken
5. Enforcement of any specific needs
6. Review and assessment of the enforced decision and its effects
7. Review, revision or even repeal, whatever is best suited in the emerging scenario

Long-term, Short-term

Decisions are normally to be taken in terms of short and long-term perceptions in achieving the ultimate objective. Often the short-term action may appear as if it has apparently nothing to do with the final objective. This may be the perception of those working at lower levels. It may not be so in reality. For example lowering the price of goods, selling them at even loss for a while may appear nonsense to lower level workers. But it is assessed that such steps would increase the sale and the loss so incurred can be made good later by increasing the sale-price. The overall course of action on long-term basis has been adjudged by the leader and short-term decisions are taken in view of the long-term objectives. The leader/manager is solely responsible for deciding the course of action. The credit, if succeeds and, discredit if it proves a failure, is all of the leader/manager. But often decisions are also required to be taken impromptu as the situation demands. The leader is therefore expected to know the overall situation and effects of varieties of variables on the possible, even future-possible decisions that he may take in a given case.

In case of planning the organisation, decision implies approval of the plan and commitment of allocation of minimum required resources like men, money, materials and otherwise, for the plan of action, in terms of long-term view of the organisation. These are all based on the overall judgment of the controller or at times even by the leader or manager. These are only broad decisions and the leader/manager may have to take varied decisions in the course of action itself.

The process of decision-making involves premising, identifying and evaluation of possible alternatives, choosing the best course and setting forth the action to achieve the objective. Since decision-making, in its ultimate analysis, is made by a human being, and shall always be as per his subjective perception and satisfaction, can never be entirely rational at all. Decision-making is always bound by the limitations of the knowledge about the thing/situation, some insurmountable and perhaps known or unknown obstacles, availability and quality of man-power at command, availability of finance, possible obstacles from socio-political interferences and many such things. These have to be assessed and judged before initiating any action whatsoever. With whatever knowledge and understanding of the situation the decision is made, it must be satisfying, as the best in a given situation, to initiate the action. If there are any doubts about the course of action then it cannot be considered as decision, since decision is expected to finally lead into success after appropriate action.

Alternatives

Usually there will always be more than one course of actions available and hence judgment about a particular course of action, in preference to others, must be the one as adjudged best. If there is only one course of action then it can be safely adjudged that the prior process of assessment has not been carried out as per expected requirements. It is a challenge to human intelligence to have **'no-alternative situation'** for achieving any human objective.

Alternatives can be evaluated both in terms of qualitative and quantitative factors that are bound to affect the final outcome. In commercial organisations everything is usually judged in terms of overall and final profit that might accrue from a certain decision. If it can be quantitatively proved that a certain course is bound to lead to higher profit, that course shall in a normal way be chosen, subject to many other social and environmental constraints. Problems come only when the qualitative and quantitative assessments come out at loggerheads.

Sixth Sense

Decision-making does involve creativity and use of creative and innovative abilities of co-workers and subordinates. Under the Newton-Cartesian influence decision-making was essentially based on objective facts, data, information and such things. However it is no more considered to be the sole criterion for making decisions. It has now been seen that human intellect, intuition, sixth sense, etc. based more on general experience and commonsense, often lead to better judgments and therefore better decisions than those based entirely on facts and figures alone. It may be because facts and figures cannot reveal the entire truth about the issue at hand. The personal judgments of controller/leader are often more relied upon than mere facts and figures because it is more based on obvious as well as tacit understanding of the issue, which may not be explicable in the form of data alone, no matter how precise these are. The sixth sense or intuition of controller/leader thus has acquired predominance over the facts and figures. The decision-making often gets complicated, if the two do not tally. The conflicting views and judgments require more information to resolve the issue. If quick experimentation is permissible, either with respect to time requirement or monetary involvement, then that can be resorted to and based on those findings final course of action may be decided.

In social, political and charitable organisations the process of decision-making is more out of intuition of the leader, as he is very much knowledgeable and involved in the whole organisational processes, through and through. It may also be due to non-availability of precise data that are needed to assess the situation and arrive at the quantitative decision. His decisions therefore often falls in the creative and innovative realm.

Blink

It is often seen that the first impression or impression formed just at the first blink, on seeing or interacting with something, is just the correct assessment of the problem, more in line with what comes out eventually after elaborate evaluation process [2]. Manager's intuition therefore has its own role and effective too, in making correct decisions. It should not however be stretched too far. Everything has its own limitations, so has the creativity and intuition in final decision-making. Decisions based both on facts and figures and on leader's intuition would perhaps be the best.

Types of Decision-making

In any organisational structure, the necessity and authority of decision-making and therefore the attendant capability must increase towards the controller, leader or the manager from the bottom level up, and vice a versa. There are basically two broad types of decision-making, namely the **programmed and the structural decision-making**. The programmed decision-making is based on the routine problems and fairly known situations, whereas the structural decision-making is required in view of emergent and more or less un-imagined problems before. Decision-making always involves some risk, though perhaps it may be a calculated one, since there is no guarantee that it will always be right. It may come out to be wrong and in such a case it has to be accepted in right spirit. All that is required is to take right decision as far as is based on given information and correct perception, intuition and foresight. It is equally needed that failures may be taken as first step towards success.

Blame-game

It is easy to criticise the decisions after they result in failures. The criticism is often sharper if the failures are serious. These are after thoughts and only fools think about anything, after it has become history. It serves no purpose. No action is deliberately taken to lead to such failures, unless some one is out to sabotage the situation from within for some ulterior reasons. But some unforeseen factors, perhaps as a result of leaders own limitations or situational limitations, beyond his control, may be the possible reasons of failure. The leader's own limitations needs to be viewed seriously even to the extent of his replacement. But the leader cannot be blamed for a situation beyond his control. Such after-assessments often tend to be more subjective rather than objective for making up the deficiencies in future course of actions. These assessments tend to blame the leader solely for the failure and are often aimed at taking some revenge clandestinely. This is what is termed as ***politics*** in any organisation, in common parlance. No organisation can be free of such politics. It is in its nature, since human beings are involved. Such blame-game in reality help retard the organisational progress. It is no good in the long run in achieving the objectives of organisations. All this can be avoided to a large extent by making the organisation more flat [3,4] and involving most, if not all, in decision-making so that no body has any personal axe to grind, in the event of any failure. Success or failure is the order of organisational functioning. All that is needed is to take it as one's own and not as a result of anybody else's specific failure.

Creativity and Innovation

One of the important areas where decision-making is quite critical is where creativity and innovation is involved in any organisation. Creativity is the ability to bring out new ideas, designs, things, etc. and innovation means using such new ideas for some useful application. Creativity is highly an individualistic phenomenon, involving the insight, logical approach, conscious evaluation, intuition and such things. The left half hemisphere of our brain is the seat of learning through repetitive practices and is sharpened through hard work and industry. The creativity and innovativeness is the property of right hemisphere of our brain, which is considered to be a nature's gift. **Basic rational training of left brain is required as a useful infra-structural aid for creative functioning of the right hand hemisphere brain.** The two hemispheres work as an integral whole brain because the left one always helps the right one to do some creative work. It depends basically on the ability of right brain to do such innovative work. For example one cannot ordinarily do creative work in say science without prior training in science. A painter without science training cannot innovate in science in a normal course. He may be able to innovate in an art. Creativity cannot be predicted before hand, because the ability of the right half brain can neither be measured, nor can it be improved by any training whatsoever. It is considered to be a nature's gift. No wonder it appears often to come out serendipitously, without any prior signal.

Crisis

Anybody's ability to perceive, judge and take appropriate decision to implement it thereafter is tested whenever there is a crisis [3]. Crisis is such a situation which is never experienced before. Hence earlier experience is least useful in responding to any crisis. The situation is such that it demands exceptional perception, equally rare acumen to judge and boldness, against all odds, to decide the course of action. Though the outcome is not certain it offers best possible opportunity to face the world. It is always a great teacher. Crisis is a double edged sword. Whatever is the response, the earlier stability is definitely threatened. It expects creative ability to cope up with it. It may cause initially even chaos if responded to but may even bring forth an astonishing outcome. For this to happen it requires extraordinary inner strength, determination and confidence in one's own self, which may surface in the form of creative response. It definitely eliminates earlier fears and teaches new meanings of life. One often discovers new meaning of life, inner strength, never experienced before, and as a result may even discover new life mission out of its perception, judgment and response.

Social Revolution

The effects of social evolution – stone-age to agriculture to industrial to information technology – on perception, judgment, decision-making and even implementation needs to be appreciated because the evolved state of individuals and also of groups in the form of organisation depends, to a large extent, on their state of evolution. It can be readily observed in India where individuals and groups belonging to all these stages of evolution appear to perceive, judge and make decisions differently as per their existing state of evolution.

In the agricultural era the rate of change in the society or even in an individual's life was perhaps negligibly small, to the extent that it appeared as if life was stagnated and has been in existence in that form for ages without change. This was more so in India, which had the longest span of agricultural era in the world. This may be the reason why the traditionalists in India think that the Hindu society has been in existence for lacs of years like this before and that Lord Rama and Lord Krishna lived here several lacs of years ago. Now we know for certain that agricultural revolution is no more than about 10-12000 years old only. But even in the span of few thousand years of that era life remained without much of a change, until almost some centuries ago. The net result was in making the society more conservative and extremely reluctant to change in all its approaches. It has almost become a part of the human genome in India as explained earlier. The challenges that were faced in perhaps the entire agricultural era were somewhat similar to one another without much difference, at least within anybody's life time. The present day challenges have almost nothing to do with those challenges. But the agricultural hangover is very strong and that comes in as a hurdle in embarking on to the modern era with full vigour. The hangover reflects in many ways. Let us see how it works.

In the agricultural era, experience counted more in their perception and decision-making. Honesty in general was rated as the top-most quality in agricultural era. The concept of efficiency was almost unknown to that era. It is the outcome of industrial era and more so as an inalienable part of current knowledge era. It is rated higher than even honesty or character in general. In agricultural era perception of elderly people predominated and was accepted without question. Creativity and innovation was practically absent in agricultural era. But these are the hall marks of industrial and knowledge era. Knowledge was not commodity for sale but now it is produced by investing money and treated as intellectual property like any other property. It is generated to make profit by its later sale. Practically no organisation existed, at least in India, except the governing organisations, in the agricultural era. Even otherwise it is dominantly a gift of industrialisation. Systemic thinking is the result of knowledge era and is affecting the present day perception immensely in all walks of life. All such variations need to be understood to develop the basic structure of science of organisation.

Experience vs. Creativity

The major hangover is in terms of experience as the sole basis for tracking solutions for the present. The experience gained in responding the challenges in that stagnant society at one or the other point of time were often found to be useful in responding somewhat similar challenges even later. Naturally the elders being more experienced came in handy for tackling similar challenges later. They were therefore usually taken as suitable guides and advisors in tackling similar problems later. This is how the philosophy that wisdom lies with elders for being more experienced came to be accepted as a standard norm in the agricultural era.

That is why, as already explained in Chapter 10 in the words of **Bhishmacharya** that whenever situation demands any answers, one should look at the intellectuals how they behaved in similar situation earlier, and follow the same path. The experience counted most in those agricultural days in responding to the challenges posed before.

The same mental make-up still continues in India in the form of utmost respect to the elders and seeking their blessings and advice for anything and everything even in the present day industrialised world, when things have drastically changed and are still changing rapidly without any respite, due to industrialisation. Hence elder's experience does not count much in tackling the present day problems. But this fact is not easily grasped in India because most of the population still lives mentally in the agricultural psyche (see also Chapter 12).

In the agricultural era in India there used to be gurus to advice people more on the path of salvation. But most of them used to guide the masses even in their day-to-day mundane affairs as well. This tradition continues even today out of the ***disciple-syndrome*** in operation in India as described earlier. It is generally believed that one who can guide about the unknown other worldly affairs, like salvation, must be equally qualified to guide even in this worldly affairs, that is material worldly affairs, as these are considered to be far too inferior to the other worldly affairs. One can find people even now who are glad to seek advice from their guru as to what course like, say, mechanical or electrical or electronics engineering, be chosen by their ward after the twelfth examination. Guru's advice even in such specialised fields of modern social system and which is fairly unknown to the old style guru, is taken as binding and acted on accordingly. Even if something goes wrong, it is accepted as if fate had it that way, with equanimity without any grudge against the guru. Many times marriages are fixed as per guru's advice without looking into any other relevant aspects.

The strange phenomena are that the effect of this conservative, stagnating and feudal lifestyle is felt in India in all walks of life even after considerable industrialisation of the society. This is typical perception of agricultural society. But the modern social and technological life is changing fast and poses every time perhaps new challenges. Experience does not help much to solve such new problems. Instead creativity and innovativeness are needed to respond the new challenges of the modern world almost in every sphere and almost every time. It is not only true with individuals but truer with organised efforts.

This is the reason why many quite young and inexperienced ones have contributed in various social spheres like, political, social, economical and even in science and technology, purely because of their creative abilities. Lack of experience did not come in the way of their progress.

Character vs. Efficiency

The other major hangover of the agricultural era is the ***guru-syndrome*** very dominant in average Indian masses. It somewhat resembles the Newton-Cartesian ghost in character.

In agriculture era, character had a very high, perhaps the top-most, place in the repertoire of good qualities. Character often means how you deal with women? Do you treat them as some kind of material thing to be enjoyed and no more or as equal human beings? Many do consider it that way since the whole world is meant for them for their physical pleasures and nothing more. Women are not treated as exceptions or equal humans because they are under the traditional influence and still subsume female under the male in the form of natural law of nature. This is where exactly **Fritjof Capra** [3] hits at them by propounding deep ecology or feminine ecology. Once his thesis is accepted, the creative power of half of human population is additionally released for developmental work and betterment of humanity. Fortunately the world in general is moving on in the correct direction. But character means much more than just perception of women.

Character also means honesty, particularly with respect to money matters. The industrialism has made it a commercial policy matter, in the sense that **'honesty has been reduced to in the form of the best policy'** and no more. It means that it can be changed if situation demands to earn profit. Then there is no value or virtue left in it. But in the agricultural era it was a virtue to be upheld even when situation was adverse and laden with danger of resulting in monetary or any other loss. That is how culture got evolved without consideration of anybody's profit or loss or hardship to be sustained, to evolve an almost all pleasing society. Character means many more things, but this much will suffice to illustrate the point here.

That is the reason why, in the agriculture era, those who renunciated material wealth and treated all females as their mothers were revered most. In India this was typified by a large number in the form of the ***sanyasis, gurus, rishis*** and such people who were revered by one and all. It still continues to a large extent even today.

The agricultural society was simple with agriculture mainly as their mainstay. It was mainly based on natural rainfall and which constituted the then economic system, supported by some production through crafts. The division of work was not complicated as is today. In such a simple lifestyle, with dominance of salvation, the ***sanyasis*** automatically occupied the pivotal role of guiding the individuals and the society, not only for salvation but even in the affairs of their day-to-day material world. As a result of a long agricultural era in India, this habit has fully entrenched in the genome of an average Indian. An average Indian even now is prepared to follow those who have renunciated all day-to-day pleasures, almost in all walks of life.

In societal affairs of today, the problems may not be solved by merely relying on selflessness. The quality that counts in such cases is first efficiency and then if at all, the honesty. Mere honesty is of no use in solving the present day societal problems, if efficiency is missing. One will have to be efficient and perhaps extremely efficient, *as a priori*. Imagine a very honest but inefficient government bureaucrat. What is good of him? He may not get anything done readily. But if someone is efficient, then the things will be achieved fast. If he is not honest then it may cost little more and that additional cost will have to be borne to avail his efficiency. If he is efficient and honest then it is the best. But such combinations are not readily available. Who should be chosen then, in the present-day world, if choice comes to that, honest or efficient?

There are many organisations where honesty is treated as the top-most quality even in the present day world where efficiency in fact should count most. Therefore the selfless ones are their leaders. Religious organisations are essentially based on this principle. Even some social, charitable or even political organisations may be based on this principle alone. The efficiency may be the first victim in such cases as is being observed.

It can be illustrated by a funny example. Let us imagine that a few are seated for dinner and a couple of dozen servers are serving the food. What does it look like? They will get their dinner alright. It means work will be done but at what efficiency? At what cost? It was alright in agricultural era when ample time was available for any and every activity, but not certainly in the modern-day world, where time and money run together. This phenomenon is readily discernible in India on a fairly large scale.

There was no concept of inputs and outputs in the agricultural era. It has come out purely in terms of profit in industrial production, distribution and sale of goods and services. Profit is the prime driving force for most of such activities. In order to earn more profit the expenditure side is kept to minimum and the recovery side is attempted to keep at the maximum. The energy efficiency has to be achieved at its maximum, to ensure minimum energy consumption and thereby cheaper production. In social context it is related to time and money, without sacrificing the quality, required for carrying out any social, political and charitable activity. Hence quick perception, proper judgment and decision-making and effective implementation are the hallmark of the present era.

Knowledge as Commodity

In the good old India it was a crime to sell knowledge and earn a living or sustenance. That is the reason why there was no fee charged at the ***guru-kul*** in those days. At the end of learning, the disciple may give something to his guru in the form of voluntary gift, called ***guru-dakshina***. It could be anything depending upon the ability of the disciple. So comes down the tradition that knowledge is not for sale.

Firstly knowledge was not generated in those days by spending money as is done today in spending on the R and D activities. Secondly knowledge was meant for salvation. It was achieved through no spending, but by one's own meditation. There was no necessity to sell it. Thirdly even if this was put out for sale nobody would have bought it, as it was not purchased but earned through meditation and other ascetic practices. Fourthly, knowledge of some kind of craft was not sold because it was available in the family by way of traditional training. Those who did not have it in their family were not allowed to practice it anyway as per the social structure. There was no other form of knowledge that was generated in those days by spending huge amounts, like the present-day R and D activities.

Even today the spiritual knowledge is not sold by any one as per the tradition. But the material's knowledge is presently quite saleable to recover the amount spent on its development and some profit as these are activities of sustenance for some at least. That is the reason why the knowledge now has been classified as intellectual property [4]. It is safeguarded through patent rights. It is like owning a tangible property. The present-day information technology organisations generate and sell knowledge on a large scale.

The traditional Indians still think it a sin to sell the knowledge. Many of those who plead it like-wise are often found themselves selling their talents by way of salary. This is a double speak. But those who have superiority complex by way of their traditions do commit such mistakes. It is hollow boasting and nothing else.

The consultants and advisors primarily sell their knowledge and nothing else in the form of their expertise. The patent holders also do the same thing by selling their patent rights in the modern-day world.

Disciple vs. Co-worker

Religion is mainly the outcome of the agricultural era and as a result the disciple-syndrome that gets developed, often leads to transforming the subordinate workers as disciples of the manager/leader. The present requirement is that everybody should contribute to the organisational endeavours by their creativity and innovativeness, rather than merely following the instructions of the bosses and that too mechanically, so that maximum efficiency is achieved. It is therefore necessary that the subordinates should not become disciples of the manager by killing their own creativity. In that case all the creative thinking, and which is a must these days, will have to be carried out by the manager alone. This is unnecessarily straining the manager and as a result reducing his efficiency as well. Hence it is necessary to cultivate true co-workmanship in place of super and sub-ordination manifesting in the form of disciple mentality. The disciple mental make-up should be bare minimum to lead to creative and innovative approach at even the lower levels in an organisation. It means the organisations should be more flat and look always for excellence [5] and every individual therein must possess passion for excellence through innovation [6].

Individual Entrepreneurship in Systems

The present day world is sustained by varieties of systems, including the organisations. By far the individuals contribute in sustaining the society through their contribution in these systems only. As far as governance of a society is concerned it is more through democratic systems only. As a result those who get elected at various levels to run the social-system are not the best ones from the society, but more often these are the average ones with only strong manipulative skills and perhaps good common sense. The executive however is made up of mostly the very intelligent and creative ones (say the IAS, IPS, IFS, etc. officers). It may not be the case with profit making organisations but it is generally true with NPOs. It is truer in a country like India where the majority of electorate is poor and illiterate.

This factual position results in managing the governance more subjectively rather than objectively. The system therefore does not get empowered to lead to better social conditions. On the contrary the system may further decay in such situations, as has been observed in India. In such situations dilemma is often faced by the executive. Whether to exert to empower the system or to exert in getting some important and useful things executed within one's own sphere of administration without bothering about the system? In reality, both types of executives are found, especially in India, because adherents of both are seen justifying their own approaches as more relevant.

Though the Indian Governmental system is too big and too inefficient it helps the individuals to deliver goods if they so desire by even disregarding the system apparently. That is what many do. The best is that system, wherein most are active but if it is not possible, for whatever reasons, then at least some should exert and thereby achieve some progress. Whether the motivated and efficient ones should work disregarding the system will always remain a dilemma to be solved at their own discretion.

In fact it is always better to empower the system for better long-term results. But the system has been damaged to such an extent that many consider it beyond redemption, at least in India. Many therefore prefer to deliver goods by taking personal initiatives without bothering about the system. In doing so the system may even be further damaged. The individual perception, judgment, decision-making and implementation thereat, even in similar or identical situations, differ considerably in such a scenario as prevalent in India.

Decentralisation

It is in human nature, in general, to shirk work and responsibility, to the extent possible without damaging own interests. The larger the organisation, the more are the rules and regulations for its management and, as a result, more scope exists to find alibis to shirk work. The centralised systems suffer more from this malady. It is therefore better to decentralise the system by making the decision-making process itself decentralised, without damaging efficiency in any way. As a result the system gets the benefit of perception and judgment of many more. It also helps to fix accountability readily. In a decentralised system the motivated ones may utilise fully their creative abilities in delivering what is expected of them. It has beneficial influence on others who otherwise have an inclination to shirk work.

In decentralised systems perception, judgment, decision and its implementation can be achieved by many more people simultaneously to contribute in achieving the common objective.

Frustration

One of the dominant obstacles in proper perception, understanding and judgment about any issue and above all its implementation is the frustration that already exists in an individual. It does not allow proper motivation for any work. Everything seems to be of no use and therefore not worth implementing. This is the psychological barrier related to ones own mental state and has to be tackled before hand for him to get motivated for the required job either on individual basis or in an organisation.

It is the duty of the leader or manager to manage the organisation in such a way that his co-workers do not get frustrated on any issue of management related to the individual co-workers or at least it is kept to the minimum.

Implementation

In case of an individual, decisions can be implemented straightaway without waiting for anything provided all other requirements can be met. But for an organisation even the decisions have to be implemented at different levels and by different people, because the actual actions thereat are to be taken by some others. It therefore involves communication, provision of required resources for its implementation, motivating the subordinates for actual actions, their guidance at every stage if they have any doubts in the implementation and so on. In other words it is the management of implementation that remains to be done even after taking the decisions.

The most important part of implementation is the timing of all actions. Success very much depends on such timings. There are ample examples in history when wrong timings led to catastrophic failures. Similarly there are instances in the commercial world of failures when a product or service was introduced at wrong times. This has acquired dominant importance in dynamic technology like space missions. As a result they have developed a system of count-down to ensure to start the operation at a correct predetermined time.

References

1. Gladwell, Malcolm, *Blink*, Penguin, London, (2006).
2. Dow, Marty, V., *Times of India*, Mumbai Daily, 31st Jan' (2010).
3. Capra Fritjof, *The web of Life,* Flamingo, London, (2003).
4. Patent Laws.
5. Tom Peters and Robert H., Waterman Jr., *In search of Excellence*, Profile, (2003).
6. Tom Peters and Nancy, Austin, *A passion for Excellence*, Profile, London, (2003).

CHAPTER 22

DECAY AND DECIMATION

CHAPTER STRUCTURE

- Decay in Organisationality
- Concept of Incarnation
- Assimilation
- Continuity through Changes
- Role of Statistics (Mechanicalness)
- Wealth Systems
- Power Structure
- Defense Structure
- Social Structure
    - Eternal Truths
- Helplessness

Decay and decimation of organisationality and of organisations have to be dealt with separately because the factors that cause decay or decimation are quite different in these two cases.

Decay in Organisationality

The rise and fall of civilizational organisationality has been dealt with in greater details by **Toynbee** [1] in the form of his well known theory of **'challenge and response'** as described in Chapter 11. When the challenges are such that adequate response is not given by the organisation of creative minority jointly with the majority, it is likely to result in decay and eventual decimation of civilizations. In reality what happens is that the organisational solidarity of the combination does not remain, with the passage of time, as effective as it was in the beginning. It is often seen that the creative minority, with the passage of time, after successfully responding to the challenges, slowly turns into ***dominant minority***, tending more towards dictatorial tendencies, and as a result of which, the bond between the two is weakened, resulting in weakening of the organisationality. The earlier success perhaps gets into its head, sharpening its ego more than necessary. It is quite human to be so. Consequently the creative minority mentally moves away from the majority, and as a result, decay starts and which unless deliberately reversed, results finally in decimation of the organisationality and along with it the civilization as well. That is how most of the civilizations have been wiped out from the earth, once and for all times. They are now left only as historical and archeological facts, to be studied for knowing the reasons of their rise and fall. It is also the reason how the situation changed from pre-independence period to post-independent period in India.

The exceptions to this rule of rise and fall are that of Hindu/Bharatiya/Indian civilization and the Confucian Chinese civilization. The Chinese also has undergone some basic changes later because of their conversion into Buddhism. But it has remained as a continuous flow all through the ages in India, albeit by assimilating whatever came its way, but without changing its basic outlook and premises.

It is often described as if it is an umbrella. An umbrella is a structure made up of cloth, some sticks, handle, supporting stem and so on. Its basic purpose is to provide protection against sun, rain, etc. If sometimes any one or more sticks are broken, they are repaired, as and when each one breaks, to retain the shape and the purpose of the umbrella. Next time if the cloth is torn it is repaired by putting pieces, perhaps appearing as kolas, while retaining the purpose intact; sometimes even the entire cloth is replaced. If better materials are available the earlier materials are replaced by the better ones. Like-wise everything changes bit by bit every time, through timely and innovative action, and the umbrella remains as umbrella to serve the basic purpose, all the time. The purpose always overrides the mechanical structure and it continues its existence perpetually.

This is how the Indian civilization, in essence, has survived, while undergoing the mechanical structural changes all through the ages but keeping the essence intact. Whatever came its way and if found to be useful, it was accepted by assimilating it in the existing structure without causing any tensions. This was made possible by great men who were born, in succession, from time to time and having understood the importance of the essential premises, kept it afloat, through appropriate changes in the outwardly structure. The essential premise was the eternal Dharma – the social forces of its sustenance - and the changes that were made form time to time were in respect of the Yug-dharma, as is understood, in the Indian parlance. The other civilizations could not do this and were therefore wiped out by the barbaric or stoneage-forces once and for all. Of course their decimation paved the way for newer civilizations to grow there in due course of time as everywhere stoneage had to evolve into further evolved structures, in the form of natural social evolution, by way of increasing organisationality.

In the agricultural era religion provided the basis for the evolution of organisationality to a large extent. In that agricultural era there was no higher corporate social life above the family level and that religion was the only alternative. The contribution of Islam and Christianity is worth mentioning for their due in this respect. Even Buddhism also provided such a basis, particularly in the south-east Asian region, but only in relation with the local cultural organisationality. The Christian organisationality, once dominant all over Europe, had to slowly give way to more localised culture- based higher order organisationality, in the form of number of nation-states. This organisationality in the form of nation-states seems to have established now all over the world, in all the different societies. Only the humanitarian organisationality has been able to stand in front of organisationality based on nation-state, without damaging it, anywhere in the world. Europe experienced this onslaught few hundred years ago. Islam also faced the same wherever it flourished. Now there are many Muslim nations, even with contagious boundaries, but behaving like foes. The pan-Islamic or pan-Christian organisationality on universal level is seen only with respect to some issues of common interests, particularly against the outsiders.

The Jewish organisationality remained intact in spite of loss of their homeland for over eighteen hundred years. That is the reason why they could get hold of their homeland even after such a long lapse of time. This is a unique example of organisationality which lasted even without support of homeland and as a result, in spite of common administrative structure, over such an extended period.

The Jewish organisationality is more based on living style, with some eternal values, like that of the Hindus and this is the reason why both survived so many onslaughts of barbarians. Being a small group it was easier for Jews to have retained it till the present times, in spite of their spreading in small groups all over the world. They maintained their Jewish character even in small groups, in spite of contact with other dominant cultures, by not getting assimilated in the local cultures any where in the world, even after such a long time.

The Hindus being not very integrated and now loosing faith in that lifestyle against the scientific and technological revolution, like the Europeans after scientific developments, they are now finding it difficult to retain their old cultural organisationality. It is certainly cracking day by day due to the onslaught of scientific and industrial revolution. Fact remains that the creative minority in India, in the form of saints and sadhus in modern times, has not been able to take along the majority in meeting these challenges. In fact the creative minority itself is cracking in India in this respect.

The basis of Hindu organisationality was essentially in the form of social order, decentralisation of powers in the social structure in the form of governance, knowledge and the wealth, at three different and counter-balancing centers; motivating individually to march on the path for the realisation of ultimate truth and establishing co-operation and co-ordination all through the society in the form of self-contained village life, with Ram-Rajya as their ideal.

Firstly all these are being challenged by the Hindus themselves, in view of the scientific and technological progress, exactly like what the Europeans did, a few centuries ago. Secondly the paradigms, in the form of values of agricultural society, have not been evolved further to suit the modern day social evolution. Thirdly the lifestyle in the form of essence of eternal Dharma was almost completely obscured by the rigid and mechanical routines, enforced by the so-called custodians of culture, which did not allow them to adapt to the required changes with time. The so-called creative minority failed to realise such challenges. Fourthly the Hindu society fell prey to the British attempts of dividing the society, on the basis of apparent distinctions and differences like caste, language, religion, etc. In fact the Hindus themselves are forgetting the essential unity in diversity amongst themselves. They are attempting to realise, as per their essential outlook, the wider Hindu Muslim organisationality, which still does not have any scientific basis for its evolution without common agreed values, and as a result it proved not only futile but resulted in further degradation of the already feeble and now uncared of and in fact abused, traditional Hindu organisationality. What started before independence, as compulsive strategy, for getting independence, under the British policy of ***'divide and rule'***, continues in the same direction as a policy, even after independence, without evolving the required foundational basis. In this process, the development of Hindu organisationality is completely disregarded. In fact attempts are made to destroy it to the extent possible. India has not been able to develop organisationality on the basis of nation-state under common constitution as was successful in Europe. As a result the Indians have lost on all fronts in consolidating their organisationality as a whole. Hence the overall degradation in social life, which is reflected in overall decay of organisations, as observed, in post-independent India.

The present day attempts in the name of so-called secularism are aimed at developing organisationality of mainly the Hindus and the Muslims, at times taking the Christians into account, assuming them more as the religious groups, like so many under the traditional Hindufold, on the basis that they are common citizens of the same country and are governed by the same constitution. In this process the first victim is the already weak traditional organisationality of Hindus, which is being weakened further. In the absence of common civil code, common constitution is unable to provide the solid basis for the evolution of organisationality of all citizens in India.

The belief to create such organisationality is based on the same lines as was used in developing the European nation-states. There are however many fundamental differences in the two situations and the foremost being that the European nations did not have two or more, almost different nationalities, to be merged into one nation-state anywhere, in that process of evolution. Wherever such situation existed the nation-state was disintegrated in due course of time to evolve nation-states on the basis of smaller groups. The example of Yugoslavia typically represents this. They had their own earlier organisationality based broadly on their own kingdom with broadly the same religious people, and the same material welfare as a common goal, to evolve their different modern nationalities. The net result has been that the small groups, with apparent difference in the form of language, caste, region, sampradaya and so on, within the Hindufold have been consolidating and developing their own organisationality, at the cost of overriding civilizational and weak Hindu traditional (not religious) cultural organisationality

Organisationality is developing in the newly liberated nation-states everywhere in the world, based on whatever is their weak but own traditional cultural and civilizational organisationalities. India is not even thinking to develop it on those lines. The net result has been the lack of spirit of India anywhere and everywhere. The example of China needs to be studied in this context.

Truly the Indians are trying to develop national integration through disintegration. They are trying to build society and nation on utterly selfish interests. They try to serve society by serving themselves or at best their near ones. They are trying to develop democratic spirit by developing intolerance and antagonism. They want to develop cohesive society by nurturing sectarian interests and abusing each other to the extreme. They would like to homogenise the society by digging out the atrocities inflicted in history and cultivating the spirit to undo history, perhaps even archeology. They talk of socialism by eulogising capitalism in its extreme. The list of such paradoxes is unending and yet they dream of making India a great organised society. There is no comparison to this approach, as it is hypocracy of the highest order, perhaps not found anywhere else in the world.

Concept of Incarnation

There is saying in Sanskrit that strength lies in organisation only

***sanghe shaktihi kalow yuge*.**

The present day organisations serve one or the other purpose to serve the society, through fulfillment of their own goals. The achievement of their goals is their own life missions. In the example of umbrella cited earlier, it was effectively kept in order through proper maintenance, in the form of appropriate entrepreneurship, at times even by innovative action when needed, to make it available for protection against rain and sun. In the absence of any such thing it is to be discarded as junk, exposing oneself to the risk of rain and sun or alternatively constructing a new one.

Peter Drukker [2] says the same thing as:

"Innovation is the specific tool by means of which leader exploits changes as an opportunity for bringing about changes in organisation. The sources of innovation need to be purposefully searched. Systematic analysis of opportunities can lead to this. These should bring about strengthening of organisation. This is possible if attention is focused in response to challenges. With time, in an organisation, such innovative leadership is a must. The key to growth is to foster the entrepreneurial culture in an organisation. The organisation must have environment of entrepreneurship".

This is the same concept enumerated by Hindus in the form of incarnation of God. In the Gita, Lord Krishna has promised that He would come again and again, whenever it is required to eliminate the demons to reset the social order. In the long Indian history, those who did not appreciate the essential life sustaining forces and mistook them for the mechanical super-structure of the society were destroyed in due course of time by such incarnations. That is how perhaps all other cultures, except the Hindu culture, were decimated in history. Only Hindu culture survived such sabotage even from within all through.

If the organisations do not fulfill the society's needs, even after possible improvements, for whatever reasons, these have to be eliminated and replaced by newer and timely organisations to cater to the emerging social order. Hence organisations have to be very flexible, accommodative and responsive to the challenges all through, to finally sustain the society at large. This is possible only if their attention is focused on the aim rather than on any other path of mechanical activities, howsoever lucrative they may appear. The alternative is to get decimated or amalgamated into some others, losing one's own form for ever. Organisational crisis manifests as a breakdown of the existing systemic balance. But it has to be harnessed as transition to a new balance, according to **Fritjof Capra** [3].

Universities of Cambridge and Oxford as cited earlier, are typical examples to illustrate this point. They were flexible enough to accommodate timely requirements, because of their visionary and enterprising leaderships all through the ages and, as a result, continue to function effectively even today with a long laudable history.

It is inherent in organisational set up to fall into the rut of mechanicalness because it is easier to grasp it, rather than the subtle meaning behind it. The majority has always been quite prone to accepting the mechanicalness of any activities. It is the duty of the creative leadership to keep on giving the majority correct direction, by changing the nature of the mechanical activities, as per the needs of the time. The creative and enterprising leadership has also to understand the difference between the two and minimise the mechanicalness and emphasise, time and again, the subtle objective set-forth before them. Historical experience is not much of use in this respect because future is never a replication of the past in any form. The challenges of every time are different from the previous ones and have to be responded to with creativity and innovativeness only.

No organisation can last long on initially set pattern of an organisation. It requires continuous assessment and changes in tune with reality to move in the direction of achieving the objective. This may include even drastic changes in one's own perceptions, in tune with time and requirements. Those who fail on this front get decimated. The attempts of communist/socialist's all over the world are typical examples to understand this syndrome.

All over the world communist/socialist governments that fell into the rut, did not understand what went wrong with them. They were wandering in a fool's paradise in organising their societies and as a result, were decimated to make way for the new order. Their organisations did not last even a century anywhere in the world. On the contrary the so-called capitalist's system, because of their continuous creative efforts, on all fronts, developed themselves into mighty societies and is now being copied even by the earlier socialists and communist countries all over the world.

Assimilation

Commercial organisations often get assimilated with some other similar organisation on account of either their inability to run them further, for fear of unsustainable financial losses or on account of getting a better price on sale, rather than continuing as independent units. That is how some have been decimated and eventually the multi-national or trans-national organisations have come of age.

Many times commercial organisations get decimated because of their total failure in running them, often with huge accumulated losses and that there is no alternative left but to close them down. It all indicates that over the years they have not bothered to assess the internal changes required in view of the external changes in environment. As a result they get more and more imbalanced and unfit to carry on their activities. It may also happen that the competitors bring out better and cheaper products and as a result the organisation is unable to compete, due to their inability in innovating as per the needs of the time. There is no alternative left for them but to get decimated in due course of time.

Government organisations are fairly perpetual, provided the social organisationality remains in tact or are growing, which normally happens under democratic style of functioning. But if there is a dictator or something resembling that, then people often get fed up with their governance, resulting in revolt of some kind. In that case the older governmental structure is decimated and a new one, in tune with time is constructed for governance as per the wider desires of the people. This is how the communist and the socialist's governments were thrown out and democratic governance was established. This is also how the feudal kingdoms, all over the world, were replaced by the democratic institutions, at the turn of industrial revolution in their societies.

Normally the religious organisations are not decimated so readily because there are always some followers who continue to have blind faith in that religious organisation and it's whatever leadership. They may somewhat lose their following and may not grow, but the faithful continue to be associated because of family attachment and teachings. It gets converted into a sort of religious ghetto but continues to exist. The western churches are typical examples of this category.

There is no scope for religious organisations to merge into one another. They are quite independent and characteristically different in their approach and invariably continue to remain so. In fact there is no similarity in any two religious organisations, except their category as religious organisations, for their merger to occur, like the commercial, charitable or political organisations. Although everyone believes in only one Supreme Power, the paths to attain the same are so different that they cannot be merged for any reason whatsoever.

Continuity through Changes

There are social or political organisations which continue their existence by way of changes in their name and/or style of functioning. Typical example of this category is the Indian National Congress. It was basically a movement, encompassing adherents of even fairly opposite view-points. The agreement was in terms of getting rid of Britishers. This was a project organisation with its limited and specific purpose and that is the reason why diverse people agreed to co-operate in achieving the common objective of getting independence. When the Britishers left, granting independence to India, the controller of Congress, **Mahatma Gandhi** in fact had then suggested for disbanding it as it had become irrelevant. But the Congress leadership converted it into a political party under the same name, changed the structure and operation to suit their altered interests. The other groups with diverse political views, being in minority, had no alternative but to separate out and form their own political parties. The original Congress was thus decimated in reality, with only the name being continued for selfish gains.

Project organisations are officially closed once their set objective is achieved or if there is no more, any objective left for it to be achieved.

Role of Statistics (Mechanicalness)

If organisations become big enough or if they are multifarious in their activities, it is not possible to take decisions based on qualitative or quantitative and subjective assessment of its performance. Then the top leadership gets to know the functioning of their organisation only in the form of some data or figures or statistics and from which they have to draw the inferences, as to whether it is making any progress or otherwise. This is precisely the beginning of mechanicalness in any organisation.

The experience over the years, of Government functioning in India, has been quite revealing in this respect. Everything got bogged down to data and nothing else. The governing machinery lost touch with the people to a large extent. All information was reaching the top managers only as data and nothing else. Data are fundamentally quite funny in character. These can be processed in suitable manner to bring out what is required rather than what it has to reveal. It depends on the skill of the middle level leadership to turn out such false progressive reports based on the same data. Prior to independence the picture was much different with leaders being in active contact with the masses. This was all lost later in the form of governmental bureaucracy, insulated from the public at large. In fact the progress drowned in the sea of statistical data of even, at times illusory progress.

This brings forth the question as to how everybody should be made to feel the progress, since the statistical figures may not convey the correct and legible picture to the concerned general masses.

Decentralisation of everything is the only possible solution for such problems. That is why in commercial organisations decentralisation is achieved through varieties of avenues like, forming fairly independent organisational groups on whatever feasible basis, forming atomised organisations, as proposed by **Deal, Kennedy and Allen** [4], developing effective vendor system, by business process out-sourcing and so on. Failure to embark on any or many such avenues is a sure sign of moving towards decimation. The decentralisation offers plenty of opportunities for more people to show their caliber in achieving the objective more effectively and efficiently. This is what has been envisaged by **Toffler** [5] as the third wave organisational structure of the future.

Wealth Systems

There was practically no wealth, worth mentioning, in the stoneage. Wealth generation started for the first time after agricultural revolution, with surplus production beyond the producer's requirements. The surplus had to be sold or bartered for something else. Whoever had more surpluses was considered wealthier. In due course of time bartering was replaced by money transactions and it acquired the status of wealth, which continues till to date. The agricultural system was perhaps the first wealth system to come into operation in any society.

The onset of industrial revolution generated far greater amounts of surplus because the production exceeded the consumption of the producer by a huge margin. As a result money became the central focus for obtaining all other needs in increasing amounts. The industrial surpluses far exceeded the agricultural surpluses in varieties and in quantities [5]. Much of the agricultural social system, in the form of its wealth system, slowly got transformed into the industrial system, to a large extent, to accommodate all the surplus agricultural population, in due course of time. Many jobs based on individual skills like, black smithy, carpentry, washing, cobbling, tailoring and so on, typically representing the agricultural wealth system, were almost completely replaced by industrial systems. In other words such artisans were replaced by machines and their operators. This went on, on ever increasing scale, to limit the agricultural wealth set-up. The net result has been that the wealth generating systems of agricultural era, being relatively inefficient, were decimated to make way for new systems suited to industrial era.

As the information technology revolution set-in its way, many of the industrial social and wealth structures were demolished to make way for new structures. For example ticket sale was made by vending machines or internet. The industrial wealth systems are fast being decimated to make way for new and more efficient wealth generating and exchange systems.

In agricultural era the wealth systems were very simple. In industrial era they became more pyramidal, run by centralised and bureaucratic power structure, characteristic of its own. This is being challenged by the knowledge era systems, almost in its entirety. The industrial systems have to give in to make way for the knowledge era systems. .

Now wealth is generated in terms of synchronisation of production, distribution and sale and related activities. It is also very much affected by the time considerations, required for any such activities. Lately the locational advantage has resulted in tremendous influence on wealth generation in terms of off-shoring and business process out-sourcing. One who can excel in any one or all these three [6] can generate more wealth efficiently. In this process those organisations that lag behind have no other alternative but to get decimated. In general the agricultural set up displaced the stoneage set-up. It was not because they ran out of stones but because of superior agricultural wealth system for better sustenance. Similarly the industrial set-up has displaced the agricultural set-up and the knowledge systems are fast replacing the industrial wealth systems. The reason is simple. That displacing the previous one is a more efficient and effective mode to provide the current human needs. This is an irreversible directional change and those not falling in line will have no option but to get decimated.

The style of capitalism as a symbol of industrialisation is being replaced by a new knowledge based systems of capitalism. As a result the industrial capitalistic, monetary, fiscal and financial organisations are slowly being decimated to make way for new knowledge era systems. For example old banking, with actual money transactions are getting practically eliminated step by step. The actual money transactions are getting replaced by mere digital transactions in the form of virtual money transactions. Even bartering between nations is becoming order of the day to balance out the adverse balance of payments. There appears to be no end in this transformation.

The old style ownership of means of production by capitalists is fast getting replaced by ownership by even the work-force by way of share holding of the same organisation. Stock-options to the work force are becoming a common practice. The more the stake of work-force is developed in this way the more they will be inclined to strive in achieving the organisational objectives. The old style functioning will therefore be decimated by the social forces of inevitable change.

In the agricultural era cultivable land was an asset as well as wealth. In industrial era the plant, machinery and such tangible things were the dominant forms of wealth. Now **in informational era knowledge is seen as the supreme wealth.** Steel plants with such huge plant and machinery was seen as a sign of wealth in industrial era. But now without much of such wealth, the information technology companies are considered to be richer, because of their accumulated knowledge. Their share price in general often far exceeds that of the general steel companies. This is how the changes in wealth systems are taking place.

Power Structure

As has already been seen that power structure is the manifestation of an organised effort. In view of the understanding of the parameters that influence the effectiveness and efficiency of an organisation, there is no confusion left any more about transforming the organisations into more flat structures, with less and less distribution of power[7]. The old pyramidal structural organisations have already become history. In fact the entire power structure in any society is undergoing paradigm changes in view of the emerging times. The overall old social structure is being decimated to give way for re-organisation on altogether new lines.

Defense Structure

What is continuously getting decimated with time is no more any thing else than the defense organisations [8]. The new structural forms are emerging, in tune with technological developments, for better effective and more efficient combat operations. Whole emphasis is on using less and less man power in direct combat operations and its place being taken by the remote controlled unmanned equipments. The defense organisations are being manned by qualified scientists and technologists on an ever increasing scale. Old defense organisational structures, their related equipments, structural forms, quality and type of human resources and management techniques employed are all getting decimated and making way for the new ones. In fact the concept of provision of credible nuclear deterrent, is replacing the old style defense structure from fundamental standpoint.

Social Structures

The social structures are essentially based on the economics of production, distribution, marketing and sale of goods and services. Since this has undergone paradigm changes with every social revolution like stoneage to agriculture to industrial to information era, the relevant social structure was inevitably decimated to make way for the emerging new era. This change is far more drastic on evolution of industrialisation. It has caused too many changes in the psychological status of even individuals, resulting in tensions unimagined before. The old structures have to be decimated to make way for the new ones to relieve these tensions to the extent possible. Those who have been able to do it with fewer tensions have generally progressed at faster speeds and are able to undergo changes required for the onset of informational technological changes.

The change from stoneage to agriculture, from that to industrial and now to information era are all irreversible changes and the earlier social systems have to get decimated to make way for the new ones [5]. This is what has been the social evolution anyway.

Eternal Truths

There are some eternal truths related to organisations and their functioning. The organisations lose their relevance when the rate of internal change lags behind the pace of external changes in the society. In profit making organisations the aim of making profit remains always active and drives organisations towards it. In NPOs the aim itself may get blurred. That is the reason why **Hamel** [9] **asked a pertinent question to religious leaders, "whether the gospel has become irrelevant, or the churches, or, is the God's message a problem, or the methods?"**

Similar questions can be asked to other social organisations who have been working for quite some time. In political fields**, is it the parties that have become irrelevant or their methodology of working?** In social organisations **is it the aim in the form of service that has become irrelevant or the way the service is delivered?** In the case of RSS **is it their aim that has become irrelevant or the way they are trying to achieve it has become out of tune with time?**

In all such cases it is normally found that the aims of most NPOs are relevant; religion is required even more than before; charitable service is still needed for the remaining have-nots; political awakening and good governance is the least what people expect from political parties and so on. On all such fronts **it is the methodology that has gone out of tune with time** and hence is unable to deliver the expected. The calcification is almost through and needs nothing less than surgery to meet the requirements of time. In the absence of such drastic changes all such institutions and organisations, which once did their job well, are decaying and are on the verge of decimation. It is true with all organisations without exceptions. Only those are surviving which have undertaken such drastic changes in tune with time. The rest are infected by the cancer of rigidity and are destined to get decimated with progressive decay. The development of disciple-syndrome, as discussed before, indicates only decay in their organisational endeavours. The evolution of sampradayas out of even social service activities, in the Indian context is the same phenomenon. In general the way organisations grow initially and decay later at some point of time is qualitatively shown in **Fig. 22.1.**

Societies do undergo changes with time as per the requirements of time. It should be remembered that if the societal deterioration is substantial then the existing institutions can not bring the necessary changes, for certain. These have to be decimated and new relevant institutions have to be created to bring in the social reforms. There is no alternative to this; no matter how painful the change.

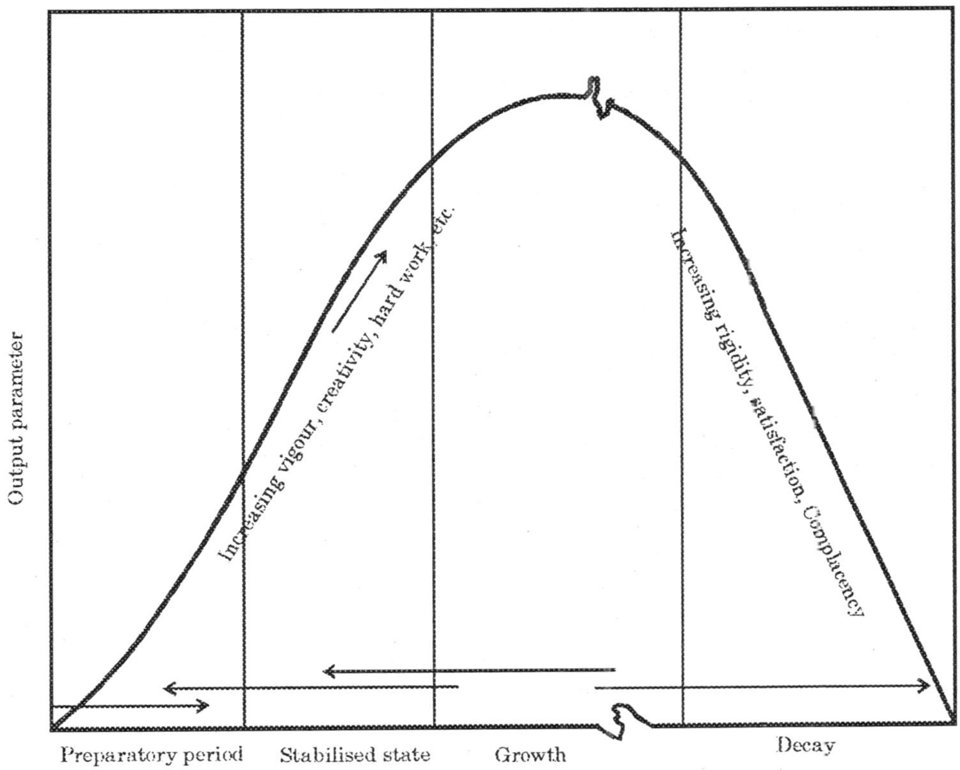

Fig. 22.1 : Schematic of growth and decay of organisations as is generally observed

Helplessness

It is seen that when social, political or even religious organisations grow they do not generally get the right type of people to manage the middle levels of their organisations. In such situations whoever is available is assigned the job by considering him to be the best available to run the show at that time. Since he is not the one suited, the job is not carried out properly, bringing in varieties of drawbacks like lack of proper perception, misjudgment, even nepotism and so on in the organisation. It is a sure path of decay for that organisation. It often breeds in disciple-syndrome and the organisation may be damaged beyond rectification. This is all done by the leader knowingly and consciously as there seems to be no alternative or else he has to forego rapid growth. This is a chance taken as a shot in the dark, with the hope that it will improve. It is surely helplessness and nothing else. The result is then anybody's guess.

References

1. Toynbee, Arnold, *A Study of History*, Abridged Edition, Oxford (1972).
2. Drukker, Peter, as quoted by Vasant Desai, *Dynamics of Entrepreneurial Development and Management*, Himalaya, Mumbai, (2004).
3. Capra Fritjof, *The Web of Life*, Flamingo, London, (2003).
4. Deal, T., Kennedy, E. and Allan, A., *Corporate Cultures (The Rites and Rituals of Corporate Life)*, Perseus, Cambridge, Mass, (1982).
5. Toffler, Alvin, *The Third Wave*, Warner, (1985).
6. Toffler, Alvin, *Revolutionary Wealth,* Bantam, (2006).
7. Tom Peters and Nancy, Austin, *A passion for Excellence*, Profile, London, (2003).
8. Toffler, Alvin, *Power Shift*, Bantam, (1990).
9. Hamel, Gary, *Blog-Organised Religion's Management and Problems* (2009).

CHAPTER 23

CONSULTANTS AND ADVISORS

CHAPTER STRUCTURE

- Necessity
- Intangible Products
- Complex Web of Industrial World
- Innovativeness
- Experts
- Consultants/Advisors
- Needs
- Choice
- Sundry Area

Necessity

The present day societies are fast converting themselves into knowledge based societies in tune with the third wave change according to Toffler [1].The consultants and advisors are those who have acquired specialised, and fairly thorough to the extent possible, knowledge of one or the other disciplines of human activities. Their job is to keep on updating knowledge in their own area of specialisation, as a matter of division of work in the modern day world. These are the people who can help others, when needed, by providing their knowledge, either on payment or as a matter of gratefulness or service. This is the way they can remain as active **consultants and advisors**. They may belong to research and development organisations as an organised group. It may be provided as an expertise in an organised manner. They may also be individuals who have acquired expertise in some discipline by practicing it over a long period and offer it on individual or organised basis. It may also be an individual or a small group who have undergone specialised university training in some discipline.

In the information technology era, knowledge base has expanded so much that it is not possible for any one to be an expert in all the areas of ones own interests. It is even more difficult to keep updating the same. This is the age of specialisation and most can be experts in some narrow field of specialisation alone or be a generalists if they so desire. **Knowledge-selling is regular sustenance of such experts**. Whenever expert knowledge is required in some other area it is better to get it, on payment or service, from those who have the requisite expertise. Such experts provide their expertise to the needy ones as and when required on payment. It is easier and cheaper to buy such knowledge as and when required. **The consultants and advisors are needed in the modern day world just to make the system more efficient,** in tune with time. In the market, basically created by industrial revolution, and as it is being updated in information technology era, it is required to generate and sell knowledge as well, as in any other profession. In other words knowledge has become a commodity just like any other tangible or intangible things.

The material knowledge is presently quite saleable to recover the amount spent on its development and additionally to make some profit, as these are activities of sustenance, at least for a sizable population. That is the reason why the knowledge has now been classified as **intellectual property** and its ownership is safeguarded through patent rights. The present-day information technology organisations generate and sell knowledge on a large scale.

The consultants and advisors primarily sell their knowledge and nothing else in the form of their expertise. The patent holders also do the same thing by selling their patent rights.

Intangible Products

Modern economy is based on manufacture and sale of products. But there are many intangible things like services, systems, transactions, etc. which are also now called as products. That is the reason why the schemes of banks, insurance companies, investment agencies, advertisements and many such things are also called products. These are sold as any other tangible products.

The tangible products were ones marketed for sale to the needy ones and earn profit. In the present knowledge era there are people who work only in developing ideas, concepts, knowledge and such intangibles. Many others provide some kind of service only. Both tangible and intangible products are required to sustain the present-day societies. These have to be sold to earn their sustenance in the money-centric world. Hence intangibles like ideas, services, suggestions, spiritual tips, and all such things are marketed and sold to earn a living. So goes the saying that **Shri Ramdeobaba,** the yoga-guru, has been able to market his perceptions well and hence he got the tremendous following. There have been many, equally competent before, but who did not get that much success, because of their lack of required marketing skill in tune with time. The agricultural hangover does not allow many to sell such valuable information in their possession. Many sell even spirituality indirectly without admitting the same explicitly. Its ones own perception of the changing era.

In the modern world it requires money to get practically anything going and more so on a large scale, including perhaps spirituality as well. The same holds true with yoga teaching. Price can either be put on the transaction, consultation, advice or alternatively it is called as voluntary contribution or entry fee of some event or by any such innovative name. Those who understand it get going and serve the society well, using modern day tools and practices. Those who are under the agricultural hangover are not able to convey or transfer what they have for want of this understanding. The society under the influence of industrialisation understands popular market language easily and readily. Those who sell such ideas in the present can be classified as modern day consultants or advisors and nothing else. Many ***babas/gurus*** in the present-day world are nothing but spiritual consultants.

Complex web of Industrial World

The present-day industrial and information technological world has no semblance with the earlier agricultural world. What is the present-day world like? It consists of several complex systems operating at the same time along with and, interacting with several other systems, at the same time. For the sake of simplicity let us understand the main ones.

With all the internationalism, humanitarian outlook and environmental worries of the globe every individual is still known by his own national identity and that all his needs and desires are met almost wholly through overall national considerations alone. It may at times be wrapped in some form of internationalism, human rights and such appealing modern names. Hence all the systems in operation have a national overtone though they may interact with international systems and their pressures, per force.

The most dominant system in the industrialised world is the economic system involving production and sale of goods and services on ever increasing scale. This may involve from the simple individualistic crafts and skills and, services to organisational activities on small medium and large scale industries. It may be as large as the trans-national corporations. With all the national freedom in manufacturing the goods and generating services, the entire system is practically under the overall supervision of World Trade Organisation. The investors, the manufacturers, the financers, the workers and the consumers form the essential supporters of this system as individuals and in an organised form. It dominates the society and the individuals to the extent that much of individual's life has become money-centric, profit-centric, selfish and more devoid of humane considerations.

The economic system needs it and is supported by equally complex monetary and financial system in the form of banks, financial institutions, insurance companies, stock market and the like. This is aided by the International Monetary Fund, World Bank and many national governments. The depositors, the workers and the loan takers form the backbone of this system in individual and in organised capacity.

The most dominant system being the knowledge or the educational system in all its possible forms. It is to train and generate the required human resource for all other systems. It includes the sub-systems of research, development and innovation to cater to all new requirements, for improving quality and efficiency of production of goods and services. It is supported by the learners, the teachers and private and, governmental financing.

There is the governmental system, including the defense, to ensure the national security and safety of the society and the individuals and also to oversee practically all the other systems operating in the society. It has several tier arrangements to look after the needs of people. In a way it controls all other systems directly or indirectly. It has therefore evolved many other systems directly under its control or in the form of autonomous corporations, like the judiciary, entertainment, infra-structural needs of all other systems, and so on. No matter what model of economic development is chosen to meet the people's present-day needs, the governmental system is becoming more and more democratic and, more and more all-pervading in its functioning. As a result many other autonomous systems in the form of legal, technical, financial, accounting and such others have been developed to cater to the emerging needs. The governmental system is supported by individuals and organisations. The economic system is controlled by the government by way of varied taxations and laws.

There is the charity system catering to provide the ***have-nots*** with whatever it can, taking help from the ***haves.*** This is supported by the social workers, financiers in the form of individuals, organisations and governments.

The most independent of all the systems and in its fairly autonomous form is the system of religious organisations. They cater to the individual's needs related to the other world. It may be tightly organised or a loose structure, as per the needs and objectives.

Human beings are associated with all these systems directly and actively or somewhat loosely depending upon individual's choice. They may be associated with many such systems at the same time.

All these put together form the complex social web, at the regional, national, or international levels. This is a highly complex web catering to meet the human needs at the physical, mental, intellectual and spiritual levels, to the extent possible, on individual and on an organised basis.

This is the present-day complex industrial world which has no similarity whatsoever with the earlier agricultural world. Nobody can live in any society now without getting entangled in this complex web fairly deeply. Great amount of knowledge in-puts at a variety of different points, in the form of science, technology, marketing, legality, taxation, accounting, construction, services and so on is required to sustain this complex system. This is more true with organised activities, although it does hold true with individuals as well, to some extent.

Innovativeness

The onset of industrialisation changed the economics of production, distribution, sale, marketing and all such things fundamentally. Being essentially profit-centric, efficiency of work, for the first time, came in question with reference to all economic activities. The input and output had to be evaluated in terms of final profits. As a result the input costs had to be decreased and output earnings improved by whatever means possible to stand in competition in open market. Persistent research and development is required to keep this system going. All this resulted in making changes in materials, processes, technologies, distribution, sale and everything else as a matter of routine practice to continuously improve upon the economics and thereby improving the profit. Nothing therefore remained stagnant, everything started changing and changing rapidly to cope up with related economics. The overall effect of industrialisation has been to develop knowledge and understanding of every aspect of economical and therefore of social life to the extent possible. It had its tremendous influence even on all other areas like sports, education, entertainment, politics, charity and so on, with the net result of making the entire society more dynamic than ever imagined before.

Everybody individually and more so the managers and leaders of organised efforts were expected to keep abreast with the up-to-date knowledge to stand competition in the sector of their interest as a routine and general working style. However it is humanly almost impossible for an individual to keep track of up-to-date knowledge of such a vast spectrum of activities related to oneself as an individual or as manager of any organisation. What is the alternative?

The process of industrialisation fortunately also resulted in development of experts in all such activities of interest to the society. They could and would continuously improve upon their knowledge of the specific area of operation or activity. It was however impossible to keep experts of all such subjects as regular employees. Firstly because such experts would be too costly to be retained on personal or even at times organisational level on regular pay roles. Secondly such experts are not available for regular employment. Thirdly they were not often required on full time basis as there was not that much necessity. They could be hired on part time basis, as and when required. Often new situations are faced and which need expert inputs for being tackled successfully.

Experts

Industrialisation as a corollary also led to develop the knowledge generating systems in developing the experts to cater to the needs in almost every field of activity. Universities started academic programmes in such varied disciplines to train experts to suit essentially the industrial requirements but along with that all such requirements of the society are also met. Academically intelligent people could pursue these programmes, carry out further research, practice for a while in their respective field of activities and thereby develop expertise which could be hired by the required individuals or organisations as and when required on appropriate payments. Many on personal level or in the form of a joint team would provide expertise in some specific area in the form of general consultancy or advisory services. The expertise included engineering design, technology, structural analysis, tax and accounts, legal aid, architectural help, medical help and any and every such need in the field of activity. In fact all such requirements are often made available not just on individual basis but on an organised basis in the form of consultants via consulting firms.

Consultants/Advisors

Industrialisation primarily and now, along with information technology, has led to evolve expertise in every possible field of activity. These are essentially knowledge oriented people, who try to keep abreast with up-to-date knowledge in the subject of their interest, to the extent possible. They offer their expertise to those who require it on appropriate payments on contractual basis or as a service. Anybody individually or for one's own organisation, can hire them for the specific job, as and when required. **These are called consultants or advisors**. These terms are often used synonymously without any distinction. Some prefer to call themselves as consultants since they are consulted for their expert opinion on the problem, related to their field of expertise. Some others call themselves as advisors.

Advisor is often referred to as that expert who is called in for a short and quick comment on some problem in the form of advice which may or may not be accepted. It may be in the form of second or additional opinion to the one already in possession from an equally competent expert to ensure the correctness of the earlier advice for its applicability in a given situation. Consultants are often hired, on the basis of their known credentials, for some project which may last for some time and may include help from many different experts simultaneously, at times provided by the same agency.

There are people who develop expertise in some subject of their interest by way of earlier practical experience or university training and/or research and so on and then make it available in the form of consultation and advice, to the extent desired. Quite often university professors, who have developed expertise in the subject of their teaching and research, are available for expert advice. In fact their knowledge is thereby fully exploited for some useful and productive purpose.

Needs

People do need expert advice in the field of their requirements on individual or collective basis. This is particularly required by those who occupy managerial positions in the form of executives. They have to take decisions on many and varied subjects and execute many such different things about which they may not possess the expert knowledge to the extent required for planning and taking the decision or executing the job. They are often generalists with adequate experience of handling varied things with their intuitional judgments. They are also good managers at managing rather than possessing detailed expertise about many things. In the absence of correct advice or professional help in installation of plants or service groups, their execution may cost dear to the organisation. They need expert people to advise them on all such matters to enable them to take best possible decisions. They also need professional executors to do some of their specific jobs, at times on turn-key basis.

The same thing applies to individuals before they take decisions on matters which otherwise may cost them dear unnecessarily. In all such situations they hire expert consultants and advisors for short duration on due payments. The tax and accounts consultants typically fall in this category.

Choice

How to pick up the right consultant or advisor? It is often a million or perhaps a trillion dollar question. Managers are supposed to keep track of such people who are around, during their growing years before becoming managers. The promotors and controllers are specifically required to keep knowledge about experts in the field of their interest because they may need their help right at the promotion stage or any time later. This information is generally obtained through discussions, gossip, personal contacts, and earlier experiences of bosses or peers before becoming managers, and so on. Even for personal use like for auditing of one's own accounts or for tax purposes or for constructional purposes advisors are required and are obtained on the same basis.

How to choose a consultant or an advisor for a specific purpose? This is a serious problem when the choice is to be made for the first time in a particular area and for a specific purpose, out of the few available ones. The so-called commercial consultants and advisors are out to make money by way of their expertise. There are people who pose to be experts when in reality they are not experts of the requisite level at all. Such people often on their own contact the probable customers and try to impress them about their expertise.

One is never sure about the real level of expertise of a particular person unless tested on specific account. How to solve the problem when it is sought for the first time? One can go by experience of friends who had earlier sought advice from the same expert in the specific area for solving their own requirements. It is no right judgment to know experts only after losing money on them for the first time advice.

In this respect, by and large, university professors are found to be better advisors on many accounts. *Firstly* they are on the whole cheaper to hire. *Secondly* they have with them other experts of adjoining areas as their colleague-professors from whom they can seek the fringe knowledge as and when required. *Thirdly* advice can be sought from the university/department/school as such so that all the expertise available in the organised form is made available for giving considered advice. They are fairly up to date in terms of their expertise. The chances of such advice being close to the truth is definitely more. *Fourthly* the name and fame of the institute is at stake and normally professors would not like to loose it by tendering wrong advice. If they tender wrong advice then they may not only damage their institute but themselves as well. This is a very common practice in USA and is copied all over the world.

Experts have to advertise their competency through subtle moves as most professionals do not approve of advertising any such thing through media. It does not fit into their professional ethics either. In this respect example is better than precept. It should be remembered that economics, technology, healthcare and the like are such areas where judgments can go wrong readily.

Sundry Areas

Advisors are not only required in commercial and finance related activities where-in profit earning is the prime motive, but they are also required in all possible areas of society like sports, music, journalism, entertainment, charity, catering, travel, social activities and above all in politics as well. It all depends on the level of expertise a person has been able to develop and is recognised as of some use by the users concerned. The real test of pudding lies in its eating, so goes the saying. Similarly the real test of expertise is only in its application and which requires someone to hire it and use it. The area where university is trying to provide training is continuously expanding to cater to such diverse needs of the society.

CHAPTER 24

VISIONING, FORECASTING AND FUTURING

CHAPTER STRUCTURE

- Necessity
- Futuring Methods
  - Scanning
  - DEGEST Method
  - Trend Analysis
  - Scenario Analysis
  - DELPHY Polling
  - Modeling, Simulations and Games
  - Brainstorming
  - Visioning
- Relevance to Organisations

Necessity

Everybody often thinks about his/her future. That makes him envision about it to the extent possible. He is often worried about the future because it is not known to him and feels that it might turn out to be bad or even worse for him. That makes him envision about the possible actions that he might take in the present to make the future more tolerable and acceptable. What an individual is afraid of is more true in the case of groups such as organisations, societies, nations, human race and even the universe as a whole. Their leaders, managers or controllers have to think about the future of their groups and act in the present, to the extent possible, to make the future more acceptable.

Therefore everybody individually or along with others in some group-form, would like to progress with minimum of any hurdles to enjoy one's own and collective lives. The world is now changing so fast that it is hard to keep abreast. New technological inventions alter the way we live. It also affects values, attitudes, beliefs and almost everything of individuals as well as groups. This pace of change has been accelerating right from since when hominids first appeared on the earth. But it has acquired too great a pace now. This march has been into the future which was never known to any individual or a group. The social revolution that has been taking place, since anatomically similar to today's human first appeared some 50,000 years ago, is the result of human, individual and collective, endeavours.

Future does not just happen. It is created through people's action or inaction in the present. Therefore everybody individually and collectively have to chalk out their own course of action in the present for onward march into the future, realising the consequences of their decisions and actions. Since future is unknown, opportunity as well as danger lies ahead. People have to envision the future to the extent possible based on past facts, requirements and the possibilities of their realisation. This is called ***visioning.*** It is thus thinking in terms of the future. **Change is inevitable**. It is up to everyone to make the change constructive and helpful. On the basis of the past, some good guesses have to be made to appreciate the possibilities in the future, to the extent possible. This act of guessing the future scenario, with respect to anything, is essentially foretelling or prediction or prognostication, which in scientific terminology is called ***'forecasting'.*** The scientific practice, and perhaps art, by which this is done is now-a-days called ***'futuring'*** by the Americans though there is no such verb as 'to future' in any English dictionary. But this term has somehow come into vogue. For correct action in the future, it has to be envisioned today. The science of futuring is often referred to as ***futurology.***

Forecasting on the basis of individuals goes on almost continuously and perhaps even sub-consciously. But the consequences of not forecasting usually do not have far reaching effects in the individual cases. This is however not so with groups such as organisations, villages, towns, cities, societies, nations and even international communities. The problems faced by them have far reaching consequences. Governments of various nations or the international community, as a whole, have always to plan most of the things for their future so that progress or development of the group takes place very smoothly without being caught unaware. The cost of being caught unaware can at times be huge but is very much avoidable through forecasting. It is precisely for this reason that the leadership of such groups always endeavour to predict, to the extent possible, knowing the past, what is there in store in future for them. This can be about anything whatsoever like how would the population, economy or government spending grow in future over the prescribed time. It may be about the likelihood of climate changes over specified durations. It may be about catastrophic climatic changes to carry out proper planning such that the damages caused by it may be minimum. It could be about health of societies. It may also be of interest from the point of view of apropriate cultivation pattern. It may be of interest to governments to know how the resources would be required for various developmental purposes in view of the requirements or possible population growth.

Organisations are equally well interested in forecasting so that they plan their future production pattern at maximum possible efficiency, both for goods and services, at minimum of losses. They can thereby stand their competitors well, continue earning profit and at times even sustain themselves against heavy odds.

It may be about the way the likes and dislikes of people may change with time, so that they can plan to provide the goods or the services needed in future. The alternative can simply lead to nothing short of decimation of that organisation and nobody would like to work towards that end. The controller, manager or leader has to steer his organisation through all such tumultuous and unknown future towards achieving their mission.

No organisation can now function without appropriate planning and which cannot be effectively worked out without forecasting of many related things. Nothing on group level is done now without thinking about the possible future scenario on short or long range perception of the future. This helps to carry out the planning properly and without which no organisation can function effectively even in the present. It only means that by adopting futuring techniques and processes, possible scenario-forecasting is attempted. This is done even on individual basis as and when required and if possible.

In fact every attempt is made these days to predict everything related to the future, well beforehand. It may be related to economics, political changes, health, population changes, environment, educational needs, technologies, human likes and dislikes, raw material sources and so on. This subject has therefore acquired tremendous importance and scientific methods have been developed for futuring to enable forecasting. **Forecasting is therefore a statement made about the future or what is likely to happen in future. This is also a sort of visioning.**

In USA World Future Society [1[has been actively engaged to unfold the possible scenario about everything related to society. It has a very large membership and well known scientists and technologists are its active members. The founder of this society, **Edward Cornish, puts futuring as not predicting the future but an attempt to improve it**. It means how we will live in future by making choices today and realising the consequences of our decisions. It therefore means forecasting is attempted to improve the future without being caught unaware to face the damaging consequences or to take full advantage of the unfolding events, to the extent possible. With all such attempts and inputs from so many great people, future cannot be predicted. The direction of its unfolding at best may be revealed.

Forecasting presumes that the future is uncertain and probable guess about it has to be made and that it can be made. It originates from worries about the future. Having lived in the agricultural set-up for so long, on an average, Indians have become fatalist. For them the future is fixed or determined and everything is moving in that direction through providential decree. There is therefore no need to worry about it but to accept it as God's grace. In fact every change comes into effect because of several factors. These include the overall social forces, including the technological ones, the desires and activities of individuals and groups, chance factor and determinism. All this makes the future most uncertain and indeterminate. Yet guess can be made as to explain the likely emerging scenario. It is important from this point of view.

Hence any worth the name organisation is not managed only by planning, organizing, staffing, leading and controlling as indicated earlier, but additionally by visioning, forecasting and futuring. Whether the visioning, forecasting and futuring is done more formally or informally is a matter of choice dictated by circumstances. In fact **formation of an organisation begins with a vision and forecasting of some human needs based on futuring.** Organisation is formed to meet these needs.

Futuring Methods [2]

Broadly eight different scientific methods have been developed for futuring to lead to appropriate forecasting. These are

1. Scanning
2. DEGEST method
3. Trend analysis
4. Scenario analysis
5. DELPHY polling
6. Modeling, Simulations and Games
7. Brainstorming
8. Visioning

All of these techniques may not be applicable to every requirement of forecasting. For evaluation of any specific area of interests one or more of these techniques may be adopted. These have all been tried and tested methods for their own area of application. Futuring based on these techniques will help better navigate uncertainties, take advantages of new opportunities and perhaps guard against potential problems.

1. *Scanning*

Scanning is a continuous and systematic examination and evaluation of current information published in print and electronic media of any type such as, newspapers, magazines, internet, government publicity material, statements of leaders of all hues and so on. The fine changes are observed over a time to finally guess the possible direction of their changes in future. By doing this exercise number of times the accuracy of one's own projections can be evaluated. This is based on historical data or past record which are extrapolated either linearly or as trend or as growth curve. It might help to remain a step ahead and take appropriate decisions for better.

This is done by scanning the information, clipping the information of interest and continuous or periodical reviews of these data for prediction. Some key words or figures or phrases or any such specific thing is identified to keep track.

This technique was extensively used by military intelligence command during the wars especially during the Second World War. By analysing these long-term trends the larger picture unfolds itself. At times it reveals that the observers themselves were a part of some emerging trend only after it has emerged. It is important to understand the trend at an early stage in their development so that enough time is available for response to the emerging risks as well as opportunities.

Constant scanning and evaluation of such information updates our knowledge of the relevant world around and acts like a radar system for business and governments.

2. *DEGEST Method*

Once the emerging trends have been understood the derived information needs to be classified, analysed and evaluated for understanding the future trends. This is effectively done by adopting the DEGEST method. This was developed by **Prof. Philip Kotler of North-Western University,** especially for marketing management. He developed six distinct categories in which the future trends have to be studied. The name DEGEST is an acronym wherein first letters of these six categories is put together. These six categories are the ***demographics*** (denoted by letter 'D'), ***economics*** (denoted by 'E'), ***government*** (denoted by 'G'), ***environment*** (denoted by 'E'), ***society*** (denoted by 'S') and ***technology*** (denoted by 'T') in the acronym.

The demographics indicate the age-wise population growth. It helps in planning for future goods and services requirements. Economy provides jobs, incomes, etc. to assess their requirements of goods and services. Government means their possible direction of making laws that affect social lives, possible direction of economic development and so on. Environment is now all pervading and is to dictate the extent of material well being and enjoyment of the society as a whole. Society means culture, the media, the education system, religious and spiritual appeal and all the ways of interactions amongst individuals and groups. Technology, particularly after the industrial revolution, has been affecting the individuals, groups as well as the society and now even humanity as a whole, almost in all aspects of their lives. It has been such a powerful force that it is in everybody's interest to know its future trends. New technologies raise living standards and alongwith pose variety of new challenges. It affects the government, the economy and consequently the environment as well.

The DEGEST system of analysis is such that some or all factors can be included in the study to work out the emerging trends. Some new parameters may be included in this scheme if required.

3. Trend analysis [3]

In the constantly changing world there is generally a trend of change in almost everything. Trend analysis is to study the nature, causes, speed and potential impact of a developing change. Trend can have primary as well as secondary impacts. Increasing longer life span is bound to provide proportionately larger number of people contributing to economy. But equally large resources will have to be provided for them to contribute.

In the business world the value of trends is well recognized and these are constantly watched so that the business is not left behind time. Knowledge of world trends in human-likes and dislikes, national feelings, religious appeals and so on of populations helps to make practical judgments about business goals and strategies. Being unaware of relevant trends means risking entire business in the competitive world by a unrecognised change. By utilising trend analysis individuals as well as groups can hope to ride the wave of change towards their goals. Trend analysis is equally important to an individual and organisations.

Trend analysis includes actual analysis of causes of the change, the rate of change and their impacts; monitoring the change and its projection into the future. Causal analysis identifies the forces that are responsible for the changes. Quite often these forces are themselves trends. In that case contributory trends will have to be analysed. Impact analysis identifies the effects of the trend. The process of anticipation can be risky as well. The trend has to be carefully monitored and watched regularly to establish its character. For example, rising unemployment can have significant impacts on many different commercial organisations in terms of its marketing of goods and services. If such a trend is not monitored then some organisations may go bust.

A trend can be analysed, if enough statistical data is available, by plotting it over time in the form of a graph. The trend curve can be extended or projected into the future, assuming it to continue likewise. The projections are never cent per cent accurate. Some other factors may crop in and change the trend in future and one should be cautious in such projections. Good trend analysis therefore takes into account all possible primary and secondary contributing factors before doing any projections, and much less, evolving strategies for tackling them. Projections are not a static process of analysis. It must be continuously tested with changing times to remain abreast.

4. Scenarios analysis [4]

This is nothing short of serious fiction and can match any good detective story. It is certainly not forecasting but down-to-earth visioning of the future. This method was first adopted formally in the 1950s by USA's defense leaders to visualise what the scenarios would be like if World War III broke out or if nuclear war occurs? How would major American cities be protected against such eventualities? This is probabilistic forecasting. The causal analysis identifies the forces that are creating and shaping such imaginary events. But it is now routinely adopted in business organisations.

These appear as fictions but aren't. In this, thoughts and ideas are put in a story form about the possibilities when a specific event occurs. All the details of how it would occur, what circumstances would lead it to occur, what consequences there would be, how it would be tackled and all such possible details are worked out. It provides reasonable guess of the future and enables one to take informed decisions, leading to minimum of damage, should it occur. Multiple scenario approach enables one to think in terms of alternative possibilities, rather than a fixed and predetermined future. It leads to creation of five different alternatives. These are:

The surprise-free scenario

This storyline assumes that current trends shall continue without many upheavals. This is often referred to as 'business-as-usual scenario'.

The optimistic scenario

It presumes that things will get definitely better than present.

The pessimistic scenario

It presumes that things will get worse

The disaster scenario

The situation shall prove to be disastrous

The miracle scenario

It presumes that some miracle might save the situation from getting worse.

Scenario analysis is not only meant for some large scale scenario predictions but can be equally applied to minor issues and issues related to individuals like spending a vacation or accepting a new assignment and so on.

5. Delphi polling

Olaf Helmer and **Normon Dalkey**, two scientists of Rand Corporation, in 1953, developed a polling process to generate more accurate predictions than mere opinion gathering approaches. They called it Delphi method.

This technique consisted of gathering some experts of a given field to work out forecasting in any area of interest. In this the problems are first put before the experts and are asked to write their own reactions independently. Their responses are then analysed to find out the area of agreement as well as of disagreement amongst them. In the second stage, summary of the outcome is prepared and is presented before the experts as a group. Now in the light of views of others, each one is allowed to change one's own predictions, if so desired and to whatever extent they wished. This is how the overall opinion of experts is obtained on the subject of interest. The method is logically very sound and tested on larger horizons of expert opinions. It is a judgmental method and individual intuition plays its role. There is definitely a subjective probability involved. Yet it allows to make better-informed, more accurate and more rational predictions.

6. Modeling, Simulations and Games

A model is something in a miniature form to show how the actual thing would look like in its real full scale. Models are static as well as dynamic. Simulations are miniature descriptions of the real process in modular form. Futuring models are usually mathematical descriptions and show how the reality would look like in the form of mathematical equations. They are dynamic descriptions of the complex systems. The interplay of real variables is played by the rules of the model. The biggest challenge in this exercise is getting these rules drafted accurately.

In fact as human beings we tend to construct models and simulate them by running them mentally. The same has been adopted by scientists from **Galileo to Einstein,** who trained their minds to accurately imagine what might occur, given a certain set of circumstances, in order to achieve breakthroughs. These days' computers do this job very well and the softwares are the models and nothing else. When these are operated they simulate the real change.

Computer games are nothing but real games played in miniature form by simulating the real game. It helps to involve people emotionally and make them think about the real problems and ways of solving the same in real life situations.

7. Brainstorming

The idea of brainstorming was introduced by **Alex F. Osborn** in 1950s to get new ideas in ad campaigns. It is the most popular technique used today for creating new ideas about any subject. It has four basic rules. These are:

1. Defer judgment on any idea
2. Try to develop a lot of ideas and not worry about their quality
3. Strive for unusual ideas (even crazy ideas to be welcomed)
4. Build on other people's ideas

There is a leader to guide the session and there is a recorder to note all the ideas. After one or more such brainstorming sessions an evaluation meeting is held to assess the ideas proposed. Ideas can be sorted and ranked with respect to their applicability and usefulness for possible action. It indicates different possibilities, opportunities and risks involved to develop innovative strategies.

8. Visioning

In reality it is thinking in future tense. It is most desirable for individuals as well as organisations before planning any strategy for action, to avoid later crises and disasters. In a group everybody is encouraged to carry out visioning so that the final strategy is evolved through a more democratic process.

The actual session of visioning is carried out in four stages:

1. **The Critique phase** – wherein all negative experiences are expressed
2. **The Fantasy phase** – in which wild thinking is allowed about possible solutions
3. **The Selection phase** – wherein selection of useful ideas is made and small working groups are formed to develop solutions and projects for their possible applications.
4. **The Implementation phase** – when the details of getting the project through are worked out to formulate the action plan, with all foreseeable hurdles in its implementation. There are now experts available who help visioning in an organisation, more so for business purposes.

Clement Bezold outlines five stages in building a vision as:

1. Identification of a problem
2. Identification of past successes
3. Identification of desires for the future
4. Identification of measurable goals
5. Identification of resources to achieve the set goals

This technique truly appeals people and has great value in generating new ideas, encouraging interaction in a group and focusing the group on a common set goal.

Relevance to Organisations

Organisational management is often carried out in terms of five main activities as indicated earlier. Planning is the most basic one without which it does not come into existence. Planning is a continuous process. It takes place even before forming an organisation. It is carried out all through the functioning of an organisation on regular basis and is carried out specifically in view of the impending future scenario so that it does not have to face problems unthought of earlier. Planning is nothing but futuring carried out to predict favourable conditions for the orgnisation to achieve its objective collectively. Planning directly affects staffing in terms of future needs. Planning influences organisational functions with long-term perspectives. Planning guides the leader to exercise organisational control effectively. Above all proper planning, that is futuring alone, enables the leader to lead effectively in all circumstances.

References

1. World Future Society, website – www.wfs.org.
2. Mack, Tim, *Futuring Methods*, www.wfs.org.
3. Gordon, Adam, *Future Savvy : Identifying Trends to Make Better Decisions and manage Uncertainty,* AMACOM, Oct., 2008, p. 294.
4. Fukuyama, Francis, *Blindside : How to Anticipate Forcing Events and Wild Cats in Global Politics,* Institution, Oct., 2007, p. 198.

CHAPTER 25

REFORM TRENDS

CHAPTER STRUCTURE

- Historical
- Efficiency
- Business Management
- Awareness
- Current Trends
- Visionary Organisations
- CSR
- Excellence
- Alternatives
- Virtual Organisations
- Person-centric Organisation
- Brands
- Quality Circle
- Learning Organisations

Historical

Although there were organisations before in the agricultural era, the onset of industrial revolution additionally required myriad types of organisations to cope up with the ever increasing production and distribution of goods and also to meet the social changes consequent upon it. As long as only few nations of Europe were industrialized and that they had much of their market in the form of their own captive colonies, there was not much of a competition amongst the organisations that they had specifically created to exploit industrial revolution and create wealth. Even otherwise the industrial production was not all that colossal, as is today, to require large market for its sale. Much of what was produced was sold readily as something not seen before by most in the societies at home and abroad. Those organisations by and large served the purpose for which they were created.

This was the early era of industrial revolution that is 18-19th centuries. That era did contribute in the evolution of science in general and scientific management practices in particular for improving organisational efficiency. Its applications however were more in defense and state governance rather than in commercial activities. It however did have an impact in improving even the commercial organisations, but at a relatively slow pace. Understanding the science of organization did not get the attention of social scientists that it deserved then. That is one of the major reasons why the developments in organisational science got mixed up with management, initially in the form of evolution of management practices, which slowly transformed and came to be accepted as management science itself. The organisational science *per se* did not therefore develop as an independent branch of social science. Ideally it should have been developed as **'organizational science'** like any other branch of basic science and management as its applied part. That is why and how it has now come to be called as management science which includes both the basic and the applied part mixed up as one whole

The evolution of management as a branch of science goes back to early part of twentieth century when **Frederick Taylor** for the first time revealed that in an organisation there are those who think and issue directions and instructions, which are to be acted upon by the rest unquestioningly, in trying to achieve the organisational objective. It was presumed that, in the absence of any alternative means of sustenance, payment would motivate the workers adequately to run such a bureaucratic set-up. In their perception therefore there were the 'thinkers' on the one hand and the 'doers' on the other in an organisation. The thinkers were the leaders, managers or the bosses and the rest were workers. This is what is now referred to as the traditional hierarchical, bureaucratic or pyramidal organisation and their management approach is described as bureaucratic or traditional hierarchical. It is based on an illusion that anyone could master the dynamics and detailed complexity, in the entire organisation, from top and offer solutions to any problems at any level in an organisation. The leadership in fact works on an illusion of being in control. The fact is that the leadership is under less and less influence on events. The bureaucrats are always doubtful as to how organisations can be controlled without controlling it. This perception is based on the perception of average worker's powerlessness, lack of any vision and inability to master the forces of change; the deficits can only be made good by a few called leaders. In reality however anybody can expand his capability to understand complexity and clarify vision. Its predominant application in defense and state governance was perhaps more responsible for such traditional perception. In the beginning it was copied in commercial organisations without question.

The overall scientific and sociological understanding of the contemporary times in a way always decides the management perceptions and practices. The bureaucratic perception must have been the result of the **Newtonian-Cartesian** perceptions that dominated those times and which looked at the world in pieces and parts. The theorem of Arnold Toynbee, as explained earlier in **Chapter 14**, with reference to the formation of organisations, in the form of creative minority mechanically joining majority, was universally accepted then as valid and it formed the basis of management.

Efficiency

The question of efficiency of commercial organisations did not come up seriously until the end of Second World War when these industrialised nations started facing competition, for the first time, as a result of increased production and therefore increasing global trade, against even with their earlier colonies and other nations. When competition came to the center stage, particularly in the commercial world, the management practices came to be scrutinised very seriously to improve upon and keep improving the organisational efficiency. The commercial world was in the vanguard of improvement because it is in its nature and is capable of experimentation to evolve better methods, strategies and practices to ensure profit.

Business Management

In the later half of twentieth century management science became a very prominent branch of knowledge to be taught at the universities, almost all over the world. The human resource trained in management at the university was sought in all walks of social life for its management. Now it is the prime branch where the best of brains, in general, seek admission to make their own carrier. These are the ones who later come to manage particularly the myriad business organisations, wherein wealth is predominantly generated. It is also the reason why the management courses at the university are known more as '**business management courses**'.

Awareness

Being at the centre of economic activities the management science has undergone paradigm changes since the Second World War. In fact it has been undergoing thorough research and their application in actual practice, on an ever increasing scale the world over. The traditional hierarchical organisations proved too inadequate to match the emerging expectations of commercial activities. The first three of the basic human requirements, food, shelter and belonging, as illustrated by **Abraham Maslow** (confirm p 57), could be met rather easily. These therefore could not motivate further to put in more efforts in an organisation. For higher efficiency the management will have to address the higher needs like self respect and self-actualisation by building organisations with perceptions more consistent with human nature. The changes should eliminate or at least minimize the diseases that afflict the bureaucratic organisations.

These changes are essentially based on the fundamentally different perception of organisations. It scrutinizes the organisational structures, amount of individual freedom and responsibility spread through and, management practices for extracting what is desired for achieving the organisational objective. It presumes that there is still a lot of untapped potential in an organisation and any improvements should aim at to realize it. Therefore current trends in management improvements dwell more on the study of human nature, individually as well as group-wise, their desires, perceptions, motivations and so on. It manifests in more effective types and extents of training to generate the required human resources. Fundamentally it dwells again and again on planning, organizing, staffing, leading and controlling – the essential and well established five point programme of management – but in the light of modern perceptions. Fundamentally it assumes that human beings would like to ascend to a higher level of awareness through deep learning, under suitable conditions and thereby contribute their might to society through organisations.

The bureaucratic organisations undergo changes by reacting to the events as they come as challenges. These are external in nature. But the real challenges are internal and are related to lack of adequate knowledge, team intelligence, individual and team mental framework, leaders as role models and adequate vision, mission and core ideology for motivation. All the innovations in management have been and are currently being directed in this direction.

Current Trends

In trying to improve organisational efficiency considerable attention was paid to understand what motivates and inspires people to work and what generates lethargy while working in an organised group. This has been discussed in some detail in **Chapter 20.**

Organisation is a social phenomenon and understanding of individual and group psychology, their perception, judgment, decision-making and execution of decision so taken became essential subjects of studies in understanding organisational science and therefrom developing better management practices. It has been dealt with in **Chapter 21**.

Minimisation of inadequacies in the traditional centralised and hierarchical structure by making it more open, decentralised and non-hierarchical in design to allow more freedom, attendant responsibility and commitment to organisational objective, is now order of the day. It reduces not only the mechanical pressure but it relives the unnecessary psychological barriers that demotivate the workers. As a result, organisations have structurally becoming more flat, to the extent possible, while reforming them. This has already been explained earlier in **Chapter 13**. In general it did improve the organisational efficiency to some extent because of increased freedom of action and accountability at even the lower levels.

Being an inalienable part of society the organisation owes full responsibility towards well being of the society. As a result the concept of corporate social responsibility has now been universally accepted by the corporate world to substantiate the obligations of commercial organisations towards the society, rather than being focused only on profit. Organisational activities should be viewed as only indirect social activities, carried out by practically self-appointed groups and nothing else. Hence social exploitation in the form of profit-making cannot be its aim. It can at best be the result that automatically follows out of essentially some social obligations. This has been dealt with earlier and also in detail in **Chapter 26**.

Future of any organisation does not just happen. It has to be created through individual and collective action without being caught unaware about anything. This improves the efficiency to a large extent. This has already been discussed in **Chapter 24** in some details.

The adoption of vendor system, development of ancillaries or contractual ***virtual*** organisations is yet another approach to improve organisational efficiency of particularly the large organisations. It is now followed to the extent possible even by promoting, educating and developing specific vendors as a matter of economical activity of large organisations. Similarly ***out-sourcing*** and ***off-shoring*** of activities, to the extent possible is being increasingly adopted to improve efficiency and economics of operation.

Development of brand name by persistently producing standard quality or even somewhat improved version of the product is yet another way of improving the efficiency and economics of commercial organisations.

Effective use of quality circles has been made to improve the efficiency of organisation since last few decades almost all over the world by major commercial companies to improve quality and productivity.

Focused efforts at varied and rigorous training, to develop the best possible human resource, are often seen to improve efficiency of commercial as well as social and political organisations.

The latest improvement in this long list is the transformation of entire organisation into a learning organisation which has been dealt with in little more details in the present chapter.

On the whole management science of feed-back and feed-forward systems, ecology-centric futurology and computer-centric super technology is now trying to replace much of the industrial world and causing the third-wave/information technology/knowledge revolution almost all over the world. It has been and is bound to further change the organisational perceptions in future.

Visionary Organisations

The study of organisations has of late developed the concept of visionary organisations as somewhat idealised organisations. The motivational studies revealed that people work more readily for some worth achieving vision in the form of better society, nation or humanity as a whole. Such visions do have the relevant mission to achieve it. People do have inborn instincts to identify with such humanitarian vision and mission, if put before them in proper perspective. They are then prepared to put in more efforts and even sacrifice to some extent for such mission. But it must be a lofty vision, more perhaps in the service of society or humanity, as a priori. Many social, religious or political organisations do have such vision and mission and therefore many toil hard, to the utmost of their capacities, in such organisations, to serve the society. With suitable training and building individual role models to follow, many may go even out of way in trying to realise the same. Even commercial organisations also understood the importance of such vision and mission while producing goods and services aimed ultimately to serve the society.

In right type of NPO's, the chief motivation is always one of service to the society or the needy ones to achieve individual peace, prosperity and security. That is always their core driving force. But the profit making organisations are fundamentally run to earn profit, along with service to the society as well. Of late they visualise themselves with such vision and mission so that profit shall follow out of their specific service to the target group, as an outcome rather than the prime motive.

Such visionary companies therefore define their core ideologies to work for. It may be service to the customers or welfare of the employees or better products and services through increased R and D efforts or better healthcare of individuals or protection of environment or establishing national spirit and so on. These are matters of highly subjective satisfactions and do not have any universal basis as applicable philosophies. They may invite criticism that these are clever ploys of concealing the real motive of profit alone. None the less they surely serve society better by becoming better. These certainly do make organisations more effective and efficient. Yet all these attempts stand on the ***us* and *they*** syndrome. The top hierarchy in such cases may be somewhat committed but the remaining major work force falls in line just to earn own living, perhaps under compulsions or as a matter of strategy. It can be improved through sustained training.

Such visions often continue as long as the activities are on the whole profitable. The moment it becomes a matter of losing proposition, perhaps against competitors, such visions are often relegated to the background per force. Those who have their monopolies established by way of some edge over the competitors may talk of such visions and core ideologies and the like. In fact a **better mental, intellectual and philosophical basis is needed to manage society via organisations.**

Collins [1,2] and his co-workers have shown from their study of variety of commercial organisations that these can be **'Built to Last'** [2], in the service of society, without much difficulties, provided they evolve lofty social needs as their organisational objectives.

Similarly **Good** organisations can be transformed into **Great** organisations [1], with high operational efficiency, by adopting core ideology in the form of their vision and mission in larger social or humanitarian interests. More and more organisations are adopting this line of approach, for certain.

In reality ideology is something for which the organisation must be in a position to sacrifice itself, if it comes to that. It is unchangeable and is a point of faith. It is quite different from policy.

CSR

The concept of corporate social responsibility has also been almost universally accepted by the corporate world to substantiate the obligations of commercial organisations towards the society. Work force can be motivated to work in such larger interests. This has been dealt with earlier but more in detail in **Chapter 26**. In a way any organisation that aims at social development as its core philosophy, is bound to be more effective and efficient, since it touches the heart of the work force readily. After all the work force is also a part of society, mentally as well as psychologically.

Excellence

In the eighties of the last century **Tom Peters** [3,4]and his associates scrutinised large number of commercial organisations to know what differentiated them to produce their differential performances in terms of productivity, quality of products or services, relative costs and above all profits and all such parameters that decide the quality of their organisations on the whole. From the enormous survey and indepth studies they concluded many things and evolved parameters that make organisations excellent, average or poor. These findings are compiled in two treatises in the form of **'In Search of Excellence'** [3] and **'Passion for Excellence'** [4].

In their opinion there are always practical, justifiable, inevitable, sensible and sane reasons to compromise on any of the variables that ultimately make organisations average or poor in their performance in terms of the quality and cost of their products. The alternative is to insist, not just on better or best but, on excellence at every major or minor part of organisational activity, leading directly or indirectly in meeting the organisational objective. Equally true is to manage the affairs, on micro as well as macro level, such that every one in the organisation feels at ease to work towards excellence in their own local areas of operation and, contribute in such a way that overall excellence is achieved. It is incumbent on the superiors at all levels to facilitate everything in this direction. It primarily starts with treating all as equal partners and, intelligent and competent enough, to contribute towards the goal of excellence. The work force will have to be trained accordingly. The lip-service and gimmick need to be avoided consciously. The all-pervading theme is respect for the individual as an equal human being.

In search of excellence or a passion for excellence does not mean uniformity with respect to vision, mission, goal, value-system or programme, in all organisations of similar types. The structure, systems, styles, values and so on shall be different in different organisations but they should all be reinforcing one another so that the individual organisation is truly unusual in its ability to achieve extraordinary results through ordinary people, who then become the winners. Such organisations become creative and innovative at all levels. This will not be achieved without proper training and human resource development. If this is the passion of the leader and is committed, then it is rather easy to make organisations excellent. The effectiveness and efficiency of such organisations shall then be automatically at their best.

Alternatives

Mere changes in organisational structures have not been found adequate enough for improving efficiency. Several alternative solutions have been suggested and have been tried, though with only partial success. Some paradigm changes in perceptions are taking place to find alternatives. These include the adoption of vendor system for getting many of the products or services supplied by other people, either individually or by their much smaller organisations where the organisational efficiency is comparatively and normally high. The other is the off-loading of work to virtual organisations led by intelligent individuals.

In the information technology era aided by computers, individuals are becoming equally strong to challenge even the mighty organised groups. It should be noted that the instances of ***'cyber-hacktivists'***, that are posing great threats to many national governments [5] should be channelised for improving organisational efficiency. It is a human trait to be either devil or saintly. Efforts should be directed to make them more saintly.

Virtual Organisations

Having realised the shortfalls of traditionally organised activities the information technologies are slowly and continuously transforming the industrial era organisations into suitable new formats [3.4]. Still it is inherent in organisations to tend to be essentially a centralised structure and such structures are always prone to exploit the have-nots, may be in subtle manner. The knowledge era is bound to destroy the organised structures of the industrial era and evolve into individualistic and decentralised organised formats.

One of the possible new formats of decentralised arrangement is ***virtual organisations*** in the form of organisations apparently looking as of just individuals. This appears to be simply a fantastic idea in view of the definition of organisation as evolved and universally accepted, in the industrial era and as described before. The meaning of organisations as understood in the form of industrial organisations requires essentially a group to form organisations. But in a virtual organisation of the third wave era, individuals work in such a way, that it will appear as if work is going on in an organised way, but without forming formally any organisational structure for working physically together. There will be the necessary power structure, in loose form, in such set-ups. Individuals will seek help from many similar individuals, as and when required, perhaps just for the time being or on the basis of specific assignment, and shall appear consequently as if the work is being carried out by an organisation in the form of all those so involved. The efficiency of such work is as good as of any individual working for own interests. There will be stiff competition amongst those who offer such services and a suitable one can be chosen or even changed, if so desired, from the lot. There is bound to be maximum possible motivation achieved in such arrangements. In fact the individual will identify himself as an organisation and nothing less than that. This is being adopted widely.

The basic requirements to form organisation, as described in **Chapter 7**, shall still be met in the form of the virtual groups. It will have a common objective and for which the involved ones agree to work with mutual help and co-ordination to fulfill their self interests, under some legal framework. It will be led by some individual for coordinating all the activities. The scientific definition of an organisation as accepted universally does not dictate that the group shall be physically working together, perhaps under one shed. The group so working may go on working together without formally forming any organisation or it may be extremely transient in its existence, for some specific assignment. People working in such a way may form and break organisations informally and therefore readily. They will resemble more closely in their style of functioning to that of informal project organisations of still more transient existence.

The commission agents typically fall in this category. This job is done by some people putting their efforts together. They charge commission on the basis of transactions they carry out. Such people are very intelligent and belong to the class of creative minority as defined by **Toynbee**. They do have the ability to form organisations but prefer to work as individuals taking help from many others from time to time, rather than on permanent basis. All such people, from time to time, when they work together, they consider themselves as organisation itself. The other examples of such activities are the increasingly becoming popular contractual system of getting work done through some contractor who may in turn hire people time to time to get the job done. The vendor system or business process outsourcing system also falls in the same category. The other examples are in the form of some individuals who get work done with the help of several other individuals on the basis of sundry work-piece contracts. This type of work does require a very motivated, intelligent and co-operative worker to act as its anchor. The working efficiency is almost at its peak in such arrangements because motivation is at its peak.

The success of virtual organisations is pointing the direction in which the future organisational set up shall be evolved, to a fair extent. It will be preferred to maintain ones own freedom at its utmost. It will have its own niche area of operation. It will also result in very high efficiency. **It eliminates the compulsions of getting saddled with some fixed work force and their attendant disinterestedness and inefficiency growing with time.** The motivational problems and resulting inefficiency in achieving set-out aim can be eliminated in this way. Each one will have to get motivated for work in such virtual organisations on their own, all along, any time and every time. This has been lucidly illustrated by **Friedman** [7] by giving an example of Dell computers, its manufacture and marketing.

Person-centric Organisation

Still other examples, particularly in the field of social activities, are in the form of individuals crusading for some public purpose, wherein the others join, as and when required purely on the basis of the issue and their interests therein, from their own places of work. Social worker **Anna Hazare** in Maharashtra or **Medha Patkar** as leader of victims of Narmada river valley or many other human-rights-activists do not have any formal organisation of their own and yet their work goes on in a much organised manner with considerable public support and participation. Often they give some name to their activity and that virtually gets recognised as an organised activity through the media. This type of virtual organisation does require morally strong individuals with equally strong commitment and who command respect out of their sterling character, to lead such organisations. These are generally not recongnised under any legal frame-work except that these activities are carried out under the fundamental rights of expression and organisation as guaranteed under democratic constitutions. Such solutions are indeed effective and efficient and need to be followed on a wider scale. Such individuals do not just think as if they are the organisations but they consider themselves as if they are the society itself and hence work for its utmost welfare. They have found their application in social and political areas. They are bound to be followed on increasing scale even in other spheres of social life. These are often found to be fairly effective and efficient in the social arena. But is it the answer for the plaguing problems of organisations on social front?

Brands

Modern organisations unlike the earlier organisations are now known more as their brands, e.g. Sony, Hitachi, Tatas, Infosys, AT and T, 3M, IBM and so on. This is not only true with commercial organisations but it is equally true with other organisations as well. The days of organisations being known by some charismatic leader are long back over. Attempts are made to make the quality of products and services known by the brand. This is rather difficult. It takes a long time to build the reputation of the brand in terms of quality of their products in whatever form. Those who rely more on individuals and their qualities find it difficult to sustain and grow over a long duration. When vision and mission of an organisation is clear and as a result the core ideology is accepted, it is rather easy to build the brand by sustainingly producing the required products and maintaining the quality of the products. People may come and people may go but the service to society through products and services, in tune with time, shall go on uninterruptedly. The actual products on getting obsolete may be discarded and newer ones introduced as per the social needs. Those who man such organisations may grow old and leave the organisation. But it should continue to serve the society. Such organisations are formed to last much longer in the service of the society, in spite of the people manning them and the products they produce, undergoing changes and even drastic ones too.

In the social sector RSS cultivated the organisation by laying extreme emphasis on collectivity rather than on any individual caliber or achievement. This was achieved by accepting an unusual guide and philosopher in the form of *Saffron Flag* as their guru, rather than building the organisation around any individual, much less even around the founder. In fact they killed individuality and the related ego, by defacing individuality, in all possible ways, to build the organisation. RSS has therefore acquired a brand name for nationalism, selflessness, sacrifice, dedication, commitment, social service and above all saver of Hindu society and never for any selfish or parochial interests. This was possible because they placed the core ideology of ***Hindu-Nation*** (not religious but cultural) as overriding above all the rest. Their vision and mission was thus fully objective and had a very long-term vision. One may agree or disagree with them but that is also the reason why it is growing even after eighty five years and changes in leadership several times during this period.

Quality Circle

This is the concept that was evolved by Kaoru Ishikawa in 1962 in Japan to improve skills, capabilities, confidence and creativity of the workers through cumulative process of education, training, work experience and participation to finally improve quality and productivity of the operation. It facilitates commitment to work, self motivation and excellence. It is basically development of human resource right from the lower-most level to improve effectiveness and efficiency of an organisation. It recognizes the value of worker as a human being capable of rational thinking. Herein people are respected and are involved in decision-making. Everyone can be made to learn and contribute to organisational goal. It changes the spirit from 'I do this' to 'we did it' stage.

Perhaps the concept of learning organisation might have its roots in quality circle perception.

Learning Organisations

The systemic thinking evolved out of Einsteinian world view and later consolidated by the deep ecological perspectives, has now come to occupy the centre stage while considering any activity, more so the organisational efficiency. But mere systemic perception is not enough to remodel any organization. It must come as a package deal along with some other parameters that are capable of fully exploiting the systemic thinking in transforming the organisations to suit the modern times. In this respect an idealized organisational model, as per their R and D efforts, has been evolved by the management group of MIT in USA led by **Peter Senge** [6], towards the end of the previous century, in the form of **'Fifth Discipline'**. It is to transform the organisation into a learning organisation. It is not just the model but it also suggests the practice how this fifth discipline shall be cultivated in any organisation.

They have worked out five apparently different but integrally holistic disciplines as an ensemble to improve organisational efficiency. Their belief is that it surpasses the results beyond imagination. It inalienably includes **building shared vision, developing suitable mental models for participants, methodology of group learning and personal mastery** to realize full potential of any organisation in achieving its objective.

They have lucidly shown how the thinking in terms of pieces, directly or indirectly, acts as a hurdle in finding right solutions of problems faced by an organisation, in modern times. Non-systemic thinking tends to attribute blame of any failure to something external that helps to wash off hands from any responsibility. Basically it prevents further learning and that is very detrimental to organisational progress. Even those who think that they are very proactive in solving the possible problems, act in reality reactively, albeit unknowingly. It should be realised that primarily threats do not come from sudden events or external events but from slow and gradual processes related to the organisation. Hence these must be thoroughly investigated to find out the solution and see that they do not recur. The consequences of any action, if are discernible in the distant past or future, the learning horizon has to be extended in time and space to that extent. It proves rather difficult and hence attempts are made to break it in pieces and understand their immediate effects which may turn out to be quite fruitless.

The non-systemic thinking makes us prisoners of own thinking and expect the events to occur that way. As a result action is at one place in time and space and the result of which may occur elsewhere. Systemic thinking enables one to see the pattern of changes and long-term trends to get prepared to tackle them. In trying to find quick-fix solutions, it often leads to thinking in terms of events which is anathema to systemic thinking. It only complicates the matter further. One must realise that today's problems have come perhaps from yesterday's solutions. Those who solved it earlier are different from those facing it today. It may only lead to blame-game and no solution. The answer to all such problems lies in holistic or systemic thinking. Unnecessary dissection of a problem may lead to creation of more problems rather than providing any solution. The origin of such thinking has to be changed at the conscious and sub-conscious level only through changes in mental models of the work-force because **systems-thinking is a discipline for seeing the whole, in terms of the pattern, rather than as parts.**

It is the age that reveals the inter-dependence in almost anything and everything. In animate systems the inter-connectedness is the chief characteristic that distinguishes it from inanimate objects. Human factor is an inalienable part of organisations and that makes the organisation dynamically a very complex and interconnected system. Human involvement inevitably makes it a goal oriented systemic process which is generally characterised by long-term considerations. Feed-back and feed-forward processes underlie all such goal oriented processes. It may support or hinder the process because there is always some form of inherent delays in such loop-systems. Any resistance to feed-processes may result in additional balancing processes coming into effect. All these factors make it a dynamically complex process which can only be understood through equally dynamic and complex systemic solutions. The systems archetypes, if developed properly, can reveal an elegant simplicity underlying the complexity, particularly in management issues. It unifies knowledge across all related fields that help create the pattern of reality. It reduces increasing dependence on quick solutions in terms of discreet events and forces. According to **Senge** it enables all involved to see the 'forest as well as the trees' more clearly. It helps to evolve coherent story of the problem and the possible solutions thereat. It can deal effectively with diversified people with equally diversified mind, and way of their thinking without offending anybody.

Any presumed structures of any phenomena tend to hold us prisoner of that presumption rather than detached thinking and that in reality prevents finding effective solutions. This is how the reality is visualised in simplistic terms. In fact each one must be able to understand reality, howsoever complex it may be and the vision to be achieved, so that tension is generated in the mind about the gap, what **Senge** calls as 'creative tension'. It is here that personal mastery is required to overcome this tension. It is different from emotional tension and structural conflict. Personal mastery is achieved through individual learning. It integrates reason with individual intuition and feels more connected through compassion and commitment to the whole. The perception that rationality is opposed to intuition stems from linear and non-systemic thinking. **Systemic thinking holds key to integration of reason and intuition.** Synergy of these two is the quality of great thinkers. This is one of the primary contributions of systemic thinking according to Senge. The more the inter-connectedness is realised the more it helps towards systemic thinking.

A learning organisation can be created wherein people are encouraged to create their own vision, inquiry and commitment to truth and where challenging the status-quo is encouraged. Personal mastery helps how to reflect on tacit assumptions or express ones own vision and listen to other's vision and participate in joint inquiry into varied views of current reality. It is possible through developing mental models compatible with such inquiries. The learning organisation is to develop vision, values and mental models to develop organisational working more congruent with human nature.

In traditional organisations, according to **Senge,** merit means doing what boss wants, openness means telling the boss what he wants to hear and localness means doing the dirty stuff that boss does not want to do himself. Therefore mental models of key decision makers are very important and must be generative rather than adaptive. The heart of learning organisation is dialogue and not discussion. It would be based on shared understanding, inter-relatedness and understanding possible patterns of change. Free flow of even conflicting ideas is critical to building shared vision.

Personal mastery without team learning is not possible to a large extent. The team IQ must be more than the sum of participants IQs put together. The ideal example of team learning can be found in Indian history when the *rishis* used to stay together in *Naimisharanya*(a specific forest abode of rishis) for four months in the rainy season when their movements, even otherwise were restricted in those days, when animals and carts were the only mode of transport. They use to deliberate on issues and problems faced by the society, spread in self-contained villages across the entire land of the then India. They would bring some kind of consensually accepted solutions which would then be disseminated in society during the rest of the eight months of the year, when the weather was conducive to their movements. That is the reason why the decentralised Indian society maintained its cultural identity all through the tumultuous times till to date, uninterruptedly even after number of aggressions to destroy it. It was a typical case of developing individual passion through collective learning by thorough deliberations in smaller or larger groups. It is the whole that can readily organise parts. It is not a case of parts trying to make the whole. It combines perception and action.

Senge emphasises that systemic thinking precludes keeping conflict between the family and the work place. Collective learning insists on personal mastery in all spheres of life, including the family. Else it results in imbalances resulting in split personality which is detrimental to collective learning even at the work place. It may be recalled here that in the traditional Indian perception the physical, mental, psychological and intellectual facets of an individual needs to be integrated to make him worth for the organisation. If one is not so then this needs to be cultivated to improve organisational efficiency. It brings in synergy at the work place through synergy at home. One cannot build a learning organisation on broken homes of workers and strained family relationships. This is achieved initially at the micro-level and built up step by step towards the entire organisation. It requires individuals to suspend their assumptions as a priori, to facilitate dialogue at the micro-level, so that integrated view of reality at that level is established. The repetition of such exercises step by step may eventually lead to integrated view at the organisational level. It builds up shared language that can tackle complexity readily. This challenges the organisational politics by openly challenging it. It will mark the end of disciple-syndrome in any organisation and the control from top shall wither away. The control is then through learning. The decision-making from top is thus replaced by decision-making at various levels; that is the real difference.

According to **Senge** the executives are expected to do jobs, different from standard management practices, in a learning organisation. They should also restrain themselves from only passing orders and instructions. The standard managing, organising and controlling is to be replaced by development of vision, values and mental models of workers suitable to leaning organisation. They have to primarily see how collective learning develops at the lower and micro-levels. That only shall lead to understand the dynamics of the underlying system. For this to happen it requires new generation of organisational architects who can master the cycle of thinking, doing, evaluating and reflecting. Without this there is no organisational learning.

On the whole it is easily said than done to build learning organisations. It has been almost two decades since the concept of learning organisation was developed and put into practice by **Senge.** But it has not been possible to establish acceptable methodology by which an organisation can readily be transformed into a learning organisation. It requires lot of preparatory training even of leaders or managers besides ordinary workers to transform an organisation into a learning organisation. It may be easy to develop social or political learning organisations. But it is still an uphill task to build profit making learning organisations.

The concept of learning organisation is certainly more abstract to grasp. It is therefore not easy to transform any organisation into a learning organisation easily. The theory is sound but practice is difficult. Is there any alternative? It has been discussed in the next chapter.

References

1. Collins, Jim, *Good to Great*, Harper-Collins, N.Y. (2001).
2. Collins, Jim and Porras, Jerry, I., *Built to Last*, Harper-Collins, N.Y. (2002).
3. Friedman Thomas, L., *Indian Express*, Delhi, 16th Dec. 2010.
3. Tom Peters and Robert H. Waterman Jr, *In search of Excellence*, Profile, (2003).
4. Tom Peters and Nancy Austin, *A Passion for Excellence,* Profile, (2003).
5. Friedman Thomas, L., *Indian Express*, Delhi, 16th Dec. 2010.
6. Senge, Peter, M., *The Fifth Discipline*, Currency Doubleday, N.Y. (1994).

CHAPTER 26

FOURTH WAVE EVOLUTION

CHAPTER STRUCTURE

- Evolutional Path
- Spirituality vs. Materialism
- Fall-outs of Material Progress
- Organisational Efficiency
- Way-out
- Basic Approach
- Social Organisational Models
- Western Model
- Thou Art That
- Fourth Wave Concept
- Advaiti Perception
- Illustrations
- Inevitability
- Westernisation
- Early Signs of Fourth Wave Change
- INFOSYS Experiment
- Guarantee
- Integral Approach
- Western Limitations
- Co-existence of Waves
- Social Extension
- Future Organisationality

Evolutional Path

Biological evolution has been taking place continuously since the birth of earth as a consolidated planet. Similarly social evolution has been taking place unabatedly since the birth of human beings in the process of evolution. That is how stoneage was replaced by agricultural society almost all over the world. The agricultural society is on the vanishing path because superior social form ensuring better sustenance, pleasant lifestyles decreasing day-to-day hardships, in the form of industrial social format got evolved through human intelligence and efforts. Most of the social development that has so far taken place is a result of individual and more so of organised efforts. But having understood the limitations of traditional organised forms as essentially evolved out of industrialisation, several new changes are taking place as discussed in the previous chapter. It is being adopted to make organisations more effective and efficient. There is no end to such paradigm social changes with time. In fact it is the result of conscious or sub-conscious efforts of all in the society. The mute question is only whether these changes are stop-gap arrangements or have more lasting influence.

It took nearly 30-40,000 years to change over from stoneage to evolve agricultural first wave society. It took almost 3-10.000 years to change over from first wave to second wave industrial society. The second wave society was characterised by factory and smoke-stacks, industrial revolution based on imperialism, development of bureaucratic management skills, Newtonian sciences and engineering. It took only few hundred years to change over from second to third wave information technological society based on feedback and feed-forward systems with computer-centric super technology. Twenty-first century will have many different characteristics distinctly different from all the previous ones. It will be de-massified, de-centralised and de-concentrated. It will have naturalistic, holistic and deep ecological overtones. It will be asynchronous and multi-polar in orientation and will be characterized by diversification. It will be informative, innovative and individualistic in approach. Will the organisations, even after taking into account the trends of its reformation, be able to cope up with these upcoming requirements? The present chapter is aimed to analyse this problem.

Every social evolution, by bringing in reforms, evolved better and better social formats to organise the society to make human beings, individually and collectively, more happy. This is how it has reached to third wave social change as described earlier. The evolutionary process can not be stagnated at this stage. Evolution to fourth wave society is therefore a logical next step in the direction of social evolution. How long will it take to evolve depends on its urgency. What kind of change will it be? Or has it already started evolving? The answers shall be based on our understanding of the increasing complexity of social systems.

Spirituality vs. Materialism

Notwithstanding the attraction to know the inaccessible other world and discovery of sure path of its realisation by the Indian seers, for most, the industrialisation and attendant production of goods and services, have been perhaps more attractive for enjoying this world at the material level. The debate over whether materialism or spiritualism should dominate one's own life has therefore sharpened fair bit in recent times. Those who have enjoyed enough material pleasures and having realised its limitations in getting lasting happiness, are now looking for spirituality as a possible way out for individual happiness. They are often resorting to some kind of rituals as a path of spirituality or Bhakti-marg as is called in Indian parlance. Those who have not enjoyed the material pleasures, particularly from the developing and under-developed countries, are looking for material pleasures with priority, at times disregarding their traditional spiritual treasure. This debate stems more from misunderstanding of spirituality. Often the term spirituality brings before, somebody in sack clothes, closing eyes and controlling breathing by closing one or the other nostrils in some odd manner. Let us not mistake spirituality with any such thing at all. The breathing exercise has its own importance but spirituality does not depend on it entirely. Spirituality is nothing but an attitude of one's own, to face everything in this world with equanimity in the form of a third person watching the things happening around, without getting involved in them unnecessarily, more perhaps like the actors in a drama. It also means that, doing whatever otherwise one would have done in this world, with certain attitude and outlook. It does require good health and the breathing exercises and yoga may be helpful to that end.

Fall-outs of Material Progress

Toffler revealed the social revolution that has taken place so far in the form of three different stages, namely the stoneage transforming into agricultural society, which later on transforming into industrial form and now is being aided by informational technology into a more effective and efficient instrument in trying to meet the human needs individually and collectively, in the form of knowledge era. It has in fact more than overstepped basic human requirements of meeting the needs into making human beings greedy, and that too, without perhaps any limits, whether sustainable by the globe or not. Acquiring material things and material enjoyments in itself has become the aim of life. In fact buying material things has become a value in itself or has second nature of human beings This is why **Toffler** calls it as ***indust-realism.*** The net result has been that if on the one hand human beings are happy for relatively less harsh lifestyles, they have become equally unhappy on the other because of unlimited increase in their material desires not being met. All through the ages the saints of all hues have been preaching that real happiness lies in giving more than receiving. The indust-realism taught us just the contrary. **Mahatma Gandhi** emphasised that there is enough in this world to meet everybody's needs, but it cannot meet anybody's greed, for sure. It has resulted in destroying the value system of individuals as well as of societies, almost beyond repair.

The indust-realism has unleashed only greed in human beings for material pleasures to the extent of even depriving the relatively weaker ones, if it comes to that, and this is the sole problem that has created immense tensions in almost everybody's lives. Why should an individual sacrifice his own selfish interests for organisational efficiency? The situation becomes worst when he finds that the bosses are getting the maximum material benefits out of his whatever organisational contributions. The industrialisation has been a boon for material pleasures but it comes with attendant and inalienable problems and personal tensions like these in the form of a package deal. There are numerous ills that accompany it. Some of them are like drug-addiction, corruption, sexual abuses, teenage violence, disintegration of family, racial hatred, general power-thirstiness, fanaticism, mistrust, power-mongering politics and political expediency, nexus between politicians and criminals and business magnets and, caste conflicts under Indian scenario and so on.

According to Toffler the third wave changes that are now sweeping are expected to bring in suitable answers to all the above ills and transform human groups into a more civilized societies with better feeling of community. Third wave is being projected as the panacea for all the ills of industrialisation. Every individual would like the society to be organised such that it meets the basic physical needs of everybody and ensures a sense of fulfillment. How can this be achieved when the basic unit of society in the form of family is being destroyed by the industrialisation and the situation is not in any way reversed by the third wave changes to the required level? Is there any way out? Would it affect the assiduously built organisations and the well organised, family-centric format of the society, to meet human material pleasures?

It would otherwise destroy even the achievements of last almost three hundred years of creative minority's creative and innovative contributions in social developments. More intricately organised format is a natural outcome of human efforts, since industrialisation began, and it cannot be destroyed to create anti-natural tendencies just like that. If the second or third wave changes continue to progress in the directions they have taken, then there is every reason to believe that the human race may be wiped out of existence from this globe as many such live-species have been in the past, for want of their sustenance. The environmentalists are worried just for that. The answers are being found in third wave change not in restricting material pleasures, but only altering their means of production. Since the modern society needs enormous amount of energy to sustain itself, in the form of various material items, and since the use of natural fossil fuels have acquired alarming dimensions, other more friendly sources of renewable energy are being tapped [1]. The change over in energy forms are not likely to offer any relief with respect to the basic ailments of material consumption and greed arising therefrom. The problem of human tensions therefore shall still remain as before and perhaps increase instead. A way out is required for this basic malady. Fundamental understanding of human nature may be required to evolve a way out.

Organisational Efficiency

The problem is serious enough since it is increasing human greed and thereby straining the global resources on the whole, to the extent that it cannot be sustained for too long. It is heading towards shirking of work by way of less and less human inputs and expecting more in return for more material pleasures at leisure. It is alarming when that reflects in decrease in human efficiency and commitment while working in organisations. How can human greed be met if the organisational objectives in general are not met effectively and efficiently to produce and supply goods and services at economical costs?

This is the main problem of managers in keeping the organisations not only going but working with increasing efficiency. Some somehow achieve it and hence pose challenges to others in competition. The others have to improve upon the efficiency to stay in competition. The alternative is only decimation. The main requirement is how to keep all motivated all the time to ensure maximum possible effectiveness and efficiency.

Way-out

Most of the human intelligence, on the whole, is spent in managing organisations and making them more effective and efficient, practically all over the world. This exceeds even the efforts put in R and D to create new relatively better products and services. Yet the problem seems to be insurmountable to the extent of satisfaction.

Because of their very nature the NPOs face relatively less of problems than the commercial profit making organisations in this respect. In NPO's the focus is often devoid of efficiency because whatever service is provided and whatever results are obtained are generally considered as achievements and nothing less. The achievements of governments typically illustrate this point. Any lack of efficiency is attributed to the inefficiency of the beneficiaries in receiving the service. The problem is therefore more serious in the case of commercial profit making organisations.

There has to be a philosophical base to sustain the core values in any organisation. In every society there will always be a small minority of pious people. These are exceptions. But it is no guarantee that these pious men will be able to transform the organisations by creating their core values. There will have to be an agreed philosophical common value-base for it to grow as characteristic of the society or at least of the elite. That is why all talks about social responsibility of organisations do not lead to much of tangible results. It remains more of rhetoric. Calling it as *professionalism* is merely another fashion. It does not have specific connotation. At times it is reduced to as merely a tactic, or may be strategy, which could be altered as per requirements, as and when needed. It must therefore have a philosophical base.

There is urgent need to find solutions for making human beings socially committed, less greedy and still happy and contented in their lifestyle. Is there a way out? Does any one know the solution? Yes, in the absence of any other solution coming from any other society world over, the Indian philosophy may be the only hope because they had once developed self a contented and happy society, albeit in the simple agricultural era when society was not as complex as is today. But the same underlying principles can be applied in the present scenario to evolve a solution for the present impasse using the presently available intelligence on global level. Fortunately interest in Indian philosophy has increased in recent times because of easy transport and communication systems.

Basic Approach

Fundamentally the problem is not of providing goods and services but it is to make human beings happy and contented. This **fine distinction needs to be appreciated and understood in all its depth**. This is not a new problem. It has been in existence along with the evolution of man with cortex brain. The Indian thinkers did think about it from this very angle unlike the rest of the societies in the world. The answer therefore lies in understanding how the Indian seers approached this problem, in principle, in their times and what they found as the right solution thereat, even in those remote times. In order to appreciate that let us first appreciate all the possible solutions so far offered by various societies all over the world to make human beings happy and contented.

Social Organisational Models

Society and its organisations are two sides of the same coin. Same is the story of international community and international organisations. In fact through organisations alone that the society is evolved or gets organised the way it likes. The basic outlook of any society determines how the organised life of that society shall be. There are essentially few basic models of outlooks, so far suggested and practiced, at least to some extent, in organising one or the other societies around the world. These are:

1. Materialistic European model essentially based on Greek and perhaps Roman civilisational values of upto around 2500 years old
2. Islamic model suggested around 1300 years back in Arabia
3. Spirituality-based Indian model perhaps 5-7,000 years old suggested and practiced, though in dilapidated conditions, in India
4. Chinese model essentially based on Confucian ideology of 2000 years old.
5. Western industrial model of only 300 years old and as an extension of essentially the same traditional materialistic European model and now supported by informational technology.
6. Marxist model, about 150 years old

Out of which the No 1 is now extinct and has now been completely replaced by a modified one as shown at No 5. The model No 6 is just the same as Model No 5, with the only difference in ownership of the means of production. Marx emphasised that it should be state owned, whereas the western model is prepared to leave it in private hands as per ones own capabilities. The basic materialistic approach remains the same in either case. The Chinese model at No 4 is more about how a king should behave so that his decisions are in the interests of the people. The Islamic model has been insisting on reversing the wheels of progress to take back the societies in the seventh century, since their adherents are not prepared to make any changes in the original design even with changed times of the day. It cannot be changed come what may, as per their beliefs and insistence. They will have to take into account the industrial revolution and the present informational technology evolution in the form of knowledge-era in re-interpreting their model. In reality the Muslim societies have been reforming themselves in this direction but are not bold enough to proclaim it, lest the wrath of the fundamentalists and terrorists in their religious fold befall them. If the industrial model is accepted by the Muslim society for material progress then the religious part can be left to individuals to follow as per their own choices. The insistence on Shariya-based society is bound to undergo the necessary changes in tune with time. Therefore there are essentially only two ideological models left in the world for organising the societies at large. These are

1. The essentially materialistic social model as manifested by the westerners, based on the industrial and now information technological perceptions for production of goods and services to cater to satisfy human beings in terms of bodily, mental and intellectual needs.

2. The spirituality-centric social model as propounded by the Indian seers in the Upanishad period itself, essentially based on the *dharma, artha, kama and moksha* (including the *vyashti, samasti, shrushti and permeshti)* perceptions, wherein the above three plus spiritual needs (not religious needs) of human beings are recognised, for sustainable production and consumption, for contented and happy individual life. The Islamic as well as Christian and all other religious perceptions can get their due place in this set-up.

Western Model

The materialistic model of the west presumes that every human being is merely a bundle of physical desires and that by providing the material needs human being can be made happy. In spite of providing such needs on increasing proportion, through industrialisation and now improving the same through the application of knowledge on ever increasing scale, they have not been able to make humans happy, that's for certain. Assuming that, in addition to bodily pleasures, human beings do have mental and intellectual needs, attempts are being made on an increasing scale, to cater to these requirements as well. This is being done more on the basis of **Maslow's** hierarchical needs [2]. Mental needs in the form of recreations, arts, music, sports, games, travel, seeing the diversities in the world, living in natural surroundings and so on are being provided to this end. For some enlightened ones, achieving power, name and fame, in some form, give mental pleasure. The more the attempts to meet the mental needs, the more shall be the wealth requirements. Intellectual needs of at least some are being met through research and developmental work. The rest can enjoy the creative products and services from such efforts. It may generate more wealth as well. But even herein more wealth will be required to meet the increasing intellectual needs. The big question is how to generate so much of wealth without adding to the already acute problems arising out of consumption? Wealth here means broadly the production of goods and services aided by more knowledge if so required.

The question of accommodating spirituality as yet does not arise in their model. Many of them therefore often look to India for the way out by adopting spirituality in one or the other form, as the basis of reforming individuals. They have not yet come to the stage of taking it into consideration as an essential basis for social reorganisation. But on individual basis many westerners are keen to understand the spirituality as propounded by the Indians. The popularity of Indian gurus and more specifically of ISCON and such other movements are good examples to illustrate their natural thirst for spirituality.

The average westerners however confuse religion with spirituality. In reality spirituality has nothing to do with religion which is nothing but some dogmas, some mechanical rituals and such things in the form of a closed system. One may or may not follow any religion as per one's own liking, but can be spiritual. In fact spirituality is nothing but an attitude to look at the world and the human life along with all the needs together, in an integral manner. The reader may refer to standard texts as those of **Ram Krishna Mission** of India to understand this in detail. The perceptions of western society to think in terms of world environment, as a whole, are a step in the direction of spirituality and nothing else. It falls under the ***srushti*** perception of Indians. The Indians however go beyond it to the level of ***permeshti,*** which has no tangible existence but is perceptible to human consciousness alone. Any human being from any background can experience it through earnestness coupled with proper ascetic practices, while still following his own religion.

Ideal organisationality however could only be evolved for the entire world on the basis of four tier evolution of self, as perceived by the Indian seers, in the form of ***vyashti to samashti to srushti to permeshti***, as discussed earlier in detail.

Indian Dilemma

Social lifestyles, as a result of second and third wave changes, are undergoing changes at such pace that it is becoming very difficult for individuals to cope up with the changes. On the one hand the material pleasures are too attractive to leave. While on the other hand the traditional lifestyle's superiority in the form of spirituality tends to override the material pleasures. It is not easy for societies like that of India, which lived for so long under the agricultural set-up, to break away and transform into the modern lifestyles readily. Many of them mentally live in agricultural era and happen to work in an industrialised world, whereas the requirement is to mentally transform them into knowledge era and beyond. They live with such split psyche and hence lose their inherent efficiency at work. The split is highly individualistic and affects different people differently. They will have to opt for required lifestyle hereafter. Some thing in this direction has already been indicated earlier.

Thou Art That

Being able to express ones own feelings because of the cortex brain, human being is the only live-form that can express what was realised as Brahma to other fellows. We are not sure whether the rest of the animate world can experience Brahma or not. Even if they do they are unable to express it anyway. The realisation of Brahma was explained to others by the then Indian seers by a mantra in the Vedic literature as, ***tat twam asi*** or ***thou art that*** (you are that Brahma). The Vedic-rishis proclaimed to fellow humans with loudest voice and complete confidence in their findings as:

"Brahma is nothing but you yourself, provided you discover it and that it pervades all the universe in its entirety, leaving nothing whatsoever outside. Once there was only the Brahma but it thought of becoming plural and in multiple, and therefore is described as *ekoham bahusyam*, and hence the world is filled with transient Maya, perceptible to senses".

The implicit meaning of this statement has to be understood with reference to societal behaviour in general and, at the organisational level in particular. This is manifested in the form of Advaita philosophy, meaning thereby that it is all one and only one, not two. It also means that one can feel as large, as great, and as big as upto the level of entire cosmos. This is the philosophical foundation of Indian social or organisational order. This is the basis of increasing one's own self from ***vyashti* to *samashti* to *srushti* to *permeshti*** in the Indian thinking. If it is so then, can it be extended from ***vyashti*** to a group in the form of organisation to manage modern day organisations? It is to increase one's own self from an individual to that of a group. Will it solve their present day basic problems and maladies?

The fall outs of Newton-Cartesian world view of 17-19th century have already been discussed in detail earlier. This view was later superseded by the Einsteinian holistic world view and systemic approach to even social problems in the later half of twentieth century. It led to system's theory of management in dealing with organisations. This perception, though closer to truth still holds that the individuals still exist, as discreet individuals, in an organisational ensemble. The organisational structures and management thereat now tend to alter themselves in this light. It has given better results in terms of their effectiveness and efficiency. It is a step further in the direction of truth, no doubt. As a result, development of emergent structure, as described by **Fritjof Capra** [3] in the form of cohesive minds of all the participants, to the extent possible, is what is aimed at in practice, in managing organisations. However the mechanicalness in perception, in the form of different people, constituting the organisation, still remains intact and is reflected in understanding organisational behaviour. The learning organisation also suffers from the same perception though it insists on collective learning. This is analogous to assuming waves constituting the sea. It will continue to be so, as long as the psychologically separate existence of individuals remains in perception, while managing the organisations. This vision is akin to assuming the various parts of our body having their own independent existence. Because of this perception the individual selfishness shall always be at the centre of all organisational activities to a more or lesser extent. The basic western perception of antagonism between individual and the organisation (society as its wider form) shall still continue at the psychological level, in the form of ***duality***.

Even the visionary and missionary organisations with core ideology represent merely some intention of higher moral values as overriding and guiding the activities without any philosophical base as to why welfare of society has to be kept at the centre of all organisational thinking. It cannot motivate people for long. It need not necessarily lead to any sacrifice on the part of individuals, when required. These values are essential to uphold society in a cohesive manner. If organisations are not going to cultivate the philosophical base then who else will? Let us see how the Indian perception helps us to find the way out. The answer is in the Advaita philosophy and in essence, organisations have to mentally adopt that first.

Fourth Wave Concept

When the Indian seers proclaimed the mantra ***'thou art that'***, they eliminated the duality altogether. What appears apparently as different is just like the appearance of waves as different from the sea; both in reality are just the same. The waves were therefore called as Maya that is of essentially transient existence. It was also explained by siting the example of human body. Nothing else is more known to anyone than one's own body itself. It is not a collection of various parts, intimately connected with each other in holistic form. It is neither a systemic ensemble of these parts in terms of systems theory evolved out of Einsteinian world view. Even an integral system accepts the existence of parts as parts. The world is far from it. All the parts of a human body appear outwardly different but each one works as a non-dual unit with respect to the body and with respect to other parts as well. After all what is a hand or a leg or any other part of the body like? It neither resembles any other part nor the body. The sum total of all parts constitutes the body. The body only outwardly appears as their ensemble; without the parts the body does not exist. Then what is it? **Each one is more than just a part because it does not have any independent existence other than that of the body.** The Indian seers thought that any part thereof is body itself, nothing less and nothing more. It only appears differently. It never behaves as a part. It always behaves as if it is body itself, forgetting that it appears differently. This is the Advaita philosophy, emphasising that there is no duality in this universe. There is only one and that is Brahma, appearing outwardly only differently as waves are observed as something different from sea.

Similarly the family was no more a collection of some members like husband, wife, children, parents and so on, in the form of an intimately related apparent whole or even an integral system. Every one of them is considered to be family itself. **Whatever individual member did was therefore of the family, by the family and for the family alone.** This concept was further extended to the society and whatever individual or family did was all for the society, of the society and on behalf of the society, since everyone was considered as society itself and nothing else than the society. Even otherwise what is society devoid of individuals or families? Does it have any existence of its own? This is the unique concept that changes the psychology of individuals in tune with the real world around. This was reflected in the proclamation of Indian seers in the form of ***vaisudhaiva kutumbkam,*** meaning thereby that just not their society but the entire human race is just one family.

All possible attempts were made to enculture everybody in this perception such that nobody wanted or thought of acquiring extra status to rule, extra wealth to enjoy and extra power to exploit anybody else. Instead every body was taught to rule one's ownself, through control of one's own mind and intellect, so that one feels the Advaita from within. That is why there was no exploitation in the early Indian Upanishadic society and the same continued for quite some time. Later some aberrations did occur but it is besides the point and that it does not disprove the earlier truth and practice.

The analogy can be extended to organisations in the modern sense. It is not a mechanical group of individuals collected together, perhaps under compulsion of earning their livelihood, as was understood earlier in the Newton-Cartesian world or as a holistic ensemble understood by the Einsteinian or even a systemic whole under post-Einsteinian world-view of today. May be some bond of understanding is developed amongst them by way of training. But it essentially still remains as an ensemble of individuals or a multifarious unit and nothing else, striving to achieve the organisational objective but still somewhat mechanically.

Under the Indian Advaiti perception every individual in the organisation is considered and trained to think that he/she is nothing less than an organisation itself, since there is no duality whatsoever. In the illustration of human body, no part of the body would like to exploit any other even if for a certain job one part may be more dominantly involved and others have to co-operate with it to get it done. What if all individuals in an organisation in reality think like this? What wonderful things shall come out of such organised efforts. How will one work when the work is considered to be ones own and just for one's ownself? He is likely to put in all his best and to the utmost extent possible, in achieving the objective as if it is his own. No additional motivation will be required for an individual to work for his ownself. He will be fully charged with all possible vigour, drive and inspiration and what not, while working in an organisation. Every one must think that he is the organisation itself, and everybody thinks alike. The participants shall automatically consider the organisational objective as their own personal objective. This will readily pave the way for everyone to identify his/her own self with the society and then with nature and further up with the cosmos. It will be worth recalling again here what **M.S. Golwakar** alias **Guruji** said and quoted earlier on page 101. The tall talk of transformation of organisations into learning organisation [4], as a great leap forward in organisational management, then appears as much short of ideal model of organisational management. It is easier to enculture every one in this way rather than transform into what a learning organisation expects.

There will be no surplus power with any one even if he is the manager. The question of exploitation of sub-ordinates would not arise. Not much managerial efforts shall be required to make the organisation effective and efficient in attaining the objective as it will be self driven. What miracle the Indian concept of ***'thou art that'*** can bring in should now be obvious. But it is easily said as a piece of advice or philosophy rather than done. It is quite difficult to realise. It is related to mind which is the most difficult to be trained. How can it be achieved? What will be needed to achieve the spirit of ***'thou art that'*?**

Advaiti Perception

Nothing is impossible for a cortex-laden human being to achieve, through his intelligence and rigorous hard work and that too in an organised manner. There are solutions for present day organisational problems on the basis of age-old but eternal perceptions of Indians. This must first be appreciated at the intellectual and rational level. It must also be appreciated, at least theoretically, as something that could be made possible and feasible in practice. Human beings are a combination of best and worst, godly and demonly qualities together, in various proportions. It should be believed that humans can be made best and godly, ideally Advaiti. At least the general social atmosphere can be built as Advaiti by those who matter and command respect in the society. The traditional Hindu family model can readily certify that human being can be encultured to think in Advaiti-fashion through proper enculturation, training and appropriate social evolution. The fact that there have been innumerable persons in India, since times immemorial, who manifested Advaita perception in their own lives, is proof enough to accept the feasibility of this proposition. It definitely took a long time to evolve such society of Advaiti perception in India. But finally it did (see Chapter 3). There is every reason to believe that the same can be duplicated anywhere and at anytime provided earnest attempts, in right directions, are made. This is a matter of appropriate teaching in academic institutions, purposeful enculturation in society and training in individual organisations. **All the three pronged strategy will be necessary.** To start with, the whole educational approach will have to undergo a paradigm change. Higher education in general and management education in particular will have to include in their curricula the basics of Advaita philosophy.

The organisational training will have to be tuned to emphasise this aspect than anything else. For achieving it, the trainers will have to understand the Indian philosophical perception as *a priori*. Any other effort to impress upon the participants the necessity of working together shall still have the tinge of emphasising the existence of distinct individuals and therefore their selfish individual interests in an organisation. Unless serious attempts in this direction are made no amount of training shall bear the expected results in any organisation. The moment all the participants forget that they are individuals and different from organisation itself, all the presently felt insurmountable problems, in getting the organisation going, and which are mostly in terms of human psychology and their characteristic individual personality, shall begin to disappear. This is not any abstract solution because it is easily felt at the family level and can be taught at the organisational level like what is expected in learning organisation, but more easily.

Illustrations

The spirit of ***'thou art that'*** was very effectively cultivated in India at the family level wherein members, through proper enculturation, do feel identified as family themselves because of their perhaps prolonged contact in the family since birth. In this respect India stands out above all other societies in the world. This is also the reason why even most of the social activities in India all through the ages, were family-centric as described earlier. It is now universally accepted that in an ideal learning organisation there is no scope for conflict in anybody's family and work-place lives [4]. It talks of personal mastery not just at the work place but in all aspects of even so-called private life. It believes in synergy between family and work place. There can not be any imbalance between the two. This is nothing but essentially the same Advaiti thinking expressed in different words. The Advaiti perception is based on solid logical and philosophical foundation. One can not build Advaiti organisation without integrating all the expressed and unexpressed desires of one and all in an organisation.

In India the family pattern was extended to small scale social level in the form of self-contained villages and small kingdoms, in the prolonged agricultural era. That is why the ideal method of governance in the form of Ram-Rajya could be evolved in India. The king therein identified himself as the subject and not as king with any additional power.

But it could not be extended on a larger corporate social level because such necessity did not arise in the agricultural era in India. In due course, as the society became more complex, the social system unfortunately became more rigid and out of tune with time. The same period was also coupled with series of external aggressions in India, when security became an overriding consideration than social reconstruction, and thereafter the social decay started unabatedly thereon. **As a result the social psychology became such as to cling on to the old system with unquestionable faith as one's own valuable cultural treasures. The system continued but with continuous decay and hence the decayed and dismal picture of today.** In the post independence India nothing has changed in the right direction in the light of the old precious philosophical treasure. Many would like to get rid of all that. But it is tantamount to ***'throwing the baby with the wash water'*** after the bath. With all this decay there have always been some enlightened ones who understood the essence of the basic Indian perception and tried to preserve it through their own lifestyles, all through the ages until today.

That is the reason why the same essential ingredients, in the form of basic principles and outlook, to re-organise the society, are still available in the form of enlightened rishis or sanyasis, who continue to study and update it. They are seen occasionally. The main Upanishadic knowledge treasure is still readily available with such people.

Now the basic unit of organising any society in the present day industrial and information technological world is organisation, unlike the family in the agricultural era. It may be aided by intellectual individuals. These must therefore be strengthened to suit the times to achieve maximum efficiency and effectiveness in not just productive but all sorts of activities. That is why now individuals will have to be encultured to develop their self from individuality to identify it with the organisation at physical, mental, intellectual and spiritual levels. Similarly individuals will have to be encultured to identify with the society like Anna Hazare. **This is the fourth wave change.**

Inevitability

All modern management techniques are evolved to make the participant work more, when the participant himself, in this materialistic world, would like to put in less, as far as is possible. This is because even the third wave has not been able to decrease the indust-reality of selfishness and human greed. How to manage organisational functions effectively and efficiently in such dichotomic circumstances? No wonder management of organisations is getting more and more difficult and as a result the mortality rate of organisations is very high. No wonder the retention rate of employees is getting poorer, since they readily join other organisations if offered more power or emoluments. No wonder all top class human intelligence and energy, all over the world, is directed in extracting work from the participants in an organisation, coming close to exploitation and nothing else. In the so-called information technological world it is common practice in India to work for 12-14 hours a day. The same is true at least in the developing world. This is sheer exploitation and nothing else, no matter how fat salary is offered. It is in fact moving towards original second wave exploitative industrial society rather than third wave information society.

The answer to such inhuman perceptions and practices is one and the only one in the form of adoption of Advaiti outlook and practicing the same in every walk of life, more so in organisational management. This is the revolutionary change that is now due and bound to come in near future after the revolutionary third wave change observed and deciphered by **Alvin Toffler** in the form of information technology. This will be yet another revolution in social thinking beyond the so-called third wave. This is the ***Fourth Wave*** change due in near future. The ***Advaiti-society*** that is bound to emerge from this shall be the ***Fourth-Wave- Society*** to emerge in very near future, originating from India.

The signs of third wave appeared only after it had already set-in for some time in USA. It was not discernible when it had just started. It always happens like that. Social change becomes discernible only after some sizeable and perceptible change has already occurred. The same thing is happening in India with respect to the fourth wave change. It is just discernible to those who can critically observe and appreciate.

The social reconstruction in the west was never the result of any pre-thought out philosophy. Whatever changes occurred was later deciphered in terms of the philosophy behind them. The agricultural revolution occurred as an evolution everywhere, without exception. The industrial and the information technological revolutions were also initially the results of evolution and not as per any pre-conceived thought or design, by social scientists.

By contrast the Indian social reconstruction even in the remote past, as in the Upanishadic era, was the result of pre-conceived philosophical thought essentially in the form of concept of Brahma to be realised by one and all without any distinction and differentiation. The Indian seers conceived of the societal design and constructed it in reality as per their perception so that everybody could realise Brahma or salvation or at least march on the path of its realisation. That is how they lived happily as society for millennia, albeit, in that remote and simple agricultural era.

Westernisation

It is true that the once golden land, India has almost been reduced to the stage of complete bankruptcy and is a pauper and that every attempt was needed to ensure the fulfillment of basic physical needs of the entire society, without any discrimination. The western industrial revolution, aided by information technology, came in handy for achieving this urgent need. But being only well versed in the western patterns and not knowing the eternal values and knowledge of Indian ethos, the so-called modern entrepreneurs in India are only blindly copying the western model of progress, for increasing the means for catering the bodily needs. Those who are well versed in Indian traditional ethos do get worried, but often do not know the way out. On the one hand it is presumed that progress means industrial production aided by information technology, expressed in terms of national product (GNP or GDP and the like) and on the other happiness means following the traditional Indian ethos including the value system. The Indians individually as well as organisationally are plagued with this dichotomy and hence suffer from ineffectiveness and inefficiency. Not many know the way out of this impasse. All that is attempted is to restructure the organisations, time and again, like taking a shot in the dark and at times it hits the right spot, by sheer luck. The same shot however rarely works a right again.

The necessity of organisational culture, as propounded by **Deal, Kennedy and Allen** [5], for proper functioning of organisations in the west, is nothing but the perception of the same fourth wave, but in a different format. It has been put forward against the western social background. It deals only with the general behaviour. It lacks necessary clarity in its philosophical base. **The fourth wave as propounded here has the entire necessary philosophical base devoid of any ambiguity.**

The same can be said about the commercial organisations that were built to last [6] and became great from good [7] by establishing the core ideology and pursuing it through relevant visions and the missions of their organisations. These are the symptoms of fourth wave change but they lack the basic philosophy, as applicable to all without discrimination. This philosophical base is provided by the Indian Advaiti perception.

Early Signs of Fourth Wave Change

Some of the Indian corporate leaders-cum-social thinkers were worried about the terrifying fall-outs of second and third wave revolutions, in spite of it being immensely useful in technological contributions and making lifestyles happier by being less rigorous. They were also worried because India had already started its journey on the same suicidal course of sheer material prosperity, by blindly copying the industrial and the informational revolutions of the west. Being well versed in traditional Indian philosophy, they were more worried to see the material prosperity overriding the traditional spirituality and the self-contentedness, which is above all supreme in life. Thorough understanding of second and third wave revolutions that are sweeping the west and knowing the traditional Indian wisdom through their family background, they were able to find possible solutions out of this blind alley.

It must have made them self-introspective, as is often recommended for realisation of Brahma in the traditional Indian *sadhana*. Wisdom has ultimately dawned on them. They have started practicing the basic Indian outlook, somewhat as mentioned above, in the form of ***'thou art that'***, in their own corporate establishments. This new practice is often referred to as ***professionalism*** out of general trend of nomenclature in tune with time. Being in hopeless minority and more so out of hesitation to emphasise the underlying basic Indian perception, they call it professionalism. The diffidence also stems from the way they were taught that India was never prosperous both materially and intellectually, as compared to the westerners. Within few years of such practice their results have been exemplary and beyond imagination, even to them. They have become embodiment of this philosophy on corporate level. The signs of this new revolution can be seen in India.

INFOSYS Experiment

INFOSYS, the most recent and popular brand in corporate IT world, is almost in the vanguard of this change. It is just about a two decade old organisation and is moving assiduously in that direction, because of the founder's earlier good enculturation in Indian ethos, certainly not through modern western-style education, but perhaps mainly through his family, acquaintances and social surroundings. INFOSYS has already transformed itself from good to great in a very short span of their existence. It now appears as if it was built to last right from the beginning. In other words all that Collins and his co-workers [6,7] thought could be built over time was achieved by the INFOSYS management in a very short span of time.

The promotors do not appear anything less than modern ***industrial rishis***. No wonder the founder of INFOSYS and its former chief mentor **N.R Narayana Murthy**, along with his other team mates, are very attentively listened to, when they speak, by those interested in management of corporate world. This includes the students of management as well as the practicing managers. The same spirit can be seen in practice in Tatas, though a little differently, and even in many others in partial fulfillment of the same objective.

Whatever qualities that are being seen in visionary organisations in the west [6,7] are all available in such late comers like INFOSYS. They had their core ideology right in place at the beginning itself. Hence they had their vision and mission fixed accordingly. It was therefore started with right spirit by the promoters like N.R.Murthy and others. They had unquestioning faith primarily in the social development through their organisation in tune with Indian perception. It was much more than mere economic activity to them. They knew what they were, what they stood for and what they were to achieve through INFOSYS. In the end they did achieve almost all that they had imagined. The 'Built to Last' and 'Good to Great' companies sited by Collins, even after more than one hundred years, are far behind the stage INFOSYS has reached within just couple of decades. This is how the philosophical Advaiti perception differentiates the mere visionary and missionary companies from the **Advaiti-Companies.**

This is the fourth wave revolution which has just begun to unfold and the fourth wave society has started to emerge out of it in India. It is the answer to the present day management problems in totality. It is no use asking all the attributes of it right at this stage when it itself is in infancy, trying to decode the age-old perceptions in the present scenario and developing itself to meet the challenges of the present time, particularly when the western thinkers are at a loss. It will reveal itself fully by unfolding slowly in due course of time. One of the sure signs of its emergence is also the ever increasing interest of corporate world in listening to those who are well versed in traditional Indian ethos and its eternal relevance. The early contributions of, particularly **Swami Jitatmanand** of **RamKrishna Mission,** Rajkot [8] may be worth recollecting by those interested in the subject.

Guarantee

There is no such structure based on ***'thou art that'*** perception elsewhere in the world as yet. It can easily be seen in the Indian family especially in the form of mother, or even father in the Indian family, even in such degenerated social conditions of today. The perception of mother can also be seen in many other shades in India as they call river Ganges, cow, the earth and many others as mothers only. She sacrifices almost her entire life considering that it will be lived by her progeny. In fact she mentally lives in the form of her sons and daughters and not as herself. There are innumerable instances, in fact it is the order, even in present day degenerated Indian society that the mother sacrifices, even her entire life for bringing up her children. She enjoys it because of this perception. This is nothing but the spirit of ***'thou art that'*** and nothing else.

That is why of late the western thinkers are getting more interested in understanding the Hindu family perception, its historical evolution, the role of Hindu perception in evolving the family structure and the role it plays in moulding the mentality and psychology of individuals in the society. The western encultured Hindus may brand it as women's subjugation without understanding it from within. The father in the Hindu family also acts in the same way, except that his method of expression is different because of man's inherent differential personality, as distinct from women, evolved during social evolution [9,10]. The same spirit is exhibited by the son when his parents grow old in return. The mythological story of young **Shravana** in India is being told to all generations through ages to cultivate the same spirit. **Lord Rama** is revered not because he was king but for his total identification with his family and with his subjects later. **He manifested himself as his father, brother and all the subjects and not as the beneficiary king** as and when required. This is how the philosophical perception is cultivated in practice to inculcate the same spirit even in most ordinary and perhaps so-called uneducated masses in India through traditional enculturation. This cannot be understood without understanding the four tier expanding vision of an individual in Indian philosophy as described earlier and how it is ingrained in average masses even now, for his overall progress. The material outlook cultivated by the western education may be somewhat reflected in so called modern mothers, but even many of these as well as the traditional mothers behave in the traditional manner.

Because of not understanding the real nature and purpose of the human being, and in the absence of any other ethereal bond, the westerners understood human relations only in the form of contracts amongst individuals and groups and nothing else, as an aid in achieving socialisation. The intense desire of keeping their individuality intact, as distinct from the others, and yet living as society, leaves no option of developing any other relationship. It also stems from their perception of anthropo-centric material enjoyment in its ultimate form. Their families are therefore breaking due to disputes, mostly over physical pleasures. Human beings cannot be happy without stable, mutually loving and co-operative family. This is the reason why the latest learning organisation insists on synergy between family and work place in the lives of its work force. This is precisely where the western society has miserably failed because of their mad pursuit of instinctual material pleasures alone.

Integral Approach

The fourth wave is not observable merely in terms of some organisational management, based on some core values, relegating profit to the background, in any sphere of social activity. All attributes of visionary organisations as depicted by **Collins** [6,7] cannot lead to fourth wave change unless the approach is integrated with the characteristic Indian outlook. It should include the acceptance of the ***vanaprasthashram*** (as described in Chapter 9), the most unique contribution of Indians in leading one's own life with full satisfaction. Fourth wave shall not evolve unless all those who matter in any society, directly or indirectly as leaders, controllers and managers of organisations, voluntarily and not per force, opt for ***vanaprasthashram*** at the right stage of their life, by giving up power in their organisation on their own. Narayana Murthy of INFOSYS did exactly this without stating it so. He was hail and hearty and in good physical and mental health. He could have continued accumulation of wealth through his work in the same way as most others do. There was no necessity for him to resign, from the top-most post and be merely their mentor, except on this account and with complete confidence that his inning was over and must be concluded, converting him into a ***vanaprasthi***. He was sure to see that INFOSYS shall get excellent leaders one after the other for ever even after him. In fact he had led it in such a way that he was confident that his team would continue on the same path on which they had set-out right in the beginning, even without him. He had full faith that the organisation shall still be managed as well, as he managed it. The same practice was followed later by his other colleagues as a matter of lifestyle and culture of INFOSYS. This is not merely a practice based on some core values. It is in fact a core ideology in the form of total philosophy based on eternal Indian values, vision and wisdom of overall existence. **It is certainly not merely a different managerial mechanical structure either.** There is definitely spirituality involved in it. It is acceptance of ***vanaprasthashram,*** a step on the path of salvation, and nothing else as per Indian ethos. Material prosperity comes automatically on this path of spirituality without asking as a by-product. No wonder INFOSYS stands out as a unique organisation in India against the backdrop of many giant ones even in India, with reference to its effectiveness and efficiency and above all its culture as referred to in common parlance. Everybody right down to the lower most strata is thus encultured to think that they are all INFOSYS themselves and nothing less.

In short the fourth wave is a package deal as per the traditional Indian perception of generalised human goal of balanced material pleasures and spirituality in the form of an attitude to life. Since everybody in the organisation is nothing less than organisation itself, the organisation shall continue in spite of the known controller-leaders relinquishing their positions any time. Murthy feels that he has trained his associates to take up the mantle and run it as if it is their own. He does not want to accumulate wealth nor enjoy power any more by working till the last breath of his life, as most would do. It is much more than mere professionalism as is understood in management parlance. **In professionalism highly individualistic culture is evolved like in Sony of Japan**. It will cultivate individual ego more than necessary. It creates its own problems which are more difficult to solve. INFOSYS experiment is quite different. Murthy and his original team managed it nearly ideally, considering it as if it was a human body and that everyone would look after it as its body-part without nurturing individual egos. As stated earlier in Chapter 9 that it is to make way for next generation to take over and keep it going.

That is the reason why the trainers hence forth will have to be trained first in the traditional Indian perception of overall existence, including that of human being, for the fourth wave to evolve in their organisations. Once a sizeable number of organisations evolve up to this level, the fourth wave will surely be felt as a social evolutionary phenomenon like the three earlier waves of social changes. It would have then achieved the **take-off stage.**

What if other major organisations attempt to study and understand why INFOSYS behaved the way it did? What if like INFOSYS, some more organisations venture on the same path of progress and attain individually peace, perhaps bliss, for themselves, perhaps the ultimate to be achieved by anyone? What if the trainers change their present strategy of leadership training and opt for traditional Indian methodology of enculturation of work force for realising the essential human goal instead of institutional goal? What if the leaders, controllers and managers set examples of their own before the rest in their own establishments? What if they motivate other organisations to behave the same way? What if there is thorough debate amongst the team managers, in evolving such or even better strategies? What if this is accepted as something feasible since practiced at least at one major place? What if the enlightened leaders, controllers and managers think that nothing like such management practice is impossible in the present-day world?

Western Limitations

Unless and until they overcome the contract theory and develop the human bonds, in terms of human nature, as the Indians did, the westerners shall always find the organisation of humans a great unsolvable challenge, in spite of their sincere efforts in that direction. Although a human is characterised by his cortex brain as a rational being, it is cortex in combination with limbic system that makes a perfect human. Organisational problems have to be solved using both, the rational mind coupled with human feelings or by integrating reason with intuition as proposed in learning organisations and not merely by legal contracts.

The westerners of late have been proposing to improve inter-connectedness. It is possible on the basis of sympathy, empathy and compassion and not by legal contracts. The learning organisation proposes development of appropriate mental models of work force to achieve this. It is again nothing but 'thou art that' in action.

All the challenges of organisations, not just of organisations for some sectarian purposes but for organisation of the society, neigh the entire human race, can be met successfully only on the basis of Indian ethos which use rationality coupled with emotion.

For this to be achieved some have to forego or sacrifice their physical pleasures; some have to give up their mental pleasures in the form of power; some have to give up their intellectual pleasures by relinquishing the egoistic creative performance and accept construction of a all-happy society as their sole creative and innovative mission of life. This is what has already been described on page 85.

Such people can be the right leaders for management of the society at large. These will be the fourth wave leaders. In India the enlightened ones behaved like this, as explained earlier in Chapter 3, and hence they sustained the society all through the challenges of times as and when necessary like in the Upanishadic era.

In an organisation no precept works better than leading the organisation by example. Now INFOSYS has revived the same spirit in their most modern organisation. Their leaders have shown the way by their own example. They do not consider INFOSYS as their own private property. They consider it as belonging to all those working in INFOSYS for the good of the society at large. **Mahatma Gandhi** had suggested the concept of ***trusty-ship*** in running organisations as a way out of lust for wealth and power until the end of one's own life. It was typically based on Indian traditional ethos as described above. INFOSYS behaved almost in the same ideal style.

The non-acceptability of the spirituality in the form of Brahma, God and the like (not religion) is the greatest of the stumbling block in the progress of western thought in the right direction.

Notwithstanding the basic approach there have been several individuals even in typically materialistic western society, who have behaved like as if they belong to the fourth wave society. The examples of **Warren Buffet** or of **Bill Gates** and several others illustrate the point. They did realise to opt out of the mad race for power and wealth at some point in their lives after realising that there has to be an end to all that. They have also decided to spend much of their life-long earnings in charitable work. They are no less inferior to Murthy. Now **Aziz Premji** of WIPRO has recently joined this illustrious band wagon. These examples do indicate the beginning of the emergence of fourth wave society even in the west. It has yet to acquire philosophical base which is missing in the west. It is however readily available in India through family enculturation.

Recent genome studies have confirmed that human race was evolved out of the original habitants of Africa and their migration via India to all over the world. This original oneness may be useful in instilling the unity of human race as an Advaiti human kind.

Co-existence of Waves

The societies belonging to the three waves as deciphered by Toffler and the fourth one being projected here do co-exist. There are hardly any hundred percent stoneage societies now in existence because even the left over ones do cultivate land in some or the other form. Those belonging essentially to agricultural form do enjoy some industrial and perhaps some information technological facilities even while cultivating their fields. Some part of even the agricultural society may belong to the information era. Similarly some part of the society may evolve into the fourth wave society as an extension of the third wave society. The examples of Warren Buffet, Bill Gates, Narayan Murthy and Aziz Premji provide the illustrative examples. As the fourth wave change picks up momentum, such examples will increase and the fourth wave shall become more obvious as a social phenomenon in due course of time.

Social Extension

The fourth wave change is not limited to only the organisational improvements. It is all encompassing because it is Advaiti in its approach. It is based on the philosophy that finally leads everyone individually, the society as a whole and the human race at large, happier, peaceful and contented in their lifestyles. It does not differentiate humans on the basis of religion and at the same time it does not discard religion either. It leaves religion purely as an individual affair. In its natural course innumerable Buffets, Gates and Murthys will certainly be produced to make it a way of life.

Future Organisationality

In the twentieth century the essentially archeology based anthropological studies suggested many contradictory theories regarding the evolution of different societies in the world. Is European race superior to others to have ruled the world for so long? Whether the human groups from Europe migrated to India or the other way round? Whether there was something like the **Aryan race** which migrated to India and that it fought with and defeated the local **Dravidian** population?

The earlier archeological excavations of **Mohenjodaro** and the latest at **Mahendragarh** (Balochisthan) [11,12] have more than proved that there was nothing like Aryan race anywhere on earth. The question of its migration to India and its onslaught on local Dravidians therefore does not arise at all. But many did not believe this theory and insisted on earlier Aryan migration theory. They did not realise that such a theory comes in the way of developing basic organisationality amongst the Indians. It was a clever ploy of

Britishers to put wedges in the Indian society, emphasising their differential racial character and, prevent them from getting consolidated in one homogeneous organisationality and challenge the British rule unitedly. The Aryan invasion theory, for having come from the so-called enlightened social scientists of Europe, was readily accepted by even many intelligent Indians and that is how it is ingrained in their psyche since then. But it has stood as the greatest of the stumbling blocks in developing good organisationality and thus good organisations in India and therefore in its progress as a whole.

The human genome structure has now been well established, beyond doubt, to indicate the ancestry of all present societies in the world. The genome studies of present Indian population from across the whole land has been carried out and has been proved to be the same. It clearly eliminates that the two, north Indians erroneously called as descendants of Aryans and the south Indians as descendants of Dravidians, are not at all people of different stocks or origin, but they are the descendents of the same race. The question of Aryans having defeated the Dravidians therefore does not arise at all. It is now possible to correlate in the same way the origin of different societies of the world.

Some recent genome studies [13] have now come out with many revealing facts of evolution of societies. It is accepted that human beings were evolved first in the African continent several millennia before. It evolved through various stages into modern day human being. It migrated from there first to India. The species in somewhat original form may be present in the Andaman and Nicobar islands, as it has retained itself in isolation so far. In the absence of any other evidence, there is no alternative origin of humans, as yet propounded by any anthropologists, anywhere in the world. But on the Indian mainland various such migrated human groups assimilated within themselves and melted into one group and parts of which later migrated from here in different directions all over the world. One group went to Indonesia then upto Australia and New Zealand. Another group migrated towards China, via south-east Asia and then on to North America and there-from to South America. Yet another group migrated towards Europe, via Middle-East and Central Asia. In other words not only all the Indians are of only one stock but various other societies in the world are also from the same stock and therefore not superior or inferior to anyone. Their present day complexion, outwardly structure, etc. are the result of exposure to the local environment for long and nothing else.

Those who were not in favour of one common ancestry of all Indians, and on that basis pleaded to be of different stocks and therefore of different nationalities in the form of different organisationalities, have no alternative but to accept the one and only one traditional cultural bondage in India and that is in the form of Indian, Hindu, Bharatiya and so on, in its civilizational form. The apparent differences, in food habits, clothings, living-styles, lack of intermixing and so on, may be due to the environmental differences across the length and breadth of the land. The varieties of paths for the realisation of God may be due to the extreme liberal values developed right in the Upanishadic society itself in India. Once this is accepted, the organisationality takes a firm root and loses any differentiality on the basis of language, cast, religion, food habits and clothings. This new-found basis could pave the way for formation of one organisationality of Indians of the present day and perhaps better organisations thereat in near future.

The four tier Hindu perception of the universe, in the form ***vyashti, samashti, srushti* and *permeshti***, is the best available perception to evolve organisationality on a wider basis, particularly in India. It will set an example for others to follow in due course.

References

1. Friedman, Thomas, L., *Hot, Flat and Crowded*, Penguin, London, (2008).
2. Maslow Abraham, *A Theory of Human Motivation,* Psychological Review (1943).
3. Fritjof Capra, *Hidden Connections,* Flamingo, (2003).
4. Sege Peter, M., *The Fifth Discipline,* Currency Doubleday, N.Y. (1994).
5. Deal, T., Kennedy, E and Allan, A., *Corporate Cultures (The Rites and Rituals of Corporate Life),* Perseus, Cambridge, (Mass), (1982).
6. Collins, Jim and Porras, Jerry, I., *Built to Last*, Harper-Collins, N.Y. (2002).
7. Collins, Jim, *Good to Great*, Harper-Collins, N.Y. (2001).
8. Swami Jitatmanand, *Indian Ethos for Management, Management Workshop,* Ramkrishna Ashram, Rajkot, 26-27th Octo. (1996).
9. Pease, Allan and Barbara, *Why Men don't Listen and Women can't Read Maps*, Manjul (2001).
10. Pease, Allan and Barbara, *Why Men Lie and Women Cry*, Manjul (2002).
11. Rajgopalan, R., *The Secrets of Indus Valley,* CBT, N.Delhi, (1995).
12. Possehl, G.L., *Harrappan Civilization*, Oxford IBH, (1993).
13. News Story in *India Today*, September, 2009.

CHAPTER 27

CORPORATE SOCIAL RESPONSIBILITY

CHAPTER STRUCTURE

- Society and Organisations
- Selfishness of Organisations
- CSR
- Hindu Perception
- CSR vs. Charity
- Western Perception
- Customer Pressure
- Fourth Wave Perception

Society and Organisations

It is not enough to evolve very efficient organisations wherein the workers think and act as per the tenets of fourth wave social change as described in the previous chapter. That may at best help-achieve the organisational interests, which in most organisations are usually selfish *vis-à-vis* those of the society or humanity at large. Therefore it still does not indicate how it will meet the broader social, humanitarian or ecological imperatives for benefit of all. This is usually the state of affairs in spite of the fact that organisations are formed to meet the larger social objectives. Organisations do not operate in vacuum. The model of organisations as depicted in Chapter-7 therefore shows the organisational interactions with the society as an inalienable part of any organisation. No society is any more small enough and simple enough to be organised as one single unit. Even if it did, it still has to act in the best interests of at least their own environment at large. In fact the societies are very large and complex such that they can be organised only through development of innumerable active organisations of varied types and sizes. Similarly the interests of humanity or environment as a whole can be served only through national or international or humanitarian organisations alone. It cannot operate devoid of social interests. In other words through organisations alone, the present-day societies are effectively and efficiently sustained. They also thereby grow more effectively. Similarly humanity as a whole is also sustained through organisations alone. The corporate leaders must understand this basic fundamental of human sustenance and existence in the present-day world and also make their co-workers aware of this fact.

Selfishness of Organisations

In the first few centuries of industrial revolution, the social psyche was very much influenced by the Newton-Cartesian perception of looking at the world and therefore organisations as well, in discreet pieces. It also marked in phenomenal increase in organisations of various types and sizes. Under those perceptions individual happiness or happiness of a small organised group reigned supreme disregarding the well being of the rest. Social exploitation for personal gains was therefore the order of those days. Feudalism in every form was the net result. The question of organisation as an integral part of society was neither understood nor accepted then even on philosophical levels. The question of responsibility of corporate organisations towards the social well-being had not been even academically thought of then in Europe. That is the reason why organisations in those days exploited the weaker sections of their own as well as any other society in the world. Feudalism and therefore colonialism dominated and ruled over such backward agricultural societies all over the world. That is also the main reason why many stoneage societies, in different parts of the world, were practically decimated from the earth, by the industrially advanced and therefore organised societies of Europe.

The selfishness of organisations was so dominant a consideration then that they, in an organised manner, damaged even the environment, once and for all, under the garb of industrial development. They also created stratified societies, in the form of haves and have-nots, with all attendant tensions, all over the world. The present-day environmentally alarming situation is the net result of exploitation of nature carried out by such organised efforts. The situation is fraught with the danger of extinction of human race from the earth. Organisational selfish interests did reach such an alarming state in the 20th century, disregarding the well being of the society or humanity at large.

It was Karl Marx who understood this exploitation of masses by a small section, perhaps more dominantly than anybody else. That is why he suggested the necessity of developing an egalitarian society by organisational working in social interests. This was in reality the beginning of thinking in terms of responsibility of corporates in social or humanitarian interests. His ideas lacked in many ways, understanding of basic human nature. That is the reason why it could not be put into practice, and organisational working yet often operates devoid of social or humanitarian interests.

CSR

Basically organised efforts started with only selfish interests of sustenance and security of those organised against the rest. It was alright until social evolution had not occurred to a perceptible extent. But it continued even in the industrially developed world without regard to social well being at large, because personal and group-selfishness is still its driving force. The Newton-Cartesian perceptions that dominated the social psyche obscured the well being of the society, humanity or environment against selfish interests of personal physical pleasures.

Organisations are in fact an integral part of evolved societies. They are meant to sustain and better the social conditions by contributing whatever best they can. The evolution of Einstienian scientific perceptions of society or nature, including human beings, as an integral whole, led to evolve the mutually acceptable inter-relationships of organisations with the society. Humanitarian considerations therefore became dominant considerations, enforced even by suitable legislations, in the corporate sector and that led ultimately to the evolution of concept of ***corporate social responsibility*** or ***CSR*** for short. This is on the rise in any organisation. Government legislations are in a way forcing them to act in such responsible manner. But in reality that does not indicate the changed mind-set in organisations.

Hindu Perception

The same CSR spirit was the underlying perception of Hindu traditional thinking. It never thought of an individual as any discreet entity, like that under Newton-Cartesian perception. Every human being was perceived to exist inalienably at various levels like individual, family, social, human and even as a part of entire existence, at the same time. It may sometimes appear as if every human being existed as one of these categories discreetly, but truly it is the entire existence as an integral whole or even cosmos. The existence in the form of an organisation came in between family and the society or humanity at large. Existence of human beings therefore must be conducive to the sustenance of all such levels of existence. All those principles, along with dos and don'ts, for individuals and for groups, to integrate the entire existence as one whole, were referred to as ***Dharma*** in India. Hence Indian Dharma is colossally different from so called every other religion on the earth. This was encultured consciously and persistently in the Hindu society from times immemorable. It was achieved through teaching that one has to expand from ***Vyashti* to *Samashti* to *Srishti* to *Permeshti*** as described in detail earlier. This is the correct corporate social outlook and consequently as responsibility of every individual or a group in relation to society or humanity or even the entire existence as a whole.

CSR vs. Charity

The CSR is currently very enthusiastically discussed amongst the corporate world, more as charity. This is however not any charity or philanthropy at all. It ought to be the prime consideration for the very existence of organisations. It is in fact the *reason d'tere* of organisations. New organisational formats are being developed to cater to these needs on priority basis. Collins refers to such organisations as ***'built to last'*** [1] or ***'good to great'*** [2] organisations. Many organisations include these considerations, provide budget thereat, and attempt to reveal such things in their annual performance reports. Such graciousness comes out of profit and not out of any philosophical value system. If an organisation is not making profit, the CSRs are diluted to the extent possible, without feeling guilt of any kind. Much legislation has been passed, in every country, to make corporates accountable to some social, humanitarian or environmental requirements and this is bound to go much further. But there is no philosophical basis for working in this fashion except that it is order of the day and is to be legally provided for. Any behaviour contrary to this is looked down upon by the fellow corporate or the society at large. It is therefore more showiness than feeling and acting responsibly as is expected. Hence it is adopted at times even as face-saving and nothing more. It is often to only show that the corporates are behaving as per legal provisions. **This has to have a philosophical basis to become a value-system for its adoption by the corporates.** Then only it will become a point of faith to be followed even in adverse situations, with good of society at heart. The organised group must feel amongst themselves as a family and similarly with the society. The Indians went a step further and felt that the whole world is their family in the form of ***vasudhaiva kutumbakam.***

But let us not mistake that the corporates have changed into very pious, peace loving and environmentally conscious groups now. They do provide additional funds for many facilities for their own workers and the societal welfare around. There were always good individuals in all societies all the time interested in such things. The redeeming feature however is that their number is increasing day-by-day. Yet they are not prepared to forego much of their profits for such charitable work. They may not be inclined to do such things when in loss. They are not yet ready to consider themselves as only trusties and not owners as suggested by **Mahatma Gandhi.**

The industrial production has immensely contributed to the present day environmental problems in the form of carbon emission in the atmosphere. The situation has already reached alarming stage of global warming [3]. The problem is how to replace the use of such enormous amount of energy, required for sustaining the present day materialistic civilization, by other non-carbon forms of energy, like the bio, sun, wind, hydraulic, geo-thermal and such other sources. These alternatives are too costly as compared to the fossil sources of energy and its use is bound to alter the entire economics and perhaps the politico-economical order of the world. Those with vested interests in fossil energy sources have as yet proved to be a hard nut to crack [3]. Mere CSR awareness is not going to achieve the required results. It will have to be transformed into a philosophical base of social values in any society.

Western Perception

The historically evolved socio-psychological load in western society prevented them from appreciating the CSR, although they developed very good organisational network to sustain their industrial revolution and its beneficial effects. Initially they did not even accept the existence of mind as a separate entity, much less intellect as discussed earlier. All they were after was bodily physical pleasures. Similarly they did not accept the importance of society over individual freedom. In fact they felt irremedial antagonism between the instinctual freedom and socialising process. Under such psychological perceptions the question of social responsibility did not arise. Colonialism, slavery and subjugation of several backward societies all over the world were justified as divine dispensation. They realised their shortcomings by the end of Second World War and hence liberated their colonies and upheld freedom as uncompromisable virtue. Slowly they also realised the ecological damage they had caused by unrestricted industrialisation and which had to be corrected. Similarly they accepted the existence of mind and intellect as different from physical existence. These led them to evolve the social responsibilities of organised efforts in the form of concept of CSR.

Customer Pressure

In the industrial and information technological social structure everybody happens to be a customer because nobody produces all that is required for sustenance and besides whatever is produced by him the rest have to be purchased from others. Soon after the Second World War when nationalism was at its peak, great thinker like **D.B. Thengri** had therefore suggested that the customer interest was the nearest equivalent of national interests. Now when internationalism or humanity's interests are reigning supreme and when the very existence of human being is at stake the **consumer interest can be called as the nearest equivalent of social and ecological interests.**

Every product that is used to sustain the present-day civilization originally comes from the earth or the ***geosphere*** which includes soil, air, water and climate. It may undergo several stages of processing before it is used by humans. In this processing it may throw away some unwanted waste materials into the ***geosphere.*** Similarly after its use, when it becomes junk, it is bound to throw something into the ***geo*** as well as ***biosphere***. Our own bodies or those of the other living world also throw away things regularly to pollute air, water and soil used by living beings. This may cause some biological damage or damage to ***biosphere***. Equally it may damage the ***geosphere*** and ***biosphere*** during its actual use. Similarly after its use it is either thrown or is reprocessed to reproduce something which undergoes the same cycle.

During processing at every stage it also affects the ***socio-sphere*** in the form of human concerns like working conditions of workers, engagement of child labour, adequate and reasonable wages and so on. It is high time that the ***life-cycle studies*** of every product need to be studied to understand the effects of production, use and disposal of every product on the ***geo, bio*** and ***socio-spheres*** or their ecological influence as a whole. This is called as ***ecological intelligence*** by **Daniel Golman** [4]

The corporates should feel responsible on all these fronts to ensure that no perceptible damage is caused to the overall ecology. This is the true CSR. But production activity particularly against usually stiff competition is mostly driven by sale and there-from the profit. Golman therefore emphasises that it is the customer who should be made aware through ***'life cycle assessment'*** (LCA) to choose only those products which cause least overall ecological damages, at times even by paying more, to develop customer pressures on production activities. Quality and price needs to be defined by the customer in this new light of ecological sustenance.

According to **Goleman, "nothing in our evolutionary past has shaped our brain for spotting less palpable threats like slow heating of the planet, insidious spread of destructive chemical particulates into the air we breathe and things we eat, or the inexorable destruction of vast swaths of flora and fauna on our planet".**

Therefore when it comes to damage to ecology, social exploitation, mental domination, etc. we tend to ignore them thinking that it will be taken care of by others. Customer intelligence of high order is required to force the corporates to accept the social responsibility in the form of CSR in its widest encompass to make human life more meaningful and almost eternal, except for slow evolutionary changes.

This proposition is based on customer awareness and which may be a slow process. It does require enculturation and evolution of some widely accepted value system. How to evolve such a value system?

Fourth Wave Perception

The necessary philosophical base can only be evolved out of Indian perception of reality. This was described as ***'fourth wave'*** in the previous chapter. It has the Advaiti basic foundation. It evolves from the realisation that one has to expand his vision from an individual through various stages to the all pervading Brahma as an ideal. It means that the corporate shall automatically think of their existence in the form of society as an extension of their organisation and further as nature and ultimately as the Brahma pervading the entire universe. This is the extension of fourth wave social change with sound philosophical basis. Once it is imbibed it will not be necessary to enculture the corporate for CSR mechanically. It will be the logical culmination of their production activities.

Sustainable development has lately been suggested to overcome the basic malady. The question arises as to how and where to draw the line demarcating the sustainable development and non-sustainable development. Sustainability has very aptly been defined as that change which does not affect anything in future to the extent of damaging it permanently. It is difficult to decide whether it does damage or not. It therefore becomes a highly subjective phenomenon. **Murli Manohar Joshi** [5] has suggested instead the concept of sustainable consumption, which anyone can decide on his own. It may vary with individuals but again how individuals will be able to judge their own individual limits? There will have to be other motivating forces for limiting one's own consumption, irrespective of what others do.

The whole issue has to be dealt with, from the point of view of individual's happiness, along with the sustenance of the globe in an integral way and not merely from the point of view of material consumption and environmental sustainability. **Deen Dayal Upaddhaya** [6] had put forward the fundamentals of integral humanism in a nut shell to tackle these issues. His philosophy is nothing more than reiteration of the same traditional Hindu perception. But it has not been elucidated further by any one of his followers for it to be applied in practice, particularly in the present day complex social world. It has remained as merely theory so far.

The solution lies in first accepting the Upanishadic philosophical foundation of expanding individual perception as elucidated above and before. This has to be a part of regular curricular programme in every school and university for imbibing the required spirit. It will have to be the basis of every training programme of corporate world. This was once done successfully in the simple agricultural society in India and the spirit still continues in Hindu society at least to some extent in spite of the fact that it has not been a part of **Macaulayan curriculum,** introduced by Britishers long ago in India. India is copying the west blindly in almost every sphere and hence the ignorance about the usefulness of traditional philosophy. **Surprisingly the west is trying to find solutions to these flexing problems by studying the Indian philosophy.** The slow fourth wave evolution is bound to change the scenario, not just in India but all over the world.

References

1. Collins, Jim, *Good to Great*, Harper-Collins, N.Y. (2001).
2. Collins, Jim and Porras, Jerry, I., *Built to Last*, Harper-Collins, N.Y. (2002).
3. Friedman, Thomas, L., *Hot, Flat and Crowded*, Penguin, London, (2008).
4. Goleman Daniel, *Ecological Intelligence,* Allane Lane (U.K.), 2009.
5. Joshi, Murli Manohar, *Sustainable Consumption* –A New Paradigm, 2nd National Technology Day Lecture, GOI, HRD Ministry, New Delhi, 11th May 2000.
6. Upaddhyaya Deen Dayal, *Integral Humanism,* Bhartiya Vichar Sadhana, Nagpur (1963).

APPENDIX

APPENDIX STRUCTURE

A - Why at all industrial revolution occurred?
B - What is the life cycle of an organisation?

Appendix - A

Why At All Industrial Revolution Occurred?

In order to appreciate organisational science it is necessary to understand why did industrial revolution at all occur? If at all it occurred, why did it occur first in England? Above all how come it occurred at the end of eighteenth century and why not at some time earlier or later? It also raises the question as to whether organisationality developed first to give rise to formation of organisations or the other way round. In order to appreciate the answers to all these questions it is better to refer to a book entitled **'Farewell to Alms'** by **Gregory Clark** of University of California, Davis, USA.

According to Clark, as more people moved from rural England to London, the urban population had to respond to the challenges of survival and which finally resulted in industrial revolution in England. The same was the situation almost all over the north-western Europe as well.

At around 1800 AD in England, as per Prof Clark, an average Englishman was getting equivalent of 2322 calories of food daily. The food availability then differed in rural and urban England. The rural population used to get a diet equivalent of 3200 cal. when the urban population got a diet only worth of 1508 cal. In other words the urban population was relatively starving. Around the same time the great economist **Thomas Malthus** published his classic entitled *'An Essay on the Principles of Population'*. It is quite likely that this led Darvin to discover his famous principle of *'survival of the fittest'* in living nature.

According to Malthus, if the growth in production is consumed by the increased population no surplus wealth is generated and hence no economic progress would be possible. According to Clark therefore when the efficiency of production and therefore rate of wealth generation surpassed the rate of population growth in urban England industrial revolution occurred. This happened around 1800 AD and that too first in England which finally resulted in industrial revolution in England. Let us see how far these arguments hold true?

At least in India, since the advent of agricultural era some 10-12000 years back the rate of production and of population has been continuously on the increase ever since. The rate of population growth must have been more than that of the rate of production in the early part of the change over from stoneage to agricultural era. But this must have been reversed at some point of time thereafter as golden era occurred in India. The surplus wealth thus generated however did not lead to industrial revolution in India as was made possible in Europe. There was never any lack of intelligence in India to think in terms of economics and improve production. But the emphasis here was more on spirituality rather than on material enjoyment. The economic activities were more or less limited to families then in India. It never crossed beyond into any social corporate activity. The industrial revolution that occurred in England around 1800 AD was itself a process rather than just a sudden change brought in by any on-off switch. Many complex social and economical processes occurred prior to that to culminate it into an industrial revolution and thereby very organized life. These are enumerated below:

1. The challenges of survival particularly in the north-western Europe were so great that it was almost impossible to earn sustenance on individual or even family basis. They

had to per force organise themselves in groups for sustenance and safety. The society therefore slowly integrated at the mental level and developed habit of working in organised fashion. The rules and regulations of working together effectively and efficiently were readily accepted by most and those had become part of their social values.

2. The harsh conditions of survival developed in them intense desire to override nature to enable them to happier life.
3. It also led them to move around and perhaps all over the globe for earning sustenance through international trade. This is how they discovered the world including its remote corners against all odds. As a result the spirit of working in organised manner became their second nature.
4. The safety requirements for international travel and trade turned out to be the mother of invention of better fighting equipments. When it was realised that with their superior strength they could rule all over the world, they fought and enslaved many societies in the world.
5. They could then plunder and exploit almost the whole world for their own enrichment and enjoyment.
6. As a general consequence their societies, in particular the English society, evolved itself into a well organised society which helped them to progress in all aspects of social life.
7. Their observations of nature and social phenomena came in direct confrontation with what was being preached by the church as the gospel truth of Bible. This led to increased atrocities by the church in every sphere of life. The reaction to such atrocities and dictatorial tendencies of church led to evolve in them the scientific temper and increased understanding of nature in the form of natural sciences.
8. Technology is the applied science in practice. But to transform science into technology requires lot of money to be invested in its development. Unless such investment is made, scientific principles remain confined as mere ideas.
9. England was in the vanguard in developing international trade and in establishing colonies all over the world before around 1800 AD. England started becoming rich through its international trade in the form of monopoly in its colonies. It made them superior entrepreneurs as well. Lot of finances was available then for investment in developing technologies based on their understanding of science. The first in developing new technologies was fully exploited by them for earning more wealth. This had a compound accelerating effect in becoming richer as a society.
10. There is every reason to believe that had James Watt invented his steam engine a hundred years earlier he would have still had to wait till 18th century to get enough finance for its commercial application because no such financially investment-friendly situation existed in England before around 1800 AD.
11. All these factors through mutual interaction were available in England at around 1800 AD only and that led to industrial revolution for the first time in north-western Europe in general and in England in particular.

Similarly better organised social life also evolved for and as a result of industrial revolution. Such a situation was never developed in India in spite of producing many different quality goods and its international trade much before the Europeans came on the scene. There was practically no competition to Indian goods. That might have dampened the rate of improvement in the variety and quality of products in India in those days. The challenges of survival were never great in India after the advent of agricultural era. That made them more spiritual than interested in material pleasures. Spirituality and renunciation certainly dominated the social life in India all through the ages.

But it is certain that whether industrial revolution was made possible through organised efforts or vice versa is just like trying to find out whether the egg came first or the chicken. They mutually nourished each other and left no alternative to anyone except to fall in line.

Appendix - B

What is Life Cycle of an Organisation?

In the Hindu pantheon entire creation is Maya and therefore characteristically transient in its existence. It is subject to birth, growth and death. This natural phenomenon has been aptly described by the legendary Trio-Gods, Brahma, Vishnu and Mahesh in action. They manifest creation in the form of Brahma, sustenance or growth in the form of Vishnu and destruction in the form of Mahesh. Whole of the evolutionary process, both biological and social, has been subject to the phenomenon of creation, sustenance and destruction. All man-made things are subject to this phenomenon. Being man-made, organisations are also subject to the phenomenon of their formation, growth and decay. Organisations are created to meet some group interest in the light of larger social interest as if Brahma is in action. It may sustain and grow in fulfilling the objectives as if Vishnu is in action. Finally, due to some reasons, it may decay and get decimated as if Mahesh is in action. These three Gods represent the forces of creation, sustenance and decay in action in every creation.

Organisations are created in sync with the social requirements. If the creative forces are not of adequate strength and stimulus it may not come into existence. There are a number of such abortive experiences. The creative strength means adequate money, men and materials coupled with adequate missionary zeal. Sustenance and growth means required harmony of all these resources vis-à-vis the social requirements. Such harmony has to be consciously maintained to sustain growth. It will grow until such harmony is maintained. The changes in aspirations of those working in the organisation and changes in the social environment tend to disturb the initial harmony. It is the responsibility of the leader/manger to try and maintain the harmony by suitable changes in policies, management, motivation and everything at command to maintain the organisation in required shape and spirit for achieving the objectives. Failure to enforce, with respect to any and many such required changes may result in decay and eventual decimation. The forces that operate in creation, growth and decay vary with every type, size and nature of organisation.

Every day new organisations are formed with fresh spirit to meet the social requirements. Similarly many get decimated everyday as a routine matter of social evolution. This is akin to birth and death of any living being. This is the life cycle of any organisation. It is therefore necessary to understand the forces that create, help-grow and decay and finally decimate organisations of one's own interests. It is equally imperative to overcome all those forces that tend to decay and decimate organisations of one's own interests. Failure to understand and appreciate forces in the form of Brahma, Vishnu and Mahesh in any organisation is a sure sign of making hara-kiri of some sort on the organisational front.

SUBJECT INDEX

P

U

V

W

XYZ

PERSON INDEX

L

M

N

O

P

R

S

T

U

V

Y

Sanskrit Terminology Used in Text

Page No.	संस्कृत पारिभाषिक शब्द
30	चिति
39, 88, 329	परमेष्टी
39	धर्मङ्कुद्ध
39	सद्गुणविकृती
39	मोक्ष
53, 66, 168, 199	संप्रदाङ्क
54, 84	सत्ङ्कुग
61	पुरुषार्थ
61, 105, 186, 188, 328	धर्म, अर्थ, काम, मोक्ष
64, 89, 100, 186, 328, 330, 344, 348	व्ङ्कष्टि, समष्टि, सृष्टि, परमेष्टी
81	श्लोक
81	गुरुकुल
82	अंगांगी भाव
88	चेतना
91	घरच्ङ्का खाऊन लष्कराच्ङ्का भाजणे.
96, 328	सृष्टि
101, 102, 329	समष्टि
102	मजेत जगावं कसं ?
105	अद्वैत
183, 189	ङ्कुगधर्म
183, 189	शाश्वत धर्म
186	धर्म
186	धर्मशाळा
186	ब्रह्मचर्ङ्काश्रम, गृहस्थाश्रम, वानप्रस्थाश्रम, संन्ङ्कासाश्रम
186	ब्राह्मण, क्षत्रिङ्क, वैश्ङ्क, शूद्र
197	साधना
202	मठ (Math)
203	अंधश्रद्धा निर्मूलन
242	कथा-कीर्तन
271	गुरुदक्षिणा

SANSKRTI SUBHASHITAS USED IN THE TEXT

54	न राज्ङ्कं न च राजासीत् न दण्डो न च दाण्डिक: । धर्मेनैव प्रजा: सर्वा: रक्षन्ति स्म परस्परम् ।।
56	आहार-निद्रा-भङ्क-मैथुनं च सामान्ङ्कमेतत् पशुभिर्नराणाम् । धर्मो हि तेषामधिको विशेषो धर्मेणहीना: पशुभि: समाना: ।।
59	खाली पेट भजन ना होवे गोपाला
85	त्ङ्कजेदेकं कुलस्ङ्कार्थे, ग्रामस्ङ्कार्थे कुलं त्ङ्कजेत् । ग्रामं जनपदस्ङ्कार्थे आत्मार्थे पृथिवीं त्ङ्कजेत् ।।
85	न त्वहं कामङ्के राज्ङ्कं न स्वर्गं नापुनर्भवम् । कामङ्के दु:खतप्तानां प्राणिनामार्तिनाशनम् ।।
98	पिण्डे पिण्डे मतिर्भिन्ना ।
112	एकोऽहम् बहु स्ङ्काम् ।
129	महाजनो ङ्केन गत: स पन्था: ।
129, 133	राजा कालस्ङ्क कारणम् ।
133	क्रिङ्कासिद्धि: सत्त्वे भवति महतां नोपकरणे ।
278	सङ्घे शक्ति: कलौ ङ्कुगे ।
39, 112, 331, 348	वसुधैव कुटुम्बकम् ।